Evolving Software Processes

Trends and Future Directions

Scrivener Publishing
100 Cummings Center, Suite 541J
Beverly, MA 01915-6106

Publishers at Scrivener
Martin Scrivener (martin@scrivenerpublishing.com)
Phillip Carmical (pcarmical@scrivenerpublishing.com)

Evolving Software Processes

Trends and Future Directions

Edited by

Arif Ali Khan
University of Jyväskylä, Finland

Dac-Nhuong Le
Haiphong University, Haiphong, Vietnam

Scrivener
Publishing

WILEY

Library of Congress Cataloging-in-Publication Data

ISBN 978-1-119-82126-7

Cover image: Pixabay.Com
Cover design by Russell Richardson

*Dedicated to our friends
and family for their
constant support during the
course of this book*

Contents

List of Figures

List of Tables

Foreword

A number of books have been written over the years about improving the software process, some of them quite good, some less so. Arif and Dac-Nhuong Le have edited a book that I will be happy to add to my library. They have been involved in software process assessment and improvement for years, so they have the experience necessary to speak knowledgeably about the topic. They have included interesting chapters in this book that I think are important for systematic process improvement and management in today's industrial evolution.

The development processes in the software industry continue to evolve tremendously and it takes innovative efforts to cope with the global challenges. For instance, the present COVID-19 pandemic situation is reshaping the software industry working environment and is driving continuous changes in the software engineering processes, methods and collaborative software development environment. Industry will see the long-term effects in the coming years. It is a struggle to reform the working environment and specifically the software processes that are seriously affected by the 2019 pandemic.

One might argue that there are already many books that include descriptions of software processes. The answer is "yes, but." Becoming acquainted with existing software processes is not enough. It is tremendously important to understand the evolution and advancement in software processes so that they appropriately address the problems, applications, and environments to which they are applied. Providing basic knowledge for these important tasks is the main goal of this book.

Industry is in search of software process management capabilities. The emergence of the COVID-19 pandemic emphasizes the industry's need for software with specific process management capabilities. Most of today's products and services are based to a significant degree on software and are the result of large-scale development programs. The success of such programs heavily depends on process management capabilities, because
they typically require the coordination of hundreds or thousands of developers across different disciplines. Additionally, software and system development is usually distributed across geographical, cultural and temporal boundaries, which make the process management activities more challenging in the current pandemic situation. It is vital for software development organizations to address the quality challenges by improving the organizational practices and processes. A mature software process can assist an organization in successfully executing software development activities.

This book provides the basic building blocks used in the evolution of software processes, such as DevOps, agile processes management, process assessment for human resources, recommendation models for process improvement and security, in order to lay a solid foundation for successful and sustainable future processes.

I would like to congratulate the editors of this volume, Arif Ali Khan and Dac-Nhuong Le, for compiling such timely and comprehensive research contributions. The diversity of topics covered by different chapters and the profiles of contributing authors, who are internationally established researchers, is very impressive. Different chapters describe cutting edge research efforts that try to get to the depth of many of the abovementioned challenges, with an overall aim of providing a detailed literature review, starting from fundamental concepts to more specific technologies and application use cases. I firmly believe that this edited book will provide a comprehensive resource to students, researchers, and practitioners, and have a long-lasting positive impact on this important and growing research and technological field.

Pekka Abrahamsson, PhD
Professor of Information Systems Science,
Empirical Cyber Security and Software Engineering,
University of Jyväskylä, Finland
September 2021

Preface

The extremely comprehensive overview of the evolution in software processes given in this book makes it very valuable for a wide audience of interested readers. This book specifically provides a platform for practitioners, students and researchers to discuss the studies used for managing aspects of the software process, including managerial, organizational, economical and technical. It provides an opportunity to present empirical evidence using available managerial, organizational, economical and technical strategies of software processes, as well as proposes new techniques, tools, frameworks and approaches to maximize the significance of software process management.

The following studies are discussed in the 14 chapters of this book.

- In Chapter 1, Sujin Choia, Dae-Kyoo Kimc, and Sooyong Park propose a novel recommendation model (i.e., ReMo), which to enables systematic development of quality recommendations through rigorous analysis of assessment findings.
- In Chapter 2, Monica Iovan, Daniela S. Cruzes, and Espen A. Johansen describe the practical solutions in one systematic model for purposely disseminating innovations in software security practices through careful attention to the stages of effective and sustainable implementation of the software security program. The goal of the proposed framework is to enable software organizations to create a sustainable security program that ensures that software teams continue to use the practices that improve and address the security of the products, hence adopting a long-term perspective.
- In Chapter 3, Luis Fernández-Sanz, Inés López Baldominos and Vera Pospelova develop the bridge between software processes and IT professionalism frameworks. They discuss the missing relationships between processes and activities in software development projects, the job profiles involved in them, and the skills recommended for effective performance.
- In Chapter 4, Avais Jan *et al.* incorporate earned value management (EVM) into agile software development. They propose a novel framework to tackle the key EVM challenges in agile environment.
- In Chapter 5, Vishal Pradhan, Ajay Kumar and Joydip Dhar propose a process model to understand the reliability of open source software (OSS) system releases. The effectiveness of the proposed model is assessed based on the experimental results, which revealed that it is an efficient reliability model for multi-release OSS.

- In Chapter 6, Murat Tahir Çaldağ and Ebru Gökalpb present an open data capability maturity model (OD-CMM) they developed to evaluate the open data capabilities of an organization and provide a road map for further improvements. The model is developed based on the concepts of ISO 330xx family of standards.

- In Chapter 7, Abdul Wahid Khan *et al.* present a systematic literature review (SLR) and industrial survey study, which they conducted to develop a conceptual map of the success factors that could impact the outsourcing of human resources in the domain of global software development (GSD). A total of thirteen success factors are identified, which are further classified across four main categories.

- In Chapter 8, Shahid Hussain proposes a process framework to address the classification problem of security and non-security bug reports. The framework identifies the important security-related keywords from the security bug reports (SBR) and removes these keywords from the non-security bug reports (NSBR) to improve classification decisions. The framework is empirically evaluated and the results indicate its significance in terms of classification of the SBRs.

- In Chapter 9, Mohammad Shameem presents an SLR study he conducted to identify the challenging factors that could negatively impact the DevOps practices in software development organizations. The SLR study revealed a total of 16 challenging factors, which were further analyzed to reveal the most significant factors. Finally, the identified factors were analyzed across the development and operation silos of DevOps practices.

- In Chapter 10, Muhammad Shoaib Khan, Abdul Wahid Khan and Javed Khan present an SLR protocol to identify the cultural challenges in the DevOps environment. The ultimate goal of the study was to develop a DevOps culture challenges model (DC2M) to improve communication, coordination, understanding, and trust, and to reduce the barriers between development and operation silos.

- In Chapter 11, Noor Rehman and Abdul Wahid Khan report on the barriers of IoTbased software architecture. The SLR approach was used to explore the available primary studies and a total of 20 barriers were identified, which were further analyzed based on different continents.

- In Chapter 12, Sher Badshah addresses the project management challenges in the GSD environment. The sutdy's findings consist of a total of 25 challenges that could be potential barriers for project management activities in GSD. Finally, the identified challenges are mapped into the knowledge areas of the project management body of knowledge (PMBOK) framework.

- In Chapter 13, Shah Zaib, Abdul Wahid Khan and Iqbal Qasim discuss cybersecurity challenges. The SLR approach was adopted and identified a total of 13 challenging factors. The challenging factors were also analyzed based on the digital repositories of the primary studies and the adopted research methods.

- In Chapter 14, Ebru Gökalp presents the capability maturity model he developed to improve the digital transformation (DX) human resource skill development process in an organization. The proposed model is based on the concepts of ISO 330xx family of standards. The industrial evaluation of the model shows that the proposed approach is applicable to assess the current DX human resource skill development capability level of an organization and provide best practices to move to the next maturity level.

Since it disseminates cutting-edge research that delivers insights into the tools, opportunities, novel strategies, techniques, and challenges for managing software processes, this book will be a useful resource for practitioners, students and researchers alike.

Practitioners and executives will learn what impact the evolving software processes can have on their projects. They will see ways in which the frequent and continuous change in today's software processes can help to develop software that is faster and more flexible with regard to customer needs. Those practitioners who need to react to the changing requirements by adapting the concepts of continuous development and integration, will read about how DevOps, agile and global software development practices help to live up to these new challenges. This book gives an overview of which methods are used today and how to apply them to a specific project, and includes practices to plan and monitor projects.

Students could benefit from the book by gaining an understanding of the recent trends in software process management. Moreover, it could be used in software engineering degree courses, specifically systematic literature review studies in software process improvement, agile software development, global software development processes, process models, and software project management.

Researchers getting involved with the advanced software processes will find a profound introduction to the subject. They will rapidly become acquainted with these new concepts and understand how these new trends could be used in future research projects.

Arif Ali Khan
Dac-Nhuong Le
October 2021

Acknowledgments

First of all, we would like to thank all our colleagues and friends for sharing our happiness at the start of this project and following up with their encouragement when it seemed too difficult to complete. We are thankful to all the members of Scrivener Publishing, especially Martin Scrivener and Phillip Carmical, for giving us the opportunity to write this book.

We would like to acknowledge and thank the most important people in our lives, our parents and partners, for their support. This book has been a long-cherished dream which would not have been turned into reality without the support and love of these amazing people, who encouraged us with their time and attention. We are also grateful to our best friends for their blessings and unconditional love, patience, and encouragement.

Arif Ali Khan
Dac-Nhuong Le

Acronyms

4GT	Fourth Generation Techniques
AES	Advanced Encryption Standard
API	Application Programming Interface
APF	Adaptive Project Framework
ACWP	Actual Cost of Work Performed
AC	Actual Cost
AHP	Analytical Hierarchy Process
BBSPI	Blockchain-Based Software Process Improvement
BSIMM	Building Security in Maturity Model
BCWS	Budgeted Cost for Work Scheduled
BTK	Bidirectional Transfer of Knowledge
BNS	Bi-Normal Separation
CBDM	Component-Based Development Model
CMMI	Capability Maturity Model Integration
CPM	Concurrent Process Model
CIO	Chief Information Officer
CPI	Cost Performance Index
CSF	Critical Success Factors
CI	Consistency Index
CR	Consistency Ratio
CSCM	Cybersecurity Challenges Model
CSS	Cascading Style Sheets
CSA	Cyber Security Agency
DAST	Dynamic Application Security Testing
DB	Database
DCM	Divide and Conquer Model
DevOps	Development and Operations
DIMM	DevOps Implementation and Management Model
DC2M	DevOps' Culture Challenges Model
DoS	Denial of Service
DX	Digital Transformation
EBSE	Evidence-Based Software Engineering

ESCO	European Skills, Competences and Occupations
e-CF	e-Competence Framework
EQF	European Qualifications Framework
EVM	Earned Value Management
EV	Earned Value
ES	Earned Schedule
FSDM	Formal Systems Development Model
FP	Function Point
FTC	Feature Transition Charts
FPR	False Positive Rate
GMWD	Generalized Modified Weibull Distribution
GSD	Global Software Development
HIPAA	Health Insurance Portability and Accountability Act
HR	Human Resource
IAST	Interactive Application Security Testing
IDC	International Data Corporation
IDR	Incremental Delivery
IoT	Internet of Things
IPs	Improvement Packages
IT	Information Technology
ITIL	Information Technology Infrastructure Library
I/O	Input/Output
ISO/IEC	International Organization for Standardization/International Electrotechnical Commission
ISCO	International Standard Classification of Occupations
ICT	Information and Communications Technology
KPI	Key Performance Indicators
KD	Kolmogorov Distance
LSE	Least Square Estimation
M&A	Measurement & Analysis
MM	Maturity Models
MLE	Maximum Likelihood Estimation
MSE	Mean Square Error
MVF	Mean Value Function
MVC	Model View Controller
NCS	Non-Cognitive Skills
NCSF	Non-Cognitive Skills Framework
NHPP	Non-Homogeneous Poisson Process

NPS	Net Promoter Scores
OMG	Object Management Group
OD-PRM	Open Data Process Reference Model
OD-CMM	Open Data Capability Maturity Model
OECD	Organization for Economic Co-operation and Development
OSS	Open Source Software
OS	Operating System
OWASP	Open Web Application Security Project
OSDO	Offshore Software Development Outsourcing
P2P	Peer-to-Peer
PAs	Process Attributes
PCI DSS	Payment Card Industry Data Security Standard
P-CMM	People Capability Maturity Model
PEOU	Perceived Ease of Use
PIO	Population, Intervention, and Outcome
PMS	Project Management System
PU	Perceived Usefulness
PV	Planned Value
QA	Quality Assurance
QFD	Quality Function Deployment
QoS	Quality of Service
RAD	Rapid Application Development Model
ReMo	Recommendation Model
RQ	Research Questions
RSA	Rivest-Shamir-Adleman
RPM	Rapid Prototyping Model
RFC	Request for Change
RM	Risk Management
RI	Random Consistency Index
SADCM	Software Architecture, Designing Challenges Model
SAMM	Software Assurance Maturity Model
SBR	Security Bug Reports
SCAMPI	Standard CMMI Appraisal Method for Process Improvement
SGA	Structured Gap Analysis
SHA	Secure Hash Algorithm
SLC	Software Life Cycle
SDL	Security Development Life Cycle
SDL-Agile	Security Development Life Cycle for Agile Development
SOA	Service-Oriented Architecture
SPD	Software Process Definition
SPEM	Software & Systems Process Engineering Meta-Model

SPCM	Software Process Certification Model
SPI	Software Process Improvement
SPICE	Software Process Improvement and Capability Determination
SPSS	Statistical Package for Social Sciences
SQL	Structured Query Language
SME	Small and Medium Enterprises
STRIDE	Spoofing, Tampering, Repudiation, Information Disclosure, Denial of Service, and Elevation of Privilege
SSDL	Software Security Development Life Cycle
SV	Schedule Variance
SLR	Systematic Literature Review
SRGM	Software Reliability Growth Model
SSE	Sum of Squares Error
TAM	Technology Acceptance Model
TAMAR	TMMi Assessment Method Application Requirements
TCP/IP	Transmission Control Protocol/Internet Protocol
TIMP	Threat Intelligence Management Platform
TMMi	Test Maturity Model integration
TS	Theil's Statistic
XP	Extreme Programming
XSS	Cross-Site Scripting
XML	Extensible Markup Language
WBS	Work Breakdown Structure
WEF	
WSM	Win-Win Spiral Model
WAN	Wide Area Network
WSN	Wireless Sensor Network
WWW	World Wide Web

ReMo: A Recommendation Development Model for Software Process Improvement Based on Correlation Analysis

Sujin Choi[1], Dae-Kyoo Kim[2]*, Sooyong Park[3]

[1] Graduate School of Information and Technology, Sogang University, Seoul, South Korea
[2] Department of Computer Engineering, Sogang University, Seoul, South Korea
[3] Department of Computer Science and Engineering, Oakland University, Rochester, Michigan, USA
 Email: sujinchoi@sogang.ac.kr, kim2@oakland.edu, sypark@sogang.ac.kr

Abstract

Continuous software process assessment and improvement are integral to the success of business objectives. Process assessment identifies the strengths and weaknesses in a software process and produces recommendations for planning improvements. The quality of recommendations is critical for constructive improvement planning and implementation. While widely practiced assessment models (e.g., CMMI, SPICE) address the identification of strengths and weaknesses and emphasize the importance of recommendations, they lack in providing concrete methods for developing quality recommendations. This leads to ad-hoc practices in building recommendations which often result in poor quality of recommendations as witnessed in a review of the current practice. To address this problem, we present ReMo, a novel recommendation development model that enables systematic development of quality recommendations through rigorous analysis of assessment findings. In ReMo, recommendations are developed through three phases: i) correlations analysis of findings and improvement package development, ii) review of improvement packages and refinement, and iii) recommendation development. ReMo is evaluated for its quality as a process and the quality of its outcomes through twelve industry case studies from various domains. The evaluation proves the effectiveness and usefulness of ReMo in building recommendations with room for improvement in its efficiency. The evaluation also witnesses the quality of resulting recommendations in terms of concreteness and comprehensiveness.

Keywords: Process assessment, process improvement, recommendation, software process

1.1 Introduction

Software process improvement (SPI) has been widely practiced in industry for its proven impact on product quality, development cost, and time-to-market [1-3]. A typical process of SPI is (1) identifying strengths and weaknesses of the current process practice in the target organization, (2) developing improvement recommendations to address identified weaknesses and encourage strengths, (3) building improvement plans to accommodate recommendations, and (4) implementing the plans by taking necessary actions [4,5]. Recommendations are requirements for process improvement and drive the development of improvement plans. That is, the success of software process improvement highly relies on the quality of recommendations [6,7]. However, there exist few established methods for constructing quality recommendations. The standard CMMI appraisal method for process improvement (SCAMPI) [8] and ISO/IEC 15504 [9], which are widely used assessment methods, discuss recommendations, but only marginally as an optional outcome. IDEAL [10], a process improvement cycle guideline, suggests brainstorming sessions in the diagnosing phase for building recommendations, but no concrete method is provided.

In the current practice, developing recommendations remains largely ad hoc and differs by individual practitioners, projects, and organizations. More specifically, the following problems are observed from field interviews involving ten process experts and reviews of twelve assessment reports:

- There exist few methods defined for building recommendations. This makes it difficult for process engineers to develop recommendations and, as such, results in less productivity and performance in SPI process.

- Low quality of recommendations. Most recommendations produced in the current practice are a simple interpretation of findings (problems) and lack concrete solutions.

- The current practice focuses on only weaknesses, while paying little attention to strengths which provide another insight for improvement from a positive perspective.

The impact of these is not limited to the quality of recommendations, but expands to the organization as a whole in coping with the ever-changing business environment and achieving their business objectives, and further affects improvement efforts afterwards.

In this work, we present ReMo (Recommendation Model), a novel recommendation development model that enables systematic development of quality recommendations in SPI through comprehensive analysis of findings, including both weaknesses and strengths and their correlations in various perspectives. Based on the prior studies on success factors for SPI [11-14] and organizational changes [15,16], interviews with practitioners, and our field experience, we define four views – process assessment model view, business value view, software life cycle view, and organizational view – to be considered in recommendation development. Recommendations are developed in three phases. In the first phase, findings are analyzed for their correlations based on related work products and grouped to identify improvement packages which form a basis for defining recommendations. In the second phase, the identified packages are reviewed and refined by the four views. In the third phase, concrete recommendations are developed upon refined packages.

We evaluate ReMo through twelve industrial case studies from various domains, including enterprise system integration, automotive, and telecommunication. There are 15 process engineers, including 10 professional consultants from three different consulting firms, involved in the case studies. Case studies are conducted based on the guidelines by Runeson and Höst [17]. The evaluation is twofold – process evaluation and outcome evaluation. The process evaluation evaluates the productivity and performance of process engineers using ReMo and their acceptance of ReMo. We use the technology acceptance model (TAM) [18, 19] for the process evaluation. The outcome evaluation evaluates the concreteness and comprehensiveness of the recommendations produced by ReMo by comparing them to those produced by the current practice. This work extends the preliminary work presented at the International Conference on Software and System Process Improvement [20]. The extension includes extensively refined ReMo, nine more industrial case studies, and feedback from the field. ReMo is refined by i) matrix-based analysis of finding correlations, ii) detailed steps for refining improvement packages, and iii) a concrete method for building recommendations.

This chapter is organized as follows. Section 1.2 motivates the work, Section 1.3 gives an overview of related work, Section 1.4 describes ReMo, Section 1.5 conducts case studies using ReMo, Section 1.6 evaluates the quality aspects of ReMo, and Section 1.8 concludes the paper with future work.

1.2 Motivation

The process improvement process starts with identifying assessment findings (e.g., strengths, weaknesses). Assessment findings are identified by process areas through a review of the current practice, process documentation, and practitioners' interviews. Based on identified findings, recommendations are built for planning improvement actions. Figure 1.1 shows the general process of process improvement. However, in the current practice, building recommendations from findings is left largely undefined and heavily depends on individual experience, which makes it difficult for novice process engineers and even for experienced ones to practice. More importantly, there is no quality control over recommendation development.

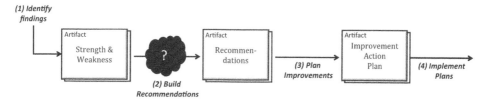

Figure 1.1: Process of improvement process.

As an example, consider the findings and recommendations in Table 1.1 from the field. The recommendations in the table show that they are directly derived from findings without any advice and simple rewriting of the findings in the reverse way. For instance, the recommendation *R1* "Identify risks during project planning" is directly derived from the finding *F1* "Lack of risk identification at project planning phase" and it is simply reworded in the reverse way without providing any concrete suggestion as to how the problem identified in the finding can be addressed. A similar observation is made for other recommendations in the table. More concrete and constructive recommendations should be developed. It can be done by considering the correlations of findings. For example, if *F1* and *F2* are considered together, it can result in a recommendation such as "*During project planning, involve test manager to identify project risks and develop mater test plan in consideration of identified risks*" which is more concrete and constructive.

Table 1.1: Recommendation examples in current practice.

Process Areas (P)		Findings (F)		Recommendations (R)	
P1	Project Planning Process	F1	Lack of risk identification at project planning phase.	R1	Identify risks during project planning
P2	Verification Process	F2	No project master test plan is developed.	R2	Develop master test plan
P3	Project Monitoring and Control Process	F3	Lack of exit criteria and formal review per milestone.	R3	Establish exit criteria and formal review on development milestone
P4	Requirement Management Process	F4	Lack of requirement change control activity.	R4	Reinforce requirement change control activity

We reviewed the recommendation development practice and the quality of recommendations in twelve process improvement assessment projects in industry provided by ten process experts who are all certified process assessors and have 15 to 22 years of industry experience. In the review, we observed similar practices to the one shown in Table 1.1 and are convinced that the practice shown in the table is pervasive in the field.

Table 1.2 shows the projects reviewed.

Table 1.2: Reviewed projects.

Project ID	Reference Model	Process Areas	Findings	Recommendations
P1	CMMI Level 2	6	18	25
P2	CMMI Level 2	6	17	19
P3	CMMI Level 2	7	38	35
P4	CMMI Level 2	6	20	20
P5	CMMI Level 3	17	145	145
P6	CMMI Level 4	19	128	128
P7	CMMI Level 2	6	59	101
P8	SPCM[a] Level 2	10	47	53
P9	CMMI Level 4	19	65	57
P10	CMMI Level 2	6	26	26
P11	A-SPICE[b] Level 2	12	23	24
P12	SPCM Level 2	10	21	22

[a] SPCM: Software Process Certification Model [21]

[b] A-SPICE: Automotive SPICE (based on ISO/IEC 15504) [22]

The current practice leads to the problems mentioned in Section 1.1, and from these problems we identify the following quality requirements for recommendations:

1. Recommendations should be detailed enough to provide concrete solutions;

2. Related findings should be considered together across process areas to provide comprehensive solutions.

The first requirement defines concreteness, while the second one defines comprehensiveness. With respect to these requirements, we conducted a focused analysis of the recommendations from the reviewed projects in Table 1.2 in terms of concreteness and comprehensiveness. Based on the practice characterization scheme in the CMMI assessment method [8], they are scaled "largely" if 60% or more recommendations in the project are found concrete/comprehensive, "partially" if 30% or more but less than 60%, and "little" if less than 30%. In the review, we took a remissive review where we considered a recommendation as concrete if it has any additional information than the information described in the finding and comprehensive if it involves information from other findings.

Figure 1.2 shows the results of the review. As shown in the graphs, more than half of the projects suffer from poor quality on both concreteness and comprehensiveness, which raises the need of solutions for improving the quality of recommendations in the current practice.

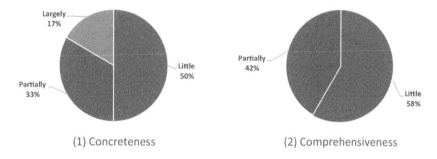

Figure 1.2: Summary of recommendation review results.

1.3   Related Work

A recommendation is a compilation of findings described in a way to improve the current practice. ISO/IEC 15504 [9] and CMMI [23] are widely used process reference models for evaluating process practices and guiding SPI practices. In process assessment, CMMI uses SCAMPI [8] as supporting assessment methods for determining the level of capability, while ISO/IEC 15504 has its own built-in assessment method defined in [9]. The roles of the assessment methods are to identify weaknesses and strengths and produce recommendations which are required in IDEAL [10], an improvement cycle model for improvement planning. While the existing assessment models provide detailed guidelines for identifying findings, the discussion on recommendations is very limited. CMMI and ISO/IEC discuss recommendations, but only conceptually as optional outcome. They lack concrete guidelines for developing recommendations. ReMo in this work addresses this problem by providing a systematic approach for developing recommendations.

Several researchers have proposed using the practice descriptions in process reference models to identify improvement recommendations. Mejía *et al.* [24] presented the SMART-SPI model which selects a process model from reference models as external best practices and analyzes it to produce a set of recommended practices. Shrestha *et al.* [25] proposed a software-mediated process assessment method for IT service management. In the method, organizational practices are assessed via an online survey, and recommendations are generated from the knowledge base DB. The knowledge base DB contains several process improvement models such as ISO/IEC 15504 and ITIL (information technology infrastructure library) [26]. Laksono *et al.* [27] presented an implementation of software test process assessment and improvement using TMMi (test maturity model integration) [28] and TAMAR [29]. TMMi is a set of best practices for software testing, and TAMAR is the official TMMi assessment method. The improvement recommendations in their work are prepared for the practices with weaknesses. However, recommendations are identified exactly as the same as the subpractice description in TMMi without analysis on assessment results. Although process reference models are generally adopted as best practices by organizations, the recommendations made from process reference models are not concrete and specific enough to guide a particular organization.

For organization-aware recommendations, several researchers use quality function deployment (QFD) [30], which is a correlation technique in process improvement planning for relating customer needs to designing, development, engineering, manufacturing, and service functions. Hierholzer *et al.* [31] used QFD for selecting mission-critical improvement proposals. Sun and Liu [32] presented a QFD framework for business-oriented process improvement based on CMMI. Business requirements and practices are analyzed for correlations, and improvement actions are identified based on correlations and prioritized by business values for each process area.

Some researchers introduced crowd-sourcing approaches for making improvement recommendations supported by experts' expertise. Raza *et al.* [33] proposed a web-based tool for analyzing software developer's personal performance and making recommendations for improvement actions. Recommendations are suggested and prioritized by invited experts as individual contributors. Farooq *et al.* [34] utilized blockchain technology for mediating and coordinating between improvement seekers and process experts. Blockchain technology is attractive for both parties in that it enables secure transactions among participants without any central trusted authority [35]. However, it still lacks a systematic procedure to produce improvement recommendations, and the quality of recommendations has to largely depend on experts.

Other assessment methods (e.g., [36-42]) focus on lightweight assessment for small organizations or self-assessment for individual developers with little attention to recommendations. Villalón *et al.* [43] presented action packages which are templates for building improvement recommendations from organizational and management views. However, no concrete method is described as to how the views should be considered. Harjumaa [44] presents a set of process patterns which provide general guidelines for improving the inspection process. The patterns to be applied are decided based on the assessment results from the inspection process. Our work can benefit from their patterns in building recommendations specific to the inspection process. Haase [45] uses a neural network method for identifying improvement points (weaknesses) that are critical for the organization to achieve the next maturity level. He uses process assessment data collected from other similar business units. Gorschek and Wohlin [46] presented DAIIPS, a method for prioritizing improvement proposals and identifying their dependencies to aid software process improvement efforts. The method is designed for small organizations that have limited resources to conduct full scale software process improvement. Improvement issues are divided into packages small enough to be managed and prioritized. The recommendations produced in our work can be used as input to their work.

Several studies emphasize the importance of understanding dependency among practices for effective process improvement. Monteiro *et al.* [47] identified dependency among process areas of CMMI at each maturity level in an effort to identify the impact on the dependencies of maturity level 2 when a process area of maturity level 3 is introduced.

Chen *et al.* [48] proposed a practice-level dependency model for 6 process areas in CMMI maturity level 2 where practice dependency is identified by workflow of work products. Both studies, however, do not discuss how identified dependencies can be used for process improvement. Calvo-Manzano *et al.* [49] present a method for identifying dependency among process areas in CMMI-ACQ [50] and suggest an implementation sequence of process areas accordingly. Arcilla *et al.* [51] proposed an implementation sequence of service management processes defined in ITIL by identifying dependencies and clusters of strongly connected processes. What these studies have in common is that dependency decisions are made solely based on the description of the reference model itself, and they are not utilized for producing and improving recommendations.

1.4 Recommendation Development Model: ReMo

Business orientation, management commitment, staff involvement, process improvement guidelines and mentoring, and automation and tools are major success factors to be considered in process improvement [11-14,52]. Organizational and business aspects are also considered important for organizational changes [15,16,52]. Considering these factors and the practitioner needs described in Section 1.2, we establish the following strategies in building improvement recommendations:

(a) Justify the importance of the change to be made and its impact. Software process is human-centric and, thus, it is important to convince people about the change to be made [53].

(b) Maximize utilization of strengths and resources of the organization. Strengths are proven practices to be exercised throughout the organization and effective use of existing resources (e.g., human resources, software tools) helps in planning practical improvement.

(c) Provide concrete and detailed guidance as to *what to do*, *why to do*, *how to do*, *who to do*, and *when to do*.

(d) Suggest a set of correlated improvement actions for synergistic effectiveness. Process activities are interrelated to each other by nature, which should be taken into account in improvement planning to avoid overlapping, conflicting, and incomplete action items.

(e) Follow the guidance of the chosen reference model. For instance, a capability-based model (e.g., CMMI, ISO/IEC 15504) describes a necessary foundation for the next level.

ReMo uses both strengths and weaknesses identified from process assessment as a base for developing recommendations. They are analyzed through three phases – *correlation analysis*, *improvement package refinement*, and *recommendation development*. As each phase is exercised, improvement packages (IPs), a preliminary form of recommendations, are formed and refined. Figure 1.3 shows the process of ReMo. Findings are related via underlying activities and their work products across process areas, and related findings should be considered together to increase synergistic effects. Correlation analysis identifies correlations of findings and defines initial IPs which establish a basis for constructing recommendations. Correlation analysis helps implement the strategies (a) and (d) in the above.

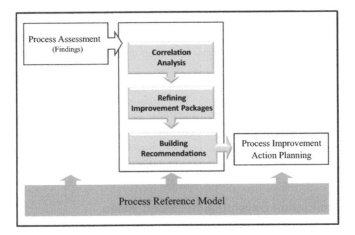

Figure 1.3: ReMo.

The IPs resulting from correlation analysis are refined by four views – *organizational view*, *software life cycle view*, *assessment model view*, and *business value view* – based on the aforementioned success factors, comments from practitioners, and our field experience. As the implementation of an IP requires resources, the organizational view reviews IPs from a resource perspective to increase utilization of existing resources in the organization [14,15], which helps implement the strategies (b) and (c). The software process is practiced per the selected software life cycle in the organization [54] and depending on the life cycle, recommendations may be changed. For instance, continuous integration of build and test is more emphasized in an agile process, while designing is more focused in a waterfall process. The software life cycle view reviews temporal relationships of practices in an IP with respect to software life cycle, which supports the strategy (c). An organization concerning process improvement uses a process reference model and its accompanying assessment methods, and any improvement effort in the organization should observe the model [10]. The assessment model view reviews an IP based on the guidance (e.g., practice sequence) of the underlying process reference model used in the organization, which supports the strategy (e). Every organization has its business objectives, and improvement efforts should be aligned with the business objectives [13,16,43]. The business value view reviews an IP for business values and prioritizes IPs per business value. This helps implement the strategy (a).

During the analysis of each view, findings in an IP may be removed or merged and new findings may be identified and added to the IP, which refines the IP. Refined IPs are further reviewed to ensure that they have their own standing point and business value. The IPs that do not have a strong standing point or have low business value are subject to be merged with other IPs. Recommendations are constructed based on the final IPs. One or more recommendations may be developed per IP. An abstract recommendation is first drafted describing the purpose of the recommendation. The abstract recommendation is then elaborated to a concrete recommendation by reviewing individual findings in the IP and defining recommendation seeds for each finding. Finally, related recommendation seeds are synthesized and evolve to a recommendation item in the final recommendation.

1.4.1   Correlation Analysis

Findings from process assessment are analyzed to identify their correlations and produce IPs. Figure 1.4 shows the activities of correlation analysis. Findings are analyzed using a symmetric matrix whose row and column have the same list of findings. The finding on each column is analyzed against all other findings on the row to identify its correlations to other findings. A column that has significant correlations becomes a candidate IP.

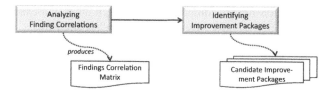

Figure 1.4: Correlation analysis.

A process reference model is defined in terms of process areas and each area defines a set of activities to achieve the goal of the area. Findings are identified for each activity in a process area. An activity may not have any finding identified. Adversely, several findings may be identified for a single activity if the activity is practiced inconsistently in different projects. Table 1.3 shows a partial list of findings from a case study (*ProjectD*) conducted in this work. The list involves 13 findings across six process areas. We use the list as a running example.

Table 1.3: Example findings of assessment.

Process Area	Finding Type	Finding id[a]	Finding Description
Design	Strength	S-DE-2	In some projects, testing strategies and test plans are developed in consideration of project characteristics and customer needs in the design phase.
	Weakness	W-DE-1	Test plans are not developed in most projects until later in the design phase.
Implement-ation	Strength	S-IM-1	Automated daily build system is used in some projects.
	Weakness	W-IM-1	Test cases are developed, but testing techniques and test coverage criteria are not considered.
	Weakness	W-IM-2	Static analysis on source code is conducted, but peer review is not involved.
Testing	Weakness	W-TE-1	In some incremental development projects, regression test strategies and release criteria are not defined.
	Weakness	W-TE-2	Test defects at several test levels are not properly collected and managed.
Measurement and Analysis	Strength	S-MA-1	Project specific metrics are defined to measure the process of development and testing in some projects.
Project Planning	Weakness	W-PP-1	Size and effort estimation process is not established.
	Weakness	W-PP-2	The risk identification activity in the early project phase is not sufficiently practiced and the risk management process is not followed.
	Weakness	W-PP-4	The rationale of selecting the project life cycle is not documented.
Quality Assurance	Weakness	W-QA-2	Resources are not sufficient to support quality assurance activities such as static analysis, performance test, and process quality audit.
	Weakness	W-QA-4	Audit results are not updated in PMS (project management system) and corrective actions to address identified non-conformance are not properly reviewed and monitored by QA auditors.

[a] T-PA-NUM: T is a finding type – S (strength) and W (weakness), PA: an abbreviation of process area, NUM: a sequential number

1.4.1.1 *Analyzing Finding Correlations*

Process areas are related to each other via input-output relationships of work products of their underlying activities. Two activities are correlated if one task uses as input the outputs of the other task. As an example, consider tasks *"Identify Project Risk"* in the Project Planning process area and *"Establish Test Plan"* in the Quality Assurance process area. In the planning test in the later task, the risks identified in the former task need to be considered to reduce the impact of the risks. Figure 1.5(a) illustrates the input-output relationships of the tasks. An input-output relationship may be bi-directional if the tasks involved in the relationship are complementary to each other. For example, consider Figure 1.5(b). In the figure, the task *"Develop QA Plan"* needs *Project Plan* as input, which is the output of *"Establish Project Plan"* for scoping and scheduling audit, and in turn *"Establish Project Plan"* needs *QA Plan* produced by the *"Develop QA Plan"* task to adjust to other project activities (e.g., configuration audit).

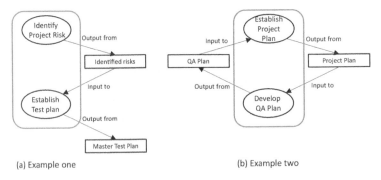

(a) Example one   (b) Example two

Figure 1.5: Correlated tasks via work products.

For a given input of identified findings and the underlying process reference model, Algorithm 1 defines the operational process of finding correlations.

Algorithm 1 Analyzing finding correlations

```
1  Input:  FindingSet, ProcessReferenceModel defining
2          activities and input and output of work products of activities
3  Output: CorrelatedFindingSet
4
5  Let inputWorkProducts be the set of input work products
of the activities associated with FindingSet;
6  Let outputWorkProducts be the set of output work products
of the activities associated with FindingSet;
7
8  findingsCorrelationAnalysis (Findings,
ProcessReferenceModel): CorrelatedFindingSet
9  {
10 /*Find correlations among findings via workflow of work product*/
11     while each iwp in inputWorkproducts{
12         while each owp in outputWorkproducts{
13             if (iwp equal to owp}){
14                 add (associatedFinding(FindingSet, iwp),
associatedFinding(FindingSet, owp))
15                     to CorrelatedFindingSet;
16         }
17     }
18     return CorrelatedFindingSet;
19 }
```

Lines 1−3 define the input and output of the operation. Lines 5−6 identify the activities that are associated with the findings in the process reference model and define sets of input work products and output work products that are associated with the activities. Lines 10−17 identify the workflow of work products that are associated with the activities identified in lines 5−6 and correlate two findings if the work products of one finding's activity are in an input-output relationship with the work products of the other finding's activity. The final set of correlated findings results in line 18.

Figure 1.6 depicts the relationships of findings, process practices, and process areas and how correlated findings are identified. In the figure, the findings *W-DE-1* and *S-DE-2* of the activity *DE.3* are related to the finding *W-PP-2* of the activity *PP.6* through the relationship of the *Design Process* area and the *Project Planning Process* area. Every finding in the design process is reviewed against the findings in the project planning process (or vice versa) to identify correlations. An activity has input and output relationships with other activities via their work products in the work product flow. So are their findings. In the workflow of CMMI [23], which is the base reference model used in the case study, the activity *PP.6* (*"project risk management planning"*) and the activity *DE.3* (*"project test planning"*) have an input-output relationship where the work products of *PP.6* are input to *DE.3*. Thus, their corresponding findings *W-PP-2* and *S-DE-2* inherit the input-output relationship of *PP.6* and *DE.3*.

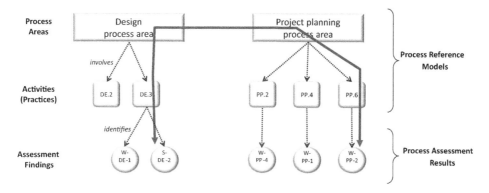

Figure 1.6: Identifying finding correlations.

Figure 1.7 shows the correlations of the findings in Table 1.3. The matrix in the figure is symmetric where the row and column have the same set of findings. For each pair of findings in the row and column, the relationship type is determined. Relationships are categorized into input, output, and input-output. A finding pair has an input relationship if the underlying activity of one finding uses the work products produced by the underlying activity of the other finding. Similarly, an output relationship is identified if the work products produced by the underlying activity of one finding are consumed by the underlying activity of the other finding. When both relationships are present, an input-output relationship is established.

For example, in Figure 1.7, the finding *S-DE-2* in the column has seven relationships with other findings in the row (excluding itself). A relationship marked *i* denotes an input relationship, *o* represents an output relationship, *i/o* represents an input-output relationship, and *1* denotes a self-relationship. For each column, the number of input and output relationships is counted for weight. An *i/o* relationship is double counted. A rule of thumb is that a column finding has at least one input and output relationship in the row. Process diagrams and meetings with stakeholders can also be used to identify finding correlations.

Correlation kinds
i: input
o: output
i/o: input-output
1: self

Findings		Design		Implementation			Testing		Project Planning			M&A	Quality Assurance	
		S-DE-2	W-DE-1	S-IM-1	W-IM-1	W-IM-2	W-TE-1	W-TE-2	W-PP-1	W-PP-2	W-PP-4	S-MA-1	W-QA-2	W-QA-4
Design	S-DE-2	1	i/o		i		o	i/o		o		i	i/o	
Design	W-DE-1	i/o	1		i		i/o					i/o		
Implementation	S-IM-1			1		o	o						i/o	
Implementation	W-IM-1	o	o		1		o	o					i/o	
Implementation	W-IM-2			i		1							i/o	
Testing	W-TE-1	i	i/o	i	i		1						i/o	
Testing	W-TE-2	i/o			i			1						
Project Planning	W-PP-1								1			i		
Project Planning	W-PP-2	i								1				i/o
Project Planning	W-PP-4										1			
M&A	S-MA-1	o	i/o						o			1		
Quality Assurance	W-QA-2	i/o		i/o	i/o	i/o	i/o						1	i
Quality Assurance	W-QA-4									i/o			o	1
'i' weight		5	3	3	5	1	2	1	-	1	-	3	5	2
'o' weight		5	4	1	1	2	5	2	1	2	-	1	6	1
total weight		8	5	4	6	3	6	3	2	3	1	4	7	3

M&A : Measurement & Analysis

Figure 1.7: Finding correlations.

1.4.1.2 Identifying Improvement Packages

Based on correlation analysis, candidate IPs are identified by reviewing the weights of columns in the matrix where a weight is the number of findings having input or output relationships. Figure 1.8 illustrates identifying IPs. Columns are reviewed for weight by process areas. In each process area, a column that has a higher total weight is chosen as a candidate IP. A higher weight implies that the column finding is significant in the process area and has a broader impact across other process areas in the row.

For example, in Figure 1.8, the finding *S-DE-2* in the column has the highest total weight, which indicates that it is the most significant finding in the design area and has a great impact on other process areas. Three candidate IPs – *IP.S-DE-2, IP.W-IM-1, and IP.W-TE-1* – are chosen in Figure 1.8 for the process areas regarding the engineering process. Candidate IPs are reviewed for a possible merge if they have similar sets of relationships. In Figure 1.8, the IP *IP.W-IM-1* is found to be a subset of *IP.S-DE-2* and thus merged with *IP.S-DE-2*. The merged IP turns out to be similar to *IP.W-TE-1*, which encourages another merge. The results of the second merge is declared as a defined IP. The columns that have similar high weights in the same process area are likely to be merged. Based on our study, IPs built upon a sound analysis of finding correlations cover up to 80% of findings.

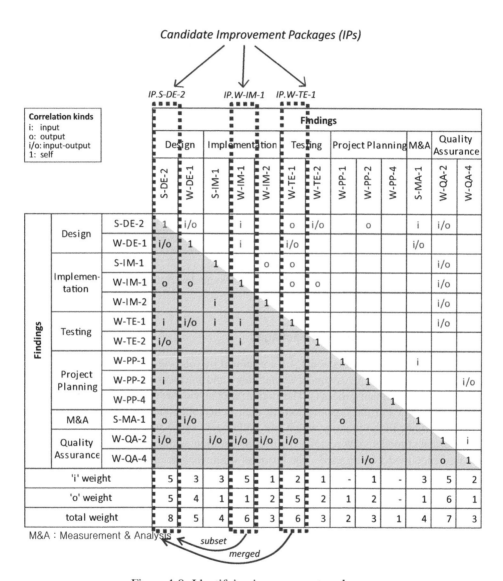

Figure 1.8: Identifying improvement packages.

Figure 1.9 shows an example of an IP description where the *Description* section describes the concern addressed by the IP and the *Correlation Analysis* section lists correlated findings in the IP.

Improvement Package ID	IP.S-DE-2	
Description	Testing process improvement	
Correlation Analysis		
Process Area		**Finding Description**
Design	S-DE-2	In some projects, testing strategies and test plans are developed in consideration of project characteristics and customer needs in the design phase.
	W-DE-1	Test plans are not developed in most projects until later in the design phase.
Implementation	S-IM-1	Automated daily build system is used in some projects.
	W-IM-1	Test cases are developed, but testing techniques and test coverage criteria are not considered.
Testing	W-TE-1	In some incremental development projects, regression test strategies and release criteria are not defined.
	W-TE-2	Test defects at several test levels are not properly collected and managed.
Project Planning	W-PP-2	The risk identification activity in the early project phase is not sufficiently practiced and the risk management process is not followed.
Measurement and Analysis	S-MA-1	Metrics are defined to measure the process of development and testing in some projects.
Quality Assurance	W-QA-2	Resources are not sufficient to support quality assurance activities such as static analysis, performance test, and process quality audit.

Figure 1.9: Improvement package description.

1.4.2 Refining Improvement Packages

The IPs resulting from Subsection 1.4.1 are refined by four views – *organizational view*, *software life cycle view*, *assessment model view*, and *business value view*. Figure 1.10 describes the refinement process. The organizational view reviews IPs in terms of the available resources of the organization for their better utilization. The software life cycle view reviews IPs to identify which life cycle needs more attention for improvement. The assessment model view reviews IPs in consideration of the characteristics of the process reference model being used. The business value view prioritizes IPs with respect to business objectives. New findings may be identified in each view and reflected in IPs for refinement. We use *IP.S-DE-1* in Figure 1.9 to demonstrate the refinement process.

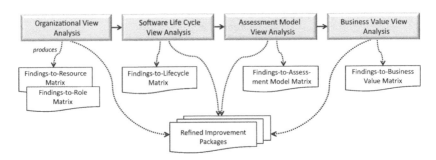

Figure 1.10: Refining improvement packages.

1.4.2.1 Organizational View

When process improvement is planned, it is important to understand organization assets for their efficient use. The organizational view reviews IPs in terms of resources and roles.

Finding-to-Resource Analysis   Depending on industry domains and types of activities, different types of resources are needed. Common types of resources include human resources and software tools. Human resources are assigned to projects usually by specialties (e.g., requirements analysis, testing). Cross-functional cooperation of human resources is integral to successful software development and delivery. Software tools and automation help improve the efficiency of process activities and operations. Availability and lack of resources can be understood in findings. For instance, from a finding "*Automated daily build system is used in some projects*," it can be understood that "*a daily build tool*" and "*a supporting source code repository*" are available in the organization. Following are the strategies for finding-to-resource analysis.

1. Understand availability and lack of resources in findings so as to enhance the utilization of existing resources and provide necessary resources.

2. Identify findings that have a dependency on resources. This increases understanding as to how resources are used in the organization.

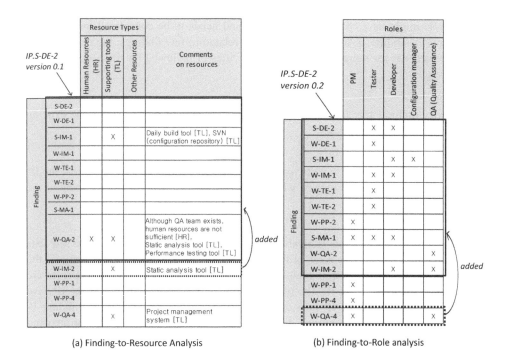

(a) Finding-to-Resource Analysis   (b) Finding-to-Role analysis

Figure 1.11: Findings-to-organization matrix.

Figure 1.11(a) shows an analysis of *IP.S-DE-1* to resources using a matrix. In the matrix, the findings of the IP in the row are analyzed against the available resource types of the organization in the column. The project team that currently conducts the improvement project is also considered in human resources. Specifics (e.g., names) of related resources may be noted in the *Comments* section. The analysis reveals that the finding *W-IM-2*, which is not part of *IP.S-DE-1*, should also be included in the IP as it is concerned with static analysis tools for testing. This implements the strategy (b) and refines *IP.S-DE-1* by adding *W-IM-2*. The comments provided in the analysis also reveal that software tools exist that are available for testing, but barely used in the current practice. This is defined as a new finding *V-ORG-1* according to the strategy (a).

Finding-to-Role Analysis   Roles are logical assets and appropriate assignment of roles is important for the success of a project [55]. Examples of roles in the software process include configuration manager, test engineer, software designer, and project manager. One person may play several roles and a single role may be played by multiple people. Depending on the organization, the definition of roles and their classification vary.

Roles are identified based on the underlying activities of findings and the knowledge about roles that assessors have acquired from assessment. As an example, in the finding "*A test strategy is developed by testers in collaboration with developers,*" whose underlying activity is "*Developing a test strategy,*" tester is found as a responsible role and developer as a consulted role. Newly identified strengths and gaps between the current practice and the expected practice with respect to involved roles are defined as new findings. The following describes the strategies for finding-to-role analysis.

1. Review the distribution of roles over findings. If a role is related to many findings, the role might have overly assigned tasks and needs to be considered for reallocating responsibilities. Adversely, if a role is related to few findings, the role needs to be considered for more involvement in activities or reviewed for the necessity of its existence.

2. Identify findings that have a role dependency. This helps better utilize the existing practices of concerned roles.

3. Suggest roles that need to participate in the process action team to implement the IP. Roles involved in an IP suggest who should participate in the implementation of the IP.

Figure 1.11(b) shows a role analysis for *IP.S-DE-1* using a matrix where the row lists findings and the column lists roles in the organization. Similar to resource analysis, the findings in the row are reviewed against the roles in the column to ensure that roles are appropriately involved in the IP. The review identifies that many activities in the IP have no QA involved, though the IP focuses on testing. This is defined as a new finding *V-ORG-2* according to the strategy (a). In a review of other activities that are not involved in the IP, but relevant to QA, a new finding *W-QA-4* is identified to include the QA audit role and added to the IP, which refines the IP. This implements the strategy (b). With a deeper understanding of the organization, the finding becomes more specific that the insufficient practice of QA is due to a lack of human resources. This is noted as another finding *V-ORG-3*. Figure 1.12 lists the three new findings identified in the organizational view analysis. They can also be used when other IPs are reviewed. The responsibility, accountability, consulted, and informed (RACI) responsibility assignment model [56], a commonly used model, may be used for detailed analysis of roles.

View	Finding ID	Finding Description
Organizational View	V-ORG-1	Testing supporting tools available, such as daily build tool, SVN(configuration reporitory), static analysis tool, and performance testing tool.
	V-ORG-2	Little QA in testing related activities.
	V-ORG-3	Though QA team exists, human resources are not sufficient. Lack of support in specialty-required areas (e.g., testing, quality assurance).

Figure 1.12: Findings from organizational view.

1.4.2.2 Software Life Cycle View

Software process activities follow the life cycle model employed in the organization. Many organizations adopt a general life cycle model (e.g., spiral model) and tailor it specifically to their needs. A process reference model, in general, also provides guidance for tailoring. When an activity is changed or newly introduced, it is important to decide where in the life cycle the activity should be carried out in consideration of other activities to increase synergy. The activity may be performed only once, repeatedly over phases, or continuously throughout the life cycle. The software life cycle review aims at identifying relevant activities to a changed activity and understanding where in the life cycle they should be exercised.

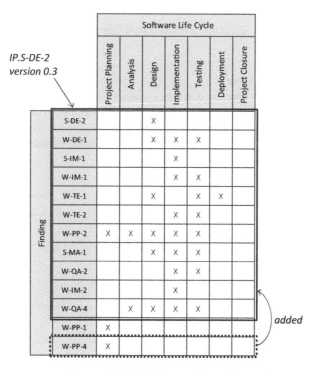

IP.S-DE-2 version 0.3

Finding	Project Planning	Analysis	Design	Implementation	Testing	Deployment	Project Closure
S-DE-2			X				
W-DE-1			X	X	X		
S-IM-1				X			
W-IM-1				X	X		
W-TE-1			X		X	X	
W-TE-2				X	X		
W-PP-2	X	X	X	X	X		
S-MA-1			X	X	X		
W-QA-2				X	X		
W-IM-2				X			
W-QA-4		X	X	X	X		
W-PP-1	X						
W-PP-4	X						

added

Figure 1.13: Finding-to-life cycle matrix.

Findings are understood in terms of life cycle phases where their underlying activities are performed. For instance, in an organization, test cases are mainly developed in the implementation and design phases, while risks and issues can be identified throughout the life cycle. New findings with respect to involved phases may be defined. Following are the strategies for finding-to-life cycle analysis:

1. Review the relation of findings to phases. A phase related to more findings should be considered more important than others when implementing the IP. Adversely, a phase related to few findings should be considered to have more activities carried out.

2. Identify the findings that have a temporal dependency. This helps to better utilize the existing practices over concerned phases.

Figure 1.13 shows an example of a life cycle view analysis. The review identifies that more testing activities are needed in the project planning, deployment, and project closure phases. This is defined as a new finding *V-SLC-1* in Figure 1.14 per the strategy (a). In review of other findings that are not involved in the IP but related to the project planning phase, *W-PP-4* is identified relevant to testing. This implements the strategy (b). The finding is concerned with selecting a life cycle model which has a great impact on planning test activities (e.g., testing strategies). The IP is refined accordingly by adding *W-PP-4*.

View	Finding ID	Finding Description
Software Life Cycle View	V-SLC-1	Insufficient testing activities in project planning, deployment, and project closure phase.

Figure 1.14: Findings from software life cycle view.

1.4.2.3 Assessment Model View

The process reference model employed in the organization provides guidance for achieving the intended benefits in the structure of the model (e.g., levels). For conformant improvement to the reference model, the guidance should be observed in the development of recommendations. For example, the important guidance of CMMI is that each level forms a necessary foundation for the next level.

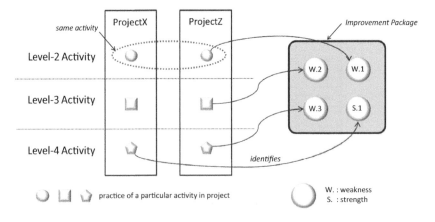

Figure 1.15: Capability-based process model guidance.

Consider the example in Figure 1.15 where process assessment is supposed to be conducted at level 4. The IP involves three weaknesses *W.1*, *W.2*, and *W.3* from *ProjectZ* and one strength *S.1* from *ProjectX*. *S.1* is a good practice that should be also exercised in *ProjectZ*. However, practicing *S.1* to improve *W.1* in *ProjectZ* is not effective as *W.1* is not ready yet to implement *S.1* because the level of *W.1* is lower than that of *S.1*. *W.2* can be explained similarly. However, *S.1* can be implemented for *W.3* since both are at the same level. The reference model used in the case study of *IP.S-DE-2* has three levels $(1-3)$ and the findings of the IP are all from level 2. This fact lends itself as a new finding *V-PAM-1* to be referenced by other IPs. Figure 1.16 defines the finding.

View	Finding ID	Finding Description
Assessment Model View	V-PAM-1	There is no disparity in capability level (All findings are from level 2).

Figure 1.16: Finding from assessment model view.

1.4.2.4 Business Value View

Process improvement should be driven by business objectives. That is, improvement actions should be prioritized based on business objectives, and improvement plans should be aligned with business objectives. No action item for important activities in business value should be missing. The business value view reviews findings against business objectives. If business objectives are not defined, stakeholders are responsible for defining them.

Figure 1.17 shows an analysis matrix of business value view. In the matrix, findings are reviewed for relevance to business objectives, strength applicability, and weakness severity. Common categories of business objectives include quality, delivery, and cost. Strength applicability reviews required costs and resources from a business value perspective for a strength to be implemented in other projects, while weakness severity reviews the impact of a weakness on business objectives. Findings are rated for these aspects on a scale of 1 to 5. The following are example questions for rating:

(Q) Is the finding related to business objectives on *Quality Improvement*?

(D) Is the finding related to business objectives on *Time to Market*?

(C) Is the finding related to business objectives on *Cost Reduction*?

(S) Is the strength applicable or expandable to other parts of organization?

(W) Is the weakness a blocking issue to achieve business objectives?

In Figure 1.17, all the three strengths in *IP.S-DE-2* are rated 4 for applicability, which means that they are highly applicable to other projects. This is defined as a new finding *V-BIS-1*. It is also observed that the findings *W-DE-1* on early test planning, *W-TE-1* on regression testing, and *W-PP-2* on early risk identification are highly relevant to business objectives and severe from a business perspective. This is defined as another finding *V-BIS-2*. The importance of the IP to each aspect of business value is measured by summing up the grades in the column. Figure 1.17 shows that *IP.S-DE-2* has the highest grade on quality improvement in business value. After refinement by the business value view, the business value of *IP.S-DE-2* is increased to 85 from 63. Note that the rating given in the matrix is for demonstration purpose and does not mean that the impact of findings on business value is known.

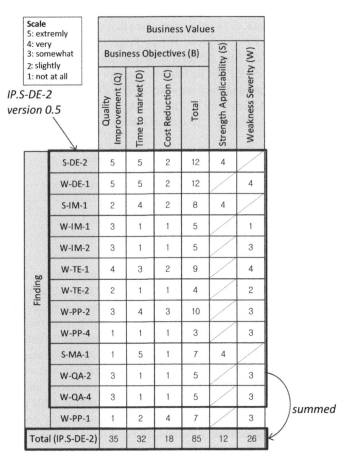

IP.S-DE-2 version 0.5 / Finding	Quality Improvement (Q)	Time to market (D)	Cost Reduction (C)	Total	Strength Applicability (S)	Weakness Severity (W)
S-DE-2	5	5	2	12	4	
W-DE-1	5	5	2	12		4
S-IM-1	2	4	2	8	4	
W-IM-1	3	1	1	5		1
W-IM-2	3	1	1	5		3
W-TE-1	4	3	2	9		4
W-TE-2	2	1	1	4		2
W-PP-2	3	4	3	10		3
W-PP-4	1	1	1	3		3
S-MA-1	1	5	1	7	4	
W-QA-2	3	1	1	5		3
W-QA-4	3	1	1	5		3
W-PP-1	1	2	4	7		3
Total (IP.S-DE-2)	35	32	18	85	12	26

Scale
5: extremly
4: very
3: somewhat
2: slightly
1: not at all

summed

Figure 1.17: Finding-to-business value matrix.

Refined IPs are reviewed for overlapping and possible re-scoping. After refinement, there might be left-out findings which do not belong to any IP. If a left-out finding has a higher business value, it may stand on its own. Otherwise, it becomes a simple corrective action. Final IPs are prioritized based on the total grade on business value. Business objectives and weakness severity are considered prior to strength applicability, which can be considered later in recommendation development. In a priority review, *IP.S-DE-2* is found to be more important for quality improvement than other IPs, which is defined as a new finding *V-BIS-3*. Figure 1.18 shows the three new findings identified in the business value view analysis.

View	Finding ID	Finding Description
Business Value View	V-BIS-1	For IP.S-DE-2, all the involving strengths are highly applicable.
	V-BIS-2	For IP.S-DE-2, Test planning in design phase, regression test strategy, and risk identification are important to business value.
	V-BIS-3	Compared to other IPs, IP.S-DE-2 is highly related to business objectives, especially quality improvement and time-to-market.

Figure 1.18: Findings from business value view.

1.4.3   Building Recommendations

The IPs resulting from Subsection 1.4.2 form a basis for building improvement recommendations. Figure 1.19 shows the activities of building recommendations. For each IP, an abstract recommendation is drafted using templates and then, a concrete recommendation is formulated based on the abstract recommendation.

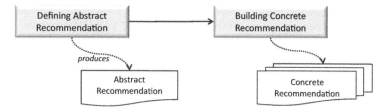

Figure 1.19: Building recommendations.

1.4.3.1 Drafting Abstract Recommendations

For each IP, an abstract recommendation is drafted with an ID, business value, traceability to the base IP, and an overview of the recommendation. Figure 1.20 shows an example of an abstract recommendation for *IP.S-DE-2*.

Recommendation ID	RECO01
Business Value	Very High
Base IP	IP.S-DE-2
Description	**IMPROVE** testing process **BY USING** testing strategy and test planning practice, and **IMPROVING** test planning process and quality assurance process **WITH** QA team and other automated tools **IN** project planning phase **TO ACHIEVE** system quality and time-to-market

Figure 1.20: Abstract recommendation.

The recommendation specifies that the ID is *RECO01*, its business value is very high, and the base IP is *IP.S-DE-2*. The description is described using the templates in Table 1.4. Four templates are defined – *W-S*, *W-W*, *S-S*, and *S-W* – for different kinds of findings (weakness and strength) based on correlation analysis and four-view analysis. *W-S* and *W-W* are designed to improve weaknesses, while *S-S* and *S-W* are for enhancing strengths. Specifically, *W-S* is used to improve a weakness using strengths, while *W-W* is for improving a weakness by improving other related weaknesses. *S-S* enhances a strength using other related strengths, while *S-W* is used to enhance a strength by improving related weaknesses. For example, in the *W-S* template

(1) The *USING <strength>* and *IMPROVING <weakness>* clauses describe finding correlations identified in correlation analysis;

(2) The *WITH <resource>* clause describes human resources and tools from the organizational view analysis;

(3) The *AT <life cycle phase>* clause describes life cycle phases to be focused on, and

(4) The *TO ACHIEVE* <*business value*> clause describes the goal of the recommendation from a business perspective.

Table 1.4: Recommendation description templates.

Type	Findings	Description Template
W-S	Strengths, Weaknesses	IMPROVE <weakness>* BY [[USING <strength>*], [IMPROVING <weakness>*]] WITH <resource>* IN <life cycle phase>* TO ACHIEVE <business objective>*
W-W	Weaknesses only	IMPROVE <weakness>* BY IMPROVING <weakness>* WITH <resource>* IN <life cycle phase>* TO ACHIEVE <business objective>*
S-S	Strengths only	ENHANCE <strength>* BY USING <strength>* WITH <resource>* IN <life cycle phase>* TO ACHIEVE <business objective>*
S-W	Strengths, Weaknesses	ENHANCE <strength>* BY [[USING <strength>*], [IMPROVING <weakness>*]] WITH <resource>* IN <life cycle phase>* TO ACHIEVE <business objective>*

Refined *IP.S-DE-2* involves both strengths and weaknesses and, thus, either *W-S* or *S-W* may be used. The dominance in the IP are weaknesses which can be improved by the involved strengths. This leads to the choice of *W-S*. The selected template is instantiated by substituting the parameters with related activities, process areas, and work products in the findings of the IP. The asterisk next to a parameter denotes that the parameter can be instantiated multiple times.

For example, the *W-S* template can be instantiated as follows. The <*weakness*> parameter in the *IMPROVE* clause is substituted by *"testing process,"* which is the major area of concern in the weaknesses of *IP.S-DE-2*. For a detailed description, it can be as specific as activities like *"testing plan, test cases, testing strategy, collecting defects."* The <*strength*> parameter in the *USING* clause is substituted by *"testing strategy"* and *"test planning practice,"* which are activities in the involved strengths. The <*weakness*> parameter in the *IMPROVING* clause is instantiated with *"test planning process"* and *"quality assurance process,"* which are sub-areas focused on in the testing process. The <*resource*> parameter in the *WITH* clause is substituted by *"QA team"* and *"testing related tools"* which are identified in the organizational view analysis. The <*life cycle phase*> parameter in the *IN* clause is replaced by *"project planning phase,"* which suggests establishing a testing strategy early on in the project planning phase. This is based on the observation that there is little test planning in the IP. The <*business objective*> parameter in the *TO ACHIEVE* clause is substituted by *"system quality"* and *"time-to-market,"* which are identified as important objectives in the business value view analysis.

1.4.3.2 *Building Concrete Recommendations*

An abstract recommendation is elaborated by identifying recommendation seeds in the base IP. A recommendation seed is a primitive recommendation item for a specific finding. A seed is identified in consideration of the context of the base IP from an improvement perspective. For a strength, the seed suggests enhancing or expanding the practice throughout the organization. For a weakness, the seed suggests improving the practice or proposes an alternative. A set of related seeds is considered together and evolves to a concrete recommendation item to be added in the final recommendation. This is where expertise and experience come into play.

Figure 1.21 shows an example of identifying recommendation seeds from the findings in *IP.S-DE-2* and their evolution. For strength *S-DE-2*, the seed suggests practicing the activity even earlier in the project planning phase than the design phase, which enhances the strength. The seed may further suggest practicing the enhanced activity throughout the organization. There are two weaknesses in the IP with respect to project characteristics – *W-TE-1* and *W-PP-2*. *W-TE-1* describes that the project life cycle is not considered in test planning. *W-PP-2* points out that it takes little effort to identify risks in project planning. There are three weaknesses – *W-TE-1*, *W-TE-2*, and *W-QA-2* – in the IP that need to be improved to support the enhancement of *S-DE-2*. These weaknesses find that regression testing (*W-TE-1*), test levels (*W-TE-2*), and performance testing strategy (*W-QA-2*), which are important constituents of a testing strategy, are not defined in the current practice. These five recommendation seeds are merged together and evolve to a recommendation item addressing the need of a testing strategy to be established in project planning in consideration of project characteristics and customer needs.

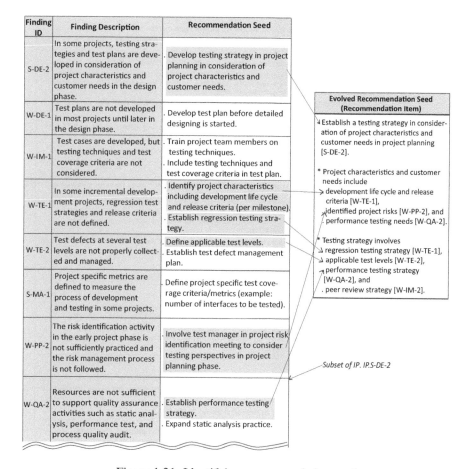

Figure 1.21: Identifying recommendation seeds.

Evolved recommendation seeds are categorized by the four views in Subsection 1.4.2. That is, recommendation seeds regarding activities belong to the software life cycle view, those regarding human resources and tools belong to the organizational view, those regarding guidance of an assessment model belong to the assessment model view, and those that are critical to business value belong to the business value view.

Figure 1.22 shows a concrete recommendation for *IP.S-DE-2*. In the figure, the evolved recommendation seed in Figure 1.21 is placed in the software life cycle view. Seeds that do not belong to any view (e.g., training programs) are described in the *Others* section. Recommendation items are tagged with related findings for traceability. Specific advice on the composition of the process action team may be specified in the *Suggested Team Composition* section.

Concrete Recommendation	
Perspectives	**Recommendation Items**

Software Life Cycle View
 	
Recommendation item in the previous figure
	. Project Planning phase
	1) Establish testing strategy in consideration of project characteristics and customer needs such as project risks, development life cycle, release criteria, and performance testing needs [S-DE-2, W-PP-2, W-PP-4, W-TE-1, W-QA-2].
	2) Establish testing strategy in project planning [S-DE-2].
	   * Test strategy may include regression test strategy [W-TE-1], applicable test levels [W-TE-2], performance testing strategy [W-QA-2], and peer review strategy [W-IM-2].
	3) Plan training on testing (e.g., test design) for project team members.
	4) Conduct formal QA review for the established testing strategy [W-QA-2, W-ORG-2].
	. Design phase
	1) Establish test plan before detailed designing is started [S-DE-2, W-DE-1, V-BIS-2].
	   * Test plan includes defect management plan [W-TE-2], project specific test coverage criteria and metrics (e.g., number of interfaces to be tested) [S-MA-1], and peer review plan (example criteria: focus peer review activity for defect-prone or changed codes) [W-IM-2]
	2) Conduct formal QA review activity for the established test plan [W-QA-2, W-ORG-2].
	. Testing Phase
	1) Review progress of testing using defined test coverage criteria and metrics [W-IM-1, W-TE-1].
	. Deployment phase
	1) Before product release, conduct formal review to ensure the test coverage is satisfied [W-IM-1, W-TE-1, W-ORG-2, V-SLC-1].
	. Project Closure phase
	1) Collect the lessons learned and good practices of the project and store them for reference in other projects [V-SLC-1].

Organizational View	**. Tools and Systems** 1) Integrate static analysis tool with auto-build system for frequent analysis with less effort [S-IM-1, W-IM-2, W-QA-2, V-ORG-1]. 2) Introduce new system or improve the existing PMS system for defect management and QA audit result management [V-ORG-1]. **. Human resources** 1) Assign QA personnel responsible for supporting testing activities [V-ORG-2, V-ORG-3] **. Role** 1) Designate test manager during project planning phase and have test manager participate in project planning such as risk identification and development life cycle selection [W-PP-2]. 2) Have QA provide guidance on establishing testing strategy and test plan of each project and conduct formal milestone review on testing activity against established testing coverage criteria and metrics [W-QA-4, V-ORG-2, V-ORG-3].
Assessment Model View	None
Business Value View	1) Establish risk identification checklist using historical risk data and encourage to use the checklist for project planning [V-BIS-3]. 2) Provide guidelines and training for regression testing [V-BIS-2]
Others	1) Improve training program on testing by referencing current good practices of projects [W-IM-1, W-TE-2, W-IM-2, V-BIS-3]. * training topics include 'test planning' for project managers and test managers and 'testing techniques' for test managers and developers.
Suggested Team Composition	
Include tester, project manager, and QA in the process action team	

Figure 1.22: Concrete recommendation.

1.5 Case Studies

We conducted case studies in collaboration with three consulting firms on twelve different software process improvement projects from various companies in business type, size, and domain. Table 1.5 shows an overview of the projects and companies involved in the case studies. The projects are to assess a specific unit in the companies. The diversity of the involved projects provides us with an opportunity to evaluate the generality of ReMo.

Table 1.5: Companies that participated in case studies.

| Case Study | Company | | | Assessed Unit | |
	Industry Domain	Size	Employees	Responsibilities	Employees
ProjectA	Automotive, Embedded Software	Large	500	Develop and maintain software platform for vehicle electric and electronic devices	32
ProjectB	Process plants Solution	SME^a	70	Develop and deploy plants software solutions	60
ProjectC	Telecommunication, IT Service, Enterprise system	Large	20,000	Develop ubiquitous city infrastructure and management systems for public services	300
ProjectD	IT Service, Enterprise system	Large	2,000	Develop and enhance public service management systems in two governmental offices	100
ProjectE	Automotive, Embedded	SME	50	Develop automotive black box system and lane departure warning system	15
ProjectF	IT Service and Engineering	Large	2,500	Develop and maintain steel software systems	200
ProjectG	Mobile and Automotive, Embedded	SME	260	Develop software on multimedia chip for mobile devices	20
ProjectH	Automotive and Mobile, Embedded	SME	50	Develop mobile platform and smart card solutions	35
ProjectI	Security Solution	SME	150	Develop and deploy security solutions	50
ProjectJ,K	Automotive	SME	150	Develop automotive electronic product (Body Control/Smart Key/Parking Aid/System, etc.)	50
ProjectL	Automotive (Car Audio & Infotainment)	SME	250	Develop car audio & infotainment system	60

^{a}SME: Small and Medium Enterprises

Table 1.6 shows the assessment data used in the case studies. Findings are produced by SCAMPI A, which is the formal assessment method for CMMI, and a structured gap analysis (SGA), which is a SCAMPI-like assessment activity for a capability-based reference model. CMMI and software process certification model (SPCM) [21] are used for SGAs. The projects *ProjectA*, *ProjectD*, *ProjectK*, and *ProjectL* include both weaknesses and strengths and we use them to demonstrate how strengths are used in ReMo. The average number of involved process areas is 12 for 41 findings.

Table 1.6: Assessment data used in case studies.

Case Study	Reference Model	Assessment Method	Num. of PAs	Finding[a] Type[a]	Num. of Findings
ProjectA	CMMI L[b]3	SCAMPI A	17	S, W	68
ProjectB	SPCM[c] L2	SGA[d]	10	W	43
ProjectC	CMMI L3	SGA	14	W	39
ProjectD	SPCM L2	SGA	10	S, W	36
ProjectE	CMMI L2	SGA	6	W	18
ProjectF	CMMI L4	SGA	19	W	65
ProjectG	SPCM L2	SGA	10	W	47
ProjectH	SPCM L2	SGA	10	W	35
ProjectI	SPCM L2	SGA	10	W	40
ProjectJ	CMMI L2	SGA	6	W	18
ProjectK	CMMI L3	SGA	17	S, W	49
ProjectL	CMMI L3	SCAMPI A	17	S, W	33

[a]Finding Type: S - Strength, W - Weakness, [b]L: Level

[c]SPCM: Software Process Certification Model, [d]SGA: Structured Gap Analysis

Table 1.7 shows the participants in the case studies. Fifteen process engineers participated in the case studies, including twelve software process consultants and three process improvement personnel from the organizations where the case studies were conducted. In particular, participants P01-7 and P12-13 are highly experienced project leaders, each having over 15 years of experience in more than 20 SPI projects. All participants are given a one-hour tutorial on ReMo. P1-P3, P7, and P13 had an experience in ReMo as a reviewer of ReMo outcomes and others actually practiced ReMo in their projects. Some consultants (P02, P04, P05, P06, P14) participated in more than one case study as noted in parenthesis.

Table 1.8 shows the summary of the case studies in terms of the number of involved process areas, findings, participants, produced IPs, recommendations, and person-hours spent. The level of details in produced recommendations varies slightly depending on the expertise level of the practitioner. *ProjectA* had more concrete recommendations produced to help less experienced participants have a better understanding of planning improvement actions. Other projects had more experienced participants involved and used simpler recommendations (e.g., without specific activities) as a result of the participants' expertise. Person-hours include execution time only. training time (one hour in each case study) and interview time are not included. Person-hours in *ProjectH* is only 1 due to the small scope (analyzing 3 process areas to 7 other areas) and the high familiarity of the participant with ReMo. Subsets of the ReMo outcomes produced in the case studies are shown in Table 1.8. A detailed evaluation including feedback is described in Section 1.6.

ReMo has been refined and evolved based on the feedback from case studies through Phases I-IV, as shown Figure 1.23.

Table 1.7: Participants in case studies.

Participant (case studies)	Responsibility	SW Eng. Experience (years)	Assessment Qualification
P01 (ProjectA)	Chief consultant for systems and software process improvement based on CMMI, SPCM, SPICE, ISO/IEC 26262, 6 Sigma, and etc.	22	Certified CMMI High Maturity Lead Appraiser, Provisional Automotive SPICE Assessor
P02 (Project C,F)	Chief consultant for systems and software process improvement based on CMMI, SPCM, Automotive SPICE, ISO/IEC 26262, and etc.	22	Certified CMMI High Maturity Lead Appraiser, Certified SPCM Lead Assessor
P03 (ProjectE)	Chief consultant for systems and software process improvement based on CMMI, SPCM, Automotive SPICE, ISO/IEC 26262, and etc.	20	Certified CMMI Lead Appraiser
P04 (ProjectC,F)	Chief consultant for systems and software process improvement based on CMMI, SPCM, Automotive SPICE, ISO/IEC 26262, and etc.	22	CMMI Appraiser, Automotive SPICE Assessor, Certified SPCM Assessor
P05 (ProjectC,E, H,I,J,K)	Principal consultant for systems and software process improvement based on CMMI, SPCM, Automotive SPICE, ISO/IEC 26262, and etc.	18	CMMI Appraiser, Certified SPCM Assessor
P06 (ProjectA,B, C,D,G,J)	Principal consultant for systems and software process improvement based on CMMI, SPCM, SPICE, Automotive SPICE, and etc.	18	CMMI Appraiser, Certified SPCM Assessor
P07 (ProjectA)	Principal consultant for systems and software process improvement based on CMMI, SPCM, SPICE, and etc.	15	CMMI Appraiser, Certified SPCM Assessor
P08 (ProjectB)	Assistant consultant for software process improvement based on CMMI, SPCM, and etc.	2	-
P09 (ProjectA)	Leading research engineer for process improvement in client organization	6	CMMI Appraiser
P10 (ProjectA)	Research engineer for process improvement in client organization	5	CMMI Appraiser
P11 (ProjectA)	Research engineer for process improvement in client organization	3	CMMI Appraiser
P12 (ProjectL)	Principal consultant for systems and software process improvement based on CMMI, SPCM, SPICE, and etc.	21	Certified SPCM Assessor
P13 (ProjectL)	Principal consultant for systems and software process improvement based on CMMI, SPCM, SPICE, and etc.	15	CMMI Appraiser
P14 (ProjectJ,K)	Principal consultant for systems and software process improvement based on CMMI, SPICE, Automotive SPICE, and etc.	12	CMMI Appraiser
P15 (ProjectK)	Assistant consultant for systems and software process improvement based on CMMI, SPCM, SPICE, Automotive SPICE, and etc.	4	CMMI Appraiser, Automotive SPICE Assessor

Table 1.8: Case study summary.

Case Study	Num. of PAs	Num. of Findings	Num. of Participants	Num. of IPs	Num. of Recomm.	Person Hours
ProjectA	17	68	6	11	11	30
ProjectB	10	43	2	5	5	8
ProjectC	14	39	4	7	7	11
ProjectD	10	36	1	6	6	8
ProjectE	6	18	2	5	3	3
ProjectF	19	65	2	4	4	8
ProjectG	10	47	1	4	4	8
ProjectH	10	35	1	3	3	1
ProjectI	10	40	1	7	7	4
ProjectJ	6	18	3	4	4	5
ProjectK	17	49	3	2	2	8
ProjectL	17	33	2	2	2	5
Average	12	41	2	5	5	8

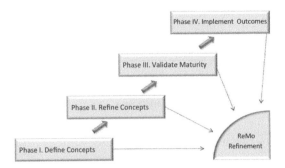

Figure 1.23: Evolution of ReMo.

In Phase I, the concepts of ReMo were defined and their feasibility was validated using posterior data from completed projects. Phase II refined ReMo based on the feedback from Phase I and validated the refined ReMo by applying it to the same data set used in Phase I. Phase III validated the maturity of the refined ReMo by applying it to live projects and Phase IV integrated ReMo with the process improvement cycle by implementing ReMo recommendations.

1.5.1   Phase I

ReMo concepts were defined and validated using the assessment findings from three completed projects – *ProjectB*, *ProjectD*, and *ProjectG* – where the authors also participated as assessors in identifying findings. The validation results were presented to process experts (*P01, P02, P04, P05, and P06*) for their feedback. While they all agreed upon the need for ReMo, they commented that correlation analysis is not concrete enough and the refinement process needs to be more detailed for each view in four-view analysis. They also commented that constructing recommendations from finding correlations needs to be more specific. The study in this phase was reported at the International Conference on Software and Systems Process [20].

1.5.2   Phase II

The ReMo was refined by addressing the concerns raised in Phase I. The concern about identifying finding correlations was addressed by defining correlation kinds and a matrix-based method for identifying correlations. The concern about the refinement process was addressed by providing specific aspects to be considered and an analysis method for each of the four views. The concern about the recommendation construction was addressed by introducing concepts of improvement packages and recommendation seeds, which serve together as a bridge between findings and recommendations. The refined ReMo was validated by applying it to the same data used in Phase I. In this phase, the resulting outcomes were compared with the existing data to observe improvements made by the refinement such as identifying missing correlations or missing improvement packages and improved quality of recommendations.

1.5.3   Phase III

The maturity of ReMo was validated through eight live projects – *ProjectC*, *ProjectE*, *ProjectF*, *ProjectH*, *ProjectI*, *ProjectJ*, *ProjectK*, and *ProjectL*. The validation focused on the producer-consumer chain of the three steps in ReMo as a project proceeds. Feedback in this phase included that the traceability from findings to recommendations is not very clear, which has been addressed by labeling IPs and recommendation items with related findings' ID. Another concern raised was the size of improvement packages being somewhat too large to keep track of the progress of recommendation development. This concern has been addressed by reducing the granularity of IPs by process areas. Feedback from *ProjectC* included that the correlation analysis involves heavy manual work. We addressed this partially by providing an Excel-based tool supporting basic data validation (e.g., consistency) in correlation analysis. Overall, the participants found ReMo efficient and effective.

1.5.4   Phase IV

In this phase, we evaluated the quality of ReMo recommendations by implementing them in improvement planning and implementation in a live project *ProjectA*. A one-day workshop on ReMo was provided before initiation. Participants were grouped into A and B. Group A executed ReMo and Group B reviewed the outcomes of ReMo. The reviewed outcomes were used by Group A to establish improvement action plans and the resulting improvement action plans were reviewed by Group B. Feedback in this phase included that (1) the resulting recommendations are concrete and detailed compared to the ones produced in the past projects and (2) the analysis results of business value view are useful for prioritizing improvement items in planning improvement actions. They also noted that ReMo reduces the quality gap between the artifacts produced by the experienced and those produced by those with less experience. Nine months after the ReMo-based improvement plan was established, most improvements, with the exception of long-term items, were successfully implemented. The lead engineer (P09) for implementing ReMo recommendations in the organization remarked that ReMo helped convince the management of the need for the changes and for the development project team to make the changes in their practice. ReMo also made improvement activities effective by encouraging people who played the roles identified in the organizational view analysis to participate in process implementation.

1.6   Evaluation

We evaluated ReMo using the data collected from the case studies in Section 1.5. Following are the research hypotheses:

- **(H1)** ReMo improves the productivity and performance of building recommendations.

- **(H2)** The resulting recommendations are concrete and comprehensive.

We evaluated H1 through surveys of the practitioners who participated in the case studies for the acceptability of ReMo based on the technology acceptance model (TAM) [18,57], which is a widely adopted method for evaluating the user acceptance of information application systems and development technologies and methodologies [19,58-60]. H2 is evaluated by comparing ReMo outcomes to those that are produced by the current practice and confirming the comparison results with practitioners.

1.6.1 Process Evaluation

To demonstrate ReMo supporting H1, we conducted surveys of the participants of the case studies in Section 1.5 on the user acceptance of ReMo in terms of perceived usefulness (PU) and perceived ease of use (PEOU) [18] using the technology acceptance model (TAM) [18]. Table 1.9 shows the questionnaires of PU and PEOU. The surveys were conducted in Phase III and IV in Figure 1.23.

Table 1.9: Measurement items for PU and PEOU.

Perceived Usefulness (PU)		Perceived Ease of Use (PEOU)	
(a)	Using ReMo in my job would enable me to accomplish tasks more quickly.	(a)	Learning to operate ReMo would be easy for me.
(b)	Using ReMo would improve my job performance.	(b)	I would find it easy to get ReMo to do what I want it to do.
(c)	Using ReMo in my job would increase my productivity.	(c)	My interaction with ReMo would be clear and understandable.
(d)	Using ReMo would enhance my effectiveness on the job.	(d)	I would find ReMo to be flexible to interact with.
(e)	Using ReMo would make it easier to do my job.	(e)	It would be easy for me to become skillful at using ReMo.
(f)	I would find ReMo useful in my job.	(f)	I would find ReMo easy to use.

1.6.1.1 Perceived Usefulness

Perceived usefulness (PU) is defined as "the degree to which a person believes that using a particular system would enhance his/her job performance" [18]. The results of PU on ReMo are shown in Table 1.10.

Table 1.10: Survey results on PU.

	Item	Mean	Median	Std. Dev
(a)	Work more quickly	5.6	6.0	1.12
(b)	Job performance	5.8	6.0	0.78
(c)	Increase productivity	5.5	6.0	0.67
(d)	Effectiveness	6.3	6.0	0.55
(e)	Makes job easier	5.7	6.0	1.07
(f)	Useful	6.1	6.0	0.79

∗ Scales : 1 extremely unlikely, 2 quite unlikely, 3 slightly unlikely,

4 neither, 5 slightly likely, 6 quite likely, 7 extremely likely

The table shows that the standard deviation of items (a) and (e) is notably higher than that of other items. This is due to the significant low score given by the participant P09, who felt that ReMo requires more effort in building recommendations than prior practice. Given that P09 has less experience in process assessment and improvement planning than others, his rating seems natural. On the other hand, P09 also commented that ReMo was helpful in getting support from the management and developers for implementing recommendations. We also observe in the table that items (d) and (f) have higher scores and lower standard deviations than other items. This can be interpreted as the practitioners having constant confidence in the effectiveness and usefulness of ReMo across projects.

The overall average of PU is 5.8 (out of 7.0) with the median 5.8 and the standard deviation 0.62. For the four most commonly used items (b), (c), (d), and (f) [19], the average is 6.0. The Cronbach alpha coefficient [61] of ReMo, which denotes reliability, is measured as 0.82, which is higher than the threshold of 0.70, which is commonly considered as being acceptable [62].

1.6.1.2 Perceived Ease of Use

Perceived ease of use (PEOU) is defined as "the degree to which a person believes that using a particular system would be free of effort" [18]. The results of the survey are shown in Table 1.11. The table shows surveyed items having similar standard deviations, which implies that ReMo is generally accepted as easy to use by both the experienced and the less experienced. The average PEOU is 6.0 with median 6.0 and standard deviation 0.40. The average of the four most commonly used items (a), (b), (d), and (f) [19] is measured the same. The reliability of the PEOU is measured as 0.73.

Table 1.11: Survey results on PEOU.

	Item	Mean	Median	Std. Dev
(a)	Easy to learn	5.9	6.0	0.52
(b)	Controllable	5.7	6.0	0.77
(c)	Clear & understandable	6.0	6.0	0.64
(d)	Flexible	6.1	6.0	0.79
(e)	Easy to become skillful	6.0	6.0	0.47
(f)	Easy to use	6.0	6.0	0.47

To gauge the generality of ReMo, we analyzed the survey results in various perspectives on the projects in which the survey participants participated. The perspectives include

(a) Organization size: the number of employees ≤ 99 (12 surveys) and > 99 (11 surveys);

(b) Assessment methods: SCAMPI A (8 surveys) and SGA (15 surveys);

(c) The number of involved process areas: ≤ 12 (6 surveys) and > 12 (17 surveys);

(d) The number of identified findings: ≤ 41 (15 surveys) and > 41 (8 surveys), and

(e) The number of years of experience of participants: ≤ 14 (6 surveys) and > 14 (17 surveys).

We adopted the Mann-Whitney U test for analyzing the differences of the two groups in each category. The Mann-Whitney U test [63] is a non-parametric test for the null hypothesis (H0) "ReMo is consistent in the two populations."

Table 1.12 shows the analysis results of p-value. Since the p-values of (a)-(e) in the table are not less than the chosen significance level of 0.05, we conclude that there is insufficient evidence to reject H0 for all five categories. This demonstrates that ReMo is general to the studied projects for the considered categories.

Table 1.12: Mann-Whitney U Test results on PU and PEOU.

	Context	Groups	PU	PEOU
(a)	Organization size	≤ 99 vs. > 99	.1.000	.566
(b)	Assessment method	SCAMPI vs. SGP	.190	.728
(c)	Number of process areas	≤ 12 vs. > 12	.227	.286
(d)	Number of findings	≤ 41 vs. > 41	.325	.115
(e)	Participant's years of experience	≤ 14 vs. > 14	.708	.658

* Mann-Whitney U Test P-values for PU and PEOU are presented

The general feedback on the usefulness of ReMo based on individual interviews is that ReMo helps in understanding the organizational state of the software development practice and considering improvement alternatives. P04, P05, and P08 commented that ReMo helps find unforeseen action items and the resulting recommendations are concrete and convincing. P04 and P09 advised extending the application of ReMo to other domains such as the system domain and the vehicle domain. The participants also commented that after practicing ReMo, its purpose and necessity are better understood. In particular, they all value four-view analysis in identifying hidden correlations of findings. On the other hand, P09 commented that identifying correlations can be somewhat difficult for less experienced people and it would be helpful if participants were advised on the expected expertise and experience in using ReMo. Besides the capability-based models used in the case studies, P04 also suggested looking into non-capability-based models. With respect to the implementation of produced recommendations, participants also commented that ReMo complements the current process assessment practice in their organization and its outcomes are concrete enough to convince the commitment of management and practitioners and facilitate communication.

1.6.2 Outcome Evaluation

With respect to H2, we evaluated the concreteness and comprehensiveness of ReMo recommendations by comparing them to those that are produced by the current practice in the case studies in Section 1.5. Concreteness is concerned with the level of details that the resulting recommendations possess. Details should contain detailed guidelines as to "how" the concern in related findings can be addressed. Comprehensiveness is concerned that a recommendation addresses related findings together across process areas for synergistic improvements.

Definition and measurement attributes for concreteness and comprehensiveness are established and refined from trial measurements by the evaluators. Measurements are made for every recommendation statement in five out of twelve case studies that have two sets of improvement recommendations – one set from ReMo (see the example in Figure 1.22) and another set from the current practice. Table 1.13 shows a recommendation example developed by the current practice. Two experts, each with over 20 years of experience, individually measured each attribute, and then a consensus is made from a structured review and discussion session using the Delphi method [64].

Table 1.13: Example recommendations produced by an ad-hoc method in current practice.

Process area	Finding Type	Finding ID	Recommendation Items
Design	Strength	S-DE-2	–
	Weakness	W-DE-1	Improve testing process . Test planning in high-level design phase
Implement-ation	Strength	S-IM-1	–
	Weakness	W-IM-1	Develop guideline and training program for testing techniques.
Testing	Weakness	W-TE-1	Develop guideline on regression test strategy and release criteria.
	Weakness	W-TE-2	Improve defect management . Introduce defect management tool

1.6.2.1 Concreteness

SPEM 2.0 [65], the standard for software process definition by the Object Management Group (OMG), defines *activity, work product, work product description (explanation of the contents), role, team (participating organization), tool,* and *phase (timing)* as core aspects to be considered in process modeling. The concreteness of recommendations is measured by process element coverage which represents the degree to which each element is covered.

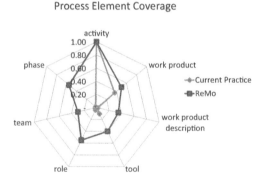

Figure 1.24: Concreteness comparison —Process element coverage.

Figure 1.24 and Table 1.14 show the comparison results in terms of process element coverage on a scale of 0 to 1. In Figure 1.24, the coverage of 1.0 for the *activity* element means that all the recommendations in the five projects specify *activity* information, and the coverage of 0.4 for the *phase* element denotes that only 40% of recommendations specify *phase* information. The average coverage is measured as 0.22 for the current practice and 0.52 for ReMo, which indicates a notable improvement by ReMo.

Table 1.14: Process element coverage.

Process Element	Activity	Work product	Work product Description	Tool	Role	Team	Phase	Average
Current Practice	1.00	0.36	0.02	0.11	0.04	0.02	0.02	0.22
ReMo	1.00	0.50	0.35	0.40	0.55	0.30	0.55	0.52
Difference	-	+0.14	+0.33	+0.29	+0.51	+0.28	+0.53	+0.35

Figure 1.25 presents the number of covered process elements by projects. With the same assessment findings, ReMo recommendations demonstrate higher concreteness than current practice ones in all five case studies. On average, the current practice produces information covering only 1.7 process elements, while ReMo covers 3.6 process elements, which demonstrates the superiority of ReMo over the current practice.

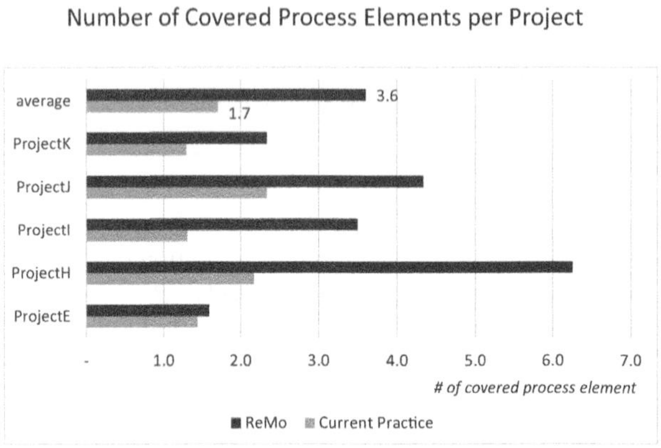

Number of Covered Process Elements per Project

Figure 1.25: Concreteness comparison per project.

Figure 1.26 demonstrates the comparison of the ReMo recommendation in Figure 1.22 with the current practice recommendation in Table 1.13 regarding test planning activity from a concretness perspective. The figure shows that the ReMo recommendation addresses the five aspects with ample details for each aspect, while the current practice recommendation describes only four aspects with limited information. Both recommendations cover the testing process.

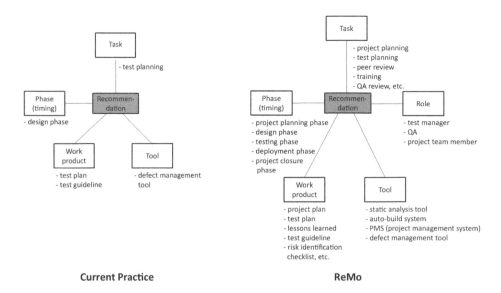

Figure 1.26: Concreteness comparison of recommendation examples.

1.6.2.2 Comprehensiveness

Comprehensiveness is measured by process area coverage which represents the degree to which relevant process areas in the composition of recommendations are covered. Figure 1.27 shows the comparison of ReMo recommendations with current practice recommendations for comprehensiveness. The process area coverage is measured on a scale of 0 to 1 where 1 means that all the relevant process areas given by the specification of the reference model are covered. In the figure, the average coverage is measured as 0.88 for ReMo and 0.27 for the current practice, which demonstrates a significant improvement by ReMo. Table 1.15 shows the process area coverage by projects. *ProjectI* and *ProjectH* are excluded from the table as their underlying reference model does not provide process correlation information. The table shows that ReMo outperforms the current practice for all the three projects.

Process Area Coverage

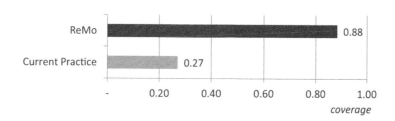

Figure 1.27: Comprehensiveness comparison —Process area coverage.

Table 1.15: Process area coverage per project.

Project	Current Practice	ReMo	Difference
ProjectE	0.27	0.90	+0.63
ProjectJ	0.37	1.00	+0.63
ProjectK	0.17	0.75	+0.58
average	0.27	0.88	+0.61

Figure 1.28 shows the comparison of ReMo with the current practice for comprehensiveness. In Figure 1.28(a), the current practice takes in single weakness *W-DE-1* and produces a recommendation based on the weakness. The produced recommendation simply suggests an activity to establish a test plan without concrete advice as to how test plans should be developed. Furthermore, it does not consider any finding about strength. On the other hand, the recommendation produced by ReMo is built upon a group of five related findings from the four process areas. In addition, the considered findings also include both weaknesses and strengths. This enables ReMo to produce detailed advice on specific items (e.g., test coverage criteria) to be considered in software test planning activity. Similarly, in Figure 1.28(b), the ReMo recommendation, which is built upon a group of the six related findings from the five process areas, provides specific activities on which test strategies should be established and the bases to be considered in developing test strategies, while the one produced by the current practice is terse and abstract.

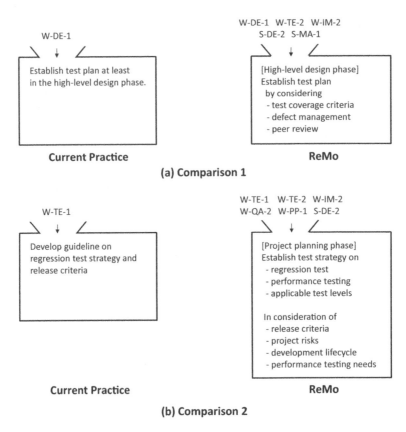

Figure 1.28: Comprehensiveness comparison —Recommendation example.

1.6.3   Threats to Validity

In this subsection, we discuss threats to validity from construct, internal, and external perspectives [66-70].

1.6.3.1   *Construct Validity*

Construct validity is concerned with failing on developing a sufficiently operational set of measures and collecting data due to subjective judgement. With respect to construct validity, the derived evaluation results in our case studies might involve subjectivity. To mitigate this threat, we used multiple sources of evidence for the results, including documentation reviews, interviews, surveys, and observations. These sources confirm that there exists consistency in the collected data. We also used an established measurement tool (i.e., TAM) to further mitigate the threat. The preliminary case study results were peer-reviewed and confirmed by a group of practitioners who participated in the case studies.

1.6.3.2   *Internal Validity*

Internal validity is concerned with the validity of causal relations of outputs. The quality of ReMo recommendations might be relative to the level of experience of the participants who participated in the case studies. It is quite natural that more experienced people would likely produce better quality outcomes. In the outcome evaluation, the participants consistently stated that ReMo helps produce better recommendations compared to their prior recommendations produced by an ad-hoc practice in the past. This testifies that although the quality of ReMo recommendations is relative to experience level, practitioners do feel that at their experience level, the quality of ReMo recommendations is better than those produced in the past practice.

1.6.3.3 External Validity

External validity is concerned with the generalization of study results. In this work, the improvements by ReMo may be justifiable only within the studied SPI projects and participants. To mitigate this threat, we strived to conduct as many case studies as possible with more process experts involved. The contexts of the studied projects vary in business domain, company size, assessed organization size, process reference model, assessment method, and the number of involved process areas and findings. The participants of the case studies also have many years of experiences in various domains, including enterprise system integration, automotive, and telecommunication. We think that the diversity of the covered contexts and domains testifies to the generality of ReMo to a reasonable extent.

1.7 Discussion

In this study, ReMo, a process model for producing process improvement recommendations, is presented and validated through multiple industrial case studies and structured reviews by experts. The results show that ReMo is applicable in industrial practice of SPI and improves the quality of improvement recommendations. The creation of improvement recommendations is known to be an essential activity in software process improvement [8-10,23,29]. However, both the commercial (e.g., CMMI, TMMI, ISO/IEC) and academic literature have so far focused mainly on establishing a set of best practices as reference models and applying the models across industries to understand organizational development capability. There exists only a little research regarding quality improvement recommendations. Table 1.16 summarizes the existing relevant studies (see Section 1.3 for details of each study) in comparison with ReMo. In practice, although improvement recommendations are regarded as essential, their creation is carried out in an ad-hoc manner, and the quality of essential activities and their outcome highly rely on the personal capability of practitioners. This should be changed. Process reference models are used to improve the software development process. In the same sense, SPI processes should be used to improve SPI. ReMo as an SPI process can serve as a guidance and training material for junior and senior practitioners to produce quality improvement recommendations.

ReMo was evaluated through diverse case studies. In the evaluation of perceived usefulness (see Table 1.10), ReMo received relatively lower scores on *work more quickly* (5.6/7) and *makes job easier* (5.7/7), which are concerned with efficiency, while receiving higher scores on *effectivenss* (6.3/7) and *useful* (6.1/7). The room for improvement in efficiency can be filled up by establishing a knowledge base of empirical SPI data (e.g., assessment findings, findings analysis results, produced recommendations, development context, etc.) and AI-assistant tool support which can accelerate buy-in of ReMo by SPI practitioners and increase the productivity of SPI activity. ReMo is ready to expand its application to other development contexts (e.g., agile, DevOps, etc.) and assessment models (ISO/IEC 15504, ITIL, TMMI, etc.) to enhance the generality and practicality of ReMo. ReMo uses findings from an assessment model to create recommendations. However, ReMo is not dependent on any specific assessment model. Although the CMMI and SPCM assessment models were used in the case studies, ReMo can also be used with other assessment models.

Table 1.16: A comparison of ReMo with existing studies.

Studies	Identification of recommendations	Correlation Analysis	Guidance on description of recommendations
McFeeley [10]	Yes	None	None
Mejía et al. [24]	Yes	None	Yes
Shrestha et al. [25]	Yes	None	Yes
Laksono et al. [27]	Yes	None	Yes
Hierholzer et al. [31]	Yes	Partially	None
Sun and Liu [32]	Yes	Partially	None
Raza et al. [33,67]	Partially	None	None
Farooq et al. [34]	Partially	None	None
Villalón et al. [43]	Partially	Partially	None
Harjumaa [44]	Yes	None	None
Gorschek and Wohlin [46]	None	Partially	None
Monteiro et al. [47]	None	Partially	None
Chen et al. [48]	None	Partially	Partially
Calvo-anzano et al. [49]	None	Partially	Partially
Arcilla et al. [51]	None	Partially	Partially
ReMo	Yes	Yes	Yes

1.8 Conclusion

We have presented ReMo, a model for systematic development of recommendations in the process improvement process. The development of ReMo is driven by practical needs from the field and its benefits and impact were evaluated through diverse case studies, and surveys and interviews of practitioners. ReMo takes as input the findings resulting from process assessment and analyzes them for correlations. Improvement packages are identified by grouping findings that have a great impact across process areas. Improvement packages are refined through four-view analysis. Recommendation seeds are identified from a refined improvement package and evolve to recommendation items to form a concrete recommendation. Twelve case studies were conducted to evaluate ReMo for outcome quality and process acceptance. The evaluation showed that ReMo recommendations are more concrete and comprehensive than those produced by the current practice. Acceptance of ReMo is evaluated as 5.8 out of 7.0 for perceived usefulness and 6.0 out of 7.0 for perceived ease of use. A statistical analysis of the evaluation results to various contextual parameters (e.g., organizational size, number of involved process areas, participants' experience) showed that ReMo is general within the considered projects in the case studies.

The consideration of process areas in correlation analysis enables identification of implicit correlations across related process areas whose relevance is not explicit. Such process areas are usually considered independently in practice, which makes it difficult to identify hidden correlations. The type of input findings (weakness, strength) influences the results of ReMo. In the twelve case studies, eight studies used only weaknesses and the other four used both strengths and weaknesses. While the sole use of weaknesses does not have a negative impact on the quality of ReMo outcomes, the combined use of both weaknesses and strengths produces more constructive outcomes. Also, the quality of input findings may have an impact on the quality of ReMo outcomes, and thus certain quality control is necessary for input findings.

ReMo is designed for the capability-based process reference models which are widely used in industry. However, ReMo can also be used for a non-capability-based model (e.g.,

ISO 26262) by tailoring (or excluding) the assessment model view in the refinement process. While ReMo helps improve the productivity of less experienced individuals, its impact can be much greater if more experienced and motivated practitioners work as a team. The most rewarding comment in the case studies was submitted by P11, who said that *"ReMo is very systematic and helped me a lot in deriving improvement action plans. I could not get it done without ReMo."*

We plan to define metamodels and tool support for establishing finding correlations and identifying improvement packages. As advised in case studies, we shall look into the extent to which ReMo can be used in other domains such as systems engineering. For instance, the life cycle view and assessment model view might need to be tailored for a specific life cycle model in the target domain.

Acknowledgments

This research was partially supported by the MSIT (Ministry of Science and ICT), Republic of Korea, under the ITRC (Information Technology Research Center) support program (IITP-2021-2017-0-01628) supervised by the IITP (Institute for Information & Communications Technology Promotion)

References

1. Staples, M., & Niazi, M. (2008). Systematic review of organizational motivations for adopting CMM-based SPI. *Information and Software Technology*, 50(7-8), 605-620.

2. Unterkalmsteiner, M., Gorschek, T., Islam, A. M., Cheng, C. K., Permadi, R. B., & Feldt, R. (2011). Evaluation and measurement of software process improvement - a systematic literature review. *IEEE Transactions on Software Engineering*, 38(2), 398-424.

3. Swinarski, M., Parente, D. H., & Kishore, R. (2012). Do small IT firms benefit from higher process capability?. *Communications of the ACM*, 55(7), 129-134.

4. Paulk, M. C., Humphrey, W. S., & Pandelios G. J. (1992). Software process assessments: Issues and lessons learned. *in ISQE92 Proceedings*, 4B41-4B58, 41-58.

5. Sommerville, I., & Ransom, J. (2005). An empirical study of industrial requirements engineering process assessment and improvement. *ACM Transactions on Software Engineering and Methodology (TOSEM)*, 14(1), 85-117.

6. Goldenson, D. R., & Herbsleb, J. D. (1995). After the Appraisal: A Systematic Survey of Process Improvement, its Benefits, and Factors that Influence Success. CMU/SEI-95-TR-009, Software Engineering Inst., Carnegie Mellon University.

7. Humphrey, W. S., Snyder, T. R., & Willis, R. R. (1991). Software process improvement at Hughes Aircraft. *IEEE Software*, 8(4), 11-23.

8. Team, S. U. (2011). Standard CMMI Appraisal Method for Process Improvement (SCAMPI) A, Version 1.3: Method Definition Document. *Software Engineering Institute*, Carnegie Mellon University, Tech. Rep. CMU/SEI-2011-HB-001.

9. ISO/IEC, ISO/IEC 15504 Information technology - Process assessment Part 1 - Part 5 (2006).

10. McFeeley, B. (1996). *IDEAL: A User's Guide for Software Process Improvement*. CMU/SEI-96-HB-001, Carnegie Mellon University Software Engineering Inst.

11. Zahra, K., Azam, F., Ilyas, F., Faisal, H., Ambreen, N., & Gondal, N. (2017, January). Success factors of organizational change in software process improvement: A systematic literature

review. In *Proceedings of the 5th International Conference on Information and Education Technology* (pp. 155-160).

12. Baddoo, N., & Hall, T. (2003). De-motivators for software process improvement: an analysis of practitioners' views. *Journal of Systems and Software*, 66(1), 23-33.

13. Dyba, T. (2005). An empirical investigation of the key factors for success in software process improvement. *IEEE transactions on Software Engineering*, 31(5), 410-424.

14. Niazi, M., Babar, M. A., & Verner, J. M. (2010). Software Process Improvement barriers: A cross-cultural comparison. *Information and Software Technology*, 52(11), 1204-1216.

15. Cattaneo, F., Fuggetta, A., & Sciuto, D. (2001). Pursuing coherence in software process assessment and improvement. *Software Process: Improvement and Practice*, 6(1), 3-22.

16. Pettigrew, A. M. (2012). Context and action in the transformation of the firm: A reprise. *Journal of Management Studies*, 49(7), 1304-1328.

17. Runeson, P., & Höst, M. (2009). Guidelines for conducting and reporting case study research in software engineering. *Empirical Software Engineering*, 14(2), 131-164.

18. Davis, F. D. (1989). Perceived usefulness, perceived ease of use, and user acceptance of information technology. *MIS Quarterly*, 319-340.

19. Legris, P., Ingham, J., & Collerette, P. (2003). Why do people use information technology? A critical review of the technology acceptance model. *Information & Management*, 40(3), 191-204.

20. Choi, S., Kim, D. K., & Park, S. (2012, June). ReMo: a recommendation model for software process improvement. In *2012 International Conference on Software and System Process (ICSSP)* (pp. 135-139). IEEE.

21. Hwang, S. M., & Im, S. (2011, May). Korean software process quality certification model. In *2011 First ACIS/JNU International Conference on Computers, Networks, Systems and Industrial Engineering* (pp. 123-128). IEEE.

22. Hörmann, K., Müller, M., Dittmann, L., & Zimmer, J. (2008). *Automotive SPICE in Practice: Surviving Implementation and Assessment*. Rocky Nook., 1st Edition.

23. CMMI Product Team (2010). *CMMI for Development*, Version 1.3, Tech. Rep. CMU/SEI-2010-TR- 033, Software Engineering Inst, Carnegie Mellon University.

24. Mejía, J., Iñiguez, F., & Muñoz, M. (2017, June). SMART-SPI: A data analysis model proposal for software process improvement. In *2017 12th Iberian Conference on Information Systems and Technologies (CISTI)* (pp. 1-7). IEEE.

25. Shrestha, A., Cater-Steel, A., Toleman, M., Behari, S., & Rajaeian, M. M. (2020). Development and evaluation of a software-mediated process assessment method for IT service management. *Information & Management*, 57(4), 103213.

26. White, S. K., & Greiner, L. (2019). What is ITIL? Your guide to the IT Infrastructure Library. Publicado em. (2019, Jan 18). URL https://www.cio.com/article/2439501/infrastructure-it-infrastructure-library-itil-definition

27. Laksono, M. A., Budiardjo, E. K., & Ferdinansyah, A. (2019, January). Assessment of Test Maturity Model: A Comparative Study for Process Improvement. In *Proceedings of the 2nd International Conference on Software Engineering and Information Management*, New York, NY, USA, (pp. 110-118).

28. Van Veenendaal, E., & Wells, B. (2012). Test maturity model integration (TMMi). *TMMI Foundation* (www. tmmifoundation. org), Uitgeverij Tutein Nolthenius.

29. T. Foundation, TMMi Assessment Method Application Requirements (TAMAR) Release 1.0, Tech. rep., TMMi Foundation (2014). URL http://www.tmmi.org

30. Yoji Akao. (2004). *Quality function deployment: integrating customer requirements into product design*. SteinerBooks.

31. Hierholzer, A., Herzwurm, G., & Schlang, H. (2003). Applying QFD for software process improvement at SAP AG, *in: Proceedings of the World Innovation and Strategy Conference*, 1998, pp. 85-95.

32. Sun, Y., & Liu, X. F. (2010). Business-oriented software process improvement based on CMMI using QFD. *Information and Software Technology*, 52(1), 79-91.

33. Raza, M., Faria, J. P., Amaro, L., & Henriques, P. C. (2017, July). WebProcessPAIR: recommendation system for software process improvement. In R. Bendraou, D. Raffo, L. Huang, F. M. Maggi (Eds.), *Proceedings of the 2017 International Conference on Software and System Process*, Paris, France, (pp. 139-140).

34. Farooq, U., Ahmed, M., Hussain, S., Hussain, F., Naseem, A., & Aslam, K. (2021). Blockchain-Based Software Process Improvement (BBSPI): An Approach for SMEs to Perform Process Improvement. *IEEE Access*, 9, 10426-10442.

35. Yli-Huumo, J., Ko, D., Choi, S., Park, S., & Smolander, K. (2016). Where is current research on blockchain technology?—a systematic review. *PloS one*, 11(10), e0163477, 1-27.

36. Pino, F. J., Pardo, C., García, F., & Piattini, M. (2010). Assessment methodology for software process improvement in small organizations. *Information and Software Technology*, 52(10), 1044-1061.

37. Wiegers, K. E., & Sturzenberger, D. C. (2000). A modular software process mini-assessment method. *IEEE Software*, 17(1), 62-69.

38. Tang, J., Jing, M., & Zhu, Q. (2012). Towards Quantitative Assessment Model for Software Process Improvement in Small Organization. *Information Technology Journal*, 11(1), 49-57.

39. Habra, N., Alexandre, S., Desharnais, J. M., Laporte, C. Y., & Renault, A. (2008). Initiating software process improvement in very small enterprises: Experience with a light assessment tool. *Information and Software Technology*, 50(7-8), 763-771.

40. Wilkie, F. G., Mc Caffery, F., McFall, D., Lester, N., & Wilkinson, E. (2007). A Low-overhead method for software process appraisal. *Software Process: Improvement and Practice*, 12(4), 339-349.

41. Pettersson, F., Ivarsson, M., Gorschek, T., & Öhman, P. (2008). A practitioner's guide to light weight software process assessment and improvement planning. *Journal of Systems and Software*, 81(6), 972-995.

42. Daily, K., & Dresner, D. (2003). Towards software excellence—informal self-assessment for software developers. *Software Process: Improvement and Practice*, 8(3), 157-168.

43. Villalón, J. A. C. M., Agustín, G. C., Gilabert, T. S. F., Seco, A. D. A., Sánchez, L. G., & Cota, M. P. (2002). Experiences in the application of software process improvement in SMES. *Software Quality Journal*, 10(3), 261-273.

44. Harjumaa, L. (2005). A pattern approach to software inspection process improvement. *Software Process: Improvement and Practice*, 10(4), 455-465.

45. Haase, V. H. (1998, August). Software process improvement planning with neural networks. In Proceedings. 24th EUROMICRO Conference (Cat. No. 98EX204) (Vol. 2, pp. 808-815). IEEE.

46. Gorschek, T., & Wohlin, C. (2004). Packaging software process improvement issues: a method and a case study. *Software: Practice and Experience*, 34(14), 1311-1344.

47. Monteiro, P., Machado, R. J., Kazman, R., & Henriques, C. (2010, June). Dependency analysis between CMMI process areas. In *International Conference on Product Focused Software Process Improvement* (pp. 263-275). Springer, Berlin, Heidelberg.

48. Chen, X., Staples, M., & Bannerman, P. (2008, September). Analysis of dependencies between specific practices in CMMI maturity level 2. In *European Conference on Software Process Improvement* (pp. 94-105). Springer, Berlin, Heidelberg.

49. Calvo-Manzano, J., Cuevas, G., Mejía, J., San Feliu, T., & Sánchez, A. (2008, September). CMMI-ACQ: A formal implementation sequences of the processes areas at maturity level 2. In *2008 Electronics, Robotics and Automotive Mechanics Conference (CERMA'08)* (pp. 212-217). IEEE. Doi:10.1109/CERMA.2008.55.

50. CMMI Product Team, CMMI for Acquisition, Version 1.3, Tech. Rep. CMU/SEI-2010-TR- 032, Software Engineering Inst., Carnegie Mellon University (2010). URL http://resources.sei.cmu.edu/library/asset-view.cfm?AssetID=9657

51. Arcilla, M., Calvo-Manzano, J., Cuevas, G., Gómez, G., Ruiz, E., & San Feliu, T. (2008, September). A solution for establishing the information technology service management processes implementation sequence. In *European Conference on Software Process Improvement* (pp. 106-116). Springer, Berlin, Heidelberg.

52. Frederiksen, H. D., & Mathiassen, L. (2008). A contextual approach to improving software metrics practices. *IEEE Transactions on Engineering Management*, 55(4), 602-616.

53. Bremer, M. (2012), Organizational Culture Change: Unleashing your Organization's Potential in Circles of 10, Kikker Groep.

54. Abran, A., Moore, J. W., Bourque, P., Dupuis, R., & Tripp, L. (2004). Software engineering body of knowledge. *IEEE Computer Society*, Angela Burgess.

55. Johansen, J., & Pries-Heje, J. (2007). Success with improvement—requires the right roles to be enacted—in symbiosis. *Software Process: Improvement and Practice*, 12(6), 529-539.

56. Smith, M. L., Erwin, J., & Diaferio, S. (2005). Role & responsibility charting (RACI). In *Project Management Forum (PMForum)* (Vol. 5). http://myclass.peelschools.org/sec/12/4268/Resources/RACIRWeb31:pdf

57. Davis, F. D., Bagozzi, R. P., & Warshaw, P. R. (1989). User acceptance of computer technology: A comparison of two theoretical models. *Management Science*, 35(8), 982-1003.

58. Umarji, M., & Seaman, C. (2005). Predicting acceptance of software process improvement. *ACM SIGSOFT Software Engineering Notes*, 30(4), 1-6.

59. Chan, F. K., & Thong, J. Y. (2009). Acceptance of agile methodologies: A critical review and conceptual framework. *Decision Support Systems*, 46(4), 803-814.

60. Riemenschneider, C. K., Hardgrave, B. C., & Davis, F. D. (2002). Explaining software developer acceptance of methodologies: a comparison of five theoretical models. *IEEE Transactions on Software Engineering*, 28(12), 1135-1145.

61. Carmines, E. G., & Zeller, R. A. (1979). *Reliability and validity assessment*. SAGE Publication.

62. Santos, J. R. A. (1999). Cronbach's alpha: A tool for assessing the reliability of scales. *Journal of Extension*, 37(2), 1-5.

63. Mann, H. B., & Whitney, D. R. (1947). On a test of whether one of two random variables is stochastically larger than the other. *The Annals of Mathematics and Statistics*, 50-60.

64. Turoff, M., & Linstone, H. A. (2002). *The Delphi method-techniques and applications*. Addison-Wesley.

65. I. Object Management Group, Software & Systems Process Engineering Meta-Model (SPEM) 2.0 (April 2008).

66. Yin, R. K. (2009). *Case Study Research. Design and Methods* 4th edn., SAGE Publications.

67. Raza, M., & Faria, J. P. (2016, August). ProcessPAIR: A tool for automated performance analysis and improvement recommendation in software development. In *Proceedings of the 31st IEEE/ACM International Conference on Automated Software Engineering* (pp. 798-803).

68. Le, D. N., Nguyen, G. N., Garg, H., Huynh, Q. T., Bao, T. N., & Tuan, N. N. (2021). Optimizing Bidders Selection of Multi-Round Procurement Problem in Software Project Management Using Parallel Max-Min Ant System Algorithm. *CMC-COMPUTERS MATERIALS & CONTINUA*, 66(1), 993-1010.

69. Bao, T. N., Huynh, Q. T., Nguyen, X. T., Nguyen, G. N., & Le, D. N. (2020). A Novel Particle Swarm Optimization Approach to Support Decision-Making in the Multi-Round of an Auction by Game Theory. *International Journal of Computational Intelligence Systems*, 13(1), 1447-1463.

70. Le, D. N. (2017). A new ant algorithm for optimal service selection with end-to-end QoS constraints. *Journal of Internet Technology*, 18(5), 1017-1030.

Appendix. Example Recommendations in Case Studies

Table 1.17: Example results in case studies.

Case Study	Correlation Analysis	Refining Improvement Package	Building Recommendations
ProjectA	(a) Relation between requirement change and peer review (b) Relation between peer review and quality assurance	(a) Relation between change impact analysis and formal decision and analysis (organizational view analysis)	Improve peer review process by following: (a) Review requirement change request from functional and non-functional views by referencing the change review checklist, (b) When the duration of implementing change is much longer than average (e.g. more than 2-3 months), plan peer review for each development phase, (c) When the impact of change is large in terms of product quality and project schedule, follow the formal decision and analysis process, (d) Review requirement specification according to the requirement checklist on quality attributes, (e) Conduct process and product audit periodically for conformance to requirement change process and peer review process by quality assurance personnel
ProjectB	(a) Relation between peer review on source code and coding standard, (b) Relation between peer review on code criteria and static analysis results, (c) Relation between process conformance review and metric-based process monitoring	(a) Importance of formalized project milestone review and requirements analysis (business value view analysis)	Improve code peer review process by following: (a) Establish coding standard for more effective code review, (b) Identify violation of coding standard in regular by introducing automated tool, (c) Focus code review for defect-prone area and new and changed area, which can be identified by build system and static analysis tool, (d) Identify code quality metrics about static analysis and code review, (e) Improve quality audit checklist for code review, and conduct quality audit regularly for the conformance of the activity.
ProjectC	(a) Relation among project progress monitoring and peer review, quality audit, and configuration management	(a) Importance of configuration audit for a software release (business value view analysis)	Enhance visibility of project progress by following: (a) Enhance visibility of work product quality by peer review results, (b) Enhance visibility of process quality by process audit results, (c) Enhance visibility on change by establishing baseline and performing configuration audit
ProjectD	(a) Relation among requirement management, requirement analysis, quality assurance, configuration management, and measurement and analysis	(a) Little involvement of testers in requirement change practice (organizational view analysis)	Improve requirement change and management by following: (a) Establish measurement program for requirement process (e.g., number of requirement, number of changed requirement, and etc.), (b) Conduct peer review on draft requirement specification, (c) Conduct customer's formal review before requirements are approved, (d) Select level of formality on requirement change process according to the size and impact of change, (e) Conduct configuration audit for requirement baseline and change management, (f) Conduct quality assurance audit for requirement change and management, (g) Have testers participate in requirement change process for requirement review from testing perspectives and test preparation in advance

Table 1.18: Example results in case studies (continued).

Case Study	Correlation Analysis	Refining Improvement Package	Building Recommendations
ProjectE	(a) Relation among project planning, project monitoring and control, requirement management, configuration management, quality assurance, and measurement and analysis	(a) Little involvement of project managers in development tasks and important decisions such as requirement change and design change. (organizational view analysis) (b) Necessity of process improvement in all the development phases in terms of project management (software life cycle view analysis)	Improve project planning by following: (a) Establish effort estimation procedure, (b) Establish standard work breakdown structure, and plan tasks and deliverables accordingly, (c) Plan project data and work product management, (d) Review lessons learned of prior projects in project planning phase, (e) Establish completion criteria for each milestone in accordance with criteria for quality audit and configuration audit, (f) At each milestone, conduct formal milestone review according to the completion criteria, (g) In project closure phase, conduct lessons learned meeting and collect measurement data for reference in other project
ProjectF	(a) Relation among product quality criteria and project planning, product integration, verification, and validation	(a) Little guidance for project activities by quality assurance team (organizational view analysis)	Improve product quality by following: (a) Establish quality criteria for each development phase, (b) According to the quality criteria, conduct requirement traceability tracking and quality review at each phase, (c) Improve defect management by introducing tool and make decisions based on defect analyses, (d) Have testing experts for test planning, (e) Perform testing and peer review in complementary way (e.g., conduct review based on testing results and vice versa)
ProjectG	(a) Relation among test planning and completion criteria of each development phase and quality criteria of software release	(a) Little involvement of testing team in release process (organizational view analysis)	Improve product quality by following: (a) Establish quality objectives for product and completion criteria of each phase with testing team, (b) Establish test plan according to the quality objectives and completion criteria of each phase, (c) Before releasing product, conduct formal review on testing team's test results based on the quality criteria
ProjectH	(a) Relation between requirement specification and testing	(a) Importance of requirement specification and requirement traceability (business value view analysis)	Improve requirement specification by following: (a) Develop requirement specification according to the standard template. Template should include i) non-functional requirements, especially performance and usability, ii) testing needs on stress and load testing, iii) User Interface (UI) scenario or use cases, (b) Involve testers in requirement review, (c) Establish requirement traceability including testing activities
ProjectI	(a) Relation among testing, peer review, development standard, milestone review, requirement tracking, establishing configuration baseline, and quality assurance audit	(a) Importance of test planning and formal milestone review (business value view analysis)	Improve testing and peer review by following: (a) Establish development standard and guideline for design and coding, and conduct peer review accordingly, (b) Establish test plan including functional and non-functional quality objectives for final product and each development phase, (c) Establish level test plan (e.g., unit test, system test, etc.), (d) Conduct formal milestone review based on quality objectives, (e) Improve quality assurance plan and checklist regarding formal milestone review

Table 1.19: Example results in case studies (continued).

Case Study	Correlation Analysis	Refining Improvement Package	Building Recommendations
ProjectI	(a) Relation among project planning, project monitoring, requirement management, quality assurance, and measurement and analysis	(a) Little involvement of QA in project management activities. (organizational view analysis)	Improve project planning and monitoring by following: (a) Establish quality objectives (e.g., defect, performance, etc.) based on functional and non-functional requirements, (b) Develop size and effort estimates based on documented requirements, (c) Identify project risks and develop mitigation plan, (d) Establish exit criteria for each milestone. Criteria would include quality objectives, monitoring metrics, and quality audit results, (e) Define project monitoring metrics and measurement data (e.g., effort, software size, progress rate etc.) (f) Provide project setup service by QA team in the project planning phase, (g) Involve QA for project plan review, (h) Periodically monitor project progress (weekly, monthly and milestone review for defined metrics, issue and risks), (i) In project closure phase, collect lessons learned, final deliverables, measurement data for reference in other project (j) Introduce project management supporting tools (especially issue/risk management tool etc.)
ProjectJ	(a) Relation among requirement development, design, testing, requirement management, quality assurance, and organizational training	(a) Requirement specification with proper level of detail in consideration of life cycle phase such as concept development, prototype, pilot development, and production (life cycle view analysis)	Improve requirement development by following: (a) Establish standard template for requirements specification for system, H/W, and S/W, (b) Plan requirement development activities with effort estimation during project planning, (c) Monitor requirement development activities using relevant monitoring metrics, (d) Identify and manage risks regarding requirement development, (e) Identify critical requirement items which requires a formal review on alternative solutions, (f) Identify interface requirements, (g) Establish traceability between requirements and associated testing strategy, (h) Develop requirement review checklist for QA review and peer review (i) Develop training program for requirement development and specification
ProjectK	(a) Relation among design, requirement development, testing, and project planning	(a) Little involvement of testing team in release process (organizational view analysis)	Improve design quality and process by following: (a) Plan required skill and training needs for project team members to improve design capability during project planning, (b) Identify detailed work environment of the project including relevant tools to design activity, (c) Develop alternative solutions and conduct formal review, (d) Provide detailed guideline on design with good practice and templates, (e) Conduct peer review on design, (f) Establish traceability among requirements, quality metrics, and test cases.

2

A Framework for a Sustainable Software Security Program

Monica Iovan[1], Daniela S. Cruzes[2], Espen A. Johansen[3]

[1,3] Visma, Romania
[2]   SINTEF Digital, Norway
[1,3] monica.iovan@visma.com, espen.johansen@visma.com
[2]   daniela.s.cruzes@sintef.no
      http://www.visma.com

Abstract

To remain competitive in the market, software development teams must innovate. Focusing on security can increase the sales of software products because software security is a proven differentiator in competitive industries. In this case, software security requires continuous innovations, which can be seen either as discrete products or as outcomes that turn into new ideas, methods or process of introducing something new. The goal of such innovations would be to create a sustainable security program that can ensure that software development teams continue to use the practices that improve and address the security of their products by adopting a long-term perspective. This chapter describes the stages of effective and sustainable implementation of a software security program while using one systematic model for purposefully disseminating innovations in software security practices.

Keywords: Security program, ambidextrous, software security, agile development, diffusion of innovations, self-managed teams

2.1   Introduction

In an age of increasingly effective cybercrime and more visible nation-state-driven cyber operations, focusing on software security is crucial because of the major risks regarding reputation and financial losses, not to mention the risks regarding the safety of the users. Software systems need to have engineering activities that ensure that the software continues to function correctly under malicious attacks while also preventing breaches from happening. Good security can increase the sales of software products because software security is a proven differentiators and may be used as a unique selling point in competitive industries.

Addressing software security is not an easy task; there are enormous technical, business, social and organizational challenges that hinder and affect a software security program. Whereas in the context of Agile and DevOps software development environments, the challenges are even bigger as security activities are not explicitly addressed by the Agile and DevOps methods, and in many ways, security can be considered to be in conflict with the current trend of "continuous development," reducing efficiency by delaying delivery of new features. As an answer to the challenges of having a security focus in Agile software development, some approaches have been proposed. The focus so far has been on proposing which activities to include without focusing on how to manage the adoption and implementation processes for these activities. One of the tensions comes from the culture differences between the involved parties in delivering software products. One of the approaches is that the development teams include infrastructure engineers, who are mainly used to work with information technology infrastructure library (ITIL) practices, developers, who are used to Agile or DevOps practices, and security engineers, who are used to working with policies and standards. Thus, having these three features under joint leadership and sharing common goals requires some translation to make sure that a shared understanding of reality can be established.

Ambidexterity is an important component of a sustainable security program. The balance between a top-down and bottom-up approach to security is key when working with self-managed teams. This ambidexterity can be translated into creating a balance between the tendency to give mandatory compliance-based security controls while ensuring that a team's empowerment is fully embedded. In addition, the program should also challenge the need to be relevant and keep activities that the teams have as routine to maintain the company's competitive advantage. At the same time, in reducing the risk from a security threat, it is critical to persist in having a relevant software security program. The security program should be composed of services that are always increasing the security of the products.

Another way of approaching ambidexterity refers to the tensions of making the best use of existing services (exploitation mode) and, contrary to this, of creating new ones (exploration mode). We put forward the hypothesis that the question of arbitration between the exploitation mode and exploration mode contributes to a sustainable software security program. We believe that to ensure the program does not become outdated, an important aspect is to include the exploration mode by continuously researching and creating new security services.

To create a sustainable security program, there is the need to add new security activities into the software development process. These new activities are seen as innovations. We define innovations following Rogers' definition [2]: *"Innovation is a broad category, relative to the current knowledge of the analyzed unit. Any idea, practice, or object that is perceived as new by an individual or other unit of adoption could be considered an in-*

novation available for study." In this chapter, software security activities are defined as scientific knowledge, new technical products, application methods or tools that facilitate problem solving for better software security. Adopting and implementing such innovations involves team member persuasion, creating new habits and establishing and maintaining a systematic and holistic approach to security on a daily basis once the teams are deploying software continuously. The goal is to ensure that software teams continue to use the practices that improve and address the security of the products, hence adopting a long-term perspective. Therefore, a security program is considered sustainable when the software teams change their attitude towards software security activities and when these become a routine that is embedded in the whole development life cycle.

In this chapter, we describe one systematic model that includes the usage of the two ways of approaching ambidexterity for introducing innovations and targeting excellence regarding the existing service for effective and sustainable implementation of the software security program. The chapter addresses the basic evaluation and procedural concepts that are involved in this implementation. The following sections describe these activities by exemplifying the approach of a real-world example of the implementation of security services in a software organization.

2.2 Software Security Best Practices

This section introduces the most commonly proposed security practices. These practices are proposed based on the state of the practice and studies conducted in organizations about what is needed for achieving good security in the software development process.

2.2.1 Microsoft Security Development Lifecycle for Agile Development

Many software development organizations, including many products and online services groups within Microsoft, use Agile software development and management methods to build their applications. Microsoft has embarked on a set of software development process improvements called the Security Development Lifecycle (SDL).[1] The SDL has been shown to reduce the number of vulnerabilities in shipping software by more than 50%. However, from an Agile viewpoint, the SDL is heavyweight because it was designed primarily to help secure very large products, such as Windows and Microsoft Office, both of which have long development cycles.

From the perspective of Microsoft, if Agile practitioners are to adopt SDL, two changes must be made. First, SDL additions to Agile processes must be lean. This means that for each feature, the team should do just enough SDL work for that feature before working on the next one. Second, the development phases (design, implementation, verification and release) associated with the classic waterfall-style SDL do not apply to Agile and must be reorganized into a more Agile-friendly format. To this end, the SDL team at Microsoft developed and put into practice a streamlined approach that melds Agile methods and security — the Security Development Lifecycle for Agile Development (SDL-Agile).

The SDL-Agile is split into three types of activities:

- **Every-Sprint Requirements**: Consists of the SDL requirements that are so essential to security that no software should ever be released without these requirements being met. Some examples of every-sprint requirements include the following:

---

[1] https://www.microsoft.com/en-us/securityengineering/sdl

- Run automatic code analysis tools daily or per build.
- Threat model all new features.
- Ensure that each project member has completed at least one security training course in the past year.
- Use filtering and escaping libraries around all web output.
- Use only strong crypto in new code (AES, RSA and SHA-256 or better).

- **Bucket Requirements**: These activities must be performed on a regular basis during the development life cycle; there are three types of such requirements (each type referred to as a bucket), and typically, one is picked from each bucket in each sprint. This category is subdivided into three separate buckets of related tasks:

  - Planning: Includes the tasks related to security documentation and planning, such as privacy support documents, security response contacts, network down plan, and so forth.
  - Design review: Conducting privacy reviews, crypto reviews, user account control, and so forth.
  - Verification: Mostly fuzzers and other analysis tools for an attack surface analysis, binary analysis, and so forth.

- **One-Time Requirements**: These activities typically only need to be performed once at the beginning of the project. The one-time requirements should generally be easy and quick to complete, with the exception of creating a baseline threat model. Examples of activities for one-time requirements are the following:

  - Determine security response standards
  - Establish a security response plan
  - Identify security and privacy experts for the project
  - Configure a bug tracking system for security bugs.

2.2.2 Building Security in Maturity Model

The building security in maturity model (BSIMM)[2] is a study of existing software security initiatives. By quantifying the practices of more than 100 different organizations, the authors have described a set of activities that are mostly found as best practices in software security programs. BSIMM describes the common ground shared by many, as well as the variations that make each unique. BSIMM is made up of a software security framework used to organize the 121 activities used to assess initiatives. It is not a how-to guide, nor is it a one-size-fits-all prescription. The framework consists of 12 practices organized into four domains:

- **Governance**: Practices that help organize, manage and measure a software security initiative:

  - The strategy and metrics practices encompasses planning, assigning roles and responsibilities, identifying software security goals, determining budgets and identifying metrics and software release conditions.

---

[2]https://www.bsimm.com/

– The compliance and policy practices is focused on identifying the controls for compliance regimens such as PCI DSS (payment card industry data security standard) and HIPAA (Health Insurance Portability and Accountability Act), developing contractual controls such as service-level agreements to help control commercial off-the-shelf software risk, setting organizational software security policy and auditing against that policy.

– Training focuses on security knowledge training for the developers, architects and managers.

- **Intelligence**: Practices that result in collections of corporate knowledge used in carrying out software security activities throughout the organization:

  – Attack models capture information used to think like an attacker: threat modeling, abuse case development and refinement, data classification and technology-specific attack patterns.

  – The security features and design practices practice is charged with creating usable security patterns for major security controls (meeting the standards defined in the standards and requirements practice), building middleware frameworks for those controls and creating and publishing other proactive security guidance.

  – The standards and requirements practice involves eliciting explicit security requirements from the organization, determining which commercial off-the-shelf software to recommend, building standards for major security controls (such as authentication, input validation and so on), creating security standards for technologies in use and creating a standards review board.

- **SSDL Touchpoints**: The practices associated with the analysis and assurance or particular software development artefacts and processes:

  – Architecture analysis encompasses capturing software architecture in concise diagrams, applying lists of risks and threats, adopting a process for review (such as STRIDE or architecture risk analysis) and building an assessment and remediation plan for the organization.

  – The code review practice includes the use of code review tools, development of tailored rules, customized profiles for tool use by different roles (e.g., developers versus auditors), manual analysis and tracking/measuring results.

  – The security testing practice is concerned with pre-release testing, including integrating security into standard quality assurance processes. The practice includes use of black-box security tools (including fuzz testing) as a smoke test, risk-driven white-box testing, application of the attack model and code coverage analysis. Security testing focuses on vulnerabilities in construction.

- **Deployment**: Practices that interfere with traditional network security and software maintenance organizations.

  – The penetration testing practice involves standard outside-in testing of the sort carried out by security specialists. Penetration testing focuses on vulnerabilities in the final configuration, providing direct feeds to defect management and mitigation.

  – The software environment practice deals with OS and platform patching (including in the cloud), WAFs (web application firewalls), installation and configuration documentation, containerization, orchestration, application monitoring, change management and code signing.

– The configuration management and vulnerability management practice is focused on patching and updating applications, version control, defect tracking and remediation and incident handling.

2.2.3 OWASP Software Assurance Maturity Model

The OWASP SAMM™ (software assurance maturity model) [3] is a community-led, open-sourced framework that allows teams and developers to assess, formulate and implement strategies for better security; the model can be easily integrated into an existing organizational software development life cycle (SDLC). The global community works to create freely available articles, methodologies, documentation, tools and technologies. The OWASP SAMM is a prescriptive model that helps organizations analyze their current software security practices, build a security program in defined iterations, show progressive improvements in secure practices and define and measure security-related activities. SAMM is based around 15 security practices grouped into 5 business functions. Every security practice contains a set of activities structured into three maturity levels. The activities on a lower maturity level are typically easier to execute and require less formalization than the ones on a higher maturity level. The five business functions are as follows:

- **Governance** focuses on the processes and activities related to how an organization manages the overall software development activities. More specifically, this concerns the impact cross-functional groups involved in development, as well as business processes established at the organization level.

- **Design** concerns the processes and activities related to how an organization defines its goals and creates software within development projects. In general, this will include requirements gathering, high-level architecture specification and detailed design.

- **Implementation** is focused on the processes and activities related to how an organization builds and deploys software components and its related defects. The activities within the implementation function have the most impact on the daily life of developers. The joint goal is to ship reliably working software with minimum defects.

- **Verification** focuses on the processes and activities related to how an organization checks and tests the artefacts produced throughout software development. This typically includes quality assurance work such as testing, but it can also include other review and evaluation activities.

- **Operations Business Function** encompasses those activities necessary to ensure that confidentiality, integrity and availability are maintained throughout the operational lifetime of an application and its associated data. Increased maturity regarding this business function provides greater assurance that the organization is resilient in the face of operational disruptions and responsive to changes in the operational landscape.

---

[3] https://owasp.org/www-project-samm/

2.2.4 Software Security Services

Based on the subsections above, there will be many services that can be created within a specific security program. This subsection shows concrete examples some of these services.

Security Awareness

- Secure development training can be achieved by having organization-level application security training across the teams; for example, through e-learning platforms where team members can learn and compete with others. Training should be targeted to all software development roles (business analysts, developers, test engineers, infrastructure engineers, support, etc.).

- General security awareness is an activity that increases the awareness of all the employees regarding different aspects of the security, including physical security, infrastructure and information security. Employees need to learn about the different types of attacks, how they can identify them and how to behave and mitigate the risks of being exploited.

Requirements

- Within security requirements, the development team or a dedicated security team will scrutinize the requirements from a security perspective. In this step, the team will identify security and privacy requirements and establish the risk level they are willing to accept.

- A security risk assessment helps identify the risks in the company, the risk due to the domain the product operates in or the risk of using a specific technology. This will also help in understanding what controls need to be implemented to safeguard against security threats. Security risk assessments are also required by compliance standards.

Design

- Threat modeling is a process by which potential threats, such as structural vulnerabilities or the absence of appropriate safeguards, can be identified and enumerated and mitigations prioritized. The purpose is to equip the software development teams with a systematic analysis of which controls or defenses need to be included given the nature of the system, the probable attacker's profile, the most likely attack vectors and the assets most desired by an attacker.

- An architecture assessment consists of identifying the architectural flaws in the product. One way of performing this activity is to create a checklist that describes the high level of cybersecurity of a product, including aspects such as analyzing and minimizing the attack surface, strategies to protect against common vulnerabilities and securely handling keys and credentials.

Security Implementation

- A manual security code review refers to a manual review of a product's source code. Teams can use predefined security review checklists, here depending on the technology used.

- Static application security testing (SAST) is an automated security code review that analyzes the source code to identify security defects from the inside while components are at rest.

- A software composition analysis tests the security of third-party components in the finished products. It also identifies the open source software in a code base.

Verification

- Dynamic application security testing (DAST) is a type of black-box security testing in which tests are performed by attacking a product from outside of the organization.

- Interactive application security testing (IAST) analyzes code for security vulnerabilities while the product is running. It works by deploying agents and sensors in the running product, analyzing all interactions done by automated tests, humans or any other activity.

- Fuzz testing is an automated black-box testing technique that involves providing malformed/semi-malformed data like invalid, unexpected or random data inputs while proving the product's behavior is being monitored for exceptions.

- Penetration testing is an in-house or external dynamic grey-box manual security testing service. Testing is done on pre-production environments with authentication credentials. The service is designed to identify application-level weaknesses and vulnerabilities, most of which are covered in OWASP Top 10, OWASP Mobile Top 10 and API Security TOP 10.

- Red teaming is an in-house or external (organic) black-box, grey-box and white-box security testing service that simulates cyber attacks to identify areas of improvement regarding attack prevention, detection and response. The red teaming activities are meant to challenge plans, policies, systems and assumptions by mimicking the tactics, techniques and procedures of advanced threat actors.

- Responsible disclosure is a vulnerability disclosure model in which a vulnerability is disclosed only after a period of time that would allow for the vulnerability to be patched.

- Bug bounty is a service offered by websites, organizations and software developers by which individuals can receive recognition and compensation for reporting bugs, especially those pertaining to security exploits and vulnerabilities. It is a great and proven way of battle testing the security of a service with ethical hackers around the world; the number of eyes and expertise in the technologies used that the hackers provide are where the strength of this service emerges.

Operations

- Incident management is a process focused on returning the performance of the organization's products to normal as quickly as possible. Ideally, this should be done in a way that has little to no negative impact on the core business. Incidents are logged, and the process of solving them is recorded.

- Security log management is the process of managing system-generated log records for the purposes of detecting and investigating threats towards the company's systems, cloud services, employees and customers.

Cyber Intelligence

- Cyber threat intelligence is a proven way to enhance the knowledge that allows for the prevention or mitigation of potential attacks against a service, application or company. Threat intelligence provides context for a proactive approach — if somebody is mentioning a specific product or is preparing an attack, what could be their motivation and capabilities and what indicators of compromise should be looked for in the specific products.

2.3 Software Security in Visma

The Visma group consists of over 200 software companies across more than 20 countries worldwide, with their headquarters being based in Norway. It consists of around 14,000 employees. The main focus of the group is to develop, deliver and operate cloud software products. The group has nearly one million customers in the private and public sectors.

The group acquires new companies every year, and the average volume of companies acquired yearly is around 40. This translates to one new company every one and a half weeks on average. The goal is for these companies to remain independent. This means that the companies maintain their way of working but can use a shared infrastructure and services. This also implies a multitude of technologies used for developing different products. Based on the technology survey that was run last year in the group, there are around 80 programming languages or frameworks used. This technology abundance creates an additional challenge regarding security.

The Visma group follows the sustainable software security program approach described in this chapter. To maintain independence under such conditions, each development company is composed of one or more self-managed teams. These teams are responsible for the entire life cycle of their products, including their security. They have full and exclusive ownership of their product's code and are expected to deliver continuous high-quality services to their customers. To accomplish such responsibility, the teams need highly skilled and motivated employees that apply modern methods and best practices in the software industry. For security, the security team enables the security excellence of all Visma's products by creating the core of the security program. It was decided that each team have at least one person responsible for security, called a security engineer. Usually, for this role, the teams select a developer who wants to be a security champion.

The security team has the role of overseeing this diverse mix of development teams to maintain the highest security standards and defend against targeted attacks across all Visma products. All the security vulnerabilities discovered are tracked in the development tracking system and will have assigned severity levels that were initially agreed upon by the management and development teams. The security team is created around the ambidextrous approach both regarding top down vs. bottom up but also regarding exploration versus exploitation.

2.4 Top-Down and Bottom-Up Approach of a Sustainable Program

The Ambidextrous Software Security Program was adapted from McDermott's [1] healthcare governance model. The model combines a top-down with bottom-up approach. The top-down formal regulatory mechanisms deter breaches of protocol and enact penalties where they occur (e.g., standard setting, monitoring and accountability), while the bottom-up capacity building and persuasive encouragement of adherence to guidance by professional self-determination, implementation and improvement support (e.g., training, stimulating interventions).

In this model, as presented in Figure 2.1, both the security team and development teams have distinct yet complementary responsibilities. The development teams are self-managed agile teams and are responsible for the security of their products, while the security team is responsible for the security services provided and for introducing the development teams to the best practices in the industry.

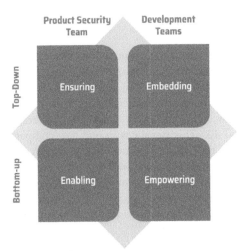

Figure 2.1: The ambidextrous security program.

The top-down approach establishes a governance-led culture where a security team is driving the security. This brings the benefits of having a standardized way of working across teams. However, top-down alone is not effective in achieving changes of behavior uniformly across and within the software development teams. The benefits come when this approach is balanced with the bottom-up approach in which development and operations teams also drive software security efforts. In this way, the attention to security becomes embedded as part of the team culture.

The model has four main activities:

- Ensuring the adoption and implementation of the software security practices;

- Enabling the adoption and implementation of the software security practices;

- Empowering software development teams to adapt and add to overall mandates of security;

- Embedding cultures of improvement within security domains.

2.4.1   Ensuring the Adoption and Implementation of Security Practices

The first activity is a top-down activity where the responsibility lies within the security team; they have the scope to create an overall strategy and ensure the adoption and success of the security program. While creating the strategy, it is recommended to use evidence-based best practices, drawing on a range of potential deterrence-oriented accountability mechanisms, such as standards, scrutiny and inspection. It is vital that both technical and non-technical staff understand the constantly changing threats; this can be done through training and regular internal awareness communications. To ease the adoption of this program, the security team can decide to build a financial platform where the development teams do not need to worry about the costs associated with the security services. Another aspect of this activity is to evaluate the performance of the program using the mechanisms that require the collection of performance information, which is "an essential prerequisite for continuous improvement."

2.4.2   Enabling the Adoption and Implementation of Security Practices

The second activity is using a bottom-up approach that focuses on persuasion, education and training, which complements other regulatory instruments. Although potentially counterintuitive for a bottom-up approach, the need to spread improvement capacity across the system means that the security team should change resources and training while also creating networks to spread learning. Many times, without building these learning networks, the software development teams are unable to make good security decisions once they lack security knowledge inside the team.

2.4.3   Empowering the Teams

The empowering activity is a crucial one for fostering innovations. For this activity, it is important to give people voice, to utilize their bottom-up improvement capacity in their own organizations and to let them know that in their context, they have the power to decide. For example, the teams have flexibility to adapt the way they adopt the practices/tools/techniques that are ensured by the top-down management. The teams also have the power to decide and reason the use of other tools in addition to or instead of the ones that have been chosen by the security team.

The judgements and interactions of individual workers are not driven directly by managerial policies or intervention but occur as real-time responses in relation to the flexibility of each worker. In this case, the security team will only provide the venue for the security knowledge sharing, while the development teams will discuss specific challenges and and innovative problem solving they encounter on their products. Creating such a supportive climate for service improvement requires attention to sharing best practice information and developing local leadership. To accomplish local leadership, some developers adopt the security engineering role; in OWASP, this is called a security champion.

Security engineer role: Security engineers are seen as ambassadors and advocates for security activities, and they "champion" the security program in their teams. They should be active team members that contribute to identifying and solving security issues early in the software development life cycle. Depending on the product's size and complexity, the team can have one or multiple security engineers that will allocate between 20% and 100% of their time on building confidence that their products are secure. Security engineers are not responsible for fixing security issues, but they need to make sure that security is considered in each step of the SDLC and that the risks and vulnerabilities that are discovered are fixed as soon as possible. The security engineer has communication channels established with the product security group; through these communication channels, the security engineers can share information about the teams, hear about other teams' approaches, become better informed about diverse threats and incident cases and ask for help. To summarize, security engineers are defined as having the following purposes/backgrounds:

- Spread and increase security awareness/culture;

- Share knowledge on the security program and how to use it;

- Scale security work in an efficient and tested way; and

- Be a point of contact to the security team.

2.4.4 Embedding the Security Activities

For maintaining a top-down and bottom-up approach, it is also important to create a culture of improvement, innovation and learning. This can be achieved through policies and priorities, clinical governance, local improvement support units and celebrating success. This culture change requires contextually sensitive interventions. For the security team's part, this requires incorporating security work into the individual's everyday tasks and rewarding good behavior while not rewarding negative behavior. Two ways of embedding security activities are establishing a trust center and creating indexes of maturity.

- A **trust center** is a publicly available website where the end customers can find answers to questions and concerns regarding privacy, security and other specific questions; they can view security and privacy information by product, learn more about the standards and protocols used and view documentation.

- The **security maturity index** measures the fulfillment of the different activities that are part of the security program. It consists of several categories that correspond to different risk-reducing activities. Each activity has a set amount of points associated with it. The amount of points are based on the risk-reducing gains the activities are supposed to give. These are the points that a product receives if the activity is not performed. Each product is assigned one of four tiers, and the application calculates the actual tier based on the points that the product gets. This can then be used by management when prioritizing resources for a specific product. The team responsible for a product can also use the details as a list of things they should perform on the required tier.

2.5 Explorability of a Sustainable Software Security Program

Besides the tensions in the bottom-up and top-down approach to security, the organization must deal with the tension between the explorability and exploitability of the services. The program needs to maintain consistency and stability while targeting excellence on the offered security services, but at the same time, the program also needs to be innovative and up to date with the constantly changing security threats. This section focuses on the explorability aspects of the framework, where new services must be explored, created and adopted by teams through a process of persuasion and onboarding.

2.5.1 Researching and Innovating Services

Because the program needs to be constantly updated to respond to new threats and add new security practices or services, it is very important to allocate a part of the existing resources to research and innovation.

Research refers to the process of determining the viability of an idea, a new service or product; it is the process conducted directly with the development teams and security specialist. The process uses data collected internally or externally while collaborating with different organizations. In a company, if there is a strong security culture, new ideas can come from many places: from academia, from other external organizations that have expertise in security, from shared experiences with other companies or from inside the organization.

Regarding academia, the organization can collaborate or follow the research topics of different professors, PhD and master students. This is a source of new approaches, tools and techniques that has not been tested widely in many other companies, and many times, there is no evidence that these will work in practice or will have an impact on the security of the products. At the same time, these are ideas that have the potential to put the company ahead of the market on new solutions for software security issues. Examples of academia research are the following: services that use machine learning for anomaly detection, developing new malware to test the protection mechanisms or adapting ambidextrous approaches for the security program.

By following other external organizations that have expertise in security, such as the OWASP, practices can be used as a source and inspiration for the software security programs with new approaches. In this case, the company's research can be conducted by organizational members accessing externally established ideas or innovations that are new to the organization. For example, they can follow the trends in the market for new tools or techniques and practices that are showing good results in other security programs. The best practices models can also be used as a source for these practices, as shown in Section 2.2.

New ideas can be created by actively searching for them together with other third-party companies or organizations that are focused on security. For example, the way the security engineer program could be gamified by other companies, hence giving the engineers a chance to look at what went well and what went wrong with that approach. Sharing experiences and ideas between different companies has proven to be a good practice. This allows the company to explore the efficacy and efficiency of the service towards security and get opinions and other feedback from others about their interest in the security product or service.

The last source of new ideas is from inside the organization. Getting ideas from the development teams is important to create a culture where they feel their opinions matter. If the company can build a strong security culture, their team members will always look for what they can improve upon and will try different solutions to understand which of them fits the company's needs. An example of this category is the reuse of the user interface for automated tests for security testing. This can be done, for example, by providing different payloads on the fields and verifying the product's behavior.

Although research is important for finding new services, innovations increase the success of these ideas. Innovation happens when combining different discovered ideas and developing useful security services out of them or when simplifying services and reducing costs. Even if there is a conflict between security standards and innovation because new technologies disrupt these standards, innovations can bring huge benefits, especially when practical wisdom is applied. Security specialists need to understand when they should bend the rules implied by standards and follow the benefits that innovation brings.

The research and innovation of new services can span from three months to a year, depending on the complexity and readiness of the idea.

2.5.2 Creating New Services

Once an innovation is shown to be promising, to reduce the risks and ensure that the new innovation has a positive impact on the security of the development teams, the new innovation is tested through some pilots. it is important to include the perspectives of the software development teams and their acceptance of the new innovation. Therefore, the owner of the new innovation should always include the target teams in its evaluation.

Then, if the results favor the new innovation, the security specialists/new service owner can establish a service around this innovation, letting it become part of the software security program and the software security development life cycle.

The creation of a new service can start with something as simple as creating a service description webpage. The service description will contain details like the following:

- What is the service?

- How is this service different from others in the program?

- What are the benefits of using this service?

- What are the prerequisites to use this service (use of other services, knowledge, tools, licenses, settings, configurations, etc.)?

- What are the expectations from the development teams (resources needed, changes in the activities of the development team, costs, etc.)?

- What is the onboarding process?

- How does this service work?

    - Where can the teams see the discovered vulnerabilities?

    - What are the rules of using this service?

- Who is the contact person?

Later on, the following details can be added to the service description:

- How many development teams are using the service?

- Who is using this service?

- What are the experiences (success stories) of using this service?

The service description will be complemented by an additional page focusing on a more strategic perspective of the service, one where the service owner describes the targeted clients, the life expectancy of the service, the risks and opportunities, the time frame for onboarding, how the service will be disseminated, the financial model of the service and how the service will be exploited.

These services will be adapted over time, starting from creating a small service description and continuing with automation of the onboarding process while implementing good support for the development teams. All these changes are important for the success of the adoption rate, as we describe next.

2.5.3 Persuasion Focusing on the Types of Software Development Teams

Once a service has been created, it must then be adopted by the teams; if this does not occur, the service will not be successful. The sustainable security program adopts Rogers' diffusion of innovation theory [2], which explains how over time, innovations (new ideas, products or services) are diffused through a specific group of people. The desired end result is that the development teams adopting the new service, which means that they change their previous behavior, use the new security service routinely, acquire and apply new knowledge to improve the security of the product based on this new service and so forth.

The adoption process includes four stages: awareness that there is a problem that the new service is trying to solve, decision to adopt (or reject) the new service, initial use to test it, and continued use of the innovation. Each of these stages are influenced by five main factors:

- Relative advantage: The degree to which the new service is seen as good for solving the issues it tries to solve.

- Compatibility: How consistent the new service is with the developer's values, experiences and needs.

- Complexity: How difficult the service is to understand and/or use, especially taking into consideration whether the developers need to make a lot of changes to the way they are currently working.

- Triability: The extent to which the service can be tested or experimented with before a commitment to adopt it is made.

- Observability: The extent to which the service provides tangible results.

To ensure a good adoption rate, the service owner needs to articulate the benefits of the new or different service. Sometimes, simply being transparent with the developers as to why things will be different going forward can help them feel more comfortable. When the new service is replacing an existing one, if the new service is clearly superior to the old one, comparing the results from both approaches will demonstrate and explain the need for a new approach.

In the persuasion process, it is important to remember that each developer/development team is different. Rogers' theory indicates that people respond in different ways to the same innovation based on their innovativeness. He defined five adopter categories, as seen in Figure 2.2, and the adopters in each category have different motivations for adopting a service and are influenced to some extent by the factors described above because they have different needs. Therefore, the service owner needs to respond to the adopter's needs in different ways. These needs and characteristics are further described by Moore [7].

Innovators are actively interested in security and are willing to allocate time to experiment and test different security products or services. They do not need state-of-the-art

Figure 2.2: Percentage of people in each adopter category.

documentation and can accept systems that come with bugs or workarounds. They want to be the first to try something new as long as they do not have to pay much for it. Based on the experience with teams, one strategy for the service owner to start the process of the diffusion of a new service is by piloting the service, identifying the teams that belong to this category and that are influential members, engaging them to gain acceptance of the new service. To convince them to try the new service, the service owner can personally invite them to try the new service. It is interesting to note that one team can be considered an innovator for one type of security service, for example, for Bug Bounty, but a laggard to others, for example, for SAST. Each security service owner must be aware of the development team's characteristics. Innovators will provide valuable feedback that must be incorporated in the service. Once these innovators are convinced of the value of the service, they need a stage to become vocal. The service owner needs to ensure that the innovators can present their impressions to the next category of adopters: the early adopters.

The **early adopters** are the development teams that understand how security impacts their business goal, for example, to use security as a selling point. The security service owners need to present the service as a fundamental breakthrough and not as an improvement. Early adopters are not so easy to please, and trialability is important for them. A good onboarding strategy is important for them. It is important to provide a good description of how this service will bring benefits to their product and the ways they can present the service usage to their customers. The success of early adopters helps drive adoption through the company because they have a large influence on the next category of teams. Many adoption processes fail because the services do not advance to the next category of adopters: the early majority.

The **early majority** have the goal of improving (incremental, measurable, predictable progress) their product. The problem is that usually, the early adopters do not have access to early majority adopters. They do not share the same interests, so the service owner needs to create a trust-filled relationship with members from the early majority category. Then, early adopters can present the service and expose their experiences with the early majority adopters. This is the moment when the onboarding process must be streamlined. If possible, the process should be automatized to minimize the impact on the development teams. Also, there is a need to focus on the compatibility of the new service with the team's working practices.

The **late majority** are against security services that require a change in their way of working. They will be convinced to try the new service only when the majority of teams are using that service successfully. The service owner will have to demonstrate that the security services are mature and that they do not cost much. They want high-quality and tested services that focus on convenience rather than performance and user experience rather than feature sets. For the late majority adopters, the service owner can use statistics to demonstrate that this is the best service on the market and that good support exists for the service. The service owner may also mention standards and/or good practices frameworks that includes these activities. For the late majority, there is a need to focus on a top-down approach. The management team will be involved to convince the teams that are more reluctant to adopt and to show that they trust and offer their support to the service.

The **laggards** are the teams that are not interested in security and believe that the new services will only make them work more for things that are not important. These are the teams that are skeptical about the new service and will try to prove that it is not important for their product or that it costs too much. For laggards, when they refuse to adopt the new service, there are two options, here depending on the risk this brings to the company. If the risk is low, they should not be forced to adopt because they will do their best to not adopt or find ways to bypass the system. If the risk is high (e.g., the use of multiple factor authentication), the team must be persuaded by using policies and a complete top-down approach by enforcing and monitoring the adoption of the service. Or the service owner needs to spend more effort to convince them by using a bottom-up approach.

Based on these categories of adopters, each service owner will build a dissemination plan with the following information for each type of team (innovators, early adopters, early majority, late majority and laggards):

- Teams that belong to the category,

- The service description according to each category's needs,

- The selected communication channels required for each category,

- The onboarding process, and

- The support offered for the service.

2.5.4   Service Onboarding

Onboarding is the process of helping the development teams get started with the security service and stay engaged. The service owner defines and adapts the onboarding process by specifying how to start with the service, which knowledge is needed and a time frame for onboarding. The service owners are also responsible for providing the support needed for the teams to have a smooth process when it comes to starting to set up the service in their context. The onboarding process is key for the success of the adoption of the service and has to be well designed by the service owners; as mentioned before, it needs to be tailored to each type of adopter. For example, if the service is met with resistance, the question is whether the root problem is that the teams are slow to change (the service owner added the teams to the wrong adoption category) or if there might be issues with the proposed service. To discover the root cause, the teams need to be heard, and the service owner should hear them going through their thought processes as they review the service. What do they like? What questions do they have? Which parts do they prefer and why? Then, he/she needs to decide if the service should continue and how to adapt the service to the teams' needs. This brings us to the service exploitability of the existing services.

2.6   Exploiting Existing Services

Once adopted by the teams, the security services must be maintained. They have to keep the relevance and impact to the security of the products to continue to be used by the teams. It is crucial that every service appoints a service owner for the maintenance of the service. The service owner is not necessarily the one who created the service, though. The skills needed for the service owner at this stage change from sales and marketing skills to focusing on quality and targeting for excellence in the provided service.

Lean [13] principles of continuous improvement are important for success in this phase. Lean is based on four capabilities [8]: identifying wastes immediately, immediate root cause analysis and waste resolution, sharing knowledge and learning, and developing these capabilities across the organization. These concepts can be used by security programs to improve their security services but also for many other benefits like lowering the cost of the services and improving their reliability. These concepts can also help with having more standardized work across services and a more proactive approach towards security issues. One way to identify waste is to continuously get feedback from the development teams but also from the security specialists.

To enable these principles in the security services, waste can be defined as work or resources that add no value to the security service, as follows:

- Defects: False positives vulnerabilities, incorrect onboarding process or service descriptions that cause rework.

- Overproduction: Resources that are scaled more than needed or before they are needed, such as buying more licenses than needed based on the adoption rate or services that do not bring value to the teams.

- Waiting: Wasted time due to unavailable or low-quality support or manual approval processes that take too much time.

- Unused potential: Using security specialists for repetitive or mundane work, something that can be automated or done with less skills or knowledge while also failing to capture ideas/innovation.

- Transport: Unnecessary travel to mitigate the impact of breaches or to perform audits.

- Inventory: Underutilized hardware, software or human resources.,

- Motion: Firefighting due to incidents.

- Extra processing: Unnecessary processing of data that do not add value or requirements for manual entries that are not important.

2.6.1 Collecting Continuous Feedback

To evaluate the effectiveness of the service, it is important to understand the effects of the service on the development teams, but also on the security specialists. To understand these effects, there is the need to continuously collect feedback. The *Merriam-Webster Dictionary* [12] defines feedback as the transmission of evaluative or corrective information about an action, event or process to the original or controlling source. Development team members are the ones who implement all the security activities and who understand the pain and gain of these activities, so they are probably the best sources of feedback.

Because feedback collection is done continuously, it requires a process. The first step is to identify different feedback sources, here considering that each source can provide different perspectives to the security service. Usually, the companies prefer to use surveys, net promoter scores (NPS), key performance indicators (KPIs), and real-time data. Each of these sources have benefits and disadvantages. All of them are fast to implement, and the responses can be analyzed in an automated way. They also can be misleading because no metric is perfect. All sources may be influenced by the team member's mood in the moment they respond.

For example, in the case of NPS, the high value indicates the quality of the service is good but does not identify if the amount is sufficient.

Another source of feedback is interviews done with the different members of the company. In the case of security specialists, because they are managing the security program, they have a very deep knowledge of how the service is used, but their opinions can also be subjective. Managers are experienced and have specialized knowledge of the tasks their teams are performing. They also have insights into company procedures, policy and roadmap prioritization.

Visma is also using a technique called security chartering [4], which is a specific focus group approach that helps in understanding the effectiveness of the product security strategy, get more focused feedback on the program, provide an additional channel of communication from the teams to the security core team, and understand the priorities of the teams towards the improvements needed for the program. Most importantly, it provides a channel to empower the security engineers by giving them a voice to raise their concerns and share success cases and experiences with the program. This also helps the service owner validate the hypotheses they had about the security services, giving them the confidence that it is working.

Once the service owner decides which sources and techniques to use, the next step is to define the periodicity for each of them. It is important to ensure that the members are requested to provide feedback often enough, but also to ensure they are not overloaded by this feedback collection. If possible, they should have the option to provide feedback at any point in time, as needed.

After the feedback has been collected, it becomes critical to make sure the feedback is considered, and actions are taken as soon as possible. If the team members do not receive a response to their feedback and do not see any changes, then they will lose the trust in the service team, which will impact the adoption of future services or even cause them to refuse to continue using the existing services.

When the service owner detects that the service needs critical improvements, the service owner may start with retrofitting the service.

2.6.2 Retrofitting the Services

Retrofitting is the process of modifying something after it has been deployed in production. It involves changing systems, services or structures after some period of use and experience with it. Security retrofitting is a way to systematically identify the areas that need changes to become more valuable for the development teams and for the security program. This work can improve the sustainability of security services and improve its performance.

The focus of this process is improvement activities, which should depend on the needs of the service. This may include the following:

- Fine-tuning the service: The ongoing day-to-day operations, either by lowering the costs or, for example, creating a better image of the service.

- Service innovation: The redesign of the service and end-to-end processes used, increasing productivity and lowering the maintenance needed.

- Making the security program anti-fragile: Releasing the stress of team members and improving the serviceability.

The retrofitting process should include collecting as much data as possible regarding the service usage, analyzing these data and then deciding on the scenarios that best increase the service's or program's value. The scenarios should also include the possibility to decommission the service or replace it with something newer. Next, the approved scenarios are implemented.

Finally, KPIs are defined in such a way that the service owner can evaluate if the retrofitting is successful or not. The end result should be better service at lower costs.

2.6.3 Focus on Investment Costs and Benefits

Analyzing the balance between the costs and benefits is a challenging step. First, it is challenging to manage all the costs of the whole set of activities in the program, but it is also very challenging to quantify the benefits of the activities for security. In addition, the whole approach for the investment analysis must be holistically structured, so the services are not seen in isolation but as part of the puzzles in the whole program [14, 15].

The service owners must find approaches to keep evaluating the costs and benefits and effects of the service to the security of the products. The service owner should establish at least the internal costs for running the services, including the licenses and personnel needed to provide the service. In addition, the service owners should also account for the costs that the development teams will incur by adopting the service, including costs of training, competence building, setup and configuration and daily maintenance of the service (e.g., following up the outputs of the analysis tools).

Regarding the benefits, the services should provide benefits to the security of the product and/or overall security approach and program. Some KPIs can be established to follow the status of the services and efficacy of the services in providing benefits to the company. For example, for a service on static analysis tools, one KPI could be based on the ratio of vulnerabilities acted on per the vulnerabilities found, and the KPI could state that the teams should act on at least 60% of the vulnerabilities found.

This analysis should be done periodically because new security tools are developed every day and others are becoming obsolete. When the service owner notices that the service is becoming obsolete, the discontinuity process should be started.

2.6.4 Discontinuing a Service

Services will eventually be discontinued. To discontinue a service, the security team should perform an analysis of the service and overall software security program. It should consider the trust the development teams have in the service, the adoption rate, the discontinuance rate and the research and innovation carried out.

The reasons for discontinuation of a service can be numerous, as follows:

- Lack on return on investment: The service is not impacting security as it was previously.

- Low efficiency in improved security of the products.

- Low impact of the service.

- Low number of adopters of the service.

- Need to prioritize resources to other more relevant services.

- The service is obsolete and no longer relevant to the program.

Once a decision has been made for discontinuation of the service, the associated costs and process required to discontinue the service should be accounted for. It is important to have a thorough communication plan to inform all stakeholders about the discontinuation of the services. Then, the teams should be off-boarded from the service, and the service should be removed from the top-down ensuring mechanisms of the company.

2.7 Pitfalls of a Sustainable Software Security Program

Achieving exploitation and exploration and a top-down and bottom-up approach to security enables the success of a software security program but increases challenging tensions. Ambidextrous organizations excel at exploiting existing services to enable incremental innovation and at exploring new opportunities to foster more radical innovation, but this demands an extensive focus on balancing the exploitation and exploration in a way that is sustainable and successful. This comes with the need to consider not only going towards a path of continuous improvement, but also creating disruptive innovations when needed. Regarding the top-down and bottom-up tensions, large software companies tend to focus on compliance approaches and lose the bottom-up focus of the teams, which cannot be ignored when dealing with self-managed teams. It is always challenging to maintain the right balance. Regarding the tension in exploitation versus exploration, it is sometimes more comfortable to keep the services that have been working well, procrastinating on the renewal of the services for better security.

In working towards this balance, there are many different aspects that should be taken into consideration. In this section, we describe the top three aspects to be mindful of.

1. **Competence management** is essential to the whole program. A robust competence management system will deliver real value to the security program by satisfying the expectations of regulators, in addition to also providing a platform for continuous improvement. Improvement decisions should not only come from the top management, but also from the teams. However, the bottom-up initiative only happens when the workforce is skilled and not only execute the tasks established by top management but are to design their own tasks. There are many different ways to build competence in the workforce, but hands-on activities have been shown to be the most effective. Visma has put effort into providing competence building in the process of executing the services that are offered to the teams. There should be a focus on creating an army of software security experts who are not implants in the software development teams but are team members who have the security competence to bring to the front the focus on security when needed.

2. **Silos shall be broken**. In any organization, there are silos of roles and responsibilities. In security, there are the traditional silos between the app-sec and the IT-sec personnel. Both can benefit from better collaboration and integration of the working procedures to achieve better security coverage. If a company only focuses on one or the other, there will be a vast amount of vulnerabilities that will be left uncovered. Some occasions require "hard" approaches. These can be moving people from one organizational unit to another, closing down units, or moving budgets to stimulate actions.

3. Managers should learn to **"speak security" to the top-level management** and learn how to get financial support from the organization for the program. The security manager should consider the need to balance the focus on security and the need to maintain the business. There should also be a focus on showing the benefits and ROI of the investments from the board. Dashboards in which data are summarized can be a powerful tool to show that the security services of the security program are running in the teams.

2.8 Further Reading

Diffusion of Innovations, Everett M. Rogers, 5th Edition, Free Press, ISBN: 9780743222099. This book explains how new ideas spread over time via communication channels. Such innovations are initially perceived as uncertain and even risky. To overcome this uncertainty, most people seek out others like themselves who have already adopted the new idea. Thus, the diffusion process consists of a few individuals who first adopt an innovation and then spread the word among their circle of acquaintances—a process that typically takes months or years.

2.9 Conclusion

This chapter described the practical solutions in one systematic model for purposely disseminating innovations in software security practice through careful attention to the stages of effective and sustainable implementation of the software security program. The goal of this framework is to enable software organizations to create a sustainable security program that ensures that software teams continue to use the practices that improve and address the security of the products, hence adopting a long-term perspective.

This is not an easy task and requires ambidextrous thinking from management and personnel. The costs associated with such a program should be continuously analyzed and reevaluated. This chapter shows that it is possible to manage a sustainable software security program if efforts are systematically channeled.

Acknowledgments

This work was partially supported by the SoS-Agile project: Science of Security in Agile Software Development, funded by the Research Council of Norway (grant number 247678).

References

1. McDermott, A. M., Hamel, L. M., Steel, D., Flood, P. C., & Mkee, L. (2015). Hybrid health care gov- ernance for improvement? Combining top-down and bottom-up approaches to public sector regulation. Public Administration, 93(2), 324-344. doi:10.1111/padm.12118

2. Rogers, E. M., Singhal, A., & Quinlan, M. M. (2014). *Diffusion of innovations* (pp. 432-448). Routledge., ISBN:9780743222099

3. Mora, M., Gómez, J. M., O'Connor, R. V., & Buchalcevová, A. (Eds.). (2020). *Balancing Agile and Disciplined Engineering and Management Approaches for IT Services and Software Products*. IGI Global.

4. Iovan, M., Cruzes, D., & Johansen, E.(2020). *Empowerment of Security Engineers through Security Chartering in Visma*, Agile Alliance .

5. May, P., Ehrlich, H.C., & Steinke, T.(2006). ZIB Structure Prediction Pipeline: Composing a Complex Biological Workflow through Web Services. In: Nagel, W.E., Walter, W.V., Lehner, W. (eds.) Euro-Par 2006. LNCS, vol. 4128, pp. 1148–1158. Springer, Heidelberg.

6. Foster, I., & Kesselman, C. (Eds.). (2003). *The Grid 2: Blueprint for a new computing infrastructure*. Elsevier.

7. Moore, G. A. (2014). *Marketing and selling disruptive products to mainstream customers.* Harper Collins Publishers: New York, NY, USA.

8. Spear, S. (2010). *The High Velocity Edge*, McGraw-Hill, 2 edition.

9. Czajkowski, K., Fitzgerald, S., Foster, I., & Kesselman, C. (2001, August). Grid information services for distributed resource sharing. In *Proceedings 10th IEEE International Symposium on High Performance Distributed Computing* (pp. 181-194), New York. IEEE.

10. Foster, I., Kesselman, C., Nick, J. M., & Tuecke, S. (2002). The Physiology of the Grid: an Open Grid Services Architecture for Distributed Systems Integration. Technical report, Global Grid Forum, 35(6), 37-46.

11. National Center for Biotechnology Information, `http://www.ncbi.nlm.nih.gov`

12. Merriam Webster Dictionary, `https://www.merriam-webster.com/dictionary/feedback`

13. Lean Enterprise Institute, `https://www.lean.org/whatslean/`

14. Le, D. N., Nguyen, G. N., Garg, H., Huynh, Q. T., Bao, T. N., & Tuan, N. N. (2021). Optimizing Bidders Selection of Multi-Round Procurement Problem in Software Project Management Using Parallel Max-Min Ant System Algorithm. *CMC-COMPUTERS MATERIALS & CONTINUA*, 66(1), 993-1010.

15. Bao, T. N., Huynh, Q. T., Nguyen, X. T., Nguyen, G. N., & Le, D. N. (2020). A Novel Particle Swarm Optimization Approach to Support Decision-Making in the Multi-Round of an Auction by Game Theory. *International Journal of Computational Intelligence Systems*, 13(1), 1447-1463.

3

Linking Software Processes to IT Professionalism Frameworks

LUIS FERNÁNDEZ-SANZ[1], INÉS LÓPEZ BALDOMINOS[1], VERA POSPELOVA[1]

[1] Department of Computer Science, University of Alcalá, Alcalá de Henares, Spain
Email: luis.fernandez.sanz@uah.es, ines.lopezb@edu.uah.es, vera.pospelova@uah.es

Abstract

Software processes have been widely studied since software engineering placed the focus on them, especially in the 1980s of the 20th century with the appearance of CMMi and other well-known proposals. Researchers and practitioners have explored most of the aspects of software processes, although the connection to the IT professionalism profiles has been neglected, probably because the work with professional roles has only recently been modeled with references like e-CF (EN16234) or ESCO. These references define skills and competences for the roles but this chapter focuses on the soft skills analysis that we can extract from these recent models for IT professionalism in the framework of software processes. This chapter explores the links between software processes, IT profiles and the recommended soft skills for them.

Keywords: Software processes, IT professionalism, ESCO, EN16234

3.1 Introduction

Software development is mainly a social activity as software project teams, groups, departments, and corporations act as social bodies. In the end, software development is a highly technical activity involving people performing diverse roles in projects, and with knowledge and experience on many different methodologies, tools, and techniques, organized to follow effective processes. Such software processes are largely influenced by the human factor, the people behind activities. The human dimension can be even more important than the technical side [1]. Human factors play a very important role in software development [2]. According to [2], "Failure to include human factors may explain some of the dissatisfaction with conventional information systems development methodologies; they do not address real organizations." Software development is in essence a human activity where human factors play a critical role. While the topic spans many different and diverse concepts, the human factor aspects most often studied in software engineering research include coordination, collaboration in the development process, trust, expert recommendation, knowledge management and culture. Many of these aspects closely embrace the concept of soft skills: something logical as people in software projects must work together to achieve project goals. So these kinds of skills and abilities, so-called "soft" or "nontechnical" skills, are considered as important as, or even more important than, traditional qualifications and technical skills for personal and professional success.

However, as analysis of the literature has already shown [2], the interest in the general topic of human factors in software engineering has been growing in general, although the research community has neglected the specific work on connecting IT profiles and software activities. One wide systematic literature review on human factors [3] identified many contributions in the area, although the part for human roles is limited, to see which main role (customer/user, developer or manager) the research was focused on [2]. An extended review on human factors and recent work limited to software quality [4] did not provide any additional useful results.

The study of software processes has resulted in many proposals expressed as official standards, such as ISO 12207 [5] or ISO 15504, as well as de facto references such as CMMI [6], methodologies, models and agile processes (e.g., SCRUM [7]). First, it is necessary to provide some definitions of the main concepts related to this chapter. Official standards do not include a definition of software process but do define process and software engineering separately. Combining both a common definition will be the application of a systematic, disciplined, quantifiable approach to the development, operation, and maintenance of software in a set of interrelated activities, which transform inputs into outputs, to achieve a given purpose [6]. This definition is consistent with the ones given in ISO 12207 and ISO 15504. The perspective is general for the complete organization; however, when talking about life cycle models the focus is on projects and the specific techniques for each approach. In the world of standards, Paulk *et al.* proposed that software development processes refer to the activities, methods, practices, and transformations that are used to develop and maintain software. All models of software processes vary in terms of benefits, limitations and applicability to the practice [8].

Decisions linked to software development processes include possible choices related to team organization and staffing, methodologies, techniques, and tools, but little research has been devoted to the human resources side. However, all processes are in the end implemented by professionals whose performance is highly determined by their skills. Although not all these references mention specific requirements and profiles for each activity and process, there is enough relevant information to outline a link to the recent IT professionalism skills frameworks, which are rapidly gaining a huge relevance in managing human resources in ICT. This connection is not limited to the emergence of new job profiles in the software domain. It also addresses the trends in IT HR management, which are already dominating the future evolution of the study of software processes and project management and organization.

What is the role of soft skills in software processes? As stated by Sukhoo *et al.* [9], the integration of soft skills as part of the management of software processes can probably lead to a higher success of software projects. The relation between soft skills and processes in software engineering has been and still is the object of study of different research works. In a recent systematic mapping [10], 44 different references were analyzed to identify and categorize the relevant skills involved in the human aspect of software engineering, concluding that investigation on this topic is highly interesting to the software engineering community and particularly to management roles. These studies are focused on specific, and even limited, datasets. Studies on skills have already been produced for specific contexts like cultural and gender influence on global software development (GSD) [11] or activities (e.g., project management [12]).

Soft skills are also called non-cognitive skills (NCS), which is the name we will use throughout this chapter. The work with soft skills is challenging as it is frequently hindered by a lack of agreement on categorization, nomenclature, or definitions [13]. For our purpose, NCS are capacities, behaviors, attitudes and personal qualities which enable a reflective ability of the individuals to effectively [14]:

- React to and interact with their environment (social side),

- React to and interact with themselves (self-image, feelings, and vision of the world),

- Act and react to conditions and problems of their work when pursuing results (context and performance side), and

- Apply thinking methods and abilities to work (methodological side).

This chapter will show detailed examples of the exploitation of the most relevant skills frameworks, such as EN16234 [15], the ESCO labor classification[1] or the Skills Match framework for soft skills[2] for the analysis of roles and competences involved in software processes. The approach is based on the use of big data from the job market (millions of online vacancies analyzed by the OVATE tool) as well as the exploration of skills profiles created by experts (using new customized complex queries to the ESCO database, which was developed over four years by more than 200 experts). The analysis of a large number of literature references will complement these data. The underlying idea is to overcome the limitations traditionally based on reduced samples of job ads (e.g., [16,17]) or the mere opinion of small groups of experts (e.g., [18]), thus, giving more precise and robust conclusions.

This chapter is organized as follows: Section 3.2 provides a general overview of software processes and their models and standards. Section 3.3 reviews the references on IT professional roles and profiles and their skill and competence models. Section 3.4 describes how the IT professionalism references can be used for analyzing big data sources and connect them to software processes in ISO 12207 and CMMi. Section 3.5 analyzes

---

[1] https://ec.europa.eu/esco/portal/home
[2] https://skillsmatch.eu/

recommended skills in software processes. Section 3.6 gives some conclusions and future lines of work.

3.2 Process Standards

There are many possible models, methodologies, and standards applicable to the area of software processes. Starting from the most basic and traditional life cycle models, we can find many proposals which have already been studied and compared to determine their benefits and limitations [8]. We can find three basic software process models on which most other models are based:

- The Waterfall Model: This is a classical model used by software developers, which is sometimes referred to as the Classical Life Cycle Model [19]. It creates a system in which fundamental activities are separated into five phases: requirement specification, design, implementation, testing, and maintenance.

- The Iterative [20] and Evolutionary [21] Process Model: In this case, progress in the development of the system is achieved in iterative small increments that receive feedback from the main stakeholders until the final validation.

- Rapid Application Development (RAD) Model [19]: This model is also incremental, with its focus on a short development cycle. In this case, software functions or components are reused in new systems with minor or no modification.

Software managers can combine these models to implement the activities which could be of interest from each process and discard the aspects less useful for a specific project. There are several alternative models and methods used for software development based on the previous three main types following this pragmatic approach, including the rapid prototyping model (RPM) [22], spiral model [23], V-model [24], divide and conquer model (DCM) [24], win-win spiral model (WSM) [25], concurrent process model (CPM) [26], formal systems development model (FSDM), and the component-based development model (CBDM) [27].

Bringing general models into practice has led to the emergence of development methodologies and practical approaches which adopt and/or combine different techniques, methods and philosophies. A good list of existing development methodologies appears in [8], including, for example, the adaptive project framework (APF) [28], family-oriented software development process (FSDP) [29], incremental delivery (IDR) [21], joint application development [30], agile software development methodologies (extreme programing [31], Scrum [32], crystal methodologies [26], etc.) or the fourth generation techniques (4GT) [19].

Software life cycle models are not enough to achieve organizational excellence. Models and methodologies focus on the product and how it evolves through each phase from a technical point of view [33], providing details on the specific techniques. As has been pointed out, the complexity of software products has increased and has led to new opportunities but also to challenges for organizations. These challenges exist in every stage of the life cycle of a system [5]. This has driven the necessary development of official processes standards. Process standards focus on the activities performed from a general perspective for the whole organization and not specifically for a project [33]. This point of view includes technical processes but also the ones for management and support.

ISO/IEC/IEEE 12207 provides the necessary framework for achieving excellence in software project planning. It provides a common framework of concepts, processes, activities and tasks for software life cycle processes [34]. These apply to the entire software life cycle, supply, development, operation, maintenance, and disposal of products. Another official standard is ISO 15504, which is based on ISO 12207. It provides process areas, and activities depending on the maturity of the organization [35].

Capability maturity model integration (CMMI) is focused on optimizing and improving processes in organizations. The specific model for development, CMMI-DEV, defines 22 process areas, grouped into five maturity levels and another continuous representation, where four levels of capability are set [36], in a similar way as ISO 15504 does. The main improvement line is the elimination of inconsistencies and the activities and deliverables being defined in every stage of a software development project. However, depending on the nature of the project, it may need to be adapted or some of the guidelines proposed may even need to be removed [36].

Since CMMI is compliant with ISO 12207 and ISO 15504 standards, organizations can work with harmonized frameworks, implement, and optimize certified processes, and deliver quality products. Moreover, some hybrid models have been developed mixing the three of them [37]. These standards are also compatible with the different methodologies; for example, an organization may develop software projects using CMMI and agile methodologies. In fact, the ISO 12207 standard explains how to combine it with agile methods in its annexes.

3.3 IT Professionalism Standards

As explained before, we can find models of processes that guide the complete software lifetime and process standards that deal with the activities performed. The less developed area in these models and standards is the definition of the professional profiles linked to each activity or the description of the competences recommended for a successful work in each process. The relation between professional profiles and the associated skills is carried out in different standards and models, but they also fail to develop the relationship between profiles and processes. In the same way that process standards describe tasks in a generic way and do not specify which profile should be involved in each activity, profile standards do not develop how these profiles explicitly relate to the specific activities associated with each software engineering process. Profile standards are focused on the description of each profile in terms of the recommended qualification, including both cognitive and NCS.

The effective analysis of the demand for NCS for the different IS profiles requires a reference framework for categorizing and classifying both skills and occupations, otherwise the lack of consistent terminology and definition of terms would impede the achievement of solid results. During the past decade, the EU has promoted several competence frameworks to enable a better coordination of the analysis of the job market. These could be applied to ICT profiles: the e-Competence Framework (e-CF) [15] and the ESCO Labor Classification [39]. e-CF is a framework which is based on competences rather than on job profiles, although there are already 30 sample profiles based on e-CF competences [40]. ESCO is a classification of occupations, which are accompanied by their recommended profile of skills and knowledge. It uses a hierarchy of relationships between them as well as metadata and mappings of the International Standard Classification of Occupations (ISCO) to structure the catalogue of occupations.

These references try to capture the essence of the labor market and can provide a standardized view of roles and occupations to all players in the field of ICT, but their underlying approaches are different. Although both consider NCS in one way or another, they do not offer a specific framework structure for these skills by themselves. So, we will use the NCS framework (NCSF) from the Skills Match project [13], which maps skills to the ESCO classification and was developed after an exhaustive analysis of sources on NCS. We will present the reference frameworks ESCO, e-CF and NCSF in the next subsections.

3.3.1 ESCO

The European classification of skills and occupations is known as ESCO. The aim of ESCO is to support job mobility across Europe and therefore a more integrated and efficient labor market, by offering a "common language" on occupations and skills that can be used by different stakeholders on employment and education and training topics. It provides descriptions for 2942 occupations and 13485 skills linked to these occupations, translated into 27 languages (all official EU languages plus Icelandic, Norwegian and Arabic). ESCO groups the occupations into ISCO-08 code groups with 4 digits on ISCO code for the narrowest group of occupations, classifying the different occupational profiles and showing the relationships between occupations, skills, competences, and qualifications. ESCO structures its pillars hierarchically and interrelated with each other. ESCO is also linked to relevant international classifications, standards, and frameworks, such as the Statistical Classification of Economic Activities in the European Community (NACE), the International Standard Classification of Occupations (ISCO) and the European Qualification Framework (EQF). It provides a repository of more than 100000 links between profiles and their essential skills, technical and nontechnical. It offers clear and updated information and intends to provide a common and standardized terminology for both, profiles, and competences. The ESCO framework provides a highly rich description of essential and optional knowledge and skills related to each occupation profile included. It identifies and categorizes skills, competences, qualifications, and occupations in a standard way, using standard terminology in all EU languages and an open format that can be used by third-party software.

More than 200 experts from all productive sectors created the ESCO classification in a process that took longer than four years. The full ESCO group was composed by relevant stakeholders from different areas from the education and training sector as well as from the labor market. ESCO also involved other stakeholders and Member States in boards, committees, reference and working groups and online experts consultation stakeholders. According to implementation acts, the use of ESCO is compulsory for all Member States of the EU from 2021 onwards. The structure of the information of ESCO for ICT occupations is summarized in the following numbers [41]: 111 profiles/occupations with a total of 631 essential skills/knowledge items and 467 optional ones with 4 occupation groups and 15 occupation subgroups.

3.3.2 European e-Competence Framework

The European Standard EN 16234-1 provides an e-Competence Framework [15] referencing 41 competences and their relation to ICT area, distinguishing five proficiency levels. The framework responds to the need for supporting mutual understanding and provides transparency of language through the articulation of competences required and deployed by ICT professionals, including both practitioners and managers. It includes relations to ICT qualification context (e.g., by the EQF) and familiar frameworks (e.g., DigComp,

ESCO, European ICT Professional Role Profiles, behavioral skills, SFIA, ISO and further ICT industry standards). The emphasis is more on competences rather than on job profiles. This framework considers 41 different competences categorized into five competence areas (Plan, Build, Run, Enable and Manage) and with up to 5 proficiency levels which are reference level specifications on competences. It adopts a competence-based approach where the competences are characterized by a specific set of knowledge items and skills, useful to achieve observable results in the context in which the competences are acted. Similarly, CWA 16458-1 [40] provided the description of 30 ICT profiles in terms of the e-CF competences and a framework to create new description for others. The e-CF universe also includes an End User Guide EN16234-2 [42] in which a list of deliverables linked to each competence is suggested while [40] shows a RACI matrix for linking deliverables and profiles and describes 30 examples of ICT role profiles based on e-competences of EN 16234-1. The e-CF framework became a standard for the ICT competences in Europe in 2016 [43]. This framework is structured in four dimensions with five competence areas (dimension 1: Plan, Build, Run, Enable and Manage) with a set of e-Competences for each area (dimension 2: 41 in total with a generic description for each one). There are proficiency levels e-1 to e-5 (dimension 3) for each e-competence and samples of knowledge and skills (dimension 4) which add value and context, although the list of these items is not intended to be exhaustive.

3.3.3 Skills Match Framework

Skills Match[3] was a project funded by the European Commission (DG CONNECT) which developed and demonstrated a European-wide assessment and learning and guiding platform to help users to adapt their NCS to the demands of the labor market. The project expanded the experience of the previous project, e-Skills Match, which worked with different competences standards and models for ICT occupations [41]. The Skills Match project created a comprehensive and solid NCSF as the basis for its work [13].

The team analyzed information from academic literature, reviewing 66 models and 403 publications with 2928 mentions of skills, as well as 527 European Projects and other NCS existing frameworks and referenced models such as OECD [44], P21 [45], UNESCO [46], WEF [47], among others. Skills Match uses ESCO as its main reference and its 36 NCS of NCSF are mapped to ESCO skills generating 3138 connections at different levels. More than 700 buzzwords associated with each of the 36 NCS complement the description and help to identify mentions of NCS in other models and references. The visualization of the framework shows seven clusters for its 36 NCS, which group those that are most related among them (see Figure 3.1).

---

[3]https://skillsmatch.eu/

Figure 3.1: Non-cognitive skills framework represented as clusters.

3.4 Linking Software Processes and IT Professionalism Frameworks

Now that the focus of each profile standard is clear, it is even more evident that the connection to processes is far from being solved. The reason is not the impossibility of finding a connection between them but the fact that both sides developed their proposals without a strong spirit of linking such information. Obviously, each profile is aimed at developing activities, which are part of the processes, and those activities and the corresponding results recommend a set of skills and competences to achieve goals with the best performance. Our approach for the analysis of skills and competences which may impact the activity in each software process is indirect as it links them through the IT profiles which work in the activities of the process.

Despite the difficulties of working with unrelated information, previous works have explored the connection between software development processes and professional roles and profiles as a first step to analyze skills and competences. One pioneering work already explored this link before the IT professional frameworks were solid enough [48]. Even the Software Engineering Institute, the source of CMMi, explored the side of talent and people management in their People Capability Maturity Model (P-CMM) [49], but it did not result in a detailed analysis of roles and profiles, hence their corresponding skills and competences.

More specific studies have explored how people's behavioral competencies influence the effectiveness and efficiency with which they perform a role in the software process [50]. The research in [51] identifies which professional profiles in software engineering better fit with the activities of the different stages of life cycle models and other processes, such as software management, tools and methods in software engineering or general software engineering processes, based on the viewpoint of 50 professionals. This information can be customized to refer to the software processes by identifying the equivalences with ISO 12207 and IT professional profiles as expressed in CWA (once identified with them, the equivalence with ESCO is direct).

In the case of [51], the authors studied the literature about professional profiles and developed 7 general profiles according to the level of experience involved in software development and general areas of competence. Starting from this data, we have developed an equivalence in nomenclature of only those profiles mentioned in e-CF and ESCO, as is shown in Table 3.1.

Table 3.1: Profile equivalence in e-CF, ESCO and Colomo's study.

Colomo	e-CF	ESCO
A	-	Chief executive officer
B	CIO	Chief information officer
C	Project manager	ICT project manager
D	Business analyst, systems analyst	ICT business analysis manager software analyst
F	Developer	Software developer, ICT system developer

We have also analyzed and mapped equivalences between the areas of competence in the study and processes in ISO 12207 and CMMi, which are the main process standards [51]. We also analyzed the level of involvement each profile has in each area of competence. For our approach, we only took the profiles that are strongly involved in each activity (values 3 or 4). Table 3.2 shows the relation between ISO 12207 processes and the profiles that take part in them.

Table 3.2: Profiles involved in ISO 12207 processes.

F	D	C	B	A	ISO 12207
					6.4.1 Business or mission analysis
2	4	3	2	1	6.4.2 Stakeholder needs and requirements definition
					6.4.3 System/Software requirements definition
3	4	3	2	1	6.4.4. Architecture
					6.4.5 Design definition
4	3	2	1	1	6.4.6 Implementation
3	4	3	2	1	6.4.9 Verification
					6.4.11 Validation
3	4	3	2	1	6.4.13 Maintenance
2	4	3	2	1	6.3.5 Configuration management
2	4	4	3	1	6.3.8 Quality assurance
2	3	4	4	3	(6.3.1 to 6.3.8) Technical management processes
2	4	4	3	2	6.2.1. Life cycle model management process
					6.3.2 Project assessment and control process

3.5 Analysis of Recommended Skills in Processes According to Participating Professional Roles

Knowing which skills in general, and NCS, are recommended in each process can be ascertained by exploiting existing tools and sources of information with large volumes of data (millions of vacancies in OVATE and thousands of relations between skills and occupations in ESCO). This provides a solid basis to identify the most requested NCS for specific occupations or groups of occupations related to software development, combining both the point of view from experts as expressed in ESCO and the data from analysis of demand in the job market collected through OVATE (compiling data from more than 30 million online vacancies across Europe).

This approach is only possible because there is a solid framework like NCSF linked to the ESCO classification, a required reference in all EU tools and initiatives, and applicable to the standard EN16234 (e-CF). Working with these references offers a common basis to overcome the traditional problem of lack of homogeneity in terminology and definition of NCS, which hindered the analysis of demand of skills in the past. The comparison of the job market data from the OVATE tool with the results of the literature contributions has shown that some of the NCS suggested by experts were also demanded in job vacancies. However, data from the job market mentioned others, so the number of NCS identified with OVATE is larger than that suggested by ESCO experts.

If we have a clear understanding of the profiles that are more involved in each process, we can work with the idea that the skills most needed in that process are those identified for those profiles in ESCO and e-CF. The skills recommendations in the profiles are for all the activities they perform; we cannot distinguish those that refer to a specific process. However, as several profiles must be involved in a process, it is reasonable to think that the common skills of all of them are the most important for the process. Based on the profiles that have been identified as most involved in each process, we have identified the most relevant skills using the data extracted from OVATE and ESCO for each profile. The results are shown in Table 3.3.

Table 3.3: Skills relevance in ISO 12207 processes.

		adaptability	coaching	communication	conflict resolution	critical thinking	customer focus	decision making	entrepreneurship	initiative	leadership	manage quality	motivate others	networking	organization	personal development	problem-solving	reliability	resilience	self-management	strategic thinking
6.4.4	Architecture Definition process	3	1	4	1	1	2	1	1	1	1	2	1	1	1	3	3	1	1	1	1
6.4.1	Business or Mission Analysis process	2	2	4	1	1	2	1	1	1	1	3	2	1	1	1	3	1	1	1	1
6.3.5	Configuration Management process	2	2	4	1	1	2	1	1	1	2	2	1	1	1	1	3	1	1	1	1
6.4.5	Design Definition process	3	1	4	1	1	2	1	1	1	1	2	1	1	1	3	3	1	1	1	1
6.2.1	Life Cycle Model Management process	2	2	4	1	1	2	1	1	1	2	2	1	1	1	1	3	1	1	1	1
6.4.13	Maintenance process	3	2	4	1	1	2	1	1	1	1	2	1	1	1	2	3	1	1	1	1
6.3.1	Project Planning process	2	2	4	1	1	2	1	1	1	2	2	1	1	1	1	3	1	1	1	1
6.3.8	Quality Assurance process	2	2	4	1	1	2	1	1	1	2	2	1	1	1	1	3	1	1	1	1
6.4.2	Stakeholder Needs and Requirements Definition process	2	2	4	1	1	2	1	1	1	1	3	2	1	1	1	3	1	1	1	1
6.4.6	System Analysis process	3	1	4	1	1	2	1	1	1	1	2	1	1	1	3	3	1	1	1	1
6.4.3	System/Software Requirements Definition process	2	2	4	1	1	2	1	1	1	1	3	2	1	1	1	3	1	1	1	1
6.4.9	Validation process	3	2	4	1	1	2	1	1	1	1	2	1	1	1	2	3	1	1	1	1
6.4.11	Verification process	3	2	4	1	1	2	1	1	1	1	2	1	1	1	2	3	1	1	1	1
6.3.2 6.3.3 6.3.4 6.3.6 6.3.7	Other technical management processes (Project Assessment and Control process, Decision Management process, Risk Management process, Information Management process and Measurement process)	2	2	4	1	1	2	1	1	1	2	2	1	1	1	1	3	1	1	1	1

This analysis shows that the development processes require profiles with soft skills, in particular, communication, problem solving, personal development, adaptability and quality management. Communication and problem solving are the ones most recommended. Table 3.4 shows the most relevant skills for each process.

Table 3.4: Link from NCSF to processes in ISO 12207.

ISO 12207		NCSF
6.4.4	Architecture Definition process	Communication Adaptability Personal development Problem solving
6.4.1	Business or Mission Analysis process	Communication Manage quality Problem solving
6.3.5	Configuration Management process	Communication Problem solving
6.4.5	Design Definition process	Communication Personal development Problem solving
6.2.1	Life Cycle Model Management process	Communication Problem solving
6.4.13	Maintenance process	Communication Adaptability Problem solving
6.3.1	Project Planning process	Communication Problem solving
6.3.8	Quality Assurance process	Communication Problem solving
6.4.2	Stakeholder Needs and Requirements Definition process	Communication Manage quality Problem solving
6.4.6	System Analysis process	Communication Adaptability Personal development Problem solving
6.4.3	System/Software Requirements Definition process	Communication Manage quality Problem solving
6.4.9	Validation process	Communication Adaptability Problem solving
6.4.11	Verification process	Communication Adaptability Problem solving
6.3.2 6.3.3 6.3.4 6.3.6 6.3.7	Other technical management processes (Project Assessment and Control process, Decision Management process, Risk Management process, Information Management process and Measurement process)	Communication Problem solving

Another way of connecting software process areas to NCS is exploring the set of work products, including artifacts, records, information items, and data stores specified for each process in ISO 12207 [5] in Annex B with the deliverables listed in Annex B of examples of deliverables related to e-CF competences CEN/TR 16234-2:2021 [43]. As work products and deliverables are connected to IT profiles in [40], we can allocate not only the equivalence in outcomes but also explore the link of IT profiles to processes. As the origins and aims of both documents are very different, the comparison is difficult due to the lack of harmonization of terminology. However, it is possible to find clear connections. From the 123 suggested work products in annex B of ISO 12207:2017 [5], there are only 23 clear equivalences to deliverables from EN16234-2 [42], as seen in Table 3.5, covering varied deliverables and products of the life cycle.

Table 3.5: Link from processes to e-CF competences through deliverables.

ISO 12207 Process	Equivalent deliverable e-CF	Competence
Acquisition process		
Agreement (e.g., Contract)	Contract	D.8
Organizational Project-Enabling processes		
Life Cycle Model Management process		
Portfolio Management process		
Project Portfolio	Project Portfolio	E.2
Quality Management process		
Quality Management Plan (Policies, Objectives)	Quality Plan	E.6
Knowledge Management process		
Knowledge Asset Records	Knowledge or Information Base	D.10
Technical Management processes		
Project Plan	Project Plan	E.2
Risk Management process		
Risk Management Plan	Risk Management Plan	E.3
Configuration Management process		
CM Change/Variance Request	RFC (Request for Change)	C.2
Information Management process		
Information Item Archive	Knowledge or Information Base	D.10
Quality Assurance process		
Quality Assurance Procedures	Quality Plan	E.6
Incident Records	Solved Incident	C.4
Technical processes		
Business or Mission Analysis process		
Stakeholder Needs and Requirements Definition process		
Stakeholder Requirements	Solution Requirements	D.11
Stakeholder Requirements Specification	Solution Specification	A.6
Stakeholder Requirements Report	NA	
Critical Performance Measures	Quality Performance Indicators	E.6
	Process KPI	E.5
System/software requirements Specification	Solution Specification	A.6
Requirements Change Request	RFC (Request for Change)	C.2
Architecture Definition process		
Architecture Description	Enterprise Architecture	E.5
Design Definition process		
Design Artifact	SW Design Description	B.1
Interface Specification	User Experience Design	A.10
Implementation process		
Software System Element	Documented Code	B.1
Integration process		
Integration and Test Procedures	Test Procedure	B.3
Integrated Software System Elements (software library)	Integrated Solution	B.2
Validation process		
Validated System	Validated Solution	B.3

There is only one single case where two deliverables from e-CF link to one from ISO 12207: Critical Performance Measures. With this information, we are already providing some insight on the competences recommended in the activities of the 15 process areas with equivalences in products. This list may suggest:

- Obvious direct relations between processes and competences: for example, the quality assurance process is linked to competence E.6 (ICT Quality Management) through the connection between quality assurance procedures and quality plan. Another example is the configuration management process linked to C.2 (Change Support) through the equivalence between CM Change/Variance Request and RFC (Request for Change).

- Other clear relations where the nature of activity in the process involves a specific competence: for example, the design definition process is linked to A.10 (User Experience) through the relation between Interface Specification and User Experience Design.

Moreover, as each competence is equipped with examples of skills and knowledge, we could exploit the links between processes and competences to add those examples to enrich the information on the recommended skill profile for a process. For example, in the case of risk management:

- Considering the relation between the risk management process and E.3 (Risk Management) the following skills are recommended for the process:

  - S1 develop risk management plan to identify required preventative actions.
  - S2 communicate and promote the organization's risk analysis outcomes and risk management processes.
  - S3 design and document the processes for risk analysis and management.
  - S4 apply mitigation and contingency actions.

Obviously not all the skills and knowledge items of a competence should be necessarily meaningful for a process, but it would be easy to decide among them after some analysis by an expert.

Thanks to this link between processes and e-CF competences, we could determine which NCS are recommended for each process. However, in the case of NCS, there is also one other missing link to determine their connection to process areas. Standard EN16234-1 [15] has not established a clear link between its 41 competences and a set of NCS involved in them. In fact, the standard suggests that attitudes and concepts like NCS are embedded and not explicitly mentioned in the details of each competence. The possible work of listing the NCS for each competence is still pending. We have started to explore this possibility of mapping competences to the NCS of the NCSF framework by locating its buzzwords within the text descriptions of level 2, 3 and 4 of each EN16234-1 competence and then analyzing the results within the conceptual view of the standard. We can see some results of this analysis in the following examples:

- The quality assurance process of ISO 12207 is linked to two e-CF competences: E.6 (ICT Quality Management) and C.4 (Problem Management). The NCS most mentioned in buzzwords in common with the contents of dimension 2 and dimension 3 of E.6 are "manage quality," "motivate others," "tenacity," and "organization." In the case of C.4, the NCS most mentioned are "leadership," "manage quality," and "motivate others." There are mentions of up to 12 other NCS in both competences (e.g., "accountability," "problem-solving," "diligence," etc.), but as their buzzwords are only mentioned once and are not shared in the two dimensions, there is not any solid evidence of their role in the competences.

3.6   Conclusions

The study presented in this chapter develops a link between software processes and IT professionalism frameworks as a way of covering a missing part of the existing research: the connection between processes and activities in software development projects and the job profiles involved in them and the skills recommended for effective performance. Unfortunately, the depicted relationship is still very indirect at the present time. We can link skills to professional profiles and the activities they perform but this relation is not so strong when focusing on a specific development process. However, this is only a starting point in this line of work, which may encourage new efforts in determining a closer relation between information from human resources (e.g., job roles, profiles, and skills) and software process activities. Therefore, there is a need to bridge the relationship between the professionals and the process activities. It will help to recommend the professionals based on their skills for project activities in order to know who is best suited for what.

One of the benefits of this relation between human resources and processes is the exploitation of existing IT professionalism standards and the tools of job market analysis constructed upon them. New knowledge can be extracted from those sources of information providing useful guidelines for assessing and clarifying the allocation of staff to processes, for training professionals in specific activities within the software processes, for enriching the information compiled in software engineering curricula, etc. The use of big data analysis and natural language processing is much more solid as a basis for decisions than the small samples of job market situations and the reduced number of experts involved in traditional studies. The key point for this exploitation is the use of common terminology and definition of concepts and terms: now, models like e-CF and ESCO, have provided this common reference to a big international labor market like Europe and the efforts are starting to pay off with results. The case of NCS is less mature but we are convinced that the NCSF framework would be very effective given its solid foundations. In fact, thanks to its links to the ESCO classification, NCSF has a clear advantage over other options, as it is possible to get a lot of information on the presence of NCS in the demand for candidates in the job market.

In future research, we will work on an in-depth study to homogenize reference terms with more detail. The lines of work will also include an explicit study of process recommendations where each IT profile is involved, possibly as part of the efforts of standardization in the EN61234 constellation of technical reports. The benefits will not only include the study of NCS but also the possibility of analysis of technical skills and knowledge recommended for each profile and process. This would obviously require a big effort in the mapping of different expressions of technical qualification into the elements already managed in the competences of e-CF and the skills covered by ESCO. However, it is already possible through the initial link between processes and profiles already established in this work, so we are planning to offer a first version of technical skills recommended for each software process.

References

1. Acuna, S. T., Juristo, N., & Moreno, A. M. (2006). Emphasizing human capabilities in software development. *IEEE Software*, 23(2), 94-101.
2. Amrit, C. A., Daneva, M., & Damian, D. (2014). Human factors in software development: On its underlying theories and the value of learning from related disciplines. A guest editorial

introduction to the special issue. *Information and Software Technology*, 56(12), 1537-1542.

3. Pirzadeh, L. (2010). *Human factors in software development: a systematic literature review* (Master's thesis).

4. Guveyi, E., Aktas, M. S., & Kalipsiz, O. (2020, July). Human factor on software quality: A systematic literature review. In *International Conference on Computational Science and Its Applications* (pp. 918-930). Springer, Cham.

5. ISO, "ISO/IEC/IEEE 12207:2017 Systems and software engineering — Software life cycle processes." ISO, 2017.

6. Chrissis, M. B., Konrad, M., & Shrum, S. (2011). *CMMI for development: guidelines for process integration and product improvement*. Pearson Education.

7. Schwaber, K. (1997). Scrum development process. In *Business Object Design and Implementation* (pp. 117-134). Springer, London.

8. Misra, S., Omorodion, M., Fernández-Sanz, L., & Pages, C. (2018). A brief overview of software process models: benefits, limitations, and application in practice. *Computer Systems and Software Engineering: Concepts, Methodologies, Tools, and Applications*, 1-14.

9. Sukhoo, A., Barnard, A., Eloff, M. M., Van der Poll, J. A., & Motah, M. (2005). Accommodating soft skills in software project management. *Issues in Informing Science & Information Technology*, 2.

10. Matturro, G., Raschetti, F., & Fontán, C. (2019). A Systematic Mapping Study on Soft Skills in Software Engineering. *Journal of Universal Computer Science*, 25(1), 16-41.

11. Fernandez-Sanz, L., & Misra, S. (2012). Analysis of cultural and gender influences on teamwork performance for software requirements analysis in multinational environments. *IET Software*, 6(3), 167-175.

12. Sanz, L. F., Pospelova, V., Castillo-Martinez, A., Villalba, M. T., de Buenaga, M., & de Sevilla, M. F. (2020). Skills for IT Project Management: The View From EU Frameworks. In *Handbook of Research on the Role of Human Factors in IT Project Management* (pp. 85-105). IGI Global.

13. Skills match consortium, "Deliverable 2.1," Skills match consortium, Mar. 2019.

14. Lippman, L. H., Ryberg, R., Carney, R., & Moore, K. A. (2015). Workforce Connections: Key "soft skills" that foster youth workforce success: toward a consensus across fields. Washington, DC: *Child Trends*.

15. CEN, "EN 16234-1:2019, e-Competence Framework (e-CF) - A common European Framework for ICT Professionals in all sectors - Part 1: Framework." 2019.

16. Matturro, G. (2013, May). Soft skills in software engineering: A study of its demand by software companies in Uruguay. In *2013 6th International Workshop on Cooperative and Human Aspects of Software Engineering (CHASE)* (pp. 133-136). IEEE.

17. Ahmed, F., Capretz, L. F., & Campbell, P. (2012). Evaluating the demand for soft skills in software development. *IT Professional*, 14(1), 44-49.

18. Lethbridge, T. C. (2000). What knowledge is important to a software professional?. *Computer*, 33(5), 44-50.

19. Pressman, R. S. (2001). *"Software Engineering A Practitioner's Approach,"* Software Engineering A Practitioner's Approach, New York: McGraw-Hill.

20. K. K. Aggarwal and Y. Singh, "Software engineering," New Delhi: New Age International Publishers, 2008.

21. Sommerville, I. (2011). *Software engineering*, 9th Edition. ISBN-10, 137035152, Addison Wesley.

22. Jawadekar, W. S. (2004). *Software Engg*. Tata McGraw-Hill Education.

23. Boehm, B. W. (1988). A spiral model of software development and enhancement. *Computer*, 21(5), 61-72.

24. Gull, H., Azam, F., Haider, W. B., & Iqbal, S. Z. (2009). A New Divide & Conquer Software Process Model World Academy of Science. *Engineering and Technology*, 60(2009), 255-260.

25. Boehm, B., Egyed, A., Kwan, J., Port, D., Shah, A., & Madachy, R. (1998). Using the WinWin spiral model: a case study. *Computer*, 31(7), 33-44.

26. A. Cockburn, "Agile software development," Reading, MA: Addison Wesley Longman, 2001.

27. I. Crnkovic, M. Chaudron, and S. Larsson, "Component-based development process and component lifecycle. 2006," p. 44.

28. Highsmith, J. (2013). *Adaptive software development: a collaborative approach to managing complex systems*. Addison-Wesley.

29. Allenby, K., Burton, S., Buttle, D., McDermid, J., Murdoch, J., Stephenson, A., ... & Hutchesson, S. (2001, September). A family-oriented software development process for engine controllers. In *International Conference on Product Focused Software Process Improvement* (pp. 210-226). Springer, Berlin, Heidelberg.

30. Scacchi, W. (2002). Process models in software engineering. *Encyclopedia of Software Engineering*.

31. Beck, K. (2003). *Test-driven development: by example*. Addison-Wesley Professional.

32. Schwaber, K., & Beedle, M. (2002). *Agile software development with Scrum* (Vol. 1). Upper Saddle River: Prentice Hall.

33. Acuña, S. T., López, M., JURISTO, N., & MORENO, A. (1999). A process model applicable to software engineering and knowledge engineering. *International Journal of Software Engineering and Knowledge Engineering*, 9(05), 663-687. doi: 10.1142/S0218194099000358.

34. Aydan, U., Yilmaz, M., Clarke, P. M., & O'Connor, R. V. (2017). Teaching ISO/IEC 12207 software lifecycle processes: A serious game approach. Computer Standards & Interfaces, 54, 129-138. doi: 10.1016/j.csi.2016.11.014.

35. Pino, F. J., Baldassarre, M. T., Piattini, M., & Visaggio, G. (2010). Harmonizing maturity levels from CMMI-DEV and ISO/IEC 15504. *Journal of Software Maintenance and Evolution: Research and Practice*, 22(4), 279-296. doi: 10.1002/spip.437.

36. Silva, F. S., Soares, F. S. F., Peres, A. L., de Azevedo, I. M., Vasconcelos, A. P. L., Kamei, F. K., & de Lemos Meira, S. R. (2015). Using CMMI together with agile software development: A systematic review. *Information and Software Technology*, 58, 20-43. doi: 10.1016/j.infsof.2014.09.012.

37. Ruiz, J. C., Osorio, Z. B., Mejia, J., Muñoz, M., Ch, A. M., & Olivares, B. A. (2011, November). Definition of a hybrid measurement process for the models ISO/IEC 15504-ISO/IEC 12207: 2008 and CMMI Dev 1.3 in SMEs. In *2011 IEEE Electronics, Robotics and Automotive Mechanics Conference* (pp. 421-426). IEEE. doi: 10.1109/CERMA.2011.74.

38. ESCO Secretariat, "ESCO Implementation Manual." European Commission, 2019.

39. CEN Workshop on ICT Skills, "CWA 16458-1:2018 European ICT Professional Role Profiles - Part 1: 30 ICT Profiles." CEN, 2018.

40. Fernández-Sanz, L., Gómez-Pérez, J., & Castillo-Martínez, A. (2017). e-Skills Match: A framework for mapping and integrating the main skills, knowledge and competence standards and models for ICT occupations. *Computer Standards & Interfaces*, 51, 30-42. doi: 10.1016/j.csi.2016.11.004.

41. CEN, "EN 16234-1:2019, e-Competence Framework (e-CF) - A common European Framework for ICT Professionals in all sectors - Part 1: Framework." 2019.

42. CEN (European Committee for Standardization), "User guide for the application of the European e-Competence Framework 3.0. CWA 16234:2014 Part 2." 2014.

43. CEN TC 428, "EN 16234-1:2016. e-Competence Framework (e-CF) - A common European Framework for ICT Professionals in all industry sectors - Part 1: Framework." CEN, Apr. 2016.

44. OECD, "Definition and Selection of Competencies (DeSeCo)," 2005.

45. The Partnership for 21st Century Learning, "P21 Framework Definitions," May 2015.

46. UNESCO, "UNESCO Competency framework," 2015.

47. World Economic Forum. (2016). The future of jobs: Employment, skills and workforce strategy for the fourth industrial revolution. *Global Challenge Insight Report*.

48. García, M. J. G., & Sanz, L. F. (2006). El factor humano en la ingeniería del software. *Novática: Revista de la Asociación de Técnicos de Informática*, (179), 48-54.

49. Curtis, B., Hefley, B., & Miller, S. (2009). People Capability Maturity Model (P-CMM). *Software Engineering Institute*.

50. Acuña, S. T., & Juristo, N. (2004). Assigning people to roles in software projects. *Software: Practice and Experience*, 34(7), 675-696.

51. Colomo-Palacios, R., Tovar-Caro, E., García-Crespo, Á., & Gómez-Berbís, J. M. (2010). Identifying technical competences of IT professionals: The case of software engineers. *International Journal of Human Capital and Information Technology Professionals (IJHCITP)*, 1(1), 31-43.

52. Le, D. N., Nguyen, G. N., Garg, H., Huynh, Q. T., Bao, T. N., & Tuan, N. N. (2021). Optimizing Bidders Selection of Multi-Round Procurement Problem in Software Project Management Using Parallel Max-Min Ant System Algorithm. *CMC-COMPUTERS MATERIALS & CONTINUA*, 66(1), 993-1010.

53. Bao, T. N., Huynh, Q. T., Nguyen, X. T., Nguyen, G. N., & Le, D. N. (2020). A Novel Particle Swarm Optimization Approach to Support Decision-Making in the Multi-Round of an Auction by Game Theory. *International Journal of Computational Intelligence Systems*, 13(1), 1447-1463.

54. Le, D. N. (2017). A new ant algorithm for optimal service selection with end-to-end QoS constraints. *Journal of Internet Technology*, 18(5), 1017-1030.

55. Seth, B., Dalal, S., Jaglan, V., Le, D. N., Mohan, S., & Srivastava, G. (2020). Integrating encryption techniques for secure data storage in the cloud. *Transactions on Emerging Telecommunications Technologies*, e4108.

Monitoring and Controlling Software Project Scope Using Agile EVM

Avais Jan[1], Assad Abbas[1], Naveed Ahmad[2]

[1] Department of Computer Science, COMSATS University Islamabad, Islamabad Campus, Pakistan
[2] National University of Computer and Emerging Sciences, Pakistan
Email: avaisjnn@gmail.com, assadabbas@comsats.edu.pk, naveed.ahmad@nu.edu.pk

Abstract

Earned value management (EVM) gauges the performance of a project against the initial plan, where budget and schedule information are provided upfront. It makes it easier for the project manager to take corrective actions by pinpointing the deviations in time and cost. Agile project management welcomes changes throughout the life of a project. Therefore, it is important to incorporate EVM with Agile to forecast scope. Several attempts have been made to integrate EVM with Agile at iteration and release level to forecast scope. However, those approaches faced the following four challenges: (i) Not knowing and incorporating the changing effects of Agile builds unrealistic project goals; (ii) the use of velocity as a metric for monitoring and controlling work is challenging because of the local nature of this metric; similarly, (iii) focusing on individual team and individual release is another challenge because it is a contrast with the large-scale implication of traditional EVM; additionally, (iv) the method of calculating "percent complete" at work item level is another issue because without an objective basis for counting this progress, projections at higher levels are called into question. To tackle these challenges, in this research, a novel approach has been proposed. The approach consists of three steps. Firstly, a systematic literature review is conducted for scope change influencing factors identification. Secondly, mapping of the identified factors with different elements of the Agile Software Project Scope Rating Index (A-SPSRI) is performed. In the final step, there is quantification, EVM integration and simulation of the universe of projects. The proposed approach has been used at the release planning phase when several agreed upon features are decided to implement their respective iterations. Unlike the one release one team method, and just relying on the velocity current approach, the universe of simulations is used with multiple teams to ensure the large-scale implication of AgileEVM. Moreover, the triad technique is used to gauge the completeness of features implementation in percentile with respect to the iterations.

Keywords: Software project management, Agile development, project scope, earned value management, software process management.

4.1 Introduction

Earned value management (EVM) is taught as the most popular approach for monitoring and controlling the progress of a project [1,2]. Previously, it has been widely used in different application areas. Furthermore, it's widely used by project managers in their software projects [3]. EVM measures the performance of a project against the initial plan, where budget and schedule information are provided upfront. It makes it easier for the project manager to take remedial actions by pinpointing the deviations in time and cost. The Project Management Institute (PMI) states that EVM is one of the most effective tools to monitor the progress of information technology (IT) projects. Additionally, the progress of IT projects can be proficiently displayed by following triple constraints.

The triple constraints consist of cost, time and scope and can be used to show how a project achieves its goals. It is imperative to consider these constraints for the favorable outcome of any project [4]. However, for the success of software projects, the scope is the most important constraint. The main reason for the failure of thousands of projects in the literature is the scope of the project [5,6]. Though scope has been used to indicate the success criteria of a project, in the literature it has been set aside while determining the progress of the projects.

Moreover, several barriers have been highlighted in the literature which prevent project managers from properly managing and defining the project scope. For instance, some of the barriers are unsatisfactory effort from stakeholders, inadequate and poor scope, non-stop flow of requirements [6], project scope not managed well, variation in requirements, inappropriate assumptions, system complexity not fully understood, unsuitable calculations, uncertain goals and project vision [7], etc. These aforementioned problems cause projects to be over schedule and over budget [8], scope creep [9], de-scoping [10], over-scoping [11], requirement volatility [8], wasted effort [12], possible risks [13], bad quality software, and eventually cause the failure of projects [6]. The main reason for the failure of many projects is the uncontrolled and unmanaged project scope [14].

Several tools and techniques are used to gauge the performance of software projects such as function point (FP), work breakdown structure (WBS), expert judgment, feature transition charts (FTC), story mapping, performance analysis, and control scope change system. The limitation of these methods is that they only consider the complete definition of project scope for project measurement.

Finally, to fully understand the influence of scope on the project, there is a need to efficiently assess the incompleteness of the software scope definition. For measuring the status of software projects, EVM methodology uses a "well-defined baseline plan against which project performance is measured in terms of time and cost" [15]. The baseline consists of the actual project plan and the accepted changes in it. Having cost execution pattern upfront, project managers can calculate the performance of the projects in terms of scope, time and cost by inserting the actual information and later comparing it with the baseline. The baseline plan used by traditional EVM considers only schedule and budget information; it does not consider the project scope. Changes occur in the project scope throughout the project life cycle; variations occur from analysis to the maintenance phase of the project [16]. A software scope change greatly affects project planning, especially project schedules and budgets [17]. The unstable nature of scope brings us to the matter of project planning since it is vital to the baseline project scope. In conclusion, there is a limitation in EVM as it does not consider the completeness of project scope, neither does it measure the effect on the project plan that occurs due to the changes in scope.

Previous studies revealed that poor project planning and improper scope definition leads to a huge failure in terms of time, cost, and quality. This study aims to propose a novel approach that can address the challenges associated with poor project planning, and the vague and unstable scope definition of agile projects by answering the following research questions (RQs):

- Q1: What are the state-of-the-art effects of agile project scope changes on the release plan?

- Q2: How can agile scope changing factors be mapped with A-SPSRI element?

- Q3: How can agile EVM measure scope deviations?

To address RQ1, a systematic literature review has been conducted to find out the effect of scope changes in agile projects in a release plan. The findings of the literature review are discussed in Section 4.2. For answering RQ2, factors that affect the scope of the agile projects are extracted from the literature and their relationship with A-SPSRI elements is determined. This relationship is shown in Section 4.2 in the mapping give table number of factors with A-SPSRI. For measuring scope deviation in RQ3, the remainder of the chapter consists of a literature review in Section 4.2, Section 4.3 provides the insights of the proposed technique, Section 4.4 shows simulation results and, finally, Section 4.5 presents the conclusion, limitations, and future work.

4.2 Related Work

It is of great concern to appropriately organize the software development process to produce quantity systems. By introducing agile software development techniques, the rise in the failure rate of software projects using traditional methodologies can be addressed effectively [18].

For delivering successful projects, project management is extremely important for any big company. The success rate of Agile projects is three time more than that of traditional projects, according to the 2011 CHAOS report from the Standish Group [19]. Another report given in 2013 by the Standish Group shows that most of the agile projects were completed within budget and on time [20]. The findings from the study [21] show that the success rate of agile over traditional methods could be summed up as "29% improvement in cost, 71% in the schedule, 122% improvement in performance, 75% improvement in quality and 70% improvement in customer satisfaction"; however, projects still fail due to many issues [22,114].

Project limitations and restrictions mainly define scope [23], which significantly increases the project's performance in terms of planning, budgeting, achievement, and failure. According to the literature, project failure is mainly due to scope and the frequent changes in it. Project managers use different metrics and tools to analyze and control scope, including function point (FP) analysis, adept judgment, WBS and performance analysis, etc. Function point analysis helps in scope estimation by considering only requirements. Work breakdown structure (WBS) helps as a means of verifying scope. Although, it can't properly help in measuring requirements and tasks into deliverables, it operates on user or system requirements and helps by including cost estimations and resources [24]. Although, deliverables can give us requirements in some partial format, we can't classify it under WBS.

In project scope, revisions are thought to be agreed upon. These revisions are necessary for the difficult and unavoidable changes in the project scope. These changes mostly take place until the deployment stages [14]. Due to its varying nature, we ought to be more careful and need to plan early to baseline project scope properly. According to the literature, changing requirements has considerably high effects on product. In this way, it can assist us to adjust the new requirements in the project plan. Barry and Legodi have indicated in their work that there is a deep connection between the interval and effort of the project [25]. However, a detailed inquiry is needed to analyze and recognize the effect of changes in scope on the project plan. Different tools and techniques are used to define scope in software projects development. The related work is further divided into three subsections. The following sections briefly explain each category.

4.2.1 Tools and Techniques Used for Scope Definition

The data provided in Table 4.1 illustrate some of the tools and techniques used for defining in the literature. These techniques and tools are used for estimating, controlling and verifying scope. However, the existing literature is limited to measuring the completeness and quantification of the project scope.

Table 4.1: Combination of different approaches used as monitoring and controlling methods in software project management.

S.No	Tool/Tech	Monitoring	Quantification	Controlling	Visualizing	Completeness	Reference
1	Earn Value Management and Gantt Chart	C		C	C		[26]
2	Earn Value Management and statistical Methods	C		C			[27]
3	Earn Value Management and Kanban	C			C		[28]
4	Value Stream Mapping and Kanban	C			C		[29]
5	Scrum and Kanban	C			C		[30][115]
6	Control charts	C		C	C		[31]
7	PRINCE 2 and Balance Scored Method	C					[32]
8	Cumulative Flow Diagram with some metrics	C		C	C		[33]
9	Earn Value Management and critical path method	C	C	C	C		[34]
10	EVM and Use Case Point	C		C	C		[35]

Further observation of the literature, revealed a study that claims to measure the completeness of project scope. The authors contributed to the topic by dividing the project scope into 45 critical elements. The authors included diversity in these elements with the aim of addressing each type of software project [36]. These 45 elements in essence were used to define scope completeness but lack in defining scope changes and their effects on the project plan. To predict the results of changes in scope on the project plan, this research aims to include scope in EVM with the research hypothesis "Using A-SPSRI elements which will quantify the effects of changes in scope."

As we know, project scope plays a vital role in the success of any project. Therefore, it is also important to use the right tools and techniques for monitoring and controlling the project scope. In Table 4.1 we have described some of the well-known tools and techniques found in the literature. In the table, "C" indicates the presence of an attribute. The next subsection discusses the traditional project scope definition.

4.2.2 Traditional Project Scope Definition

These tools and techniques are differentiated with respect to their use in traditional and agile development. Tools and techniques used for scope definition in traditional software development are described in Table 4.2; whereas Table 4.3 describes the tools and techniques used for scope definition in the agile development process. Following are the details regarding the tools and techniques for agile project scope definition.

Table 4.2: Tools/techniques used for traditional project scope definition.

Techniques /Tools	Traditional project scope definition					
	Controlling Scope	Scope Estimation	Measure Completeness	Identifying Features	Scope Quantification	Reference
Function Points	C	C		C	C	[37]
Expert Judgment				C		[38]
Performance Analysis	C					[39]
Work-Breakdown Structure (WBS)	C				C	[24]
Feature Transition charts	C					[40]
Stakeholder Analysis				C		[41]
Benefits Analysis				C		[42]
Scope Change Control System	C					[43]
Functional Size Measurement (FSM)	C	C		C	C	[44]
Feature Survival Charts	C					[40]
SEER-SEM		C				[40]
Feature Growth Charts	C					[45]
SPSRI	C		C	C		[36]

Table 4.3: Tools/techniques used for agile project scope definition.

Techniques /Tools	Agile project scope definition					
	Controlling Scope	Scope Estimation	Measure Completeness	Identifying Features	Scope Quantification	Reference
Feature-Breakdown Structure (WBS)	C	C		C		[46]
Feature Transition charts	C					[40]
Story Mapping	C	C		C		[47] [48]
Agile EVM	C	C				[49]
Burn Up charts	C	C				[50]
Feature Survival Charts	C					[45]
Burn Down Chart	C	C				[50] [51]
Requirement Matrix	C					[52]
TinyPM, ScrumDesk, Agile for Trac, Version one	C			C		[53]
Cumulative Flow	C					[51]
Stacked Area Chart	C					[48]
Iteration Status Chart	C					[54]
Agilefant	C					[55]
Iceberg List	C					[54]
Kanban Board	C					[56]
Tree Map	C					[57]
Parking Lot Diagram	C					[57]
Planning Poker	C	C		C	C	[58]
Wideband Delphi		C		C	C	[59] [60]
Constructive Cost Model					C	[59] [60]
AgileMOW		C			C	[59] [61]

4.2.3 Tools and Techniques for Agile Project Scope Definition

Scope monitoring and control is very different in agile projects because scope in agile projects frequently changes as compared to traditional projects. That's why agile project scope monitoring and control is very difficult task. Therefore, it is necessary to use effective and different tools and techniques for agile projects. Table 4.3 shows some of the tools and techniques used for agile project scope definition. In the table, "C" indicates the presence of an attribute. Some of the widely used tools and techniques are mentioned in Table 4.3. In this research, we have used AgileEVM. Though it has been already used as it is very effective for scope monitoring and control, there are still many issues and challenges with using this tool, such as the volatile nature of agile scope, local nature of metric velocity, focus on one team one release approach, and percent completion rather than percentile completion. All these issues are addressed in this chapter.

4.3 EVM Applications and Calculation

The EVM project management method is used for gauging the project performance, which helps the project manager (PM) calculate time and cost. This helps project managers in making correct decisions. At any time during the project it indicates work done and the work that must be done up to that time. EVM consists of three terms: earned value (EV), planned value (PV), and actual cost (AC) [62,63].

- PV: The amount of money to be spent on the project for that specific time; it is also known as budgeted cost for work scheduled (BCWS).

- EV: The amount of work that has to be completed at a specific time; it is also known as budgeted cost for work performed (BCWP).

- AC: The amount of money that has been spent on the project; it is also known as actual cost of work performed (ACWP).

Though we are using EVM for predicting project schedule, initially it was used for cost management. At the end of the project it is seen that the schedule indicator shows incorrect results and project managers start depending on the cost indicator. The reason for putting the emphasis on the cost indicator may be due to schedule indicator because of the solid relationship between project cost and schedule; however, there is a need for a clear mathematical representation in order to demonstrate this relationship. Consequently, we cannot rely on useless and incorrect results of schedule indicator; besides measuring the project performance with the cost indicator, the project performance must also be measured with the schedule indicator.

The amount of value that should have been achieved at a specific time is known as earned schedule (ES) [63]. It is used for addressing the schedule performance of the project. We could get this data if we know the value of the cost baseline in conditions where EV and PV are equal. To control project schedule, EVM methodology is used. This methodology is used in the domain of schedule management. To find the relationship between EVM and schedule, P-factor is presented. Most of the time projects don't follow the actual plan and this could lead to project overschedule, therefore project schedule management is very crucial [64].

$$ES = N + \frac{EV - PV_N}{PV_{N+1} - PV_N)} \tag{4.1}$$

Here, N is the raise in time of PV, PV_N is the planned value at N and $PV - N + 1$ is planned value at $N + 1$ [65]. P-factor value is between 0 and 1. The value of 1 is not good news for the PM. It means that the project is not going well due to constraints or undisciplined employees [66].

Earned schedule (ES) is used to represent completed activities; however, it isn't used for the activities which come later on in the critical path. Furthermore, the purpose of ES is to estimate incomplete activities.

$$SV_t = ES - AT \tag{4.2}$$

$$SPI_t = \frac{ES}{AT} \tag{4.3}$$

Here, AT represents the real time.

The term S-curve has been used in [67] for predicting project estimation. To predict the project performance,the S-curve project actual performance on the project plan is later combined with the project completion probability. In studies it is shown that for the purpose of monitoring and scheduling, there is another term used; the learning curve (S-shaped). For measuring project performance, EVM technique has been used related to resources and schedule of the project. In the existing literature it is shown that EVM has been used for measuring performance by predicting project cost and its completion date.

It consists of schedule variance (SV), cost performance index (CPI), cost variance (CV), and schedule performance index (SPI). SV predicts project schedule to understand whether a project is overscheduled or not. We can represent it by $(SV = EV - PV)$. To determine how efficiently the project team is using its time, the schedule performance is used, $(SPI = EV - PV)$ [68].

If $(SV < 0)$ and $(SPI < 1)$, it means that the project is behind schedule. And if $(SV > 0)$ and $(SPI > 1)$, it means that the project is going well and is ahead of schedule.

When schedule variance (SV) moves towards zero and SPI becomes equal to one, this means the project is nearly finished. However, if the project gets delayed remarkably in its later stages, then the mentioned index cannot provide accurate information. In [68], the cost variance (CV) shows that if the project is over or under budget, the cost performance index (CPI) measures the efficient use of project resources.

- The project is over cost, when $(CV < 0)$ and $(CPI < 1)$

- The project is under budget, when $(CV > 0)$ and $(CPI > 1)$

Equation (4.4) represents the formula which is "Estimation at Completion," which is used for the estimation of the future cost of the project only if the project is running with uniform performance. We can also calculate the remaining work of the project, which is "Estimate to Compute." We can use it to subtract the actual completion budget divided by cost performance index, which is given in Equation (4.5).

$$EAC = \frac{BAC}{CPI} \tag{4.4}$$

$$ETC = \frac{(BAC - EV)}{CPI} \tag{4.5}$$

To trace and monitor project progress, EVM can be used in diverse disciplines such as IT companies, construction, etc. It is also used in agile software development projects in which the estimation for every iteration is separately calculated. It requires both the burn-down and burn-up charts and projected finalized data for estimation at completion (EAT) [50]. EVM is also used as a control technique for the time and cost of software projects because it identifies possible delays and cost overruns in the project. The previous literature shows that the EVM support project manager (PM) controls the project cost and schedules changes for taking active action earlier [69,111,112].

The EVM methodology is used as a control technique to avoid cost and schedule over-runs by presenting the idea of a cumulative buffer. To control ambiguity in the project, schedule control ($SCol(t)$) and cost control ($CCol(t)$) indexes were introduced. Using these indices, EVM shows high value if the project was running under an uncertainty. Positive value of the indices indicates that the project is under budget and schedule, while the negative value shows the problematic situation for both cost and schedule overrun [70,113]. To estimate the future state of a current project, EVM- and risk management (RM)-based WBS techniques are integrated to get better results. This integrated approach of both EVM- and RM-based WBS will help the project manager consider project risks together with the past performance, which is the history of the projects [15].

In [62], a graphical framework is introduced to manage the uncertainty of projects. The introduced framework uses a cumulative buffer at runtime execution of the project. The author of the framework integrated EVM methodology with risk management to control the uncertainty of the project. Furthermore, a Monte Carlo simulation is used to generate universe of projects and to calculate statistical distribution function for both time and cost. For controlling the project, the concept of triads is introduced. Triads define the state of the project $(x\%, Tx_j, CX_j)$, here x is the estimated percentage of the project, Tx_j is the estimated time at $x\%$ and CX_j is the estimated cost that was spent when project is completed at $x\%$. Once the spreading is calculated, it is also possible to estimate the different percentiles of the project by varying the value of x for each standard deviation. This includes percentile of cost (Pc90, Pc70, etc.) and percentile of schedule (Pd90, Pd70, etc.). These percentiles can lead us to identify and trace the project risk. EVM triad methodology is limited to identifying deviations in scope of the project as it is done for time and cost at diverse monitoring periods of the project. In order, to better understand the outcome indexes of the project, it is imperative to include scope while measuring the performance (i.e., time and cost) of the project.

4.4 Research Methodology

Our research methodology consists of three main steps. In the first step, a systematic literature review is conducted by using a specific search string. Then paper selection criteria and quality assessment of studies is performed. At the end of first step a list of scope changing factors is generated as an output. This list of factors becomes the input for the second step. In this step we further map this list of factors with A-SPSRI elements. To get the valid mapping, we went through the process of using questionnaires and surveys.

Now our third step of research methodology starts with research question three (RQ3). AgileEVM mapped and valid factors are input for this step. We quantify A-SPSRI elements and run several simulations. After simulation we integrate AgileEVM. After that we examine the scope and statistical evaluation is performed. So, at the end of this whole process we can forecast the scope deviation and statistically proved simulated data is presented. We have research question 1, 2 and 3 as an input for the three steps of our research methodology. At the end of each step we have the output of each step. This whole process is shown in Figure 4.1.

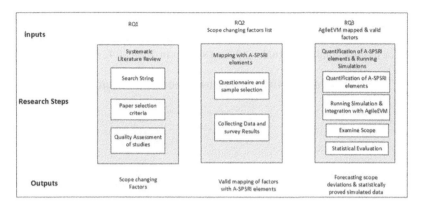

Figure 4.1: Research methodology.

4.4.1   Systematic Literature Review

A systematic review of literature (SLR) is conducted precisely by following a set of guidelines for the impartial and repeatable collection and assessment of all available evidence on a specific issue [71]. We went through the process by describing the protocol constructed and pilot examined by the first author (student) and analyzed by the second author (supervisor). We now describe the steps taken in this SLR.

4.4.1.1   Search Databases

For the identification of factors effecting scope in agile software development, an extensive literature review is conducted to answer RQ1. To search for all possible effects of agile project scope changes on the release plan, we get help from different databases. We got a plethora of good quality research papers in this way. Some famous online journal databases which were discovered for this purpose are IEEE Xplore, Science Direct, Springer Link and Google Scholar.

4.4.1.2   Search String Used

The search string used for the literature review is shown below.

((Scope change OR Scope vari* OR effects of scope changes OR effects on planning OR effect of scope changes on schedule estimation OR effect of scope changes on time estimation OR effects of scope problems OR change project scope) AND (Software risks OR software risk changes scope) AND (Scope creep OR de-scoping OR over-scoping OR requirement volatility OR requirement uncertainty) AND (Software failure, hardware and software failure) AND (Predefined budget, predefined schedule) AND (Agile Project Management OR APM)).

4.4.1.3   Inclusion and Exclusion Criteria

The identified factors were first collected in a spread sheet and afterwards these factors were aggregated into a single unique effect to make an integrated list. After finding factors of scope changes, these were grouped under a single unique factor, i.e., f1, f2, f3, etc. Factors such as failure of software, unavailability of labor, transformation and availability of resources, physical damage of hardware, and supplier issues were considered a single unique effect named change project resources. The process repeated until distinguishing results were attained. A list of about 62 unique factors with their descriptions that had an impact on project planning can be seen in Table 4.4.

4.4.1.4   Factors Identification

To find different types of factors that affect agile project scope, different articles were searched for in good quality journals and then shown in Table 4.4.

Table 4.4: Extracted factors from the literature.

Variables	Factors	References	Variables	Factors	References
f1	Priority Features	[72, 73]	f32	Missing a clear prioritization	[83]
f2	Developers and customer's discussion	[72, 46]	f33	Missing a definition of done	[83]
f3	Poor delivery Strategy	[74, 75]	f34	Conflicting priorities within the company	[83]
f4	Failing to fulfil competing Priorities	[74]	f35	Low committing to the plan	[83]
f5	Effect of constant Revision	[74]	f36	Distributed agile software development	[84]
f6	Productionized for customers	[76]	f37	Improper organization of daily work and meetings	[84]
f7	User Reviews	[76]	f38	Rare customer involvement	[80]
f8	Short Progress Meeting	[76]	f39	Customer satisfaction	[80] [85]
f9	Short release	[76]	f40	Customer collaboration	[85]
f10	Effort estimation	[77]	f41	Customer commitment	[80] [85]
f11	Project Nature	[72]	f42	Allow Teams to self-organize	[86]
f12	Project Schedule	[72]	f43	Lack of training	[86]
f13	less developer skill sets	[78]	f44	Too high workload	[86]
f14	Extremely Complex Techniques and Tools	[67]	f45	Global distribution challenges	[86]
f15	project plan document	[79]	f46	Achieving technical consistency	[86]
f16	Strict security policies	[79]	f47	Lack of necessary skill set	[87]
f17	Strict organizational policies	[79]	f48	Lack of project management competence	[87]
f18	Minimum regulatory constraints	[79]	f49	Lack of team work	[87]
f19	Poor operational performance characteristics	[79]	f50	Resistance from groups and individuals	[87]
f20	Completion time	[79]	f51	Recognition the importance of product owner role	[86]
f21	Unavailability of a business process	[79]	f52	Management in waterfall mode	[86]
f22	Neglecting non-functional requirements	[80]	f53	Keeping the old bureaucracy	[86]
f23	Unclear objectives of project	[81]	f54	Customer inability and agreement	[80]
f24	Requirement unclear to the team	[81]	f55	Contractual limitations	[80]
f25	Requirement conflicts among multiple product owners	[81]	f56	Lack of complete set of correct agile practices	[88]
f26	In-adequate communication about end-user requirements	[81]	f57	Inappropriateness of technology and tools	[88]
f27	In-adequate prioritization of requirements	[81]	f58	General resistance to change	[86]
f28	Frequent architectural changes	[81]	f59	Skepticism towards the new way of working	[86]
f29	Minimum client participation and collaboration in the process	[82]	f60	Challenges in rearranging physical spaces	[86]
f30	developer participation	[82]	f61	Developer Fear of Skill-Deficiency Exposure	[89]
f31	Important decisions not aligned	[83]	f62	Efficiency in finding potential risk	[77]

4.4.2   Mapping of Factors with A-SPSRI Elements

A-SPSRI elements [57] are selected as a baseline to deeply understand the individual effects of changes in scope. This could lead us to analyze possible effects against each scope element on the project plan. To achieve the second main objective of this research, literature-based mapping is performed between extracted effects of scope changes and A-SPSRI elements and are evaluated by the software industry via questionnaire for the purpose of identifying the least and most influencing factors for each A-SPSRI element. These extracted effects are explained in terms of time and cost, to be further used for scope quantification. Table 4.5 shows the mapping between extracted scope changing factors and A-SPSRI elements. The process of mapping is shown in Table 4.5.

4.4.2.1   Questionnaire and Sample Selection

To evaluate this mapping, a survey from the software industry was conducted by questionnaire. The data was gathered from 40 software industry experts from about 22 software companies in Islamabad, where our questionnaire was filled out by project managers and senior software engineers. They prioritized all the factors, from which we could see the most and least influencing factors. Our questionnaire consisted of two sections:

1) Designation and Experience

2) Prioritize Influencing Factors

Table 4.5: Mapping of factors elements.

S.NO	Elements	Factors	Ref
1	Product Future Statement	f1, f2	[72] [73] [90] [91] [92] [30]
2	Market strategy VS project Strategy	f3, f4, f5	[93] [74] [75] [94]
3	Release Definition and Selection	f6, f7, f8, f9	[76] [95]
4	Release plan	f6, f7, f8, f9	[96] [30]
5	Iteration Mission	f6, f7, f8, f9	[96] [30]
6	Resource Estimation	f10	[77]
7	Iteration Schedule	f11, f12	[72] [97] [98] [99]
8	Task Identification	f13	[78] [100] [101] [102]
9	Managing Dependencies	f14	[103] [104]
10	Key Deliverables	f15	[79] [102] [92]
11	Identifying Constraints	f16, f17, f18, f19, f20, f21	[105] [93] [106]
12	Managing Risk / Uncertainties	f22, f23, f24, f25, f26, f27, f28	[80] [107] [81] [102]
13	Adjust Priorities	f29, f30, f31, f32, f33, f34, f35	[82] [108] [97]
14	Review / Update Release Plan	f36, f37	[85] [81]
15	User/ Client Involvement	f38, f39, f40, f41	[80] [85]
16	Building Trust in Team	f38, f43, f44, f45, f46	[86] [104] [87] [81]
17	Manager's Role	f51, f52, f53,	[86] [102]
18	Contractual terms and conditions	f54, f55	[80] [108] [102]
19	Use of technology	f56, f57	[88] [92] [109] [102]
20	Client Acceptance and change control	f44, f58, f59, f60	[86] [92]
21	Collaborative Development Environment	f61	[89] [102] [92] [110] [99] [85] [92] [108] [86]
22	Daily Meetings	f61, f62	[89] [92] [16]

A five-point Likert scale is used for the questionnaire to prioritize these factors by obtaining data from different software industry experts. Results of the survey weighted mean approach [139,140] is used. The weighted mean is calculated for each response of each element using the following formula:

$$\overline{x} = \frac{\sum_{i=1}^{n}(X_i \times W_i)}{\sum_{i=1}^{n} X_i} \tag{4.6}$$

Where W_i is the weight given to different options for each question, and X_i is the total number of respondents.

4.4.2.2 Data Collected from Respondents and Descriptive Statistics

We performed descriptive analysis through a survey from a software company in Islamabad, Pakistan. We developed a questionnaire of 22 elements and 62 factors, where project managers and senior developers rank each factor against each element, which shows how important the element is and what factor has an effect on what element and how much of an effect. From this survey we generated a graph where we could see the effect of all 62 factors. We also generated a table where each factor has specific value of mean, standard deviation (SD) and mean+, which shows the effect of that factor on the corresponding element. The element e3, i.e., Release Definition and Selection, has the highest value of 3.381, which shows that this element is the most important element among all 22 elements. We can select the most important top 8 elements from the table based on Mean+. We have already mentioned the top element, which is Release Definition and Selection. This element has two factors, which are f8 and f9. The second most important element is Product Future Statement, which has only one factor, i.e., f1. On the third number we have Market Strategy vs Project Strategy, which has three factors, f3, f4 and f5. Here f4 has the value 3.45, which indicates that this factor has more influence on the corresponding element as compared to other factors.

Table 4.6: Descriptive statistics.

Elements	Mean & SD	Factors						Mean+
Product Future Statement		F1						
	Mean	2.35						2.35
	SD	0.759						
Market Strategy VS Project Strategy		F3	F4	F5				
	Mean	2.2	2.45	2.375				2.341
	SD	0.6	0.835	0.913				
Release Definition and Selection		F8	F9					
	Mean	2.44	2.33					2.381
	SD	0.804	0.695					
Release Plan		F8	F9					
	Mean	2.2	2.4					2.3
	SD	0.714	0.830					
Iteration Mission		F6	F7	f8				
	Mean	2.2	1.7	1.5				1.84
	SD	0.274	0.116	0.927				
Resource Estimation		F10						
	Mean	1.725						1.725
	SD	1.024						
Iteration Schedule		F11	F10	F12				
	Mean	2.55	2.575	1.775				2.3
	SD	0.893	0.833	0.651				
Task Identification		F13	F27					
	Mean	2.2	2.1					2.15
	SD	0.953	0.663					
Managing Dependencies		F14	F16					
	Mean	1.975	1.875					1.925
	SD	0.821	0.979					
Key Deliverable		F15	F7					
	Mean	2.3	2.25					2.275
	SD	0.842	0.733					
Identifying Constraints		F16	F17	F18	F19	F20	F21	
	Mean	2.525	2.2	2.4	2.2	2.1	2	2.291
	SD	0.999	0.9	0.860	0.9	0.830	1	
Managing Risk/Uncertainties		F22	F23	F24	F25			
	Mean	2.175	2.15	1.975	2.175			2.110
	SD	1.021	0.909	0.790	1.021			
Adjust Priorities		F29	F31	F32	F34			
	Mean	1.925	2.1	2.1	2			2.03
	SD	0.720	0.848	0.907	0.630			
Review/Update Release Plan		F36	F37	F17				
	Mean	2.175	2.125	2.175				2.158
	SD	0.770	0.899	0.862				
User/ Client involvement		F38	F39	F40	F41			
	Mean	2.125	1.775	2	2.175			2.018
	SD	0.780	0.987	0.894	0.997			
Building Trust in Team		F42	F49	F50	F43	F44		
	Mean	2.1	2	2.4	2.5	1.8		2.117
	SD	0.953	1.004	0.999	0.921	0.864		
Manager's Role		F51	F25	F52	F53	F62		
	Mean	2.025	1.825	2.15	1.925	2.2		2.025
	SD	0.757	0.770	0.852	0.848	0.812		
Contractual terms and Conditions		F54	F55	F56				
	Mean	2	2.15	2.15				2.1
	SD	0.836	0.936	0.988				
Use of Technology		F56	F57	F47				
	Mean	2.025	1.975	1.85				1.943
	SD	0.724	0.611	0.792				
Client Acceptance & Change Control		F58	F59	F60	F50	F43	F44	
	Mean	1.975	1.925	2	1.825	2.325	1.925	2.061
	SD	0.757	0.787	0.921	0.891	0.848	0.720	
Collaborative Development Environment		F61	F45	F48	F29			
	Mean	2.15	2.05	2.05	2.05			2.075
	SD	0.852	0.947	0.920	0.947			
Daily Meetings		F61						
	Mean	2.190						2.190
	SD	1.22						

Then we have the Release Plan and Iteration Schedule, which have the same value of 2.3. However, Release Plan has two factors and Iteration Schedule has three factors. So, here we can say that both Release Plan and Iteration Schedule have the same importance. The sixth most important element is Identifying Constraints, which has six factors affecting it with different values. Among these factors, f16 is the most influencing on this element. The seventh element is the Key Deliverable, which has two factors effecting it, i.e., f15 and f7. The last element is Review/Update Release Plan, which has three factors, i.e., f36, f37, f17. Here f36 and f37 equally affect the Review/Update Release Plan element. The Mean, standard deviation and Mean+ of all 22 elements are shown in Table 4.6. Figure 4.2 shows the evaluation results of different respondents. In this figure we can see the percentage of respondents and 62 factors. Each factor in different percentage of color indicates the respondent is strongly agrees, agrees, is neutral, disagrees or strongly disagrees.

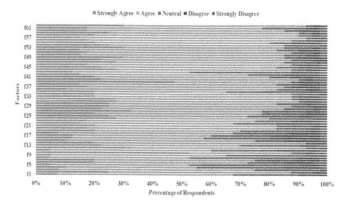

Figure 4.2: Evaluation results.

4.5   Quantification of A-SPSRI Elements and Running Simulation

4.5.1   Quantification of A-SPSRI Elements

There is a need to represent A-SPSRI elements in a mathematical form after the mapping of extracted factors with A-SPSRI components. This mathematical form has been used as input for the quantification of scope. To closely understand change information in each scope element, influencing factors of A-SPSRI elements (1-22) are defined.

General form of quantification of each factor with A-SPSRI elements could be represented as:

$$ASPSRIElement = \sum_{i=0}^{n}(f1 + f2 + f3 + .. + fn) \tag{4.7}$$

Equation (4.7) defines the effect of each factor on its corresponding A-SPSRI element using weight assigned to each factor. Where "f1" describes factor1, i.e., (Priority Features) up to "fn", i.e, (f62).

4.5.2   Running Simulations and Their Integration with Agile EVM

The research used graphical environment to monitor and control effects of changes in scope on the project plan. This graphical representation was proposed by Acebes *et al.* [62], in which different margins of confidence (that match the percentiles of statistical distribution function of the project) are shown and include representation of the project to be monitored. This framework helps us understand and analyze what degree of deviation presents in the project at each checkpoint. The main objective behind this research is to know deviations in the software scope of the project during its execution. Assuming a particular distribution function for initial scope (using dl and cost we can compute statistical distribution functions of scope (updated (dl')) and cost. When universe of the projects is generated through simulations, we can get the area of possible dl and cost to compute the statistical distribution functions. Once the distribution is computed, we can compute separate distributions, one for score (using dl') and the other for cost of the project. Using this information, we can draw percentiles for cost ($Pc10$, $Pc30$, $Pc70$, and $Pc90$) and score ($Ps10$, $Ps30$, $Ps70$, and $Ps90$). In general, we define a triad ($x\%; Sx_j; Cx_j$), where x is the percentage completion of the project, $Cx_j = xC_j$ is the amount of money that has been spent when project is completed at $x\%$, Sx_j is the score of the project when cost Cx_j has been achieved, and C_j is the total cost of the project at jth simulation.

For example, when $x = 0.5$ it represents 50% completion of the project with triad represented as ($x50\%$, $S50$, $C50$). Similarly, if the triad is split into two-dimensional graphs, a Cartesian axis of (score, cost) could be obtained with different distribution of the project up to corresponding 'J' simulation till project is 100% completed at $x = 1$. Using this statistical distribution, we could have obtained mean value and corresponding percentiles ($P10$, $P30$, $P70$, and $P90$) for both the score and cost of the project. Continuing with percentiles, we have joined the points projected on vertical axes of cost and horizontal axes of score. By joining these points a rectangle is formed, where one can determine completion of the project according to the probabilities of cost and score of the resulting project shown in Figure 4.1. If, for example, controlled lines percentiles of both cost and score variables are respectively 90% and 10%. We obtain the rectangle formed by the points Pc10, Pc90, Ps10 and Ps90. We can perform the same, i.e., for percentiles Ps30 and Ps70, etc., for percentage completion of the project progress "x", and different percentiles of the project could be created. The same procedure is repeated to get different values of x knowing that $x = \frac{EV}{BAC}$, value of x at any definition level of score could be calculated using the total cost of the work that has been completed till now and then divide it by the budget at completion (BAC). For each x, y number of j simulations are performed by means of Monte Carlo simulations and defined triads. Thus, for each x, by varying influencing factors (dl) we can obtain a desired percentile of the project scope.

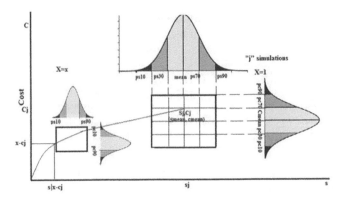

Figure 4.3: Projections of percentiles for score and cost (F. Acebes [62]).

4.5.3 Case Study 1

The current approach will be used at release planning phase where a number of agreed upon features are decided upon to implement in their respective iterations. Our method works at the release planning phase. A-SPSRI is used at iteration level to generate scores for the scope, which are used in scope definition of iteration and to select the fully defined iteration to implement first. Application of A-SPSRI is shown in Figure 4.5. In this study, the researchers have determined the influence of changes in scope on initial cost estimation of the project. A-SPSRI elements have been selected for the purpose of identifying changes in scope. These elements measure the completeness of the project scope [30]. The case study performed by F. Acebes [35] is adopted for this study. In this case study, two planned values (PVs) were drawn: one PV is collected using PERT scheduling technique (termed PVP ERT) and the other PV is collected using mean of all the simulations for project progress x (termed PVMEAN). We have demonstrated the case study using two commonly used scheduling techniques in the literature, PVP ERT and PVMEAN; however, any other scheduling techniques could be used as a benchmark. Following is the flow of steps for performing simulations, as shown in Figure 4.1.

4.5.3.1 Selection of A-SPSRI Elements

When gauging the completeness of the project scope, not all the 22 elements are vital for contributing to the project's success. In a study by S. Amjad *et al.* [57], they assigned rank and weight to A-SPSRI elements, while considering the element critical for the software projects. They considered frequency (f_i): occurrence of element in the research articles, and rank (r_i): importance of element from 1 (most important) to 22 (least important), to prioritize the elements. The A-SPSRI elements' weights were assigned using rank order centroid (ROC) method. ROC accredits individual weight to each element on a normalized scale, which shows the contribution of each element in the possible score of the project. Taking these calculations from the aforementioned article into account, the top eight critical elements for the software project in descending order turn out to be

1) Market Strategy vs Project Strategy

2) Release Definition and Selection

3) Release Plan

4) Task Identification

5) Key Deliverable

6) Adjust Priorities

7) Building Trust in Team

8) Daily Meetings Weight: Weight of the definition level (*dl*) and score (*scr*) of each element is calculated according to the following equations used by [57].

$$We_i = \frac{1}{N} \sum_{i=1}^{2} 2\frac{i}{j} \times MAX \tag{4.8}$$

$$W_{dli} = \frac{1}{Z} \sum_{x=i}^{Z} \left(\frac{1}{X}\right) \tag{4.9}$$

$$Wscr_{ei} = (Wei \times W_{dli}) \qquad (4.10)$$

Equation (4.8) defines weight of elements, where Wei is the weight of "ith" element and $(\frac{1}{N})$ is the total number of elements, i.e., 22, and $(\frac{i}{j})$ is the "jth" element. The definition level of these top contributing A-SPSRI elements shown in Table 4.10 were selected for scheduling.

A scale for definition level of each element is defined for determining their level, where the range of the scale was 0-4. Equation (4.9) calculates the weight of dl, for scale 0, 1, 2, 3, 4, while Equation (4.10) calculates the score of each element. Where Wei is the weight of "ith" element and W_{dli} is the wight of definition level of "ith" definition level.

4.5.3.2 *Total Scope Score Calculation*

In a study by S. Amjad *et al.* [57], the final step is the calculation of total scope score T_{scr} of the project. But before this, they have defined planning levels of the project. These planning levels are given below:

- PL1: Product Vision Planning

- PL2: Product Roadmap

- PL3: Product Release Planning

- PL4: Iteration Planning

- PL5: Daily Commitment Planning

For planning these projects, they have calculated scope score depending upon their corresponding elements. The scope score for each planning is calculated according to the following equations.

- Score Calculation for Product Vision Planning

$$S_{crPLI} = \sum_{i=1}^{2} Scr_{e1} + Scr_{e2} \qquad (4.11)$$

- Product Roadmap

$$Scr_{PL2} = Scr_{e3} \qquad (4.12)$$

- Product Release Planning

$$Scr_{PL3} = Scr_{e4} \qquad (4.13)$$

- Iteration planning

$$S_{crPL4} = \sum_{i=5}^{2} 1Scr_{e5} + Scr_{e6} + ... + Scr_{e21} \qquad (4.14)$$

- Daily Commitment Planning

$$Scr_{PL5} = Scr_{e22} \qquad (4.15)$$

$$T_{scr} = \sum_{i=1}^{m} S_{crPLi} \qquad (4.16)$$

Equation (4.16) calculates the total scope score of the project with respect to each planning level.

4.5.3.3 *Symbols and Notations*

The basic symbols and notations used in our research are described in Table 4.7.

Table 4.7: Description of notations.

Notation	Meaning
$X\%$	Percentage of the project progress
jth	Number of simulations
dl	Definition level
C_j	Cost at jth simulation
S_j	Score at jth simulation
Cx_i	Cost at $x\%$ completion of the project
Sx_i	Score at $x\%$ completion of the project
Pc	Percentile for project cost
Ps	Percentile for project score
Scr_{ei}	Score of the ith element
Wdli	Weight of the ith definition level
MAX	1000 (Maximum score of A-SPSRI)
Wei	Weight of the ith element

Algorithm 4.1. Algorithm for Simulation.

```
BEGIN
    Result: Cost and Score
    Initialization.
    Ai = Schedule activities;
    Ci = Assign cost to each activity;
    for k=1 to total number of releases do
        for j=1 to n (number of Iterations) do
            Aij = Duration of each activity.
            while (y > 0) do
                Calculate xCx ;
                Calculate S1Cx;
                y = y-dl%;
            endwhile
            PV = Cost at each Iteration
        endfor
        PV sum = sum of all PV at each iteration
    endfor
    Total Cost = Sum of PV sum
    Return total Cost for k releases
END
```

We have selected the project model presented in Figure 4.4 in light of past research to compare different monitoring and control methodologies. This (AON) network has been used in previous research to identify the effect of information presentation on project control. Furthermore, a study found in [59] applied this distribution for monitoring and controlling uncertainty. The researchers generated all possible variations of the planned project schedule. Figure 4.4 shows the AON network diagram.

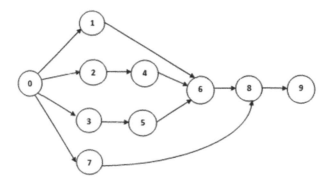

Figure 4.4: AON network diagram.

In the AON network, durations are displayed as exponential rather than typical appropriation (normal distribution and beta distribution). In the literature, exponential distribution is used to identify uncertainty in the project [59]. Similarly, in our case this type of distribution helped us to understand deviations/changes in scope for project progress x in which dl varies with respect to its baseline. Using this framework, we can forecast and compare overruns in the project with respect to an optimistic method like PERT analysis.

Table 4.8: A-SPSRI elements.

S.No	Elements	Weight	dl	Scr_{ei}
1	e1	2.06	1.00	2.06
2	e2	8.89	0.51	4.53
3	e3	26.70	0.51	13.61
4	e4	56.40	0.51	28.76
5	e5	30.49	0.51	15.54
6	e6	63.97	1.00	63.97
7	e7	49.90	1.00	49.90
8	e8	122.30	0.28	34.24
9	e9	23.21	1.00	23.21
10	e10	99.58	0.11	10.95
11	e11	11.42	1.00	11.42
12	e12	34.62	1.00	34.62
13	e13	84.43	1.00	84.43
14	e14	19.96	1.00	19.96
15	e15	73.06	0.28	20.42
16	e16	167.76	1.00	167.76
17	e17	16.93	0.28	4.74
18	e18	4.23	1.00	4.23
19	e19	14.09	0.11	1.54
20	e20	44.22	0.28	12.38
21	e21	6.50	0.28	1.82
22	e22	39.17	1.00	39.17

The planned work package is included in Table 4.10, with each portion having its expected length and cost. In the conceptual case of the executed project scope, this detail is used as a baseline.

Table 4.9: Top contributing A-SPSRI elements.

No	Scope Element	Weight
1	e2	8.89
2	e3	26.70
3	e4	56.40
4	e8	122.30
5	e10	99.58
6	e13	84.43
7	e16	167.76
8	e22	9.17

Table 4.10: Top 8 contributing A-SPSRI elements.

No	ASPSRI Element	Duration	Total Cost
1	e2	5	2240
2	e3	1	1900
3	e4	3	1110
4	e8	4	430
5	e10	2	1800
6	e13	3	900
7	e16	8	700
8	e22	3	960

1. **Assign score and cost to the elements**: First, each selected A-SPSRI element is assigned a score and cost to get the baseline plan. The score is assigned to each of the A-SPSRI elements depending on the quality of their explanation. In previous work [54], quality is referred to as definition level (dl) and a five-point scale from (0-5) is defined for determining dl. The scale used to determine definition level are described as follows:

   - 0- Not Applicable,
   - 1- Poor Definition,
   - 2- Major Deficiencies,
   - 3- Minor Deficiencies,
   - 4- Complete Definition.

2. **Features in single release**: The Agile burn-up chart is very similar to the EV and PV plots of the classical EVM. A 3-line graph of cumulative EV, AC, and PV is shown in

Figure 4.5; for a SCRUM project, the top line represents planned feature completion, which is like PV, over the five iterations of the project, and the lower line shows actual feature completions like EV, through Iteration number 4. As seen in Figure 4.5, at the completion of Iteration number 4, the project is approximately 59% complete at release level (41 features/ 70 feature) and it currently has a negative schedule variance (SV) of approximately 32% (41 features completed; 60 features planned). Keeping in mind that in the given example each iteration is of a duration of 10 days, the 32% negative SV represents about 16 days behind planned schedule, which is 32% of 50 days total.

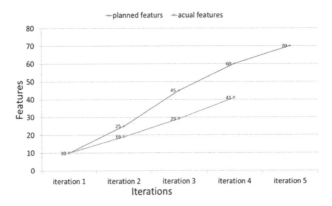

Figure 4.5: Sample burn-up chart showing schedule variance.

4.5.3.4   *Projection into Score and Cost*

To find the variations in cost and score at a different percentage of the project, the information of Triad $(x\%, Sx_j, Cx_j)$ was used. The Triad was split into a two-dimensional graph or in the form of Cartesian product of the percentage, cost $(x\%, Cx_j)$ and percentage, score $(x\%, Sx_j)$ by varying the value of 'x' as shown in Figure 4.6.

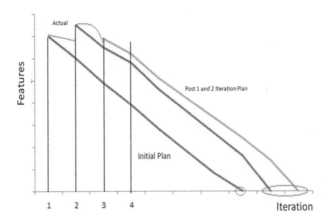

Figure 4.6: Burn-down chart reflecting scope change and schedule variance.

For any instance of x, the planned value was gauged using $x = \frac{PVs}{BAC}$, which is the budget at completion. Variations in cost were computed using the aforementioned influencing factors to get dl' for any percentage completion of the project.

4.5.3.5 *Projection of Project into Different Percentiles*

Using the percentage completion, the project is divided into different percentiles ($p10$, $p30, p70, p90$). By comparing PVMEAN (computed through Monte Carlo simulations) and PVP ERT (computed through PERT analysis), deviation or changes in scope were computed. This information was divided into different percentiles as shown in Figure 4.7.

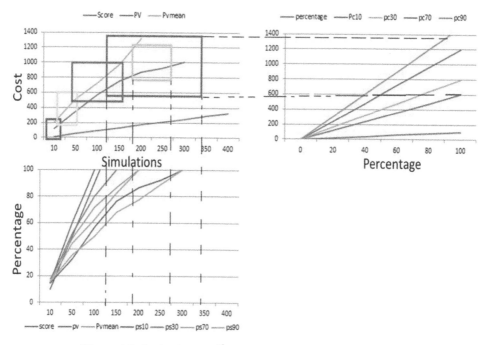

Figure 4.7: Projection of ith iteration into different percentiles.

This includes percentiles of cost ($Pc10$, $Pc30$, $Pc70$, $Pc90$) and percentiles of the score ($Ps10$, $Ps30$, $Ps70$, $Ps90$) based on the percentage completion of the project. Each square is represented by different percentage completion of the project. The smallest square shows 25% completion of the project, whereas the largest square shows the 100% completion of the project. Each square is divided into percentiles of 10 and 90 using mean and standard deviation of project progress "x". At $s = 135$, overrun on the project can be clearly seen with respect to the percentile $p70$; however, the project remains within its boundaries as compared to the percentile $p90$. Therefore, the mean and standard deviation, etc., were determined under the normal distribution curve. Cost values near the mean have a high confidence interval, while values further from the mean have a low confidence interval, i.e., the high value of the confidence interval of the standard deviation gets smaller. For any project progress "x" the standard distribution and confidence intervals of costs and the score can be calculated using this framework.

Table 4.11: Assign definition level.

No.	A-SPSRI elements	Definition level						P_score
		0(0.0)	1(1.0)	2(0.51)	3(0.28)	4(0.11)	Weight	
1	E2				C		8.89	4.53
2	E3			C			26.7	13.61
3	E4					C	56.4	28.76
4	E8				C		122.3	34.24
5	E10		C				99.5	10.95
6	E13			C			84.43	84.43
7	E16				C		167.76	167.76
8	E22		C				39.17	39.13

According to [91], the addition of burned budget or actual cost, to the Agile burn-up chart, along with the addition of monetary values to the ordinate of the graph, represents the burn-up chart in a new way, which is the same as the traditional EVM 3-line graph of PV, EV, and AC.

Cabri and Griffiths demonstrated how the addition of burned budget (AC) to the Agile burn-up chart, along with the addition of monetary values to the ordinate of the graph, creates a new look for the burn-up chart, which is very similar to the traditional EVM 3-line graph of PV, EV, and AC. After completing the monitoring and control process we have represented the planed cost vs actual cost, and planed features vs features completed; the schedule is also projected here.

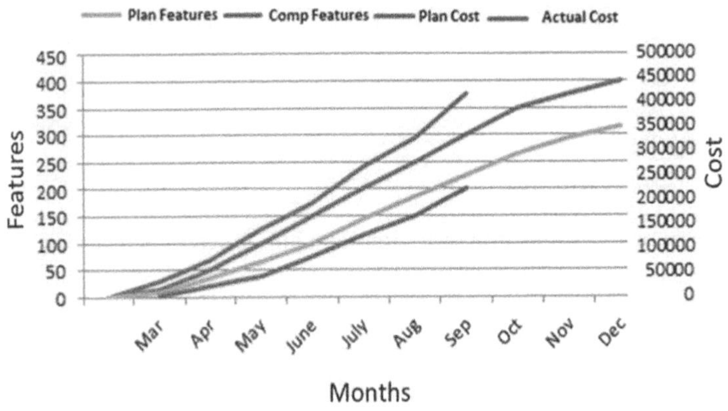

Figure 4.8: Burn-up chart incorporating cost.

4.5.4 Case Study 2

The data used in Case Study 1 was based on real-life assumptions; however, Case Study 2 is based on real-time project data obtained from a software company located in Islamabad, Pakistan. Due to the confidentiality, the name and the information of the company is undisclosed. The project is a web application related to the Myers-Briggs type indicator (MBTI) used to identify a person's personality type, strengths, and preferences in 360 environments. It has five releases. Each release consists of five iterations, whereas each iteration is composed of three features. The plan cost, actual cost and schedule is also mentioned with each feature.

We have made a graphical representation of features on release bases. Moreover, we have computed weight, definition level and score of features, iterations and releases as shown in Table 4.12. In this table the weight, definition level and score of each element is calculated by using Equation (4.8), (4.9), and (4.10), respectively.

Table 4.12: Weight, dl and score of elements in Case Study 2.

Project Elements	Definition level(dl)						Scr
	0(0.0)	1(1.0)	2(0.51)	3(0.28)	4(0.11)	Weight	
ZB1			C			221.21	112.81
ZB2					C	154.54	16.991
ZB3				C		121.21	33.93
ZB4					C	98.99	10.88
ZB5				C		82.32	23.04
ZB6		C				68.99	68.99
ZB7		C				57.88	57.88
ZB8			C			48.35	24.65
ZB9					C	40.02	4.4
ZB10			C			32.61	16.63
ZB11			C			25.95	13.23
ZB12					C	19.89	2.18
ZB13				C		14.33	4.01
ZB14					C	9.2	1.01
ZB15			C			4.44	2.26

The universe of simulations was performed at release level. Algorithm 4.1 shows how the simulations were performed at release level and further releases were computed for the entire project. The project can be monitored and controlled at each release level. The number of planned features for one release was 15, which means each iteration will implement 3 features. However, Figure 4.9 shows two lines, i.e., planned features to complete per iteration and actual features completed per iteration. At the completion of iteration 4, the release is approximately 60% completed (9 features/15 features). Whereas, it currently has negative schedule variance of approximately 25%.

The score and cost variation at different percentile levels were computed with the help of the triad $(x\%, Sxj, cxj)$ technique. It works as it is splattered into a 2D graph like a Cartesian product of the percentage, i.e., $(x\%, cxj)$ and $(x\%, sxj)$ by varying the values of x as shown in Figure 4.9.

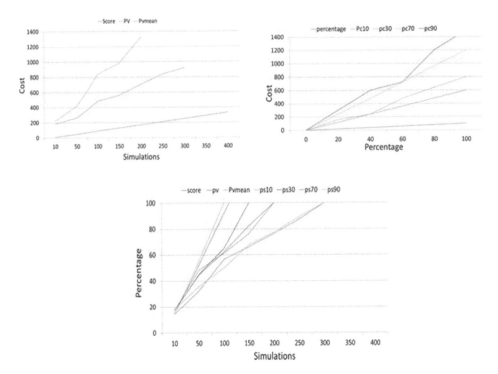

Figure 4.9: Projection into score and cost.

4.6 Experimental Evaluation of Simulated Results

These simulated results were proved statistically using the multiple linear regression test. This test not only finds the correlation between the dependent variable (overall cost) and independent variable A-SPSRI elements, but also identifies the contribution of each element on overall cost of the project. All the components selected indicated their contribution to the total project cost growth. The following four models have been developed (see Table 4.13). The normality of the data is clear before the implication of the regression linear model.

Table 4.13: Assign cost to A-SPSRI elements.

Model	R	R square
1	.350a	0.352
2	.424b	0.508
3	.675c	0.53
4	.760d	0.692

4.6.1 Regression Model Interpretation

The overall cost of Model 1, Model 2 and Model 3 explain the overall cost 35%, 51% and 53%. Therefore, Model 4 was only considered as it explains the overall cost 69%.

Model 4:

$$Y = a + b1X1 + b2X2 + b3X3 + b4X4 \tag{4.17}$$

$$Y = 3991.550 + 0.660(e1) + 0.538(e2) + 0.373(e3) + 0.625(e4) \tag{4.18}$$

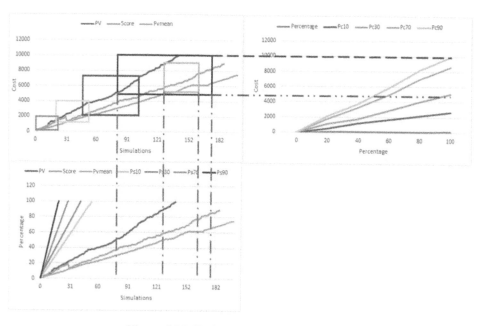

Figure 4.10: Projection into score and cost.

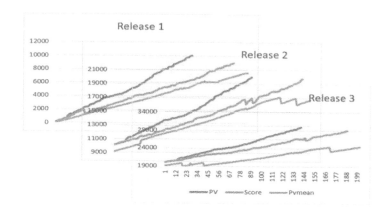

Figure 4.11: Multiple releases.

4.6.2 Interpretation

For one (unit) increase in e1, there is a 0.660 units increase in the total cost (units). At one unit increase in e2 there is a 0.538 units increase in total cost. Moreover, for one unit increase in e3 indicator there is a 0.373 units increase in total cost. Also,for one unit increase in e4 there is a 0.625 units increase in total cost. The R-Square of Model 4 (0.760) shows

the four independent indicators. Duration of elements is modeled as exponential distribution. Variables (e1-e4) explain 69 percent of total cost, while the rest of the variation is explained by other factors.

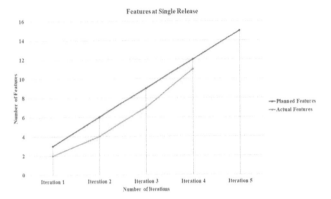

Figure 4.12: Features at single release.

The multiple linear regression test identifies the correlation between the elements. The test results are defined as follows; the 1st component (e1) is closely correlated. The 2nd aspect (e2) is interconnected. The 3rd variable (e3) does not correlate. The 4th factor (e4) has a low correlation. This measure also helps to statistically prove our values using the significance of sigma. Our results have statistically shown that all chosen components of the agile scope have an impact on the total project expense. Cronbach's alpha was calculated to figure out the internal accuracy of the questionnaire (how problems are closely connected collectively). For the suggested questionnaire, the alpha co-efficient was roughly .69, which is considered appropriate. Thus, the problems have relative internal continuity.

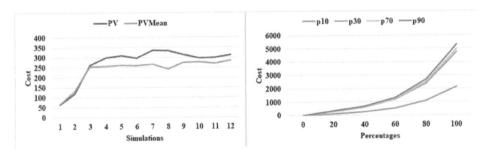

Figure 4.13: Projection into score and cost.

4.7 Conclusion

The AgileEVM approach uses knowledge from the budget and plan to track and manage the software project's performance. It is possible to calculate the performance of any software project more accurately by juggling triple project management constraints. Time and cost targets are generally straightforward, but the scope of the project is difficult to define, agree on and accomplish. Whenever adjustments are made, the cost and schedule changes associated with the project scope are included. There are several cases of failure in software projects in the literature, with a few classic examples being the following: What went wrong? What was happening with the features? etc. For this purpose, over the life of the project, there is a need to track project scope and establish a mechanism for controlling changes in scope, AgileEVM does not, however, provide project scope when assessing the project's success.

In this chapter, the factors that influence the scope changes were recorded and incorporated into AgileEVM to identify variations in scope. To find out about factors of changes an extensive literature review was conducted. As a result of this review, 62 unique factors were defined and mapped with A-SPSRI elements. This mapping process was literature-based and was evaluated by the software industry. The data of 40 respondents were collected via a questionnaire in the software industries located in Pakistan. The respondents of this research were the PMs (project managers) and senior developers. The idea behind conducting this survey was to evaluate the most influential factors against each scope element according to the industry. Furthermore, descriptive statistics were applied to find the most influential element and factor of each element. Additionally, the quantification of elements was completed. Finally, two case studies were carried out for simulation purposes using Monte Carlo simulation. The first case study was taken from the literature, whereas the second case study was the real-time data of an agile project. This study shows how to monitor and control agile project scope variations.

References

1. Anbari, F. T. (2003). Earned value project management method and extensions. *Project Management Journal*, 34(4), 12-23.

2. Warburton, R. D. (2011). A time-dependent earned value model for software projects. *International Journal of Project Management*, 29(8), 1082-1090.

3. Chen, S., & Zhang, X. (2012). An analytic review of earned value management studies in the construction industry. In *Construction Research Congress 2012: Construction Challenges in a Flat World* (pp. 236-246).

4. P. M. Institute, "Project management body of knowledge (pmbok)." Project Management Institute, 1987.

5. Nolan, A. J., Abrahão, S., Clements, P. C., & Pickard, A. (2011, August). Requirements uncertainty in a software product line. In *2011 15th International Software Product Line Conference* (pp. 223-231). IEEE.

6. Verner, J., Sampson, J., & Cerpa, N. (2008, June). What factors lead to software project failure?. In *2008 Second International Conference on Research Challenges in Information Science* (pp. 71-80). IEEE.

7. Ebert, C., & De Man, J. (2005, May). Requirements uncertainty: influencing factors and concrete improvements. In *Proceedings of the 27th international conference on Software engineering* (pp. 553-560).

8. Zowghi, D., & Nurmuliani, N. (2002, December). A study of the impact of requirements volatility on software project performance. In *Ninth Asia-Pacific Software Engineering Conference*, 2002. (pp. 3-11). IEEE.

9. Madhuri, K. L., & Suma, V. (2014, October). Influence of domain and technology upon scope creep in software projects. In *2014 International Conference on Advances in Electronics Computers and Communications* (pp. 1-6). IEEE.

10. Berry, D. M., Czarnecki, K., Antkiewicz, M., & AbdElRazik, M. (2010, September). Requirements determination is unstoppable: an experience report. In *2010 18th IEEE International Requirements Engineering Conference* (pp. 311-316). IEEE.

11. Bjarnason, E., Wnuk, K., & Regnell, B. (2010, September). Overscoping: Reasons and consequences—A case study on decision making in software product management. In *2010 Fourth International Workshop on Software Product Management* (pp. 30-39). IEEE.

12. Bjarnason, E., Wnuk, K., & Regnell, B. (2011, August). Requirements are slipping through the gaps—A case study on causes & effects of communication gaps in large-scale software development. In *2011 IEEE 19th international requirements engineering conference* (pp. 37-46). IEEE.

13. Williams, B. J., Carver, J., & Vaughn, R. B. (2006). Change Risk Assessment: Understanding Risks Involved in Changing Software Requirements. In *Software Engineering Research and Practice* (pp. 966-971).

14. Bano, M., Imtiaz, S., Ikram, N., Niazi, M., & Usman, M. (2012). Causes of requirement change-a systematic literature review.

15. Shah, A. H. (2014). Examining the perceived value of integration of earned value management with risk management-based performance measurement baseline (Doctoral dissertation, Capella University).

16. Kumari, N., & Pillai, A. S. (2014, March). A study on project scope as a requirements elicitation issue. In *2014 International Conference on Computing for Sustainable Global Development (INDIACom)* (pp. 510-514). IEEE.

17. Mirza, M. N., Pourzolfaghar, Z., & Shahnazari, M. (2013). Significance of scope in project success. *Procedia Technology*, 9, 722-729.

18. Dybå, T., & Dingsøyr, T. (2008). Empirical studies of agile software development: A systematic review. *Information and Software Technology*, 50(9-10), 833-859.

19. Layton, M. C., Ostermiller, S. J., & Kynaston, D. J. (2020). *Agile Project Management for Dummies*. John Wiley & Sons.

20. Cline, A. (2015). *Agile development in the real world*. Springer.

21. Rico, D. F., Sayani, H. H., & Sone, S. (2009). *The business value of agile software methods: maximizing ROI with just-in-time processes and documentation*. J. Ross Publishing.

22. Cho, J. (2008). Issues and Challenges of agile software development with SCRUM. *Issues in Information Systems*, 9(2), 188-195.

23. Khan, A. A., & Shameem, M. (2020). Multicriteria decision-making taxonomy for DevOps challenging factors using analytical hierarchy process. *Journal of Software: Evolution and Process*, 32(10), e2263. Doi: 10.1002/smr.2263

24. Hans, R. T. (2013). Work breakdown structure: A tool for software project scope verification. *arXiv preprint* arXiv:1308.2876.

25. Legodi, I., & Barry, M. L. (2010, July). The current challenges and status of risk management in enterprise data warehouse projects in South Africa. In *PICMET 2010 Technology Management for Global Economic Growth* (pp. 1-5). IEEE.

26. Ong, H. Y., Wang, C., & Zainon, N. (2016). Integrated earned value Gantt chart (EV-Gantt) tool for project portfolio planning and monitoring optimization. *Engineering Management Journal*, 28(1), 39-53.

27. Hazır, Ö. (2015). A review of analytical models, approaches and decision support tools in project monitoring and control. *International Journal of Project Management*, 33(4), 808-815.

28. Roy, P. K., & Goutam, P. (2014). Agile With EVM. *International Journal of Core Engineering & Management*, 1(8).

29. Abdulmalek, F. A., & Rajgopal, J. (2007). Analyzing the benefits of lean manufacturing and value stream mapping via simulation: A process sector case study. *International Journal of Production Economics*, 107(1), 223-236.

30. Mahnic, V. (2011). A case study on agile estimating and planning using scrum. *Elektronika ir Elektrotechnika*, 111(5), 123-128.

31. Chang, C. W., & Tong, L. I. (2013). Monitoring the software development process using a short-run control chart. *Software Quality Journal*, 21(3), 479-499.

32. Kazi, L., Radulovic, B., & Kazi, Z. (2012, September). Performance indicators in software project monitoring: Balanced scorecard approach. In *2012 IEEE 10th Jubilee International Symposium on Intelligent Systems and Informatics* (pp. 19-25). IEEE.

33. Petersen, K., & Wohlin, C. (2011). Measuring the flow in lean software development. *Software: Practice and experience*, 41(9), 975-996.

34. Xu, Z., Wang, S., & Mao, J. Y. (2011). Project performance analysis based on weight earned value method by simulation. *Computer Integrated Manufacturing Systems*, 17(7), 1553-1561.

35. Li, J., Ma, Z., & Dong, H. (2008, May). Monitoring software projects with earned value analysis and use case point. In *Seventh IEEE/ACIS International Conference on Computer and Information Science (ICIS 2008)* (pp. 475-480). IEEE.

36. ul Hassan, I., Ahmad, N., & Zuhaira, B. (2018). Calculating completeness of software project scope definition. *Information and Software Technology*, 94, 208-233.

37. Zheng, Y., Wang, B., Zheng, Y., & Shi, L. (2009, July). Estimation of software projects effort based on function point. In *2009 4th International Conference on Computer Science & Education* (pp. 941-943). IEEE.

38. Wohlin, C., & Andrews, A. A. (2001). Assessing project success using subjective evaluation factors. *Software Quality Journal*, 9(1), 43-70.

39. Corral, L., Sillitti, A., Succi, G., Garibbo, A., & Ramella, P. (2012, March). Evolution of mobile software development from platform-specific to web-based multiplatform paradigm. In *Proceedings of the 10th SIGPLAN symposium on New ideas, new paradigms, and reflections on programming and software* (pp. 181-183).

40. Wnuk, K., Regnell, B., & Karlsson, L. (2009, September). Feature transition charts for visualization of cross-project scope evolution in large-scale requirements engineering for product lines. In *2009 Fourth International Workshop on Requirements Engineering Visualization* (pp. 11-20). IEEE.

41. Marinho, M. L., Sampaio, S. C. B., Lima, T. L. A., & Moura, H. P. (2014). A guide to deal with uncertainties in software project management. *arXiv preprint arXiv:1411.1920*.

42. Bhatti, M. W., Hayat, F., Ehsan, N., Ishaque, A., Ahmed, S., & Mirza, E. (2010, October). A methodology to manage the changing requirements of a software project. In *2010 International Conference on Computer Information Systems and Industrial Management Applications (CISIM)* (pp. 319-322). IEEE.

43. Abrantes, R., & Figueiredo, J. (2014). Feature based process framework to manage scope in dynamic NPD portfolios. *International Journal of Project Management*, 32(5), 874-884.

44. Khelifi, A., Abran, A., & Buglione, L. (2016). 2.4 a system of reference for software measurements with ISO 19761 (COSMIC FFP). *COSMIC Function Points: Theory and Advanced Practices*, 142.

45. Wnuk, K., Regnell, B., & Karlsson, L. (2008, September). Visualization of feature survival in platform-based embedded systems development for improved understanding of scope dynamics. In *2008 Requirements Engineering Visualization* (pp. 41-50). IEEE.

46. Sliger, M., & Broderick, S. (2008). *The software project manager's bridge to agility*. Addison-Wesley Professional.

47. Patton, J., & Economy, P. (2014). *User story mapping: discover the whole story, build the right product.* "O'Reilly Media, Inc.".

48. Gregory, J., & Crispin, L. (2014). *More agile testing: learning journeys for the whole team.* Addison-Wesley Professional.

49. Sulaiman, T., Barton, B., & Blackburn, T. (2006, July). AgileEVM-earned value management in Scrum Projects. In *AGILE 2006 (AGILE'06)* (pp. 10-pp). IEEE.

50. Ghosh, S. (2015). Systemic comparison of the application of EVM in traditional and agile software project. *Integration*, 5(3).

51. Javdani, T., Zulzalil, H., Ghani, A. A. A., Sultan, A. B. M., & Parizi, R. M. (2013). On the current measurement practices in agile software development. *arXiv preprint arXiv:1301.5964*.

52. Gautam, T. (2014). Software measurement metrics in project scope management (Master's thesis).

53. Dimitrijević, S., Jovanović, J., & Devedžić, V. (2015). A comparative study of software tools for user story management. *Information and Software Technology*, 57, 352-368.

54. Wu, S. C. (2012). *Traditional and agile earned value management processes.* Boston University, 1-32.

55. Boschetti, M. A., Golfarelli, M., Rizzi, S., & Turricchia, E. (2014). A Lagrangian heuristic for sprint planning in agile software development. Computers & Operations Research, 43, 116-128.

56. Matharu, G. S., Mishra, A., Singh, H., & Upadhyay, P. (2015). Empirical study of agile software development methodologies: A comparative analysis. *ACM SIGSOFT Software Engineering Notes*, 40(1), 1-6.

57. Amjad, S., Ahmad, N., Saba, T., Anjum, A., Manzoor, U., Balubaid, M. A., & Malik, S. U. R. (2017). Calculating completeness of agile scope in scaled agile development. *IEEE Access*, 6, 5822-5847.

58. Calefato, F., & Lanubile, F. (2011). A planning poker tool for supporting collaborative estimation in distributed agile development. In *Proc. 6th Int. Conf. Softw. Eng. Adv.(ICSEA)* (pp. 14-19).

59. Munialo, S. W., & Muketha, G. M. (2016). *A review of agile software effort estimation methods.*

60. Ren A. , & Yun C. (2013). Research of software size estimation method. In *2013 International Conference on Cloud and Service Computing.* pp. 154-155.

61. Litoriya, R., & Kothari, A. (2013). An efficient approach for agile web based project estimation: AgileMOW. *Journal of Software Engineering and Applications*, 6(6), p.297.

62. Acebes, F., Pajares, J., Galán, J. M., & López-Paredes, A. (2014). A new approach for project control under uncertainty. Going back to the basics. *International Journal of Project Management*, 32(3), 423-434.

63. W. Lipke, "Schedule is different, the measurable news, 10-15," 2003.

64. Buyse, P., Vandenbussche, T., & Vanhoucke, M. (2010). Performance analysis of Earned Value Management in the construction industry. UNIVERSITEIT GENT.

65. Vandevoorde, S., & Vanhoucke, M. (2006). A comparison of different project duration forecasting methods using earned value metrics. *International Journal of Project Management*, 24(4), 289-302.

66. Lipke, W. (2004). Connecting earned value to the schedule. *The Measurable News*, 1(Winter), 6-16.

67. Barraza, G. A., Back, W. E., & Mata, F. (2004). Probabilistic forecasting of project performance using stochastic S curves. *Journal of Construction Engineering and Management*, 130(1), 25-32.

68. Khamooshi, H., & Golafshani, H. (2014). EDM: Earned Duration Management, a new approach to schedule performance management and measurement. *International Journal of Project Management*, 32(6), 1019-1041.

69. Hanna, A. S. (2012). Using the earned value management system to improve electrical project control. *Journal of Construction Engineering and Management*, 138(3), 449-457.

70. Pajares, J., & Lopez-Paredes, A. (2011). An extension of the EVM analysis for project monitoring: The Cost Control Index and the Schedule Control Index. *International Journal of Project Management*, 29(5), 615-621.

71. Keele, S. (2007). Guidelines for performing systematic literature reviews in software engineering (Vol. 5). *Technical report*, Ver. 2.3 EBSE Technical Report. EBSE.

72. Paetsch, F., Eberlein, A., & Maurer, F. (2003, June). Requirements engineering and agile software development. In *WET ICE 2003. Proceedings. Twelfth IEEE International Workshops on Enabling Technologies: Infrastructure for Collaborative Enterprises*, 2003. (pp. 308-313). IEEE.

73. Najafi, M., & Toyoshiba, L. (2008, August). Two case studies of user experience design and agile development. In *Agile 2008 Conference* (pp. 531-536). IEEE.

74. Sutherland, J. (2001). Inventing and Reinventing SCRUM in five Companies. *Cutter IT journal*, 14, 5-11.

75. Milanov, G., & Njegus, A. (2012). Analysis of return on investment in different types of agile software development project teams. *Informatica Economica*, 16(4), 7.

76. Abrahamsson, P., Salo, O., Ronkainen, J., & Warsta, J. (2017). Agile software development methods: Review and analysis. *arXiv preprint arXiv:1709.08439*.

77. Khatri, S. K., Bahri, K., & Johri, P. (2014, October). Best practices for managing risk in adaptive agile process. In *Proceedings of 3rd International Conference on Reliability, Infocom Technologies and Optimization* (pp. 1-5). IEEE.

78. Soundararajan, S., & Arthur, J. D. (2009, April). A soft-structured agile framework for larger scale systems development. In *2009 16th Annual IEEE International Conference and Workshop on the Engineering of Computer Based Systems* (pp. 187-195). IEEE.

79. Sliger, M., & Broderick, S. (2008). *The software project manager's bridge to agility*. Addison-Wesley Professional. .

80. Inayat, I., Salim, S. S., Marczak, S., Daneva, M., & Shamshirband, S. (2015). A systematic literature review on agile requirements engineering practices and challenges. *Computers in Human Behavior*, 51, 915-929.

81. Shrivastava, S. V., & Rathod, U. (2015). Categorization of risk factors for distributed agile projects. *Information and Software Technology*, 58, 373-387.

82. Racheva, Z., Daneva, M., Sikkel, K., Herrmann, A., & Wieringa, R. (2010, September). Do we know enough about requirements prioritization in agile projects: insights from a case study. In *2010 18th IEEE International Requirements Engineering Conference* (pp. 147-156). IEEE.

83. Moe, N. B., Aurum, A., & Dybå, T. (2012). Challenges of shared decision-making: A multiple case study of agile software development. *Information and Software Technology*, 54(8), 853-865.

84. Kontio, J., Hoglund, M., Ryden, J., & Abrahamsson, P. (2004, May). Managing commitments and risks: challenges in distributed agile development. In *Proceedings 26th International Conference on Software Engineering* (pp. 732-733). IEEE.

85. Misra, S. C., Kumar, V., & Kumar, U. (2009). Identifying some important success factors in adopting agile software development practices. *Journal of Systems and Software*, 82(11), 1869-1890.

86. Dikert, K., Paasivaara, M., & Lassenius, C. (2016). Challenges and success factors for large-scale agile transformations: A systematic literature review. *Journal of Systems and Software*, 119, 87-108.

87. Stankovic, D., Nikolic, V., Djordjevic, M., & Cao, D. B. (2013). A survey study of critical success factors in agile software projects in former Yugoslavia IT companies. *Journal of Systems and Software*, 86(6), 1663-1678.

88. Khan, A. A., Shameem, M., Kumar, R. R., Hussain, S., & Yan, X. (2019). Fuzzy AHP based prioritization and taxonomy of software process improvement success factors in global software development. *Applied Soft Computing*, 83, 105648.

89. Conboy, K., Coyle, S., Wang, X., & Pikkarainen, M. (2011). People over process: key people challenges in agile development.

90. Fitzgerald, B., & Stol, K. J. (2014, June). Continuous software engineering and beyond: trends and challenges. In *Proceedings of the 1st International Workshop on Rapid Continuous Software Engineering* (pp. 1-9).

91. Geras, A., Smith, M., & Miller, J. (2004, September). A prototype empirical evaluation of test driven development. In *2004 Proceedings 10th International Symposium on Software Metrics*, (pp. 405-416). IEEE.

92. Yagüe, A., Garbajosa, J., Díaz, J., & González, E. (2016). An exploratory study in communication in Agile Global Software Development. *Computer Standards & Interfaces*, 48, 184-197.

93. Ebert, C., Abrahamsson, P., & Oza, N. (2012). Lean software development. *IEEE Computer Architecture Letters*, 29(05), 22-25.

94. Cockburn, A. (2006). *Agile software development: the cooperative game*. Pearson Education.

95. Lindstrom, L., & Jeffries, R. (2003). Extreme programming and agile software development methodologies. In *Information Systems Management handbook* (pp. 531-550). Auerbach Publications.

96. Rumpe, B., & Schröder, A. (2014). Quantitative survey on extreme programming projects. *arXiv preprint arXiv:1409.6599*.

97. Rautiainen, K., Lassenius, C., & Sulonen, R. (2002). 4CC: A framework for managing software product development. *Engineering Management Journal*, 14(2), 27-32.

98. Szőke, Á. (2009, June). Decision support for iteration scheduling in agile environments. In *International Conference on Product-Focused Software Process Improvement* (pp. 156-170). Springer, Berlin, Heidelberg.

99. Berry, D. M. (2002, October). The inevitable pain of software development: Why there is no silver bullet. In *International Workshop On Radical Innovations Of Software and Systems Engineering in the Future* (pp. 50-74). Springer, Berlin, Heidelberg.

100. Helmy, W., Kamel, A., & Hegazy, O. (2012). Requirements engineering methodology in agile environment. *International Journal of Computer Science Issues (IJCSI)*, 9(5), 293.

101. Grapenthin, S., Poggel, S., Book, M., & Gruhn, V. (2015). Improving task breakdown comprehensiveness in agile projects with an Interaction Room. *Information and Software Technology*, 67, 254-264.

102. Khan, A. A., Keung, J., Hussain, S., Niazi, M., & Kieffer, S. (2018). Systematic literature study for dimensional classification of success factors affecting process improvement in global software development: client-vendor perspective. *IET Software*, 12(4), 333-344.

103. Babar, M. A., Chen, L., & Shull, F. (2010). Managing variability in software product lines. *IEEE Software*, 27(3), 89-91.

104. Rohunen, A., Rodriguez, P., Kuvaja, P., Krzanik, L., & Markkula, J. (2010, June). Approaches to agile adoption in large settings: a comparison of the results from a literature analysis and

an industrial inventory. In *International Conference on Product Focused Software Process Improvement* (pp. 77-91). Springer, Berlin, Heidelberg.

105. Pavlovski, C. J., & Zou, J. (2008, January). Non-Functional Requirements in Business Process Modeling. In *Proceedings of the fifth Asia-Pacific conference on Conceptual Modelling-Volume 79. Australian Computer Society, Inc.* (Vol. 8, pp. 103-112).

106. Ozkaya, I., Akin, Ö., & Tomayko, J. E. (2005). Teaching to think in software terms: An interdisciplinary graduate software requirement engineering course for AEC students. In *Computing in Civil Engineering* (2005) (pp. 1-10).

107. Shrivastava, S. V., & Rathod, U. (2017). A risk management framework for distributed agile projects. *Information and Software Technology*, 85, 1-15.

108. Drury, M., Conboy, K., & Power, K. (2012). Obstacles to decision making in Agile software development teams. *Journal of Systems and Software*, 85(6), 1239-1254.

109. Nerur, S., Mahapatra, R., & Mangalaraj, G. (2005). Challenges of migrating to agile methodologies. *Communications of the ACM*, 48(5), 72-78.

110. Kamaruddin, N. K., Arshad, N. H., & Mohamed, A. (2012, April). Chaos issues on communication in agile global software development. In *2012 IEEE Business, Engineering & Industrial Applications Colloquium (BEIAC)* (pp. 394-398). IEEE.

111. Khan, A. A., Shameem, M., Nadeem, M., & Akbar, M. A. (2021). Agile trends in Chinese global software development industry: Fuzzy AHP based conceptual mapping. *Applied Soft Computing*, 102, 107090.

112. Khan, A. A., Keung, J., Niazi, M., Hussain, S., & Ahmad, A. (2017). Systematic literature review and empirical investigation of barriers to process improvement in global software development: Client–vendor perspective. *Information and Software Technology*, 87, 180-205.

113. Khan, A. A., & Akbar, M. A. (2020). Systematic literature review and empirical investigation of motivators for requirements change management process in global software development. *Journal of Software: Evolution and Process*, 32(4), e2242.

114. Badshah, S., Khan, A. A., & Khan, B. (2020). Towards process improvement in DevOps: a systematic literature review. *Proceedings of the Evaluation and Assessment in Software Engineering*, 427-433.

115. Zhou, P., Khan, A. A., Liang, P., & Badshah, S. (2021). System and Software Processes in Practice: Insights from Chinese Industry. In *Evaluation and Assessment in Software Engineering* (pp. 394-401).

5

Modeling Multi-Release Open Source Software Reliability Growth Process with Generalized Modified Weibull Distribution

VISHAL PRADHAN[1], AJAY KUMAR[1], JOYDIP DHAR[1]

[1] Department of Applied Sciences, ABV-Indian Institute of Information Technology and Management, Gwalior, India
Email: vishalp@iiitm.ac.in, vishal.iiitmg@gmail.com

Abstract

To stay competitive in the industry, software companies are constantly adding new features and upgrading their software. In the last few years, open source software (OSS) has gained a lot of attention because it is free and easy to use. Closed source commercial projects follow a somewhat different protocol than open source projects. The frequency of OSS releases is high. As a result, the multi-release software reliability growth model (SRGM) has been addressed in this study. A non-homogeneous Poisson process (NHPP)-based model is built for reliability analysis, assuming that the software failure distribution is defined by a generalized modified Weibull distribution (GMWD). The experimental results are based on bug tracking data from a common open source project's multi-release failure dataset. The proposed model's efficiency is calculated based on the experimental results. The proposed model is an efficient reliability model for multi-release OSS, according to the results. The model presented in this study is extremely useful for assessing the reliability of OSS.

Keywords: Non-homogeneous Poisson process, software testing, software reliability growth model, open source software, generalized modified Weibull distribution, multi-release.

Evolving Software Processes.
Edited by Arif Ali Khan and Dac-Nhuong Le, Copyright © 2022 Scrivener Publishing

5.1 Introduction

Software is embedded in most of the digital systems used in our daily life, such as home appliances, consumer electronics, nuclear power plants, healthcare systems, and monitoring systems. As the world rapidly moves into a technological era, it has become one of the most important components in day-to-day life. It's quickly expanding to include a broad range of service-based applications. Therefore, the dependency of our society on software-driven systems has also increased. Software size is also increasing rapidly because of the various functions added into a single software component. Software development requires a lot of mental effort. As the size of software increases, the development of software becomes very complex and time-consuming. There are two types of software projects: open source project and closed source project. In recent years, open source software (OSS) has attracted significant attention because it is easily available, does not pose a risk, and continuously upgrades [1-5].

The development of OSS is a modern way of producing massive software on a global scale. In several respects, it differs from conventional software engineering principles [6]. OSS is classified as software whose source code is available alongside the software and the user has the freedom to copy, run, modify, distribute, and develop the software [7]. The OSS approach adds value to consumers while also increasing income for OSS companies. The OSS can be developed by a diverse group of developers, users, and co-developers. OSS development is often started by a single developer or a single community, who develops software to satisfy their own "unique itch." According to the study, a few major OSS products have outperformed their commercial equivalents in terms of quality and market share. They not only appeal to people who want better-quality software but also to those who cannot pay for the more costly commercial version. OSS also fits well into the various technological plans of many companies and governments.

According to a CIO survey conducted in late 2002, the IT community is becoming more comfortable with the open source development model, with the majority (64%) of companies surveyed most commonly using OSS as a web development, web server, and for server operating system [8]. There are several OSS that can be run on a variety of platforms or computers, including PCs, cell phones, and hand-held devices. In the operating system space and server, where two dominant open source products, Linux and Apache, have already established their brand names with validated quality, adoption rates are also rapidly increasing. According to Forrester's recent empirical study, most European companies have clear OSS adoption plans. As a result, it's critical to investigate and evaluate the likely fault distribution of OSS. Many software companies, such as Mozilla, Codeplex, Launchpad, GitHub, MySQL database system, Google Code, SourceForge, Linux operating system and others, will develop high-quality OSS.

These firms not only provide open source packages to users, but also provide a forum for developers, with lots of OSS projects in various stages of development on these platforms. Single-release software products are no longer sufficient to satisfy the ever-increasing consumer demands. As a result, it's important to release several versions of software in order to add new functionality in the next release and patch any lingering flaws in the previous one. As software grows in size and complexity, software organizations must grapple with how to enhance software reliability and quality, manage overall cost, and provide adequate and appealing features. Since our modern society is becoming increasingly reliant on software systems, software flaws could result in a massive catastrophe. The probability of failure-free software operation for a specified period of time in a specified environment is defined as one of the most important attributes of software quality. As a result, software reliability testing should be done correctly and in a justifiable manner.

A large number of software reliability growth models (SRGMs) have been developed in the last four decades to measure the consistency of software systems [9,10]. One of the most effective models for studying software reliability is the non-homogeneous Poisson process (NHPP). Multiple-release planning not only allows software organizations to efficiently balance conflicting stakeholder needs and benefits based on available resources, but it also reduces the likelihood of failing to meet customer requirements [11]. The most critical and influential predictor of software quality has long been the software reliability model. The workflow diagram of this study is presented in Figure 5.1.

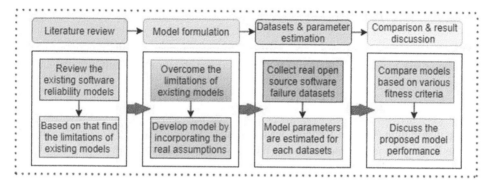

Figure 5.1: Workflow diagram.

Additionally, notation and acronyms used in this paper is given in Table 5.1

Table 5.1: Acronyms and notations.

Acronyms	Notations
$SRGMs$	Software reliability growth models
$NHPP$	Non-homogeneous Poisson process
$GMWD$	Generalized modified Weibull distribution
OSS	Open source software
$u(t)$	Mean value function
$\lambda(t)$	Failure intensity
$F(t)$	Distribution function for fault detection
Λ	Total number of faults

This chapter is organized as follows. The preliminaries and literature review are discussed in Section 5.2. The proposed single- and multi-release SRGMs are described in Section 5.3. Section 5.4 presents the numerical analysis of dataset and comparison of the results of the proposed and competing models. Finally, Section 5.5 concludes the work with future directions.

5.2 Background

The cumulative number of detected faults is represented by $\{\mathcal{N}(t), t \geq 0\}$ in the counting process, which follows NHPP with time-dependent failure intensity $\lambda(t)$, i.e.,

$$u(t) = \int_0^t \lambda(t)dt \tag{5.1}$$

where $u(t)$ is the mean value function (MVF), i.e., expected total number of faults present in the system. So the probability that the k failure occurs by time t is,

$$Pr\{\mathcal{N}(t) = k\} = \frac{u^k(t) \cdot e^{-u(t)}}{k!}, \qquad k = 0, 1, 2 \ldots \tag{5.2}$$

The failure rate of software is proportional to the number of faults remaining in the software at any given time. As a result, the difference equation for fault removal can be written as:

$$\frac{du(t)}{dt} = \lambda(t) = \frac{F'(t)}{1 - F(t)} \cdot [\Lambda - u(t)] \tag{5.3}$$

The distribution function for fault detection process is denoted by $F(t)$. In the case of a finite failure, the instantaneous failure intensity $\lambda(t)$ can be calculated using the above equation. The NHPP models are provided by

$$\lambda(t) = \Lambda \cdot f(t). \tag{5.4}$$

Failure with a finite duration infinite failures models presume that an infinite number of faults will be found in an infinite amount of testing time, while NHPP models assume that an infinite number of faults will be detected in an infinite amount of testing time [12]. The finite failure mean value function models for NHPPs can also be written as:

$$u(t) = \Lambda \cdot F(t). \tag{5.5}$$

We may derive MVF for the SRGM by choosing an appropriate $F(t)$. The MVF of G-O model can be expressed as [13]:

$$u(t) = \Lambda \cdot (1 - e^{-\beta t}). \tag{5.6}$$

where Λ is the initial number of faults to be detected and β is the fault detection rate.

Similarly, generalized G-O is also developed by adding shape parameter θ. The MVF of G-GO model is expressed as [14]:

$$u(t) = \Lambda \cdot (1 - e^{-\beta t^\theta}). \tag{5.7}$$

The probability that no errors occur in the interval $(t, t + \Delta t)$ given time t. In addition, software reliability can be defined as

$$\begin{aligned} R(\Delta t | t) &= e^{- \int_t^{T+\Delta T} \lambda(\Delta T)\, d\Delta T} \\ &= \exp\left[- \left(u(T + \Delta T) - u(T) \right) \right], \; T \geq 0, \; \Delta T > 0. \end{aligned} \tag{5.8}$$

The probability that a software failure will not occur in a given time period $(t, t + \Delta t]$ is represented by the equation.

In the proposed reliability growth models, the GMWD has been incorporated to represent the $F(t)$.

Generalized Modified Weibull Distribution (GMWD)

In the literature, failure behavior can be reflected by various distributions. Pachauri *et al.* [15] suggested a very scalable GMWD distribution with two distinct characteristics. First, they have individual cases that cover a vast number of models, as shown in Table 5.2. Second, they make it possible to model non-monotonic failure rates per fault feature. These two characteristics have a huge bearing on functional applicability. The GMWD demonstrates a strong balance between simplicity and versatility. As failure distribution $F(t)$, the GMWD is expressed as:

$$F(t) = \left[1 - e^{-\beta t^{\theta} e^{\varpi t}}\right]^{\zeta}, \tag{5.9}$$

The density function is described as:

$$f(t) = \frac{\zeta \beta e^{\varpi t} \left[1 - e^{-\beta t^{\theta} e^{\varpi t}}\right]^{\zeta} (\theta t^{\theta-1} + \varpi t^{\theta})}{e^{-\beta t^{\theta} e^{\varpi t}} - 1}, \tag{5.10}$$

Here, β is scale, θ and ζ are shape parameter and ϖ is accelerating factor that index the failure behavior of GMWD.

Table 5.2: Special cases of GMWD function with different values of parameters.

Model Name	GG NHPP [14]	G-O [13]
$F(t)$	$\left[1 - e^{-\beta t^{\theta}}\right]$	$\left[1 - e^{-\beta t}\right]$
Parameter conditions	$\zeta = 1, \varpi = 0$	$\zeta = 1, \varpi = 0, \theta = 1$

5.3 Proposed Models

In this section, we address the GMWD distribution for failure distribution to develop SRGMs.

1. The fault detection process follows the NHPP.

2. Faults are present in the system, and so the software systems are subject to failure at random.

3. All faults in a program are mutually independent.

4. Failure distribution is modeled by GMWD ($F(t)$).

5.3.1 Model-1 (General Model)

Here, we proposed an SRGM with GMWD in a perfect debugging environment. This proposed model can be used for single-release. From Equation (5.5) the proposed model is represented as:

$$
\begin{aligned}
u(t) &= \Lambda \cdot F(t) \\
&= \Lambda \cdot \left[1 - e^{-\beta t^{\theta} e^{\varpi t}} \right]^{\zeta}
\end{aligned}
\tag{5.11}
$$

where Λ is total number of faults. The MVF obtained above is the solution of the proposed perfect debugging SRGM with GMWD.

5.3.2   Model-2 (Multi-Release Model)

In this model, we enhance the previous model from single-release to multi-release by considering the assumption that the previous release's uncorrected faults are added in the next release, and the new fault is the sum of the previous uncorrected and current number of faults. By adding this assumption, the initial number of faults becomes a function of current and previously remaining faults. Therefore, the proposed multi-release model is:

- **First release:**

$$
u_1(t) = \Lambda_1 \cdot F_1(t) = \Lambda_1 \cdot \left[1 - e^{-\beta_1 t^{\theta_1} e^{\varpi_1 t}} \right]^{\zeta_1} \qquad 0 \leq t \leq t_1.
\tag{5.12}
$$

- **Second release:**

$$
u_2(t) = \Lambda_2 \cdot F_2(t) = (\Lambda_2 + (\Lambda_1 - u_1(t))) \cdot \left[1 - e^{-\beta_2 t^{\theta_2} e^{\varpi_2 t}} \right]^{\zeta_2} \qquad t_1 \leq t \leq t_2.
\tag{5.13}
$$

- **Subsequent releases:**

$$
u_i(t) = \Lambda_i \cdot F_i(t) = (\Lambda_i + (\Lambda_{i-1} - u_{i-1}(t))) \cdot \left[1 - e^{-\beta_i t^{\theta_i} e^{\varpi_i t}} \right]^{\zeta_i} \qquad t_{i-1} \leq t \leq t_i.
\tag{5.14}
$$

After model formulation, the next step is dataset collection and the most important part is parameter estimation. In the next section, dataset and parameter estimation is discussed.

5.4   Performance Evaluation with Data Analysis

5.4.1   Dataset and Parameter Estimation

Here, a single dataset with three releases is used for analysis and comparison. Details of datasets are given below. The testing time for first, second and third releases are 26, 24 and 24 months, respectively.

The dataset is taken from [16] and shown in Table 5.3. The software defects were detected using V&V. This dataset is from real failure. After the data collection, the important task is parameter estimation. The popular technique for parameter estimation are least square estimation (LSE), meta-heuristic techniques, and maximum likelihood estimation (MLE). Here, we estimate the SRGMs parameters on real-life failure datasets by LSE. All the estimated values of the model's parameter and goodness of fit are given in Table 5.5 below. We also see the performance of SRGMs in Figure 5.2.

Table 5.3: Dataset: Beam 2.0.0, Beam 2.1.0, and Beam 2.2.0.

Beam 2.0.0				Beam 2.1.0				Beam 2.2.0			
Month	Detected faults	Month	Detected faults	Month	Detected faults	Month	Detected faults	Month	Detected faults	Month	Detected faults
1	2	16	348	1	1	16	98	1	1	16	28
2	5	17	349	2	3	17	112	2	2	17	41
3	5	18	349	3	4	18	114	3	2	18	73
4	6	19	349	4	5	19	114	4	3	19	101
5	7	20	349	5	5	20	114	5	4	20	127
6	10	21	349	6	6	21	114	6	4	21	137
7	12	22	349	7	7	22	114	7	4	22	142
8	16	23	350	8	8	23	114	8	4	23	145
9	29	24	350	9	10	24	116	9	4	24	146
10	38	25	350	10	12			10	8		
11	51	26	351	11	16			11	10		
12	66			12	22			12	11		
13	95			13	25			13	13		
14	186			14	27			14	18		
15	294			15	64			15	21		

5.4.2 Competing Models and Comparison Criteria

Here, we consider four existing models for comparison with proposed model: GO model, delayed S-shaped model, generalized GO model and Li-model. These models are listed in Table 5.4.

Table 5.4: Competing and proposed models with MVF.

Model	Type	Mean value function
GO	Closed Source Software model	$\Lambda\left(1-e^{-\beta t}\right)$
DSS	Closed Source Software model	$\Lambda\left((1-(1+\beta t)e^{-\beta t}\right)$
G-GO	Closed Source Software model	$\Lambda\left(1-e^{-\beta t^{\theta}}\right)$
Li-model	Open Source Software model	$\Lambda\left(1-e^{-N\left[\frac{1}{1+Ke^{-\beta t}}-\frac{1}{1+K}\right]}\right)$
Proposed (GMWD)	Open Source Software model	$\Lambda\left(1-e^{-\beta t^{\theta}e^{\varpi t}}\right)^{\zeta}$

5.4.3 Least Square Estimation (LSE)

The LSE is a mathematical method for estimating the parameters of a statistical model that minimizes the number of squared errors (SSE) residuals between the expected and actual data. For example, the SSE of a function $f(x)$ with parameters a and b between expected and actual data. The LSE reduces the SSE of the deviations between what was expected and what was received. LSE is usually used for medium-sized samples and provides the most accurate point estimates [20]. The evaluation formula $S(a,b)$ for "least square number" is as follows:

$$\text{Minimize } S(\Lambda,\beta,\theta,\varpi,\zeta)=\sum_{k=1}^{n}\left[u_k-u(t_k)\right]^2 \tag{5.15}$$

$$\frac{\partial S}{\partial \Lambda} = \frac{\partial S}{\partial \beta} = \frac{\partial S}{\partial \theta} = \frac{\partial S}{\partial \varpi} = \frac{\partial S}{\partial \zeta} = 0 \qquad (5.16)$$

By solving the above equation, we can obtain the estimated values of the parameters.

5.4.4 Goodness of Fit

Here, SRGMs descriptive performance is measured by three comparison criteria. These criteria are explained below.

5.4.4.1 Mean Square Error (MSE)

The MSE is used for a quantitative comparison between prediction models. In MSE, the difference between the actual and predicted value is measured [17]. It is defined as:

$$\text{MSE} = \frac{1}{n} \sum_{i=1}^{n} \left[u(t_i) - u_i \right]^2, \qquad (5.17)$$

where u_i is the observed number of detected faults by time t_i and $u(t_i)$ is the MVF at time t_i. If the value of MSE is less than the fitted model it is better.

5.4.4.2 Coefficient of Determination (R^2)

The coefficient of determination measures the complete variation concerning the fitted curve. The value obtained by this is a percentage and it is equal to 1, which is 100%. Here, the larger value of R^2 means that the fitted curve is more appropriate for the given failure data [18-20].

$$R^2 = 1 - \frac{\sum_{i=1}^{n} \left(u(t_i) - u_i \right)^2}{\sum_{i=1}^{n} [u(t_i) - \bar{u}_i]^2}, \qquad (5.18)$$

where $\bar{u}_i = \frac{1}{n} \sum_{i=1}^{n} u_i$.

5.4.4.3 Theil's Statistic (TS)

The average variance percentage over all data points is the TS. The model's prediction accuracy improves as Theil's statistic approaches zero. It's defined as:

$$TS = \sqrt{\frac{\sum_{i=1}^{n} (u(t_i) - u_i)^2}{\sum_{i=1}^{n} u_i^2}} \cdot 100\% \qquad (5.19)$$

5.4.4.4 Kolmogorov Distance (KD)

$F^*(t)$ and $F(t)$ represent the cumulative distribution of the normalized observation and expectation by time t, respectively. It's defined as:

$$KD = Sup_t |F^*(x) - F(t)| \qquad (5.20)$$

5.4.5 Comparison of Results

This section tests SRGM efficiency on real failure dataset. This study also analyzes and compares the goodness-of-fit and predictive capacity of the proposed model with competing models. Since the proposed model is new for predicting/estimating software reliability, we will evaluate its accuracy with a few well-known SRGMs, such as the G-O model, DSS model, G-GO model, and Li model. After the GOF criteria were implemented, the proposed model fit best on failure dataset. Table 5.5 shows the value of estimated parameters,

MSE, R^2, R^2_{adj}, TS and KD. Figure 5.2 shows a graphical comparison of the proposed model with existing models on failure dataset. Additionally, Figure 5.2 also shows the residual evaluation of the proposed and competing models.

Table 5.5: Competing and proposed models with MVF.

Release	Model	Mean value function	MSE	R^2	R^2_{adj}	TS	KD
	GO	Λ=23576, β=0.000628	5309.9	0.7861	0.7858	30.52	0.3741
	DSS	Λ=844.91, β=0.063811	3468.1	0.8603	0.8601	24.66	0.4409
Beam 2.0.0	G-GO	Λ=333.28, β=7.9×10⁵, θ=3.5423	1610.0	0.9352	0.9347	16.80	0.2317
	Li-model	Λ=379.32, β=0.011677, K=0.5581, N=22.194	8701.0	0.6496	0.6484	39.06	0.4697
	Proposed (GMWD)	Λ=351.1, β=1.115×10⁻⁴, θ=3.82×10⁻⁷, ϖ=0.6399, N=1.076	97.885	0.9961	0.9953	6.201	0.0982
	GO	Λ=18030, β=0.000259	589.37	0.7549	0.7543	34.30	0.3513
	DSS	Λ=1433.4, β=0.021707	292.42	0.8784	0.8772	24.16	0.4124
Beam 2.1.0	G-GO	Λ=113.28, β=3.10-6, θ=4.6331	102.93	0.9572	0.9550	14.33	0.2256
	Li-model	Λ=400.16, β=0.16661, K=8.9155, N=0.4079	476.37	0.8019	0.7980	30.84	0.3785
	Proposed (GMWD)	Λ=115.3, β=2.334×10⁻⁴, θ=5.495×10⁻⁶, ϖ=0.5507, ζ=1.085	31.238	0.9870	0.9843	7.111	0.1041
	GO	Λ=29729, β=0.000144	1121.9	0.6200	0.6198	48.03	0.4816
	DSS	Λ=1.2512×10⁵, β=0.063811	400.23	0.8645	0.8623	28.69	0.2574
Beam 2.2.0	G-GO	Λ=638.89, β=8.2×10⁻⁵, θ=2.5493	261.93	0.9113	0.9105	23.21	0.2104
	Li-model	Λ=472.97, β=0.32318, K=502.44, N=0.4557	125.39	0.9575	0.9523	16.06	0.1630
	Proposed (GMWD)	Λ=146.4, β=7.479×10⁻⁴, θ=5.495×10⁻⁶, ϖ=0.3963, ζ=1.398	18.433	0.9938	0.9924	4.231	0.0504

5.5 Conclusion

In this chapter, the reliability of an OSS was investigated in a perfect debugging environment. Since OSS is a multi-release product, and the new release is an expansion of the previous release, reliability analysis has been addressed, taking into account faults that were not removed or found in the previous release, as well as the OSS detection rate. In this study, the behavior of generalized modified Weibull distribution has been used as fault detection process failure distribution. This model has been proposed by considering the single- and multi-releases of a software system. The proposed model was tested on real-life dataset, and the findings were discussed. From the results, it is observed that our proposed models with GMWD outperformed the existing compared models. The results may be useful for the system analyst to decide the release time of a software system based on cost and reliability criterion. The models may further be extended by incorporating the concept of imperfect debugging and optimal release time.

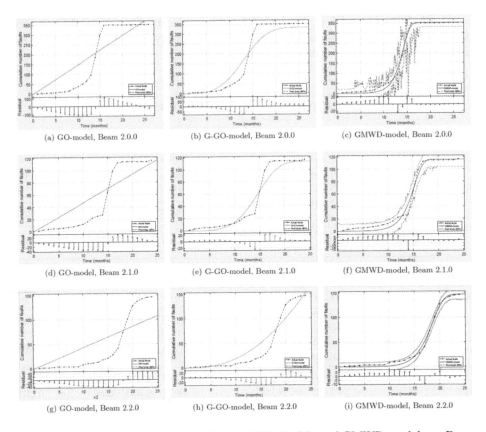

Figure 5.2: (a-i) Fitted shapes and residuals of GO, G-GO, and GMWD models on Beam 2.0.0, 2.1.0, and 2.2.0 failure datasets.

References

1. Adewumi, A., Misra, S., Omoregbe, N., Crawford, B., & Soto, R. (2016). A systematic literature review of open source software quality assessment models. *SpringerPlus*, 5(1), 1-13.

2. Aggarwal, A. G., Dhaka, V., & Nijhawan, N. (2017). Reliability analysis for multi-release open-source software systems with change point and exponentiated Weibull fault reduction factor. *Life Cycle Reliability and Safety Engineering*, 6(1), 3-14.

3. Gandhi, N., Sharma, H., Aggarwal, A. G., & Tandon, A. (2019). Reliability growth modeling for oss: a method combining the bass model and imperfect debugging. In *Smart Innovations in Communication and Computational Sciences* (pp. 23-34). Springer, Singapore.

4. Kapur, P. K., Pham, H., Aggarwal, A. G., & Kaur, G. (2012). Two dimensional multi-release software reliability modeling and optimal release planning. *IEEE Transactions on Reliability*, 61(3), 758-768.

5. Li, X., Li, Y. F., Xie, M., & Ng, S. H. (2011). Reliability analysis and optimal version-updating for open source software. *Information and Software Technology*, 53(9), 929-936.

6. Aggarwal, A. G., Dhaka, V., Nijhawan, N., & Tandon, A. (2019). Reliability growth analysis for multi-release open source software systems with change point. In *System Performance and Management Analytics* (pp. 125-137). Springer, Singapore.

7. Pachauri, B., Kumar, A., & Dhar, J. (2019). Reliability analysis of open source software systems considering the effect of previously released version. *International Journal of Computers and Applications*, 41(1), 31-38.

8. Cosgrove, L. (2003). Conffidence in open source growing, *Technical report, CIO Research Report*.

9. Chatterjee, S., Shukla, A., & Pham, H. (2019). Modeling and analysis of software fault detectability and removability with time variant fault exposure ratio, fault removal efficiency, and change point. *Proceedings of the Institution of Mechanical Engineers, Part O: Journal of Risk and Reliability*, 233(2), 246-256.

10. Pradhan, V., Dhar, J., Kumar, A., & Bhargava, A. (2020). An S-Shaped Fault Detection and Correction SRGM Subject to Gamma-Distributed Random Field Environment and Release Time Optimization. In *Decision Analytics Applications in Industry* (pp. 285-300). Springer, Singapore.

11. Westland, J. C. (2002). The cost of errors in software development: evidence from industry. *Journal of Systems and Software*, 62(1), 1-9.

12. Kapur, P. K., Pham, H., Anand, S., & Yadav, K. (2011). A unified approach for developing software reliability growth models in the presence of imperfect debugging and error generation. *IEEE Transactions on Reliability*, 60(1), 331-340.

13. Goel, A. L., & Okumoto, K. (1979). Time-dependent error-detection rate model for software reliability and other performance measures. *IEEE Transactions on Reliability*, 28(3), 206-211.

14. Goel, A. L. (1983). A Guidebook for Software Reliability Assessment. SYRACUSE UNIV NY.

15. Pachauri, B., Kumar, A., & Dhar, J. (2014). Software reliability growth modeling with dynamic faults and release time optimization using GA and MAUT. *Applied Mathematics and Computation*, 242, 500-509.

16. Wang, J. (2021). Model of Open Source Software Reliability with Fault Introduction Obeying the Generalized Pareto Distribution. *Arabian Journal for Science and Engineering*, 46(4), 3981-4000.

17. Li, Q., & Pham, H. (2017). A testing-coverage software reliability model considering fault removal efficiency and error generation. *PloS One*, 12(7), e0181524.

18. Khurshid, S., Shrivastava, A. K., & Iqbal, J. (2019). Effort based software reliability model with fault reduction factor, change point and imperfect debugging. *International Journal of Information Technology*, 1-10.

19. Le, D. N., Nguyen, G. N., Garg, H., Huynh, Q. T., Bao, T. N., & Tuan, N. N. (2021). Optimizing Bidders Selection of Multi-Round Procurement Problem in Software Project Management Using Parallel Max-Min Ant System Algorithm. *CMC-COMPUTERS MATERIALS & CONTINUA*, 66(1), 993-1010.

20. Bao, T. N., Huynh, Q. T., Nguyen, X. T., Nguyen, G. N., & Le, D. N. (2020). A Novel Particle Swarm Optimization Approach to Support Decision-Making in the Multi-Round of an Auction by Game Theory. *International Journal of Computational Intelligence Systems*, 13(1), 1447-1463.

6

Developing a Reference Model for Open Data Capability Maturity Assessment

Murat Tahir Çaldağ [1], Ebru Gökalp[2,3]

[1] Department of Technology and Knowledge Management, Başkent University, Ankara, Turkey
[2] Department of Computer Engineering, Hacettepe University, Ankara, Turkey
[3] Institute for Manufacturing, Cambridge University, Cambridge, England
 Email: mtcaldag@baskent.edu.tr, ebrugokalp@hacettepe.edu.tr

Abstract

Governments and organizations want to reap observed open data benefits like trust, participation, collaboration, transparency, anti-corruption, decreased bureaucracy, and improved organizational capacity and innovative practices. However, they face challenges during this transition since they need a holistic roadmap, including where to start and what to do to utilize the open data concept. To satisfy this need, we developed a theoretically grounded and methodologically rigorous process reference model for the open data domain to assess the current situation and provide a road map for improvements. The open data process reference model (OD-PRM), consisting of 23 open data-specific process definitions with a comprehensive perspective on the domain, is developed based upon the ISO/IEC 330xx family of standards. Owing to the OD-PRM, an organization's open data process capability and maturity levels can be assessed based on ISO/IEC 3300xx to provide a current level assessment and a roadmap for improvement to implement, use, maintain, and publish open data in a standardized manner.

Keywords: Open data, maturity model, process assessment, reference model

6.1 Introduction

Data has been changing the world every day with exponential growth in volume and variety. According to the International Data Corporation (IDC), data volume creation in 2025 is forecasted to be 163 zettabytes from 16.1 zettabytes generated in 2016 and 64.2 zettabytes in 2020 [1]. While data present a substantial resource, opening the data for commercial and non-commercial use provides new opportunities for businesses, governments, societies, and individuals. This has led to the open data concept, which can be defined as providing everyone access, use, and redistribution of data free of charge without any restrictions [2-4]. As a result of observing many advantages, such as transparency, participation, self-empowerment, accountability, collaboration, trust, legitimacy, improvement of civil rights, and corruption prevention [4-9] as well as improving operational capacity, reducing bureaucratic red tape, and providing innovative practices [4,6,10-14], open data initiatives have been increased in organizations. While the recent history of open data is inspired and affected by the open-source movement, open innovation, and open access, the administration of former U.S. president Barack Obama introduced the Open Government Initiative in 2009, which caused governments and businesses to become highly interested in open data for its beneficial promises [15,16]. After more than a decade, the popularity of opening data and its reusability is still an ongoing subject. A global open data indicator, ODIN, indicates that there was a 30 percent increase in openness and 18 percent in coverage of publicly available data from national statistical offices from 2016 to 2020 [17]. In accordance with the impact of revising the Public Sector Information Directive with open data and reusability perspectives, the total economic value of Public Sector Information will increase from €52 billion in 2018 to €194 billion in 2030 [18].

Even though organizations initiate many projects for open data, they face plenty of barriers, such as copyright problems, knowledge gaps on open data, insufficient financial resources, lack of support from administration, lack of training resources, inadequate technological infrastructure/data, data management related complications, and insufficient social awareness on open data [19,20]. Organizations that desire to achieve the benefits of open data do not know where to start, what to do, and how to execute open data strategies. There is a need for a guideline to follow. Maturity models (MMs) offer organizations the structural approach by providing step-by-step improvements with multiple capability levels. An MM consists of a sequence of maturity levels for objects representing the anticipated or desired path of progress as discrete stages [21]. MMs provide benefits like cost reduction, quality improvements, productivity, and gaining a competitive advantage for the organizations. Although MMs are used extensively in software development, they are also applied to different domains such as business process management, knowledge management, information technology management, medical, industry 4.0, and automation [22-27].

This study aims to utilize the same approach for the open data domain by developing a structured MM based on a well-known process improvement and capability determination model, also known as ISO 330xx set standards, to provide a step-by-step roadmap for organizations that want to transition to open data. The developed model, called the open data capability maturity model (OD-CMM), consists of two dimensions: process and capability. The process dimension includes the open data process reference model (OD-PRM), consisting of the process definition of open-data-specific processes. It is aimed at assessing the open data process capability and maturity levels of an organization based on ISO/IEC 3300xx owing to the developed OD-PRM.

The remainder of this chapter is organized as follows: The related works section includes the identification and evaluation of existing MMs developed for the open data domain in the literature. Then, the development and design of the OD-CMM are given in the model development section, followed by the description of the developed model; and then the study is concluded.

6.2 Literature Review

6.2.1 Theoretical Background

"Process improvement" is defined as a structured approach to performance improvement of business process designs and implementations [28]. Process improvement benefits are described as product/service quality improvements, cost reductions, productivity, employee empowerment, ease of cultural change, and decentralized governance [22,29]. Process capability/maturity models provide a roadmap that can be used by organizations to gain these benefits. Process capability/maturity models provide measurable and standard improvement processes from ad-hoc level to innovating level.

Capability maturity model integration (CMMI) and software process improvement and capability determination (SPICE) are well-accepted models in both the literature and in practice. CMMI, developed by Carnegie Mellon University, is a model that aims to improve the ability of organizations to manage the supply, development, and maintenance processes of their products and services by guiding their processes [30]. SPICE provides a structured process evaluation framework for process improvement and process-capability-maturity determination for software development and related management processes. Both CMMI and SPICE models present benefits such as reducing costs, gaining a competitive advantage, improving quality, and reducing delivery times [31]. The implementation of both models in different business sectors is a rising trend [32].

ISO 330xx [33], a revised version of SPICE, provides a well-accepted, standardized structure. It is developed for software process improvement and capability determination; however, as a result of observing benefits in the software development domain, the standard has been used in several domains other than the software development domain, like automotive [27], enterprise [34], government [29,35], and Industry 4.0 [26]. The first reason behind the selection of the SPICE model is that it is a well-accepted trendy structured model. Another reason is the presenting references on technical standards, design requirements, planning, and process implications on developing a maturity model. The final reason is that the SPICE model provides more technical details on processes than CMMI [36].

6.2.2 Related Works

Even though the number of studies in the open data domain has been exponentially increasing in the literature, there is a limited number of MMs developed for this domain. As a result of reviewing the literature, it was observed that there exists only seven MMs developed for the open data domain. The details of these seven MMs are given in Appendix A. According to [37], an MM assessment result should be unambiguous, repeatable, complete, clear, and objective. An MM assessment framework [38,39] also emphasizes that the observability, generalizability, theory-based interpretation, extrapolation, and implication criteria should be satisfied for an MM. Accordingly, the existing seven MMs developed for the open-data domain were evaluated based on the quality assessment criteria described in Table 6.1.

Table 6.1: Quality assessment criteria.

No	Criterion	Description
1	Theory-Based Framework	Every dimension, aspect, measurement of the model needs to be based upon a theoretical framework.
2	Observability	Every dimension and aspect must be appropriate according to the scope and measurements of the model. Observation criterion includes the completeness, level of detail, and definitive descriptions of maturity model levels, dimensions, measurement attributes.
3	Generalizability	Generalizability is the requirement that emphasizes the holistic approach and standardization of the processes on the model for similar and different entities, regions. A holistic perspective requires every perspective to be accounted for; therefore, the dimensions should cover all the domains.
4	Extrapolation	Extrapolation requirement emphasizes constructs and the maturity levels connection within suitability, objectivity, and assessment.
5	Improvement Implications	Improvement implication requirement regulates if the model provides a solution to an existing problem, creates a guideline, road-map for implementation, or improving the efficiency of the process.

The 5-point Likert scale was used for the quality assessment of the existing MMs to rate the degree of achievement of each criterion. The rating scale is as follows: (-) Not applicable; (1) Not at all satisfied; (2) Slightly satisfied; (3) Moderately satisfied; (4) Very satisfied; (5) Fully satisfied. Table 6.2 presents the assessment results of MMs according to the criteria given in Table 6.1.

Table 6.2: Existing MMs assessment results.

Model	Theory-Based Framework	Observability	Generalizability	Extrapolation	Improvement Implications
MM1 [40,41]	5	4	4	4	2
MM2 [42]	5	2	1	2	1
MM3 [43]	5	2	1	1	0
MM4 [44]	0	4	3	4	2
MM5 [45]	5	1	1	2	0
MM6 [46]	5	4	3	3	0
MM7 [47]	5	3	1	4	0

As an example of MM assessment, MM2: An Open Government MM for social media-based public engagement was evaluated as follows. The model is developed based upon theoretical grounds, so the first criterion was rated as five (fully satisfied). However, the observability criterion was rated as two (slightly satisfied) since the model lacked detailed descriptions and methodologies for dimensions, maturity levels, and measurement attributes. The generalizability criterion was rated as one (not at all satisfied) because the MM focuses on data, participation, and collaboration perspectives while it does not cover strategic governance, organizational management, human resource management, legal perspectives, and financial management. The extrapolation criterion was rated as two (slightly satisfied) since the research dimensions and assessment connections are not precise. The improvement implications criterion was rated as one (not at all satisfied) since there is no standardized outcome for each maturity level. The recommendation provided is based upon the authors' field studies, archival analysis, and prior literature.

As seen in Table 6.2, none of the existing MMs fully satisfies the required criteria. However, these criteria are necessary to establish an objective, consistent and comprehensive MM. Although all MMs developed in the open data domain present unique and helpful perspectives, none present a comprehensive perspective for observability and generalizability criteria. According to extrapolation criteria, the constructs and their relations are not fully suitable for the scope and assessment of the model. Additionally, none of them provides improvement implications on open-data processes with a holistic approach.

In conclusion, there is not any MM in the open data domain satisfying all MM evaluation criteria. Correspondingly, this research aims to fulfill this research gap by developing an MM for the open data domain, entitled OD-CMM, based on a well-established process improvement and capability determination standard set, ISO 330xx, satisfying all these MM evaluation criteria. The development process of OD-CMM is explained in the following section.

6.3 Model Development

The OD-CMM was developed by following the MM development framework proposed by De Bruin *et al.* [48] because it is well-accepted in business process and knowledge management domains. The framework consists of six generic stages containing scope, design, populate, test, deploy and maintain for MM development. These steps were followed to develop the OD-CMM, as described below.

6.3.1 Scope

The first step of the MM development is the determination of the model scope. The OD-CMM aims to assess current capability maturity levels of open data processes and create a roadmap for improvement of these processes. Therefore, the scope of the MM was determined as domain-specific for open data. The OD-CMM differs from other MMs developed for the open data domain with its framework based upon well-established ISO 330xx family of standards and holistic perspective that includes strategic, organizational, stakeholder related, data related, and legal aspects. Thus, the stakeholders involved in the development phase of the model were academicians and practitioners experienced in the field of open data.

6.3.2 Design

The design step of the framework aims to determine the foundation of the architecture of the model. The decision of this step includes the determination of the model's targeted audience, method of application, driver of application, respondents, and application. The OD-CMM's target audience consists of all stakeholders involved in open data processes (employees, community, non-governmental organizations, shareholders, government). The OD-CMM is designed to be developed based on ISO 330xx by developing a process reference model (OD-PRM), including open data-specific processes. The level-1 process assessment could be done owing to the OD-PRM. The process capability level assessment is conducted based on ISO 33020 [49]. The driver of the application is the need to improve an organization's open data capability maturity levels, which are determined by internal requirements. An exploratory case study was conducted to check the applicability and usability of the approach before populating. The exploratory case study showed that the approach is applicable and usable. Then, the populate step was initiated.

6.3.3 Populate

The populate step of the development framework aims to identify domain components and the maturity assessment criteria. The capability dimensions of the OD-CMM are adapted from ISO 33002 [50], which has six capability and maturity levels. The OD-PRM was developed by following an iterative approach. The first input was from a literature review related to MMs developed for the open data domain. The second input was from an expert panel conducted by experts from the industry and academicians working in the field of open data. A consensus about the critical open data processes was reached at the end of the expert panel discussion. As a result, the developed OD-PRM includes 23 open data-related processes under six main process groups: strategic governance, organizational management, stakeholder engagement management, data governance, open data management, and supplementary processes, as given in Table 6.3.

6.3.4 Test

The test stage of the development framework aims to validate the model for validity, reliability, and generalizability. An exploratory case study was conducted in the design phase. The case study determined that the approach is suitable and applicable. The final version of the OD-CMM is planned, which will be tested with a qualitative case study method on three different organizations.

6.3.5 Deploy and Maintain

The deploy and maintain stages are necessary for the developed and tested models' survivability for further use and research. Therefore, the model is planned to be made available for use, and several adjustments for tracking the evolution of the model must be made for improvement.

As a result of the development phase, the achieved model, the OD-CMM, is described in the next section.

6.4 Open Data Capability Maturity Model

The OD-CMM is developed based on the set of standards: ISO 330xx [33], which has two dimensions – process and capability. The process dimension consists of 23 open data-specific processes. The OD-PRM consists of the process definitions of these processes, developed by following the requirements defined in ISO/IEC 33004 [51]. The capability dimension is adapted from ISO 33020 [49], as described below.

6.4.1 Process Dimension

A PRM needs to establish the focused domain of the model, define the processes and their relationship with the domain and create the connection with the requirements of the process assessment model [51]. The OD-PRM consists of the process definition of 23 open-data-specific processes under six process groups, as shown in Table 6.3. The process definition requires several elements, which are process ID, name, context, purpose, and outcomes, according to ISO/IEC 33004 [51-55]. An example process definition for ODM2 Data Discovery Process is given in Appendix B.

Table 6.3: The process dimension of the OD-CMM.

Process Groups	Descriptions	Processes	Descriptions
Strategic Governance	The open data strategy and policies affect all other dimensions with the critical insight and guidelines for the open data process [40,46]. The strategic governance aspect of open data is the foundation of the vision, goals, policies, strategy, and macro-management of projects, programs, and portfolios	Open Data Strategy Management	Creation of vision, mission, goals, and objectives, policies related to the open data in the organization.
		Portfolio and Project Management	Prioritizing, allocating resources, determining the relationships between projects, programs, and portfolios.
Organizational Management	The organizational management aspect is concerned with the management of the organizational activities, processes and responsibilities concerning and supporting open data [40,46].	Organizational Structure Management	Definition of the roles, rules, and responsibilities between units throughout the organization for efficiency and higher coordination
		Human Resources Training & Skill Development	Train, Schedule activities and Develop skills on open data to organization's staff.
		Organizational Change Management	Implement new processes, create an open data culture throughout the organization, establish and maintain open communication channels.
Stakeholder Engagement Management	Participation and collaboration are core pillars of open data; therefore, stakeholder engagement is crucial to managing. The absence of stakeholder management in an open data program or project creates a barrier to success [4,52]. The purpose of stakeholder engagement is the creation of active communication and engagement channels with all parties.	Stakeholder Engagement Planning	Plan engagement scope, goals, and methods, create communication channels, schedule activities, define tools for engagement with stakeholders.
		Requirements Collecting, Analysing, and Enhancement	Gather information and feedback, establish requirements, maintain and enhance engagement requirements.
Data Governance	Data governance is one of the core processes on implementing, executing, maintaining, and achieving open data benefits [4,5,11,46]. The data governance aspect of the model is concerned with establishing of standards and oversight on data concerning the lifecycle of open data. The process group consists of 6 core data processes which are adapted from [53].	Data Strategy and Policy Management	Create a standardized plan for data quality, integrity, security, storage, access, and all processes. Determine the fundamental rules on creating, using, distributing an organization's data.
		Metadata Management	Management of information about technology and business processes, data rules and constraints, and logical and physical data structures. Describes data itself, the concepts data represents the connections between the data and concepts.
		Data Integration	Includes the movement and consolidation of data within and between data stores, applications, and organizations.
		Privacy and Security Management	Planning, developing and executing the security policies and procedures to provide proper authentication, authorization, access, and auditing of data and information assets to protect information assets in alignment with privacy and confidentiality regulations, contractual agreements, and business requirements.
		Data Storage and Archive Management	Designing, implementing, and supporting the stored data to maximize its value throughout its lifecycle, from creation/acquisition to disposal.
		Data Quality Management	Management of data through its lifecycle by setting standards and building quality into the processes that create, transform, store data, and measure data against standards.

Process Groups	Descriptions	Processes	Descriptions
Open Data Management	The objective is to understand, discover, prepare, evaluate, manage, publish and maintain the open data of the organization.	Business Understanding	Defining the organization's field of operations, products/services, and work processes. Establishing the organization's open data requirements.
		Open Data Discovery	Define and discover the organization's datasets for open data.
		Digitization and Data Preparation	Creation of the physical data of an organization to digital. Prepare the organization's data according to open data principles.
		Prototyping and Evaluating	Discover the faults, errors, and evaluation of the datasets before deployment.
		License Management	Establish and manage organization's open data licenses.
		Open Data Deployment and Publishing	Creation and management of an open data portal for deployment.
		Open Data Maintenance	Analysing open data related problems, implementing changes, providing periodic maintenance
		Information and Technology Management	Hardware, software and configuration management on organization's open data requirements.
Supplementary Processes	Supplementary processes include quantitative management and process improvement in the organizational unit. Processes support the achievement of high process capability and organizational maturity.	Quantitative performance management	Measurement and the use of appropriate quantitative techniques to ensure that performance of the organization's implemented processes support the achievement of the organization's relevant business goals.
		Quantitative process improvement	Improvement of the performance of the process with quantitative analysis.

- Process ID: For identifying the process groups and process, an identification number consisting of abbreviations of the process group and the sequence number of the process in the group is given as Process ID.

- Name: To distinguish the process from others, a name that emphasizes the aim, scope, and objectives of the process is given.

- Purpose: The goals and objectives the process aims to accomplish.

- Outcomes: The observable and measurable results of the successful execution of the process with the accomplishment of its purpose.

- Work Products: They provide evidence related to outcomes of the base practices to help the assessment process.

6.4.2 Capability Dimension

The capability dimension of the OD-CMM is adapted from ISO/IEC 33020 [49], which has six levels, from level 0 to level 5, shown in Table 6.4. Capability levels are measured with process attributes (PAs) defined to their individual levels. PAs provide an evaluation of the level with measurable properties with a rating system to present the degree of achievement.

Table 6.4: Capability levels.

Capability Level	Capability	Description
Level 0	Incomplete	The process is not applied, implemented, or is unsuccessful in acquiring process objectives. The evidence on process goals and objectives success are little or none at level 0.
Level 1	Performed	The process is successful in the accomplishment of its purpose. At this level, the process is performed.
Level 2	Managed	The process is established in a standardized way, including planning, monitoring, and adjusting. The work products of the process are also established, controlled, and maintained in a managed way.
Level 3	Established	The process is evolved by the usage of defined processes that are capable of successfully acquiring the process outcomes.
Level 4	Predictable	The process operates to achieve the process outcomes with a proactive approach. Quantitative management and analysis were performed to identify any causes for further corrective action.
Level 5	Innovating / Optimizing	The process is in continuous improvement for achieving organization's objectives and goals in changing environments.

The capability dimension of the OD-CMM is given in Figure 6.1.

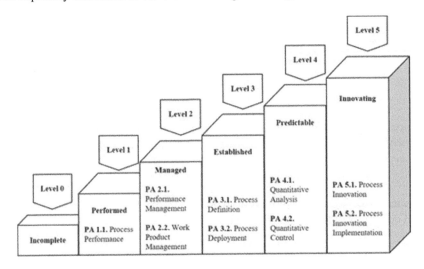

Figure 6.1: The capability dimension of the OD-CMM (adapted from [49]).

6.5   Conclusion

As a result of observing the benefits of the transition to open data, such as transparency, participation, collaboration, accountability, and accessibility, organizations and governments want to adopt open data to gain a competitive advantage. However, governments and organizations do not have a proper guideline on open data practices, which results in unsuccessful projects and attempts. Therefore, a guideline for open data implementation, management, and publication is required. The evaluation of the existing MMs based on the predefined criteria showed the necessity of a comprehensive MM that satisfies the requirements of having a theory-based framework, observability, generalizability, extrapolation, and improvement implication. Correspondingly, this study aims to develop an MM for the open data domain, called OD-CMM, by fully satisfying these requirements and having a comprehensive approach. In line with this purpose, the OD-CMM aims to provide open data capability maturity assessment based on a well-established standard, ISO 330xx. It consists of process and capability dimensions. The process dimension includes the OD-PRM, consisting of 23 open data-specific process definitions developed by following the requirements defined in ISO 33004 [51]. The OD-CMM provides a road map with strategic, organizational, technical, and stakeholder aspects to achieve open data-based programs and projects based on the SPICE framework.

The contribution of this study is to identify the requirement of OD-CMM by analyzing the existing MMs developed in the field of open data and the development of the OD-PRM holistic perspective. Future studies include the validation of OD-CMM with multiple case studies on organizations with differing countries, sizes, and business sectors.

References

1. Reinsel, D., Gantz, J., & Rydning, J. (2017) Data Age 2025: Don't Focus on Big Data; Focus on the Data That's Big. *IDC White Paper*, (April), 1-25.

2. Janssen, M., Charalabidis, Y., & Zuiderwijk, A. (2012). Benefits, adoption barriers and myths of open data and open government. *Information Systems Management*, 29(4), 258-268.

3. Braunschweig, K., Eberius, J., Thiele, M., & Lehner, W. (2012). *The state of open data. Limits of current open data platforms.*

4. Çaldağ, M. T., Gökalp, M. O., & Gökalp, E. (2019, November). Open Government Data: Analysing Benefits and Challenges. In *2019 1st International Informatics and Software Engineering Conference (UBMYK)* (pp. 1-6). IEEE.

5. Lee, G., & Kwak, Y. H. (2012). An open government maturity model for social media-based public engagement. *Government Information Quarterly*, 29(4), 492-503.

6. Altayar, M. S. (2018). Motivations for open data adoption: An institutional theory perspective. *Government Information Quarterly*, 35(4), 633-643.

7. Mayernik, M. S. (2017). Open data: Accountability and transparency. *Big Data & Society*, 4(2), 2053951717718853.

8. Sá, C., & Grieco, J. (2016). Open data for science, policy, and the public good. *Review of Policy Research*, 33(5), 526-543.

9. Open Knowledge Foundation Why Open Data?

10. Schmidthuber, L., Stütz, S., & Hilgers, D. (2019). Outcomes of open government: Does an online platform improve citizens' perception of local government?. *International Journal of Public Sector Management*.

11. Çaldağ, M. T., Gökalp, E., & Alkış, N. (2019). Analyzing determinants of open government based technologies and applications adoption in the context of organizations. In *Proceedings of the International Conference on e-Learning, e-Business, Enterprise Information Systems, and e-Government (EEE)* (pp. 50-56). The Steering Committee of The World Congress in Computer Science, Computer Engineering and Applied Computing (WorldComp).

12. Lucas Amin (2017). Making the Case for Open Contracting in Healthcare Procurement, *Transparency International*.

13. OECD (2011). Together for Better Public Services: Partnering with Citizens and Civil Society, OECD Publishing.

14. Open Government Partnership (2019). Open Government Partnership Global Report - Executive Summary.

15. Piotrowski, S. J. (2017). The "Open Government Reform" movement: The case of the open government partnership and US transparency policies. *The American Review of Public Administration*, 47(2), 155-171.

16. Lindman, J., Rossi, M., & Tuunainen, V. K. (2013, January). Open data services: Research agenda. In *2013 46th Hawaii International Conference on System Sciences* (pp. 1239-1246). IEEE.

17. Open Data Watch (2021). *Open data inventory 2020/21: Executive summary*. Open Data Watch.

18. European Commission (2018). Impact Assessment Support Study for the Revision of the Public Sector Information Directive.

19. Ubaldi, B. (2013). Open Government Data: Towards Empirical Analysis of Open Government Data Initiatives. OECD Work. Pap. Public Gov., NO.22 (22), 61.

20. Sandoval-Almazan, R., & Gil-Garcia, J. R. (2016). Toward an integrative assessment of open government: Proposing conceptual lenses and practical components. *Journal of Organizational Computing and Electronic Commerce*, 26(1-2), 170-192.

21. Becker, J., Knackstedt, R., & Pöppelbuß, J. (2009). Developing maturity models for IT management. *Business & Information Systems Engineering*, 1(3), 213-222.

22. Röglinger, M., Pöppelbuß, J., & Becker, J. (2012). Maturity models in business process management. *Business Process Management Journal*, 18(2), 328-346.

23. Tarhan, A., Turetken, O., & Reijers, H. A. (2016). Business process maturity models: A systematic literature review. *Information and Software Technology*, 75, 122-134.

24. Wendler, R. (2012). The maturity of maturity model research: A systematic mapping study. *Information and Software Technology*, 54(12), 1317-1339.

25. Oliveira, M., & Pedron, C. D. (2014). Maturity model for knowledge management and strategic benefits. In *European Conference on Knowledge Management-ECKM 2014*, 2014, Brasil, 748-756.

26. Gökalp, E., Şener, U., & Eren, P. E. (2017, October). Development of an assessment model for industry 4.0: industry 4.0-MM. In *International Conference on Software Process Improvement and Capability Determination* (pp. 128-142). Springer, Cham.

27. ISO AutomativeSPICE.

28. Hammer, M. (2002). Process management and the future of Six Sigma. *MIT Sloan Management Review*, 43(2), 26.

29. Gökalp, E. (2016). *Gov-PCDM: GOVERNMENT PROCESS CAPABILITY DETERMINATION MODEL*. Middle East Technical University.

30. Team, C. P. (2002). Capability maturity model® integration (CMMI SM), version 1.1. *CMMI for systems engineering, software engineering, integrated product and process development, and supplier sourcing* (CMMI-SE/SW/IPPD/SS, V1. 1), 2.

31. De Bruin, T., Rosemann, M., Freeze, R., & Kaulkarni, U. (2005). Understanding the main phases of developing a maturity assessment model. In *Australasian Conference on Information Systems (ACIS)*: (pp. 8-19). Australasian Chapter of the Association for Information Systems.

32. Goldenson, D., and Gibson, D.L. (2003). Demonstrating the impact and benefits of CMMI: an update and preliminary results.

33. ISO/IEC 33001 (2015). Information technology – Process assessment – Concepts and terminology.

34. Ibrahim, L. (2008). Improving process capability across your enterprise. 4th World Congr. Softw. Qual. (4WCSQ), Bethesda/USA.

35. Gökalp, E., & Demirörs, O. (2016, June). Towards a process capability assessment model for government domain. In *International Conference on Software Process Improvement and Capability Determination* (pp. 210-224). Springer, Cham.

36. Ehsan, N., Perwaiz, A., Arif, J., Mirza, E., & Ishaque, A. (2010, June). CMMI/SPICE based process improvement. In *2010 IEEE International Conference on Management of Innovation & Technology* (pp. 859-862). IEEE.

37. Rout, T., Tuffley, A., and Cahill, B. (2001). *CMMI evaluation: capability maturity model integration mapping to ISO/IEC 15504 2*: 1998. Software Quality Institute (QSI), Griffith University.

38. Kane, M., Crooks, T., & Cohen, A. (1999). Validating measures of performance. *Educational measurement: Issues and Practice*, 18(2), 5-17.

39. Thordsen, T., Murawski, M., & Bick, M. (2020, April). How to Measure Digitalization? A Critical Evaluation of Digital Maturity Models. In *Conference on e-Business, e-Services and e-Society* (pp. 358-369). Springer, Cham.

40. Solar, M., Concha, G., & Meijueiro, L. (2012, September). A model to assess open government data in public agencies. In *International Conference on Electronic Government* (pp. 210-221). Springer, Berlin, Heidelberg.

41. Solar, M., Daniels, F., López, R., & Meijueiro, L. (2014). A Model to Guide the Open Government Data Implementation in Public Agencies. *Journal of Universal Computer Science*, 20(11), 1564-1582.

42. Lee, G., & Kwak, Y. H. (2012). An open government maturity model for social media-based public engagement. *Government Information Quarterly*, 29(4), 492-503.

43. Bel, N., Forcada, M. L., & Gómez-Pérez, A. (2016). A Maturity Model for Public Administration as Open Translation Data Providers. *arXiv preprint arXiv:1607.01990*.

44. Doodds, L., and Newman, A. (2015). *Open Data Maturity Model*. 32.

45. Kalampokis, E., Tambouris, E., & Tarabanis, K. (2011, August). Open government data: A stage model. In *International conference on electronic government* (pp. 235-246). Lecture Note Computer Science 6846, Springer, Berlin, Heidelberg.

46. Silva, P. N., & Pinheiro, M. M. K. (2018). DGABr: Metric for evaluating Brazilian open government data. *Informação & Sociedade*, 28(3).

47. Veljković, N., Bogdanović-Dinić, S., & Stoimenov, L. (2014). Benchmarking open government: An open data perspective. *Government Information Quarterly*, 31(2), 278-290.

48. De Bruin, T., Rosemann, M., Freeze, R., & Kaulkarni, U. (2005). Understanding the main phases of developing a maturity assessment model. In *Australasian Conference on Information Systems (ACIS)*: (pp. 8-19). Australasian Chapter of the Association for Information Systems.

49. ISO/IEC 33020 (2015) Information technology - Process assessment - Process measurement framework for assessment of process capability.

50. ISO/IEC 33002 (2015) Information technology - Process assessment - Requirements for performing process assessment.

51. ISO/IEC 33004 (2015) Information technology - Process assessment - Requirements for Process Reference, Process Assessment and Organizational Maturity Models.

52. Donald Shao, D., & Saxena, S. (2019). Barriers to open government data (OGD) initiative in Tanzania: Stakeholders' perspectives. *Growth and Change*, 50(1), 470-485.

53. DAMA International (2017). DAMA-DMBOK Data Management Body of Knowledge, New Jersey.

54. Le, D. N., Nguyen, G. N., Garg, H., Huynh, Q. T., Bao, T. N., & Tuan, N. N. (2021). Optimizing Bidders Selection of Multi-Round Procurement Problem in Software Project Management

Using Parallel Max-Min Ant System Algorithm. *CMC-COMPUTERS MATERIALS & CONTINUA*, 66(1), 993-1010.

55. Bao, T. N., Huynh, Q. T., Nguyen, X. T., Nguyen, G. N., & Le, D. N. (2020). A Novel Particle Swarm Optimization Approach to Support Decision-Making in the Multi-Round of an Auction by Game Theory. *International Journal of Computational Intelligence Systems*, 13(1), 1447-1463.

Appendix A. Existing maturity models in the open data domain

Table 6.5: Existing maturity models in the open data domain.

Model	Year	Name	Dimensions	Description
MM1 [40,41]	2014 / 2012	A Model to Guide the Open Government Data Implementation in Public Agencies / A Model to Assess Open Government Data in Public Agencies	• Data Governance • Strategic Oversight • Stakeholder Engagement • Legal Perspective • Technology Infrastructure • Management	The model proposed aims to evaluate the capabilities of public agencies' progress on open data practices.
MM2 [42]	2012	An Open Government Maturity Model for social media-based public engagement	• Data Governance • Stakeholder Engagement	The model presented assess open government initiatives that establish public engagement through social media. The model was tested on five healthcare organizations throughout the United States.
MM3 [43]	2016	A Maturity Model for Public Administration as Open Translation Data Providers	• Data Governance	The model is established with the purpose of solving the need for public organizations' translation data.
MM4 [44]	2015	Open Data Maturity Model	• Data Governance • Human Resources • Stakeholder Engagement • Financial Management • Strategic Oversight	The model aims to aid organizations in the publishment and consumption of open data.
MM5 [45]	2011	Open Government Data: A Stage Model	• Data	The model proposed is a stage model on open government data, including dimensions of organizational & technological complexity and added value for data consumers.
MM6 [46]	2018	DGABr: Metric for evaluating Brazilian OGD	• Data Governance • Legal Management • Technical Infrastructure • Management	The model proposed evaluates open government data on public administrations of Brazil.
MM7 [47]	2014	Benchmarking open government: An open data perspective	• Data Governance • Stakeholder Engagement	The model presents a benchmark for open government data on the United States government's open data portals.

Appendix B. An example process definition of ODM2 open data discovery process

Table 6.6: An example process definition of ODM2 open data discovery process.

Process ID	ODM2
Process	Data Discovery
Purpose	The purpose of the open data discovery process is to find all the datasets and data created and used in organization's business processes. Another goal is to determine which data and datasets to open.
Outcomes	As a result of Successful Open Data Discovery; 1.All structured, semi-structured, and unstructured datasets currently used or produced in the organization are defined.
	2.All the required datasets of the organization are defined.
	3.The lacking datasets of the organization are discovered and defined.
	4.Organization's datasets are categorized for entrepreneurial use and confidentiality.
	5.Datasets that should be opened are determined.
	6.Prioritization of the datasets to open is determined.
Base Practices	**1. Define the Current Datasets of the Organization:** Find all structured, semi-structured, and unstructured datasets that are currently used, produced in the organization. (Outcome:1) 1.1. Identify Structured Datasets 1.2. Identify Semi-Structured Datasets 1.3. Identify Unstructured Datasets
	2. Define Required Datasets for Organization Processes: Determine the organizations used and produced datasets that should be defined. (Outcome:2)
	3.Compare Required and Current Datasets: Compare and determine the lacking datasets of the organization (Outcome:3)
	4.Categorize the Datasets of the Organization: Determine the category of the datasets as useful for entrepreneurs, confidential and other. (Outcome:4) 4.1. Identify Datasets for stakeholders 4.2. Categorize the Datasets.
	5.Determine and Prioritize Datasets to Open: Determine and prioritize the datasets to Open. (Outcome:5,6) 5.1.Determine which datasets to Open 5.2.Prioritize Datasets to Open
Work Products	

Input	Output
Data Management Strategy Document (Outcome:1,2,3,4,5)	Organization's Datasets List (Outcome:1,2,3,4,5)
Business Understanding Document (Outcome:1,2,3,4,5)	
Open Data Strategy Document (Outcome:1,2,3,4,5)	

7

AHP-Based Prioritization Framework for Software Outsourcing Human Resource Success Factors in Global Software Development

Abdul Wahid Khan[1], Ghulam Yaseen[2], Muhammad Imran Khan[1], Faheem Khan[3]

[1] Department of Computer Science, University of Science & Technology Bannu, KP, Pakistan
[2] Department of Computer Science, Qurtuba University of Science & Information Technology D.I.Khan, KP, Pakistan
[3] Department of Computer Science, University of Lakki Marwat University, KP, Pakistan
Email: wahidkn@gmail.com, yasin11786@gmail.com, imranktk1745@yahoo.com, kfaheem81@gmail.com

Abstract

Software outsourcing enhances the concept of developing a valuable product at a low price in order to continually increase business. The purpose of this study is to assist vendors of software development organizations in the selection of successful human resources from the vendors' perspective with the aim of accomplishing software development projects effectively. As a methodology, we used a systematic literature review (SLR) and found thirteen critical success factors in all. Next, we conducted a questionnaire survey for the validation of identified success factors. In the last step, an analytical hierarchy process (AHP) approach was adopted for the prioritization of identified success factors and their categories (based on their comparative importance). We grouped the identified success factors into four categories: procurement, organization, reliance, and quality. The category "organization" is more critical than the others based on research findings. Similarly, effective communication, trust development, competence of vendor and good governance, etc., are considered the most critical success factors as compare to others.

Keywords: Analytical hierarchical process (AHP), global software development (GSD), systematic literature review (SLR), human resources (HR), offshore software development outsourcing (OSDO), success factors (SF), critical success factors (CSF)

7.1 Introduction

In this age of science and technology, no field is free from competition. Every vendor wants to lead others in all fields and especially in the software development business. Every vendor struggles to fulfill the needs of their customers in efficient ways and at low cost. Offshore software development outsourcing is a new recently emerging approach adopted by many vendors for the development of software. Outsourcing is the best way to fulfill organization needs according to customer preferences [1]. Software outsourcing development provides the key advantages of easily accessed labor, development of high quality software and fast development [2].

Money assets, physical assets and human resources are considered as core aspects for the fruitful outcomes of all types of businesses [3, 4]. But in this research, we tried to discuss human resource assets that help vendors factors using HR factors effectively [5]. The purpose of this research is to discover HR success apply SLR [6] because of the significant role it has in making an organization viable and competitive in outsourcing. The focus of our research is to highlight which human resource success factors play a vital role in successful outsourcing of software development. Khan *et al.* [7] described important factors that are necessary for the competitiveness of vendors. They explain in their research that "skilled human resources" are very important in successful software development with client perspective. Fjermestad and Saitta [8] discussed the great importance of "management support" in software development outsourcing. At the time of software development, the vendors select successful HR for the successful outsourcing software development.

The vendor organization concentrates on the selection of different success factors that assist vendors in the successful development of software. Khan *et al.* [9] declared that the success factors in efficient project management play a vital role in the selection of outsourcing vendors for client. For the competence of vendors and successful outsourcing, it is necessary to select successful HR. Ali and Khan [10] stated that a "collaborative relationship" is an important success factor in successful outsourcing. Khan and Khan [11] showed that a "trustworthy," relationship management consultation and negotiation are critical success factors for a successful outsourcing organization. Khan and Keung [12] described how "management commitment" and "staff involvement" play vital roles in successful outsourcing software process improvement.

In outsourcing software development, all factors are important but the significance of HR success factor is very vital and unique for successful outsourcing software development from the vendor's perspective [13-16]. Our research assists vendors to identify and prioritize human resource critical success factors that play a very important role in the success of vendors in software development. We divided our research work into 7 sections. Section 7.2 contains a literature review in which we briefly discuss topic-related issues. In section 7.3, we describe research methodology in which we adopt SLR for the identification of CSFs from the existing literature, and also discuss a questionnaire survey for validation, and AHP prioritizing success factors. In Section 7.4, we discuss the results given. Research limitations are discussed in Section 7.5. In Section 7.6 the implications of the study are discussed. In Section 7.7 conclusions and future work on the study are discussed. Our research work is based on the following three research questions:

- RQ1. What are the success factors of human resources that keep them on the right track in order to have a positive impact on software outsourcing development from the seller's point of view?

- RQ2. What practices are available in the literature to be considered by vendor organizations regarding HR for OSDO?

- RQ3. How do we allocate values to identify success and how do we categorize and prioritize identified critical success factors?

7.2 Literature Review

Kitchenham recommended that software engineering-related researchers should adopt evidence-based software engineering (EBSE). An evidence-based approach to software engineering is applied to this method in software engineering research and practice. These types of approaches were first applied in medicine but with the passage of time, many other fields adopted this approach, including criminology, sociology, nursing, etc. [17]. Keele presents the guidelines of SLR methodology for existing literature [18]. Many researchers use SLR for the identification of success factors and questionnaire surveys for validation of SLR outputs [19, 20]. Ali *et al.* [21] used SLR to find the success factors of mutual trust and commitment, which are important for the success of the client and vendor relationship.

Vizcaino *et al.* [22] describe the HR success factors that affect the success of GSD vendors. Due to these factors, the vendors or suppliers can win market competencies to achieve company goals [23-25]. Niazi *et al.* [26] discuss the HR success factors that are important for the success of software project management in GSD environment. Rashid and Khan [27] tried to identify the HR success factors that are affected at outsourcing software development. Various researchers described success factors in their research that are affected at successful outsourcing [28]. Abdulkader [29] identified and analyzed the success factors and issues faced by GSD outsourcing organizations.

Ali *et al.* [21] claimed in their research that HR success factors like "mutual trust," "effective communication," "mutual interdependence and shared values," and "3Cs" are important for successful outsourcing. Khan *et al.* [30] identified success factors and developed a SPIIMM model in their research that assists vendors in the selection of successful outsourcing. Wibisono *et al.* [31] illustrated how some outsourcing organizations are successful and some are not successful, and how the HR interaction coordination and cooperation factor is important for a successful IT outsourcing vendor.

In our research, we make an effort to sum up human resource critical success factors that assist GSD vendors for the selection of successful HR, which plays a vital role in the success of outsourcing vendors. In past studies, researchers attempted to draw attention to GSD outsourcing vendors' HR factors. Our contribution is not only to include some new critical success factors through consistent methodology SLR but also validate these CSFs through a questionnaire survey with different practitioners. Moreover, we prioritized the identified success factors by using AHP methodology. We showed which HR success factors are critical compared to others and determined their criticality level locally and globally as well. The AHP and Fuzzy AHP prioritization approach was previously adopted by various other researchers in the same research domain [53-55].

7.3 Research Methodology

A systematic and scientific way of data compilation, analysis, verification, and validation of problem is called a research method. Methodology is an approach used to solve a specified problem. SLR is a method of searching out or solving an occurring research problem.

It provides guidelines for solving research issues with specific mechanisms like systematic process, task, method, tools, and techniques. In research methodology, according to the problems, different researchers use different criteria for solving problems and getting outcomes. Research methodology is classified into different types, which describe purpose of study, research design and nature of study. However, in our work we apply methodology in three phases. In phase-1 we use SLR for identification of CSFs that assist vendors in the selection of successful HR factors in outsourcing. In phase-2 we apply a questionnaire survey to validate SLR results. In phase-3 we apply AHP methodology for categorizing and prioritizing CSFs and finding their criticality level.

7.3.1 Systematic Literature Review

In online digital libraries, SLR is the best methodology for extracting data from existing literature. The main purpose of SLR is recognizing, estimating and understanding all available studies particular to the research questions, field and experience of significance [32]. However, a SLR is a secondary study [33, 34]. Khan *et al.* [35] adopted SLR methodology for extracting data. Khan *et al.* [36] used SLR in their research for extracting critical success factors and critical challenges. The advantage of using SLR over other traditional data extracting methodologies is that its results are perfect compared to others [37]. Khan and Keung [12] used SLR methodology for extraction of data in their research. Kitchenham *et al.* [38] used SLR methodology in software engineering on existing literature for data extraction. The main steps involved in the construction of SLR are planning, conducting and reporting [39]. Using the same SLR, we tried to sum up the related data for the numerical judgment about our results. We also tuned up these solutions to design an empirical study for the evaluation of SLR. We exactly followed the process and steps of a SLR procedure discussed by different researchers.

7.3.2 Search String Process

We followed the search string formation process of different researchers in [12, 24, 40].

- Research Question I:

  - **Success factors**: "success factors" OR "winner factors" OR "important factors" OR "sensational factors" OR "key factors".

  - **Vendors**: "Vendors" OR "suppliers" OR "contractors" OR "sellers" OR "organization" OR "associations" OR "company".

  - **Offshore software development outsourcing**: "offshore software development sourcing" OR "contractor software development outsourcing" OR "offshore software development.

- Research Question II:

  - **Vendor**: "vendor" OR "supplier" OR "contractor" OR "brokers" OR "sellers"

  - **Practices**: "practices" OR "outcomes" OR "Outputs" OR "manners" OR "results"

  Research Question I: (("outsourcing" OR "subcontracting") AND ("software outsourcing development") AND ("outsourcing model") AND ("success factor" OR "winner factor" OR "good factor" OR "important factor"))

Research Question I and II: (("Software outsourcing" OR "software outsourcing development" OR "Offshore software development outsourcing" OR "software subcontracting") AND (Vendor OR supplier OR Seller) AND ("success factor" OR "success reason" OR "Winner Factor") AND (Solution OR Solution OR Practice OR Practices OR advice) AND ("Human Resource"))

7.3.3   Search String Development

According to the research questions, we developed a search term and applied different types of digital libraries and online databases. We constructed a search string for the RQ1 and RQ2. Two libraries, i.e., Google Scholar and Science Direct, do not execute long search string, so we used a substring of this final search string. The second reason for a two-search string is that a single search string it is a very tiresome and time-consuming task. The search strings for research question 1 and 2 follow.

> (("Software outsourcing" OR "software outsourcing development" OR "Offshore software development outsourcing" OR "software subcontracting") AND (Vendor OR supplier OR Seller) AND ("success factor" OR "success reason" OR "Winner Factor") AND (Solution OR Solution OR Practice OR Practices OR advice) AND ("Human Resource"))

7.3.4   Selection of Publications

Basically, the initial selection of journal and article or research papers of publications takes place based on the abstract of the paper, keywords of paper, and the title of the paper. The result of this basic selection of papers are displayed in Table 7.1.

Table 7.1: Search outcomes of different resources/libraries and databases.

Resource to be search	Search result	Access	Primary selection	Final selection
Google Scholar				
Substring 1	112	91	39	18
Substring 2	23	14	13	1
Duplication			-07	-
Total	135	105	45	19
IEEE Explore	1423	1423	40	18
Emerlad insight	23	23	05	2
HEC Digital Library	187	160	16	3
Science Direct				
Substring 1	07	07	07	2
Substring 2	04	04	04	1
Duplication			-01	-
Total	11	11	10	03
Total	**2165**	**2108**	**117**	**45**

After the initial selection, we read out all selected papers by following inclusion criteria and exclusion criteria for the final selection of papers.

7.3.4.1 Inclusion Techniques

Inclusion techniques identify which part of the data extraction process should be included in the existing literature. We use criteria based on the study of the following main inclusion criteria to define which part of the literature will be used for the data extraction process. Our criteria for inclusion is base on the study of the following topics of the software engineering field:

- Offshore outsourcing

- Human resource offshore outsourcing

- Human resource outsourcing software development

- HR success factor in outsourcing

- HR success factors in outsourcing for vendors' perspective

- Global software development success factor related to our research question

- Confirm success factor related to HR outsourcing from vendors perspectives

Therefore, we include the research paper that consists of the English language and title, abstract, and keywords that are the same as our search string.

7.3.4.2 Exclusion Criteria

The reason for the exclusion process is that it ignores part of the literature which is not used for data extraction. Our process for exclusion is based on the study of the following:

- Is not related to outsourcing

- Does not fulfill our research question issues

- Is not the same title as our search string

- Is not the same abstract as our search string

- Is not the same keyword as our search string

- Does not fulfill the criteria of HR outsourcing success factors

- Research paper consists of other languages; not in the English language

7.3.4.3 Secondary Reviewer Support

As far as the initial or primary sources of choice are concerned, it's entirely based on only the assessment of the title, summary, and reserve words of different literature and research papers. For the final choice of a research paper, it only checks the results on specified defined criteria of inclusion and exclusion. If there are sometimes unconvinced conditions about inclusion and exclusion criteria then a secondary assessor calls for a review of the selected data.

7.3.5 Commencement of Data Extraction

After studying the primary selection of research papers data extraction phase, this part entirely studies the purpose of filling out the research questions. The following results were collected during this phase. The data extraction phase will start after studying primary selected publications and it will totally emphasize filling out our research questions. The following data will be collected during the data extraction phase. The details are displayed in the following Table 7.2.

Table 7.2: Details of extracted data.

P NO	Paper ID	Year	Continents	Organization Type	Paper Type	Methodology	Size	Database
1	GS-1	2011	Asia	Software development industry	Journal	SLR, Survey	Large	G.Scholar
2	GS-2	2014	Asia	Company	Journal	SLR, Survey	Large	G.Scholar
3	GS-3	2010	Asia	Software industry	Journal	Interview Survey	Large	G.Scholar
4	GS-5	2016	Asia	Company	Journal	Case study Survey	Large	G.Scholar
5	GS-6	2013	Asia	Software development industry	Journal	Interview, case study	Large	G.Scholar
6	GS(sii)-9	2018	Europe	Outsourcing Organization	Journal Research paper	Interview, Case Study	Large	G.Scholar
7	GS-15	2010	Africa	Marketing Organization	Research Conference	Interview Case Study	Large	G.Scholar
8	GS-21	2015	North America	Research institute Software development industry	Journal	Project life cycle ,Survey	Large	G.Scholar
9	GS-22	2011	Australia	Company	Thesis	Case Study, Survey	Small, Medium	G.Scholar
10	GS-26	2010	North America	Firm (Outsourcing Offshore)	Journal	Questionnaire Survey	Small, Medium	G.Scholar
11	GS-27	2015	Asia	Company	Conference	SLR Case Study	Small	G.Scholar
12	GS-36	2015	Asia	Software Development Industry	Research Article	SLR ,Survey ,Case Study	Large	G.Scholar
13	GS-41	2017	North America	Company	Journal	Interview Case study	Large	G.Scholar
14	GS-43	2004	Europe, Asia Mix	Software Industry	Article	Interview Survey	Large	G.Scholar
15	GS-49	2012	Europe	Company	Conference	Case Study	Large	G.Scholar
16	GS-54	2016	Europe	Outsourcing Company	Article	Interview Case Study	Large	G.Scholar
17	GS-57	2016	Asia	Outsourcing Firm	Thesis	Interview, Case study, Survey	Large	G.Scholar
18	GS-60	2016	North America	Software Industry	Journal	Questionnaire Survey	Large	G.Scholar
19	GS-80	2017	North America	Software Industry	Thesis	Case Study, Survey	Large	G.Scholar
20	IEEE-03	2009	Europe	Software Development Industry	Conference	Survey ,Interview	Large	IEEE
21	IEEE-07	2010	Asia	Software Development Industry	Conference	Agile Method	Small	IEEE
22	IEEE-10	2017	Asia	Industry	Journal	Interview, Case Study	Large	IEEE
23	IEEE-11	2011	Asia	Outsourcing Organization	Journal	Survey, Interview	Large	IEEE
24	IEEE-13	2006	Asia	IT Industry	Case Study	Case study	Large	IEEE
25	IEEE-17	2016	Asia	IT Outsourcing Industry	Journal	Interview Survey	Large	IEEE

P NO	Paper ID	Year	Continents	Organization Type	Paper Type	Methodology	Size	Database
26	IEEE-24	2018	Europe	Industry	Article	Case Study Survey	Large	IEEE
27	IEEE-38	2007	North America	Company	Journal	Case Study, Questionnaire	Large	IEEE
28	IEEE-44	2016	Asia	Software Developing Industry	Conference	SLR	Large	IEEE
29	IEEE-45	2018	Asia	Software Development, Organization	Article	SLR, Questionnaire Survey	large	IEEE
30	IEEE-48	2016	Asia	Software Industry	Article	SLR, Survey	Large	IEEE
31	IEEE-76	2006	Asia	Software Engineering Industry	Conference	Survey	Large	IEEE
32	IEEE-112	2002	North America	Industry	Journal Proceeding	Interview, Case Study	Small	IEEE
33	IEEE-128	2010	Asia	Company	Conference	SLR, Fuzzy linguistic Method	Large	IEEE
34	IEEE-325	2010	Australia	Company	Conference	Interview, Survey	Small, Large	IEEE
35	IEEE-359	2012	Europe	Company	Conference	SLR	Small Large	IEEE
36	Sci-Dii-02	2016	Europe	Business Industry	Conference	SLR	Large	Science, Direct
37	Sci-D-05	2008	Monmouth University (Europe)	GSD Industry	Advancement	Interview, Survey	Large	Science Direct
38	Sci-D-06	2009	Asia	IT Industry	Article	Questionnaire Survey	Large	Science Direct
39	HEC-12	2013	Europe	GSD Industry	Article	Interview, Survey	Large	HEC
40	HEC-25	2016	Asia	Company	Journal	SLR, Survey	Large	HEC
41	EMER-05	2005	Europe	IT Outsourcing Industry	Journal	Case Study, Survey	Large	Emerland
42	EMER-11	2002	North America	Global IT Outsourcing Firm	Journal	Case study, Survey	Large	Emerland
43	HEC-54	2012	Europe	Mobile APP Company	Journal	Interview, Case Study	Small	HEC
44	IEEE-52	2011	Asia	Software Development Industry	Journal	Questionnaire Survey	Medium	IEEE
45	IEEE-53	2017	Asia	IT Outsourcing Company	Conference	Questionnaire Survey	Small	IEEE

7.3.6   Result Generated for Research Questions through SLR by Applying Final Search String

By applying the final search string on five digital libraries, we collected the different number of research papers. Total search results contained 2165 research papers, total accessed 2108, primary selection 117 and final selection contain just 45 papers that are related to our research work. The details of the final selections of research papers and publications are mentioned above in Table 7.2.

We find 45 research papers in the final selection. In the first phase, we found 20 SFs after analyzing and synthesizing some of them merged the thirteen critical success factors that remain in our final selected success factors described in Table 7.3. By using the SPSS tool, we found percentage and frequency of every CSF cited in the table. The details of SFs are described as under. To answer RQ1 we found the results shown in Table 7.3. The 1st critical success factor (CSF) in our findings is "competence of vendor," its frequency is 23 out of 45, which means that the success factor repeats in the 45 papers 23 times. Its percentage is about 57% so we declare it a critical success factor because we include success factor as a critical when its percentage is greater than or equal to 36%.

The 2nd critical success factors in our research work are "well trained" and "technical capability"; the frequency of these success factors is 28 and percentage is 63%. The 3rd CSF is "good governance"; the frequency of this success factor is 17 and percentage is 38%. The 4th CSF is "proper procurement"; the frequency of this success factor is 32 and percentage is 72%. The 5th CSFs are "collaboration coordination" and "cooperation 3Cs"; the frequency of these success factors is 19 and percentage is 43%.

The 6th CSF is "effective communication"; the frequency of this success factor is 24 and percentage is 54%. The 7th CSF is "bidirectional transfer of knowledge (BTK) and exchange of knowledge"; the frequency of this success factor is 16 and percentage is 36%. The 8th CSF is "relationships enhancement"; the frequency of this success factor is 26 and percentage is 58%. The 9th CSF is "trust development"; the frequency of this success factor is 17 and percentage is 38%. The 10th CSF is "quality management"; the frequency of this success factor is 22 and percentage is 49%. The 11th CSF is "quality management"; the frequency of this success factor is 17 and percentage is 38%. The 12th CSF is "aware of standard"; the frequency of this success factor is 22 and percentage is 49%. The 13th CSF is "performance-based evaluation"; the frequency of this success factor is 22 and percentage is 49%. All the CSFs are explained below in Table 7.3.

Table 7.3: Synthesis of details of success factors.

Sr.No.	Group Name	Frequency N=45	Percentage %
1	Competence of vendor	23	52
2	Well trained and technical capability	28	63
3	Good Governance	17	38
4	Proper Procurement	32	72
5	Coordination, Cooperation and Collaboration 3Cs	19	43
6	Effective Communication	24	54
7	Bidirectional transfer of knowledge (BTK)	16	36
8	Relationships enhancement	26	58
9	Trust development	17	38
10	Innovative skill	22	49
11	Quality management	17	38
12	Aware of standards	22	49
13	Performance based evaluation	22	49

7.3.7 Categorization of Identified Success Factors

We listed the identified success factors in four groups. The investigation of success factors performed according to their group, which are shown in detail in Table 7.4. The questionnaire survey is based on the abovementioned success factors in the field of software development organizations. The identified success factors by SLR provide knowledge to the survey participants. The category-wise grouping of the success factors creates a strong structure that assists practitioners in the most critical area of the field and also assists vendors in the selection of successful HR factors.

Table 7.4: Success factors for software outsourcing human resource.

Sr. No.	Category of Success Factors	Success Factors
1	Procurement	Competence of vendor(SF-01)
		Well trained and technical capability(SF -02)
		Good Governance(SF -03)
		Proper Procurement(SF -04)
2	Organization	Coordination, cooperation and collaboration 3Cs (SF -05)
		Effective communication(SF -06)
		Bidirectional transfer of knowledge (BTK)' Exchange of Knowledge(SF -07)
3	Reliance	Relationships enhancement(SF -08)
		Trust development(SF -09)
		Innovative skill(SF -10)
4	Quality	Quality management(SF -11)
		Aware of standards(SF -12)
		Performance based evaluation(SF-13)

7.3.8 Analytical Hierarchical Process (AHP)

The most recent popular decision-making technique used is AHP. Saaty [41] is the developer of AHP and was the first to use this technique. After that, AHP has been used by various researchers in various fields for solving different complex decision-making problems [42]. We studied different research papers that used AHP methodology for analysis and prioritizing of SLR findings [43, 44]. The AHP methodology consists of the following three phases:

- Divide complex problem into a hierarchical structure shown in Figure 7.1.

- Find out the priority weight of each factor and its subfactor by using pairwise matrix comparison.

- Check the consistency of judgment.

The details of the above three phases are given below.

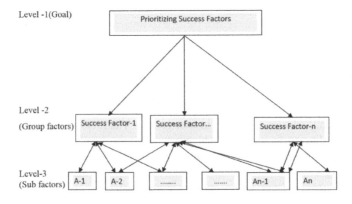

Figure 7.1: Division of complex problem into a hierarchical structure.

Phase-1: Decompose a complex decision problem into a hierarchical structure. In this phase, the complex problem is divided into hierarchical interconnected components [45]. The hierarchy of every success factor category contains a minimum of three phases, which are shown in Figure 7.1. The first phase describes the goal of the problem, the second phase shows the factors, and the third phase shows the subfactors of phase two.

Phase-2: Determine the priority weight of each factor and subfactor with the help of pairwise comparisons [46]. After performing the first phase in the second phase, the priority and weight are calculated by pairwise comparison decision matrix. The 9-point standardized comparison scaled in AHP is cited in Table 7.5. The pairwise comparison matrix is developed for every factor and its related subfactors.

Table 7.5: Description of 9-point scale for intensity of importance.

Definition	Intensity of Importance
Significant	1
Moderate significant	3
Very significant	5
Very strongly significant	7
Very extremely significant	9
Medium value	2,4,6,8

Suppose $C = \{C_j | j = 1, 2 \dots n\}$ where n is an evaluation factor and every element of the evaluation matrix A, i.e., $a_{ij}(i, j = 1, 2, .., n)$ represents its normalized relative weight, as illustrated in Equation (7.1).

$$A = \begin{bmatrix} 1 & a_{12} & \cdots & a_{1n} \\ a_{21} & 1 & \cdots & a_{2n} \\ \vdots & \vdots & \cdots & \vdots \\ a_{n1} & a_{n2} & \cdots & 1 \end{bmatrix} \tag{7.1}$$

where $a_{ij} = 1 a_{ij}, a_{ij} > 0$.

The weight vector w is identified using the characteristic equation, as shown in Equation (7.2).

$$Aw = \lambda maxw, \tag{7.2}$$

where A is the pairwise comparison matrix for the factor, w is the weight vector, and *max* is the largest Eigen value.

Phase-3: Test the consistency of the pairwise comparison matrix. In phase three, the pairwise matrix is consistent. The pairwise matrix consistency is found through the consistency index (CI) and consistency ratio (CR) with the help of Equation (7.3) and (7.4).

$$CI = \frac{(\lambda max - n)}{(n - 1)} \tag{7.3}$$

$$CR = \frac{CI}{RI} \tag{7.4}$$

where λ max is the maximum Eigen value of matrix A and n denotes the order of the factors. RI is the value of a random index of consistency, which has different values based on the number of factors, as listed in Table 7.6. The accepted value of CR is up to 0.10. If the calculated value of CR must be less than 0.10, then the priority vector (weight) of the factor is acceptable and we can conclude that matrix A has sufficient consistency. Otherwise, to improve the consistency, we repeat the evaluation procedure from Phase-1.

Table 7.6: Relationship between size of matrix and random consistency index.

Size of matrix	1	2	3	4
Random consistency index	0	0	0.025	0.087

7.4 Proposed Methodology

The final goal of this study is to find the success factors through SLR and prioritize them through AHP based on their significance [47, 48]. In our study, we prepared three phases. In the first phase we collected success factors using SLR; in the second phase the success factors were validated through a questionnaire survey; and in the third phase the success factors were prioritized through AHP.

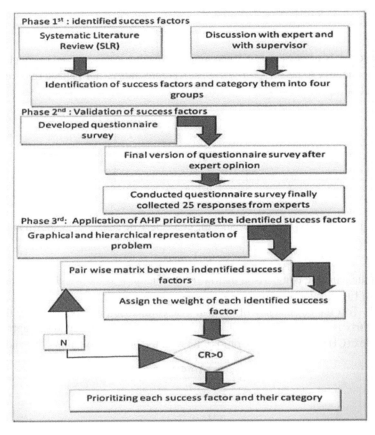

Figure 7.2: Schematic diagram of proposed research design of the analytic hierarchy process (AHP) consistency ratio.

We discarded many random expert selections and selected top expert software organizations, including DigiLynx, NESPAK, Arfa Karim Software House, Three C Technology, etc., from Pakistan. We identified the 13 success factors that are important for software outsourcing vendors and categorized them into 4 levels: Procurement, Organization, Reliance, and Quality. These categories of success factors are validated through a questionnaire survey by collecting the responses of 25 practitioners and their experience in the field of software outsourcing human resource environment. Finally, the method used for prioritizing was AHP.

The success factors were prioritized after performing pairwise matrix comparison of success factors. The following subsection describes the application of the proposed AHP methodology, on questionnaire survey findings for validating and prioritizing success factors.

7.4.1 Questionnaire Development

We found success factors through SLR and identified those success factors by questionnaire survey. Different researchers also preferred to use a questionnaire survey based on empirical study. Khan *et al.* [49] used this method for collecting responses of experts. The questionnaire survey contains 13 success factors and for every success factor five options are mentioned like strongly agree, agree, neutral, disagree, and strongly disagree. In the past, most of the researchers only used four options, but now they also use the option "neutral." Neutral plays a significant role in collecting responses of experts [50, 51]. When we requested a response on the questionnaire survey the participant guaranteed that the collected data would not be shared with any third party at any cost and that the survey raw data would only be used for research purposes.

7.4.2 Data Sources

The purpose of our study is to prioritize and evaluate the identifying success factors. It is very important in our research that we collect expert responses from different global software development (GSD) outsourcing organizations that have different experiences and designations. We collect questionnaire survey responses from different experts mostly through email and some responses were received through the post. Data was collected from November 2019 to December 2020. Our data collection process was completed six months later; data was received from a total of 25 experts and we managed the questionnaire survey responses manually. The responsibilities of the experts in the organizations included developer, manager, engineer and others in the last mixed category.

7.4.3 Validation of Identified Success Factors

The success factors were collected through SLR and validated through a questionnaire survey. The success factors are cited below in Table 7.7. The table is divided into three columns labeled positive, negative and neutral: the positive column contains the success factors that belong to the strongly agree and agree options; the negative column contains the success factors that belong to the disagree and strongly disagree options; and the neutral category contains the neutral results.

The category of positive option in Table 7.7 describes the percentage of responses of questionnaire survey experts who agree with the success factors identified through SLR. The negative category contains the expert responses of those who do not agree with our identified success factors. The neutral category contains the expert responses of those whose feelings are neither negative or positive. In the positive category in Table 7.7, the success factors contain a greater than or equal to 45% score in the positive category. These success factors are applicable for further analysis.

Table 7.7: Success factors identified in the questionnaire study.

Sr.No.	Success Factors	Positive				Neutral		Negative		
		SA	A	Total	%	Total	%	DA	SDA	%
SF-01	Competence of vendors	12	8	20	80	2	8	3	0	12
SF-02	Well trained and technical capability	20	5	25	100	0	0	0	0	0
SF-03	Good Governance	13	9	22	88	2	8	1	0	4
SF-04	Proper Procurement	18	7	25	100	0	0	0	0	0
SF-05	Coordination, Cooperation and Collaboration 3Cs	13	4	17	68	3	12	5	1	20
SF-06	Effective communication	18	6	24	96	1	4	0	0	0
SF-07	Bidirectional Transfer of Knowledge (BTK)'Exchange of Knowledge	9	3	12	48	4	16	9	0	36
SF-08	Relationship enhancement	5	14	19	76	2	8	4	0	16
SF-09	Trust development	19	6	25	100	0	0	0	0	0
SF-10	Innovative skill	17	6	23	92	0	0	0	0	0
SF-11	Quality management	10	13	23	92	1	4	1	0	4
SF-12	Aware of standards	15	9	24	96	1	4	0	0	0
SF-13	Performance based evaluation	11	5	16	64	4	16	5	0	20

7.4.4 Application of AHP to Prioritize Success Factors

For prioritizing identified success factors, we use the AHP method described below in detail.

- Step 1. The grouping of success factors and their subfactors are identified in this first step.

- Step 2. In this step, we divided our problem into pictorial and hierarchical structures, level one, level two, and level three, respectively.

- Step 3. The comparison of each success factor and each category was conducted in this step. Table 7.5 displays the scale values and Tables 7.8, 7.10, 7.12 and 7.14 present comparisons and display results. The priority vector of each success factor is listed group-wise in Tables 7.9, 7.11, 7.13, and 7.15. All priority vector sums are equal to -1. These vectors show the relative weight of success subfactors.

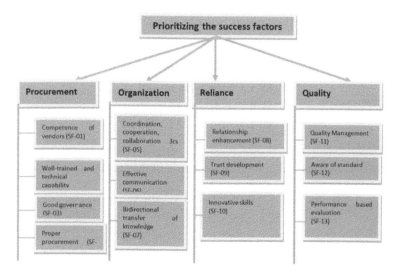

Figure 7.3: Hierarchical structure of the present study for the analytic hierarchy process (AHP) method.

Table 7.8: Pairwise comparison matrix between the success factors of the "procurement" category.

SF- No	SF-1	SF-2	SF-3	SF-4
SF-1	1	5	0.25	2
SF-2	0.33	1	4	0.25
SF-3	0.5	2	1	6
SF-4	0.25	0.33	0.5	1

Table 7.9: Synthesized or normalized matrix of the "procurement" category.

SF- No	SF-1	SF-2	SF-3	SF-4	Priority Vector (Weight)
SF-1	0.48	0.6	0.04	0.22	0.335
SF-2	0.16	0.12	0.7	0.03	0.251
SF-3	0.24	0.24	0.17	0.65	0.326
SF-4	0.12	0.04	0.09	0.11	0.089
					$\sum = 1.00$

Used short forms:

- CI: consistency index ($CI = 0.078$);

- CR: consistency ratio ($RI = 0.9$);

- RI: random consistency index ($CR = 0.09 < 0.1$ [Consistency is OK]).

- $\lambda_{max} = 4.175$;

Table 7.10: Pairwise comparison matrix between the success factors of the "organization" category.

SF- No	SF-5	SF-6	SF-7
SF-5	1	0.2	2
SF-6	5	1	6
SF-7	0.5	0.17	1

Table 7.11: Synthesized or normalized matrix of the "organization" category.

SF- No	SF-5	SF-6	SF-7	Priority Vector (Weight)
SF-5	0.15	0.15	0.22	0.174
SF-6	0.77	0.73	0.67	0.723
SF-7	0.08	0.12	0.11	0.103
				$\sum = 1.00$

Used short forms:

- CI: consistency index $(CI = 0.015)$;

- CR: consistency ratio $(RI = 0.58)$;

- RI: random consistency index $(CR = 0.03 < 0.1$ [Consistency is OK]).

- $\lambda_{max} = 3.029$;

Table 7.12: Pairwise comparison matrix between the success factors of the "reliance" category.

SF- No	SF-08	SF-09	SF-10
SF-08	1	0.25	3
SF-09	4	1	7
SF-10	0.33	0.14	1

Table 7.13: Synthesized or normalized matrix of the "reliance" category.

SF- No	SF-08	SF-09	SF-10	Priority Vector (Weight)
SF-08	0.19	0.18	0.27	0.213
SF-09	0.75	0.72	0.64	0.701
SF-10	0.06	0.1	0.09	0.085
				$\sum = 1.00$

Used short forms:

- CI: consistency index $(CI = 0.016)$;

- CR: consistency ratio $(RI = 0.58)$;

- RI: random consistency index ($CR = 0.03 < 0.1$ [Consistency is OK]).
- $\lambda_{max} = 3.033$;

Table 7.14: Pairwise comparison matrix between the success factors of the "reliance" category.

SF- No	SF-11	SF-12	SF-13
SF-11	1	0.95	3
SF-12	0.33	1	5
SF-13	0.5	0.2	1

Table 7.15: Synthesized or normalized matrix of the "quality" category.

SF- No	SF-11	SF-12	SF-13	Priority Vector (Weight)
SF-11	0.55	0.44	0.33	0.441
SF-12	0.18	0.47	0.56	0.4
SF-13	0.27	0.09	0.11	0.159
				$\sum = 1.00$

Used short forms:

- CI: consistency index ($CI = 0.031$);
- CR: consistency ratio ($RI = 0.58$);
- RI: random consistency index ($CR = 0.05 < 0.1$ [Consistency is OK]).
- $\lambda_{max} = 3.062$;

Table 7.16: Pairwise comparison matrix between the categories of success factors.

Categories	Procurement	Organization	Reliance	Quality
Procurement	1	0.65	2	3
Organization	0.33	1	4	8
Reliance	0.5	2	1	6
Quality	0.25	0.33	0.5	1

Table 7.17: Synthesized or normalized matrixes of the categories of success factors.

Categories	Procurement	Organization	Reliance	Quality	Priority Vector (Weight)
Procurement	0.48	0.16	0.27	0.17	0.269
Organization	0.16	0.25	0.53	0.44	0.347
Reliance	0.24	0.5	0.13	0.33	0.302
Quality	0.12	0.08	0.07	0.06	0.081
					$\sum = 1.00$

Used short forms:

- CI: consistency index ($CI = 0.084$);

- CR: consistency ratio ($RI = 0.9$);

- RI: random consistency index ($CR = 0.09 < 0.1$ [Consistency is OK]).

- $\lambda_{max} = 4.24$;

In Table 7.17 above, we identified the value of consistency of ratio (CR) that is less than 0.1 and declared it to be an accepted priority of the success factors. Likewise, we also identified the priority of vector for all remaining success factors. The detail of these priority vector results are shown in Tables 7.9, 7.11, 7.13, 7.15, and 7.17.

- Step 4. Table 7.18, column 4, shows the local weight of success factors and their corresponding category ranking, and the particular success factors and category ranking are shown in Table 7.18, column 5.

Table 7.18: Summary of local and global weights issues and their rankings.

Category	Weight of categories	Critical Success Factors	Local Weight	Local Ranking	Global Weight	Global Ranking
Procurement	0.269	SF-01	0.335	5	0.0901	3
		SF-02	0.251	7	0.0675	5
		SF-03	0.326	6	0.0876	4
		SF-04	0.089	12	0.0239	12
Organization	0.347	SF-05	0.174	9	0.0603	7
		SF-06	0.723	1	0.2508	1
		SF-07	0.103	11	0.03574	8
Reliance	0.302	SF-08	0.213	8	0.0643	6
		SF-09	0.701	2	0.2117	2
		SF-10	0.085	13	0.0256	11
Quality	0.081	SF-11	0.441	3	0.03572	9
		SF-12	0.400	4	0.0324	10
		SF-13	0.159	10	0.0128	13

- Step 5. In this step we identified the global weight of success factors for final ranking of success factors by using AHP; for example, the weight of success factor SF-01 (0.0901), SF-02 (0.0675), SF-03 (0.0876), etc., cited in Table 7.18, column 6.

- Step 6. In this final step, a total of 13 success factors are prioritized and categorized according to weight. In this step, we find which success factor is very important among all of the 13 success factors of the software outsourcing human resource model. Table 7.18, column 6, shows that the success factor SF-06 is extremely important.

7.4.5 Comparison of Proposed Framework

The identified success factors of AHP-based prioritization framework for software outsourcing human resource are compared in Table 7.13. Shrivastava and Rathod [52] identified risk factors and compared them in their research; therefore, like these, we compare success factors of the proposed framework. In their research, they identified the factors that negatively affect software development. However, in our research, we identified success factors that affect positively on software outsourcing development activities.

Table 7.19: Prioritizing the success factors.

Sr. No.	Name of Success Factors	Priority
SF-06	Effective communication	1.00
SF-09	Trust development	2.00
SF-01	Competence of vendors	3.00
SF-03	Good Governance	4.00
SF-02	Well trained and technical capability	5.00
SF-08	Relationship enhancement	6.00
SF-05	Coordination, Cooperation and Collaboration 3Cs	7.00
SF-07	Bidirectional Transfer of Knowledge (BTK)'Exchange of Knowledge	8.00
SF-11	Quality management	9.00
SF-12	Aware of standards	10.00
SF-10	Innovative skill	11.00
SF-04	Proper Procurement	12.00
SF-13	Performance based evaluation	13.00

7.5 Limitations

This study is conducted using the SLR approach and the two major study limitations are given below.

- Internal validity: Some authors may not give the valid reasons behind critical success factors that arise during software outsourcing human resources.

- External validity: In the questionnaire survey and case study, there may be a lack of interest of participants due to their busy schedules or responsibilities. There is also a chance that we have missed some of the key points in the literature review process.

7.6 Implications of the Study

Implementation of our research work is very useful for both practitioners and researchers. Our study proposed a framework based on 13 success factors identified through SLR and validated by a questionnaire survey, prioritizing through the AHP methodology. This research may help researchers imitate the AHP method in their research work for evaluating the ranking of issues based on their importance. The findings of this study have real-world industrial implications for vendor organizations. Similarly, the researchers could replicate the study findings and conduct the future studies in the same research domain. Moreover, AHP methodology can be used for complex and group decision-making problems that will help researchers evaluate the success factors ranking based on their importance.

7.7 Conclusions and Future Work

Mostly offshore software development vendors are faced with many problems when selecting successful HR for successful software development projects. We identified 13 critical success factors through SLR to evaluate these success factors with the input from 25 practitioners who participated in the questionnaire survey. Next, the ranking of success factors was performed through AHP on the responses of experts. The results of this study show that the "effective communication" success factor belongs to the most critical category, "organization" the second most critical success factor, and "trust development" belongs to "reliance," which assists vendors in selecting successful HR. Many researchers in the past have identified HR success factors and HR challenges; however, no such model like our model assists vendors for the selection of HR success factors from the vendor's perspective through AHP methodology.

In future work our research aims to develop a model that may assist GSD vendors for the selection of successful HR. To enhance our study, researchers need to identify additional success factors for software outsourcing human resources by conducting the SLR to get different results by the selection of a large sample size in the questionnaire survey. Our work is based on critical success factors; for future work, researchers need to take the critical challenges and best practices from these challenges and success factors.

References

1. Ahmad, J., Khan, A. W., & Qasim, I. (2018). Software Outsourcing Cost Estimation Model (SOCEM). A Systematic Literature Review Protocol. *University of Sindh Journal of Information and Communication Technology*, 2(1), 25-30.

2. Azeem, M. I., & Khan, S. U. (2011, December). Intercultural challenges in offshore software development outsourcing relationships: A systematic literature review protocol. In *2011 Malaysian Conference in Software Engineering* (pp. 475-480). IEEE.

3. Gautam, D. K. (2015). Strategic integration of HRM for organizational performance: Nepalese reality. *South Asian Journal of Global Business Research*.

4. Abdul-Halim, H., Ee, E., Ramayah, T., & Ahmad, N. H. (2014). Human resource outsourcing success: leveraging on partnership and service quality. *Sage Open*, 4(3), 2158244014545475.

5. Kodwani, A. D. (2007). Human resource outsourcing: Issues and challenges. *Journal of Nepalese Business Studies*, 4(1), 38-46.

6. Usman, A., & Khan, A. W. (2018). Software outsourcing quality challenges model systematic literature review (SLR) protocol. *University of Sindh Journal of Information and Communication Technology*, 2(4), 196-201.

7. Khan, S. U., Niazi, M., & Ahmad, R. (2011). Factors influencing clients in the selection of offshore software outsourcing vendors: An exploratory study using a systematic literature review. *Journal of Systems and Software*, 84(4), 686-699.

8. Fjermestad, J., & Saitta, J. A. (2005). A strategic management framework for IT outsourcing: A review of the literature and the development of a success factors model. *Journal of Information Technology Case and Application Research*, 7(3), 42-60.

9. Khan, S. U., Niazi, M., & Ahmad, R. (2010, June). Critical success factors for offshore software development outsourcing vendors: an empirical study. In *International Conference on Product Focused Software Process Improvement* (pp. 146-160). Springer, Berlin, Heidelberg.

10. Ali, S., & Khan, S. U. (2016). Software outsourcing partnership model: An evaluation framework for vendor organizations. *Journal of Systems and Software*, 117, 402-425.

11. Khan, A. W., & Khan, S. U. (2013). Critical success factors for offshore software outsourcing contract management from vendors' perspective: an exploratory study using a systematic literature review. *IET Software*, 7(6), 327-338.

12. Khan, A. A., & Keung, J. (2016). Systematic review of success factors and barriers for software process improvement in global software development. *IET Software*, 10(5), 125-135.

13. Khan, A. A., Keung, J., Hussain, S., Niazi, M., & Tamimy, M. M. I. (2017). Understanding software process improvement in global software development: a theoretical framework of human factors. *ACM SIGAPP Applied Computing Review*, 17(2), 5-15.

14. Alam, A. U., Khan, S. U., & Ali, I. (2012). Knowledge sharing management risks in outsourcing from various continents perspective: a systematic literature review. *International Journal of Digital Content Technology and Its Applications*, 6(21), 27.

15. McCracken, M., & McIvor, R. (2013). Transforming the HR function through outsourced shared services: insights from the public sector. *The International Journal of Human Resource Management*, 24(8), 1685-1707.

16. Keegan, A., & Francis, H. (2010). Practitioner talk: the changing textscape of HRM and emergence of HR business partnership. The *International Journal of Human Resource Management*, 21(6), 873-898.

17. Savolainen, P., Ahonen, J. J., & Richardson, I. (2012). Software development project success and failure from the supplier's perspective: A systematic literature review. *International Journal of Project Management*, 30(4), 458-469.

18. Keele, S. (2007). Guidelines for performing systematic literature reviews in software engineering (Vol. 5). *Technical Report*, Ver. 2.3 EBSE Technical Report. EBSE. Software Engineering Group School of Computer Science and Mathematics Keele University Keele, Staffs ST5 5BG, UK. p. 65.

19. Noroz, A. K., Khan, S. U., Alam, A. U., & Alam, S. U. Multi-Sourcing Human Resource Management from Vendor's Perspective: A Systematic Literature Review Protocol.

20. Khan, S. U., Niazi, M., & Ahmad, R. (2009, July). Critical success factors for offshore software development outsourcing vendors: A systematic literature review. In *2009 Fourth IEEE International Conference on Global Software Engineering* (pp. 207-216). IEEE.

21. Ali, S., Hongqi, L., Khan, S. U., Zhongguo, Y., & Liping, Z. (2017). Success factors for software outsourcing partnership management: An exploratory study using systematic literature review. *IEEE Access*, 5, 23589-23612.

22. Vizcaíno, A., García, F., Villar, J. C., Piattini, M., & Portillo, J. (2013). Applying Q-methodology to analyse the success factors in GSD. *Information and Software Technology*, 55(7), 1200-1211.

23. Khan, S. U., Niazi, M., & Ahmad, R. (2012). Empirical investigation of success factors for offshore software development outsourcing vendors. *IET Software*, 6(1), 1-15.

24. Ahmad, J., Khan, A. W., & Qasim, I. (2018). Software Outsourcing Cost Estimation Model (SOCEM). A Systematic Literature Review Protocol. *University of Sindh Journal of Information and Communication Technology*, 2(1), 25-30.

25. J. D. Lilly, M. V., D. A. Gray (2015). Investigation of success factors for offshore software development outsourcing vendors. San Jose State University SJSU ScholarWorks, January, p.20.

26. Niazi, M., Mahmood, S., Alshayeb, M., Qureshi, A. M., Faisal, K., & Cerpa, N. (2016). Toward successful project management in global software development. *International Journal of Project Management*, 34(8), 1553-1567.

27. Rashid, N., & Khan, S. U. (2015). Green agility for global software development vendors: A systematic literature review protocol. *Proceedings of the Pakistan Academy of Sciences*, 52(4), 301-313.

28. Yang, Y. H., & Tamir, G. (2015). Offshore software project management: mapping project success factors. *International Journal of Project Organisation and Management*, 7(2), 111-131.

29. Abdulkader, Z. (2016). A study on how outsourcing creates challenges and issues to the human resource in an organisation, a case study on Dell Ireland (Doctoral dissertation, Human Resources Management, Dublin Business School).

30. Khan, A. A., Keung, J. W., & Abdullah-Al-Wadud, M. (2017). SPIIMM: toward a model for software process improvement implementation and management in global software development. *IEEE Access*, 5, 13720-13741.

31. Wibisono, Y. W., Govindaraju, R., Irianto, D., & Sudirman, I. (2016, December). Interaction capability, process quality, and outsourcing success: A vendor perspective in offshore IT outsourcing. In *2016 IEEE International Conference on Industrial Engineering and Engineering Management (IEEM)* (pp. 1780-1784). IEEE.

32. Siddaway, A. (2014). What is a systematic literature review and how do I do one. University of Stirling, 1(1): p. 1-13.

33. Keele, S. (2007). Guidelines for performing systematic literature reviews in software engineering (Vol. 5). *Technical Report*, Ver. 2.3 EBSE Technical Report. EBSE.

34. Kitchenham, B., Pretorius, R., Budgen, D., Brereton, O. P., Turner, M., Niazi, M., & Linkman, S. (2010). Systematic literature reviews in software engineering–a tertiary study. *Information and Software Technology*, 52(8), 792-805.

35. Khan, A. W., & Imran, M. (2017, August). A Comparative Study of Critical Challenges of Outsourcing Contract Management Identified through SLR and Empirical Study. In *Proceedings of the International Conference on Advances in Image Processing* (pp. 161-164).

36. Khan, A. A., Keung, J., Hussain, S., Niazi, M., & Kieffer, S. (2018). Systematic literature study for dimensional classification of success factors affecting process improvement in global software development: client–vendor perspective. *IET Software*, 12(4), 333-344.

37. Fernández-Alemán, J. L., Señor, I. C., Lozoya, P. Á. O., & Toval, A. (2013). Security and privacy in electronic health records: A systematic literature review. *Journal of Biomedical Informatics*, 46(3), 541-562.

38. Kitchenham, B., Brereton, O. P., Budgen, D., Turner, M., Bailey, J., & Linkman, S. (2009). Systematic literature reviews in software engineering–a systematic literature review. *Information and Software Technology*, 51(1), 7-15.

39. Okoli, C., & Schabram, K. (2010). A guide to conducting a systematic literature review of information systems research.

40. Salam, M., & Khan, S. U. (2016, August). Developing green and sustainable software: Success factors for vendors. In *2016 7th IEEE International Conference on Software Engineering and Service Science (ICSESS)* (pp. 1059-1062). IEEE.

41. Saaty, T.L. (1988). What is the analytic hierarchy process?, in Mathematical models for decision support. Springer. p. 109-121.

42. Chatzimouratidis, A., Theotokas, I., & Lagoudis, I. N. (2012). Decision support systems for human resource training and development. The *International Journal of Human Resource Management*, 23(4), 662-693.

43. Nurhayati, S. (2019, November). Application of Computer-assisted Analytic Hierarchy Process Method to Evaluate Employee Performance. In *IOP Conference Series: Materials Science and Engineering* (Vol. 662, No. 2, p. 022033). IOP Publishing.

44. Hussain, M., Khan, H. U., Khan, A. W., & Khan, S. U. (2021). Prioritizing the Issues extracted for Getting Right People on Right Project in Software Project Management From Vendors' Perspective. *IEEE Access*, 9, 8718-8732.

45. Badri, M. A. (2001). A combined AHP-GP model for quality control systems. *International Journal of Production Economics*, 72(1), 27-40.

46. Albayrak, E., & Erensal, Y. C. (2004). Using analytic hierarchy process (AHP) to improve human performance: An application of multiple criteria decision making problem. *Journal of Intelligent Manufacturing*, 15(4), 491-503.

47. Bozbura, F. T., Beskese, A., & Kahraman, C. (2007). Prioritization of human capital measurement indicators using fuzzy AHP. *Expert Systems with Applications*, 32(4), 1100-1112.

48. Akbar, M. A., Khan, A. A., Khan, A. W., & Mahmood, S. (2020). Requirement change management challenges in GSD: An analytical hierarchy process approach. *Journal of Software: Evolution and Process*, 32(7), e2246.

49. Khan, A. A., Keung, J., Niazi, M., Hussain, S., & Ahmad, A. (2017). Systematic literature review and empirical investigation of barriers to process improvement in global software development: Client–vendor perspective. *Information and Software Technology*, 87, 180-205.

50. Niazi, M., Mahmood, S., Alshayeb, M., Riaz, M. R., Faisal, K., Cerpa, N., ... & Richardson, I. (2016). Challenges of project management in global software development: A client-vendor analysis. *Information and Software Technology*, 80, 1-19.

51. Khan, A. W., Hussain, I., & Zamir, M. (2020). Analytic hierarchy process-based prioritization framework for vendor's reliability challenges in global software development. *Journal of Software: Evolution and Process*, e2310.

52. Shrivastava, S. V., & Rathod, U. (2015). Categorization of risk factors for distributed agile projects. *Information and Software Technology*, 58, 373-387.

53. Khan, A. A., Shameem, M., Nadeem, M., & Akbar, M. A. (2021). Agile trends in Chinese global software development industry: Fuzzy AHP based conceptual mapping. Applied Soft Computing, 102, 107090.

54. Khan, A. A., & Shameem, M. (2020). Multicriteria decision-making taxonomy for DevOps challenging factors using analytical hierarchy process. *Journal of Software: Evolution and Process*, 32(10), e2263. DOI: 10.1002/smr.2263

55. Khan, A. A., Shameem, M., Kumar, R. R., Hussain, S., & Yan, X. (2019). Fuzzy AHP based prioritization and taxonomy of software process improvement success factors in global software development. Applied Soft Computing, 83, 105648.

8

A Process Framework for the Classification of Security Bug Reports

Shahid Hussain

Department of Computer and Information Science, University of Oregon, Eugene, Oregon, USA
Email: shussain@uoregon.edu

Abstract

Numerous organizations keep records of bug reports ruled by different types of sources. For example, in the context of software development, bugs are reported by developers, designers, testers and end users. Various studies have been performed to introduce models for the identification of security-related bugs; however, the number of security-related bug reports are misclassified due to their small ratio as compared to non-security bug reports due to the presence of security-related keywords in non-security bug reports, which might increase the time and efforts of bug engineers. In order to mitigate this issue, we have proposed a methodology to identify the important security-related keywords from the security-related bug report (SBR) and remove these keywords from non-security bug reports (NSBR) to improve the classification decisions. Firstly, the proposed method is evaluated with state-of-the-art feature selection methods to increase the classifier's performance. Secondly, the classifier's performance is evaluated to decrease the false positive rate (FPR) of classifiers via proposed method. The promising results indicate the significance of the proposed methodology in terms of effective identification of the bug security report.

Keywords: Bug reports, odd ratio, classification, performance

8.1 Introduction

In order to maintain software products, there is a strong need to continually assess the system and integrate changes based on user needs and demands. A bug tracking system (BTS) does this by allowing users to report bugs when using software products. This allows developers to improve the system to be less vulnerable and error-free. Bug fixing is one of the most important parts of software maintenance for client satisfaction. There are various types of bug reports reported in the BTS, but the most critical ones are those that are related to security. A security bug report (SBR) is a system security loophole that can be easily exploited; therefore, it is important to find and repair SBR [1]. Bug detection is a key concern in the current era, as we have seen a number of security breach incidents, such as the Equifax data breach, which compromised the privacy of millions of Americans [2], and the Careem ride application data breach, which affected 14 million people [3].

Over the past few years, detecting security bugs has attracted the attention of the research community, which is working on helping bug engineers immediately identify and resolve safety-related bugs. In this respect, different text-based predictive models have been developed [4-6]. These models are intended to effectively identify and classify a security bug report. However, they face the issue of misclassification of SBRs as NSBRS. There are two major reasons why SBRs are mislabeled. The first is the issue of class imbalance, because SBRs are less numerous than NSBRs in the corpus. The second reason is the lack of familiarity with the security domain, i.e., the presence of security crosswords. Security crosswords are security-related keywords that present both SBR and SNRB. Previous studies have attempted to address the misclassification issue by extracting relevant keywords and frequencies from the corpus terms [7, 8]. They used these word frequencies as features to train machine learning (ML) algorithms.

However, these studies gave rise to an increased rate of false positives. All previous studies lack in-depth exploration of security crosswords (presence of security-related keywords in SBR and NSBR). In [9], the authors introduced a bug report prediction model by first identifying the security-related keywords and then scoring them using different support functions. However, their research focused on keyword occurrences rather than their relevance to each class. We replicated the FARSEC study [9] and proposed to improve it by using a different and improved bi-normal separation (BNS) scoring method for security-related keywords. The scoring process for keywords in FARSEC has certain limitations, such as:

- It adds bias towards the SBR class by using support functions to reduce the false positive rate. However, this may lead to ignoring the relevance of words with their labels and effect the discriminating ability to select features that are very relevant.

- Scoring is based on the frequency of occurrence of words, which is not the correct indicator of keyword importance due to the tagging class as FARSEC has not considered the context of the presence of security crosswords in SBR and NSBR.

- This leads to function redundancy because functions were extracted from a subset of data.

We have overcome this problem by proposing a method for scoring keywords using the feature selection technique known as BNS. The contributions contained in this document are:

- Automatic retrieval of security-relevant keywords.

- Scoring these security-related keywords using a more effective and improved BNS feature selection method.

- BNS has helped us to get rid of the redundancy of features and gives unique keywords that are very impactful for efficient classification.

- The SNB technique has helped to combat class imbalance because the model is formed only on characteristics that are strongly related to the positive class and produces correct classification results.

- Scoring of each bug report according to key word score.

- Removed NSBRs having words present in keywords in order to remove false positive cases.

- Prediction models are constructed using the most appropriate features.

- The results showed that extracting important safety keywords significantly improved the results both in terms of classification and in terms of reducing the rate of false positives.

We used the publicly available bug report data from five projects, i.e., one from Chromium projects and four from Apache projects (Ambari, Derby, Camel and Wicket). The total number of bug reports amounts to approximately 45,940. The dataset is highly imbalanced as only 0.8% of the bug reports are related to the security class. The formulated research questions are as follows:

- **Research Question 1** (RQ1): How is the proposed methodology effective in constructing an effective model since SBR data is very small compared to NSBR data?

- **Research Question 2** (RQ2): How is the proposed methodology effective in addressing the issue of cross-security words that are present in the NSBR and contributing to the misclassification of SBR?

The remainder of this chapter is organized as follows: Related research is presented in Section 8.2, the system model is provided in Section 8.3, and Section 8.4 outlines the proposed regime's results.

8.2   Related Work

8.2.1   Text Mining for Security Bug Report Prediction

Security bug report tracking system analyzes a large number of security reports. One of the important tasks is to identify security bug reports and classify them as security and non-security related. Goseva-Popstojanova and Tyo [7] proposed a supervised as well as unsupervised automated algorithm for rating security bug reports. Both approaches employ three kinds of feature vectors. This approach analyzes the effect of different classifiers and the varying size of training data in the supervised technique. It also investigates the unsupervised domain in context of anomaly detection. The evaluation was carried out on three NASA datasets. Though it is high-performing, it does not take into account security words that are not present in the vocabulary and also requires labeling of test data.

In [9], the authors introduced the IDF N-gram technique that extracts the keyword from any length and these keywords can be used as features. Its performance was better than thematic modeling models, but only a small number of domain-specific datasets were tested and the performance changed as the number of grams changed. In their study [12], the authors used several types of characteristics, i.e., meta-characteristics and textual characteristics, for automatically identifying the security bug report. The extracted multi-type functionality is then used to predict bug reports. In [9], the authors introduced a bug report prediction template by first identifying relevant security-related keywords using the scoring method and then removing the NSBRs having these security crosswords in order to decrease the false positive rate. However, their study was based on the presence of security-related keywords and did not consider the optimal way to select a key word as a security crossword. To overcome this problem, we have proposed a framework that automatically extracts safety-related keywords and these keywords are scaled using bi-normal separation (BNS).

8.2.2 Machine Learning Algorithms-Based Prediction

Our research uses a Naïve Bayes classifier and this algorithm uses Bayes' theorem. Moreover, it predicts the class according to the probability of a data instance related to this particular class.

8.2.3 Bi-Normal Separation for Feature Selection

Feature selection is one of the most important factors to boost the performance of the classifier. The most relevant and robust features will affect the best performance of the classifier. There are different types of feature selection techniques, including filter techniques, wrap techniques and embedded techniques. This study implemented various feature selection techniques on the textual data and the results showed that BNS has the second best performance on short document data [13, 14, 25].

In this study, the authors have indicated that BNS is the most feasible feature selection technique when the data is highly biased. A recent study has also shown that BNS outperforms TF-IDF in textual analysis [16]. Keep this research in mind and analyze it since our document data is short and the data set is heavily biased. We took advantage of the BNS feature selection technique to score safety keywords. Scaling BNS helps us understand the underlying context and appropriateness of safety-related keywords for each class. As a result of this stage, we get very important and influential security-related keywords and these keywords are treated as functionalities to train classifiers.

8.3 Proposed Methodology

Figure 8.1 illustrates the proposed system design. It is an extension of [9] and the steps involved are given in subsection 8.3.1.

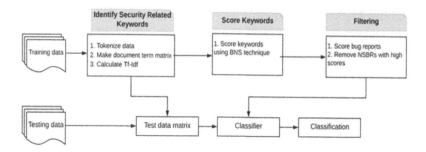

Figure 8.1: Proposed system model.

8.3.1 Data Gathering and Preprocessing

- **Data Gathering**: We collected bug report data from the publicly available Chromium project as well as 4 Apache projects (Ambari, Wicket, Camel and Derby). These datasets are highly imbalanced in terms of the number of security bug reports and are much less numerous than non-security bug reports. That makes a total of 45940 bug reports.

- **Text Preprocessing**: Pre-processing text is the key to extracting text. It not only reduces the size of the document file, but it also cleans up the text by deleting useless data like punctuations, links, numbers and so on. In addition, the data are prepared to form the classifiers used in the proposed study. The pre-processing of texts considerably improves the results of the classification. We used the Scikit library [22] to carry out the pre-processing. The steps involved are:

- **Tokenization**: This is the method by which the phrase or text is divided into small pieces called tokens. These tokens can consist of words, characters and even phrases, which become inputs to the text mining algorithm. Tokenization helps to explore the document in the form needed for mining.

- **Text Cleaning**: It consists of filtering the text by deleting figures, punctuations, stop words and unnecessary data. Stop words are common words that occur but are not important and used to form the sentence structure, such as a, and, the, in, about, etc. They have to be taken out of the text.

- **Text Lemmatization**: This is the phenomenon where words that are morphologically linked are considered to be a single word. It groups together words that relate to a common word, noun or verb and treats them as a single word.

- **Text Stemming**: This is one of the most widely used and common approaches to text preprocessing. The idea of stem is to cut out words that are made by stretching a specific root word.

8.3.2 Identifying Security-Related Keywords

In this subsection, we explain how security-related keywords are identified from the corpus.

- **Tokenization**: This is the process of converting text into little chunks (words) called tokens.

- **Weighting Method**: We employed term frequency-inverse document frequency (TF-IDF) weighting methods. It filters words associated with a document. We used TF-IDF to get a list of security-relevant keywords.

- **Indexing**: We used the document-term matrix for indexing, where rows refer to bug reports while columns are the security-related keywords obtained in the previous step.

8.3.3 Scoring Keywords

The security keywords obtained in the previous section are now scored in accordance with Algorithm 8.1 proposed using the BNS scale. This step makes it possible to identify the underlying context of the security crossword. Each security keyword will be checked against the SBR and NSBR. If the keyword gets high scores against the SBR class, it means that the keyword is very influential and important for the SBR class. Furthermore, this keyword will act as a security crossword in NSBR. NSBR with security crosswords will be eliminated to decrease the rate of false positives.

Algorithm 8.1. Keywords Scoring.

Require: $KW_1, \ldots KW_N$
Here *KW* is the set of security related keywords
Ensure: KeywordScores
Function **RETURNSCORES** (SBR, N SBR, KW)
BEGIN

- Here SBR is the security bug report data, NSBR is the non-security bug report data and KW is the set of security related keywords
- tp: number of positive cases with word
- tn: number of positive cases without word
- fp: number of negative cases with word
- fn: number of negative cases without word
- pos: positives/all
- neg: negatives/all
- tpr: tp/pos true positive ratio
- fpr: fp/neg false positive ratio

  for KW_i in KW **do**
    if (KW_i in *SBR*) **then**
      $tp = tp + 0;$
    if (KW_i not in *SBR*) **then**
      $tn = tn + 0;$
    if (KW_i in *NSBR*) **then**
      $fp = fp + 0;$
    if (KW_i not in *NSBR*) **then**
      $fn = fn + 0;$
    $tpr = \frac{tp}{(tp+fn)};$
    $fpr = \frac{fp}{(fp+tn)};$
    //Here F^{-1} is the inverse normal cumulative distribution function.
    $Score_i \leftarrow |F^{-1}(tpr) - F^{-1}(fpr)|$
  endfor
  return $Score_i$
END

8.3.4 Scoring Bug Reports

Algorithm 8.2 is designed to record bug reports. Each bug report is noted on the basis of security-related keywords present in a bug report. If a security keyword is present in a bug report, the corresponding score will be added. Otherwise, zero will be added to the sum. If the total NSBR score is above the threshold, i.e., 0.75, then the NSBR will be selected. If the score is below the threshold, the NSBR is considered to be falsely positive and is pruned.

Algorithm 8.2. Score Bug Report.

Function **SCOREREPORT** (BR, KW)
BEGIN
    Keywords ← ReturnScores (SBR, NSBR, KW);
    KeywordsScore ← list of keywords score;
    KeywordsScore' ← list of keywords score;
    For w in *BR* **do**
        $P(w) \leftarrow GetScore(w, Keywords)$ returns score if present in dictionary else return 0;
        $KeywordsScore \leftarrow P(w);$
    endfor
    For k in *KeywordsScore* **do**
        $KeywordsScore' \leftarrow 1 - k;$
    endfor
    return $\dfrac{\prod_{i=1}^{|KeywordsScore|} k_i}{\prod_{i=1}^{|KeywordsScore|} k_i + \prod_{i=1}^{|KeywordsScore'|}(1-k_i)};$
END

8.4 Experimental Setup

Experimental parameters, applied algorithm and performance assessment parameters, are addressed in this section. We performed an experiment using Python's Scikit library.

8.4.1 Machine Learning Algorithm

The machine learning algorithm used in this approach is Naïve Bayes. Naïve Bayes is considered to be the most effective and efficient machine learning algorithm. Using various studies and research, Lessmann *et al.* [23], Menzies *et al.* [24] and Hussain *et al.* [26] concluded that for software flaw prediction, Naïve Bayes works extremely well compared with other machine learning algorithms [27-30].

8.4.2 Dataset

We used 5 labeled datasets of bug reports, making a total of about 45940 bug reports. The dataset characteristics are presented in Table 8.1.

8.4.3 Performance Evaluation

To evaluate the proposed approach, we used Precision, Recall and F-measure to evaluate the effectiveness of the proposed approach. We also compared the recall change to FAR-SEC with better results.

8.5   Results and Discussion

We have performed certain experiments by considering public datasets and Naïve Bayes classifier.

8.5.1   Response to RQ1

It is possible to build an efficient model in spite of having a class imbalance problem if one works on an efficient selection of features. We built it in with the help of Algorithm 8.1, because we assessed security-related keywords and used very relevant words as characteristics. We used Naïve Bayes as our basic classifier and compared our feature selection technique with FARSEC.

The results showed that integrating our methodology with this classifier was more effective. Figure 8.2 provides a more detailed illustration of the findings.

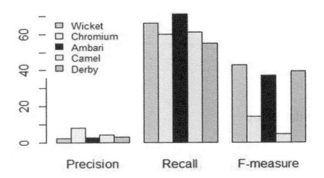

Figure 8.2: Performance evaluation of datasets using precision, recall and F-measure.

In Figure 8.2, precision, recall and F-measure values for NB were presented with each dataset considered in the proposed study. We performed higher recalls for every dataset. The highest recall value of NB on each dataset indicates the effectiveness of the model in terms of prediction of the most relevant cases. Therefore, we considered the performance measurement of the recall when we responded to RQ2.

8.5.2   Response to RQ2

The issue of the presence of security crosswords in NSBRs is removed by Algorithm 8.2, which scores the bug report. This algorithm calculates the scores for each bug report and deletes the NSBRs according to the defined threshold. If we look at Figure 8.3, we can compare the change in recalls of the FARSEC methodology and our proposed methodology. The graph may predict that the recall rate is higher than that of FARSEC, implying that the algorithm predicted the relevant results more precisely.

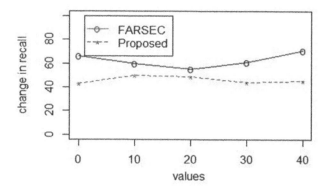

Figure 8.3: Change in recall.

8.6 Conclusion

This research study provided a framework for mitigating labeling errors in security bug reports. One of the factors contributing to the misclassification is class imbalance, because security bug reports are less numerous than non-security bug reports, and secondly, there are crosswords. We have proposed a methodology to mitigate the crossword issue by giving scores in favor of the security bug report to each word and using highly relevant words as features of the classification. In order to address the question of class imbalance, we noted each bug report based on the score reached earlier and deleted the NSBRs that have a score higher than the specified threshold.

In the future, we plan to work on how we can improve and resolve the problem of class imbalance. Apart from this, we can work to improve how learners can choose the automatic cut-off threshold for NSBR.

References

1. Shu, R., Xia, T., Williams, L., & Menzies, T. (2019). Better security bug report classification via hyperparameter optimization. *arXiv preprint arXiv:1905.06872.*

2. Gressin, Seena. "*The equifax data breach: What to do.*" Federal Trade Commission 8 (2017). https://www.ftc.gov/equifax-data-breach.

3. https://blog.careem.com/en/security/

4. Chawla, I., & Singh, S. K. (2014, August). Automatic bug labeling using semantic information from LSI. In *2014 Seventh International Conference on Contemporary Computing (IC3)* (pp. 376-381). IEEE.

5. Xia, X., Lo, D., Qiu, W., Wang, X., & Zhou, B. (2014, July). Automated configuration bug report prediction using text mining. In *2014 IEEE 38th Annual Computer Software and Applications Conference* (pp. 107-116). IEEE.

6. Xia, X., Lo, D., Shihab, E., & Wang, X. (2015). Automated bug report field reassignment and refinement prediction. *IEEE Transactions on Reliability*, 65(3), 1094-1113.

7. Goseva-Popstojanova, K., & Tyo, J. (2018, July). Identification of security related bug reports via text mining using supervised and unsupervised classification. In *2018 IEEE International Conference on Software Quality, Reliability and Security (QRS)* (pp. 344-355). IEEE.

8. Khan, A. A., Shameem, M., Nadeem, M., & Akbar, M. A. (2021). Agile trends in Chinese global software development industry: Fuzzy AHP based conceptual mapping. *Applied Soft Computing*, 102, 107090.

9. Peters, F., Tun, T. T., Yu, Y., & Nuseibeh, B. (2017). Text filtering and ranking for security bug report prediction. *IEEE Transactions on Software Engineering*, 45(6), 615-631.

10. Terdchanakul, P., Hata, H., Phannachitta, P., & Matsumoto, K. (2017, September). Bug or not? bug report classification using n-gram idf. In *2017 IEEE International Conference on Software Maintenance and Evolution (ICSME)* (pp. 534-538). IEEE.

11. Le, D. N., Nguyen, G. N., Garg, H., Huynh, Q. T., Bao, T. N., & Tuan, N. N. (2021). Optimizing Bidders Selection of Multi-Round Procurement Problem in Software Project Management Using Parallel Max-Min Ant System Algorithm. *CMC-COMPUTERS MATERIALS & CONTINUA*, 66(1), 993-1010.

12. Zou, D., Deng, Z., Li, Z., & Jin, H. (2018, July). Automatically identifying security bug reports via multitype features analysis. In *Australasian Conference on Information Security and Privacy* (pp. 619-633). Springer, Cham.

13. Abbasi, B. Z., Hussain, S., Bibi, S., & Shah, M. A. (2018, September). Impact of Membership and Non-membership Features on Classification Decision: An Empirical Study for Appraisal of Feature Selection Methods. In *2018 24th International Conference on Automation and Computing (ICAC)* (pp. 1-6). IEEE.

14. Asim, M. N., Wasim, M., Ali, M. S., & Rehman, A. (2017, November). Comparison of feature selection methods in text classification on highly skewed datasets. In *2017 First International Conference on Latest trends in Electrical Engineering and Computing Technologies (INTELLECT)* (pp. 1-8). IEEE.

15. Tang, L., & Liu, H. (2005, November). Bias analysis in text classification for highly skewed data. In *Fifth IEEE International Conference on Data Mining (ICDM'05)* (pp. 4-pp). IEEE.

16. Baillargeon, J. T., Lamontagne, L., & Marceau, É. (2019, May). Weighting Words Using Bi-Normal Separation for Text Classification Tasks with Multiple Classes. In *Canadian Conference on Artificial Intelligence* (pp. 433-439). Springer, Cham.

17. Bishop, C.M. (1995). *Neural networks for pattern recognition*. Ox-ford University Press.

18. Rish, I. (2001, August). An empirical study of the naive Bayes classifier. In *IJCAI 2001 workshop on empirical methods in artificial intelligence* (Vol. 3, No. 22, pp. 41-46).

19. Keller, J. M., Gray, M. R., & Givens, J. A. (1985). A fuzzy k-nearest neighbor algorithm. *IEEE Transactions on Systems, Man, and Cybernetics*, (4), 580-585.

20. Breiman, L. (2001). Random forests. *Machine Learning*, 45(1), 5-32.

21. Hosmer Jr, D. W., Lemeshow, S., & Sturdivant, R. X. (2013). *Applied logistic regression* (Vol. 398). John Wiley & Sons.

22. Pedregosa, F., Varoquaux, G., Gramfort, A., Michel, V., Thirion, B., Grisel, O., ... & Duchesnay, E. (2011). Scikit-learn: Machine learning in Python. *The Journal of Machine Learning Research*, 12, 2825-2830.

23. Lessmann, S., Baesens, B., Mues, C., & Pietsch, S. (2008). Benchmarking classification models for software defect prediction: A proposed framework and novel findings. *IEEE Transactions on Software Engineering*, 34(4), 485-496.

24. Menzies, T., Greenwald, J., & Frank, A. (2006). Data mining static code attributes to learn defect predictors. *IEEE Transactions on Software Engineering*, 33(1), 2-13.

25. Hussain, S., Mufti, M. R., Sohail, M. K., Afzal, H., Ahmad, G., & Khan, A. A. (2019). A Step towards the Improvement in the Performance of Text Classification. *KSII Transactions on Internet and Information Systems (TIIS)*, 13(4), 2162-2179.

26. Hussain, S., Keung, J., Khan, A. A., & Bennin, K. E. (2015, September). Performance evaluation of ensemble methods for software fault prediction: An experiment. In *Proceedings of the ASWEC 2015 24th Australasian Software Engineering Conference* (pp. 91-95).

27. Hussain, S., Keung, J., Sohail, M. K., Khan, A. A., Ahmad, G., Mufti, M. R., & Khatak, H. A. (2019). Methodology for the quantification of the effect of patterns and anti-patterns association on the software quality. *IET Software*, 13(5), 414-422.

28. Khan, A. A., Shameem, M., Kumar, R. R., Hussain, S., & Yan, X. (2019). Fuzzy AHP based prioritization and taxonomy of software process improvement success factors in global software development. *Applied Soft Computing*, 83, 105648.

29. Bao, T. N., Huynh, Q. T., Nguyen, X. T., Nguyen, G. N., & Le, D. N. (2020). A Novel Particle Swarm Optimization Approach to Support Decision-Making in the Multi-Round of an Auction by Game Theory. *International Journal of Computational Intelligence Systems*, 13(1), 1447-1463.

30. Le, D. N. (2017). A new ant algorithm for optimal service selection with end-to-end QoS constraints. *Journal of Internet Technology*, 18(5), 1017-1030.

9

A Systematic Literature Review of Challenges Factors for Implementing DevOps Practices in Software Development Organizations: A Development and Operation Teams Perspective

Mohammad Shameem[1]

[1] Department of CSE, K L University, Vijayawada, Andhra Pradesh, India
Email: shameem.ism@gmail.com

Abstract

Development and operations (DevOps) culture significantly accelerates and automates the continuous delivery and deployment of software development activities. However, presently the majority of client organizations outsource software development projects to vendor firms. The vendor organizations might be located across geographical, socio-cultural and temporal boundaries, which makes the DevOps continuous delivery and deployment process more challenging. In this chapter, the authors will address this problem by systematically reviewing the available literature and identifying the key challenges (barriers) that impact the DevOps practices between client and vendor organizations. The identified factors will be analyzed based on different perspectives, e.g., organization size, study type and experts experience. The reported factors and their analysis will provide a robust framework for both researchers and practitioners in order to address the DevOps issues in client and vendor organizations.

Keywords: DevOps, process, SLR

9.1 Introduction

DevOps is a set of collaborative and multidisciplinary efforts with an organization that has emerged in software development organizations. Although the concept of DevOps has been introduced nearly a decade before, various researchers have defined DevOps in different ways [1]. According to Díaz *et al.* [2], DevOps is defined as "a collaborative and multidisciplinary effort within an organization to automate continuous delivery of new software versions, while guaranteeing their correctness and reliability." And as defined by Lwakatare *et al.* [3], DevOps is "a portmanteau of 'development' and 'operations' and is an approach where software developers' team and operation team work in a close collaborative environment." DevOps was introduced initially to resolve the 10 conflicts between development and operations teams when they need to provide a quick response to customer requirements [2,3].

Nowadays, the software organizations are following DevOps practices to efficiently and effectively develop software product in order to develop a quality product to satisfy their clients. According to the State of DevOps Report [4] published by Puppet, the deployment rate in the DevOps environment is 30 times faster than the enterprises that have not adopted DevOps in their software development cycle. Moreover, CA Technologies conducted their study over the adoption of DevOps practices and they have predicted that 88 percent of 1892 software organizations will be using DevOps practices in the next five years [4, 5]. The goal in creating effective communication and integration between DevOps teams is to obtain the benefits of modern software development approaches that increase software development performance, process productivity, rapid deployment of new high-quality software features, and team effectiveness; resulting in faster delivery to market, better software quality, and better alignment of developers and operations with business goals and customer requirements. [6, 7, 19, 21-25]. Although DevOps offers multiple advantages and is being continuously adopted by the software development organizations, it is not a straightforward process to implement in software organizations because of a number of challenges faced by the development teams. This could be because of the limited attention given by the researchers to the development of a readiness model for effectively implementing in software organizations.

Models and framework have been developed by various organizations in order to effectively bridge the gap between development and operational teams for continuous integration, and deployment. The Unicorn framework is used for service improvement strategy, and IBM introduced the DORA platform for DevOps performance analysis, which is used for the assessment of software product delivery value stream; and an ontology-based DevOps maturity model is used to perform DevOps tasks [8, 7, 18]. However, even though these frameworks and models were developed to implement DevOps, few studies discuss how to implement them in software development activities. Therefore, the continuously increasing trend of using DevOps practices in software organizations motivated us to initiate the development of the DevOps Implementation and Management Model (DIMM), which can help software organizations measure and improve their practices for implementing DevOps. In this research work, an initial step is taken towards the development of DIMM by investigating the challenges which could have a negative impact on implementing DevOps practices. Moreover, understanding the challenges can also assist the software organizations in addressing the key areas which the organizations need to focus on to effectively implement DevOps before using the DevOps practices [9, 10, 12]. Moreover, the identified challenges also need to be classified in the context of the development team and operations team (Dev-Ops). The ultimate goal of this classification is to highlight the significance of each challenge for both the development and operation teams. Based on the above discussion, the following research questions have been designed:

- RQ1: What are the challenges identified in the literature to implementing DevOps practices in software development organizations?

- RQ2: What are the most significant challenges that need to be focused on to implement DevOps practices in the software development?

- RQ3: What are the challenges as identified in the literature related to the development team and operation team of DevOps?

This chapter is presented as follows: Section 9.2 discusses the SLR process, which is followed by the findings of the study discussed in Section 9.3. In Section 9.4, the discussions and summary about the findings are presented. The possible limitations of the study are discussed in Section 9.5. Finally, the conclusions and future directions of the study are discussed in Section 9.6.

9.2 Research Methodology

In this study, the systematic literature review (SLR) approach was selected in order to investigate the challenges for implementing DevOps in software organizations. An SLR is a type of secondary study that reviews all primary studies by analyzing and exploring all the evidences related to questions of interest [13, 15]. We have opted for the SLR process given by Kitchenham [13] in which SLR is implemented in three main stages:

- Stage-1: Planning the review,

- Stage-2: Conducting the review, and

- Stage-3: Reporting the review as briefly discussed in the following subsections. The SLR process has been used by various other researchers in a variety of domains [12, 14, 15, 20].

9.2.1 Stage-1: Planning the Review

This is the first phase of SLR in which a complete protocol is discussed, which includes developing the research questions, search process of primary studies, inclusion and exclusion criteria for the selection of primary studies, quality evaluation of primary studies, and data extraction from the finally selected articles [14].

- *Research Questions (RQs)*: All the developed research questions are discussed in Section 9.1.

- *Searching Process*: A complete search process used to find the most relevant primary studies was conducted to address the mentioned research questions. The relevant keywords and their alternatives are extracted from the available literature. The major search strings have been developed using Boolean OR and AND operators. A complete detail of search strings for the selection of primary studies from the selected digital repositories are discussed in Table 9.1. The selection of digital libraries is based on the prior studies and suggestions provided by other researchers [14, 15].

Table 9.1: Search strings and digital libraries.

Search Strings	Digital Libraries
("Challenges" OR "Barriers" OR "Hurdles" OR "Problems" OR "Difficulties" OR "Negative Impact" OR "Implement" OR "Utilize" OR "") AND ("DevOps" OR "Development and Operation team" OR "High performance team" OR "Continuous streamline" OR "Continuous development" OR "Continuous Deployment")	a. "ACM Digital Library (http://dl.acm.org)" b. "IEEE Explorer (http://ieeexplore.ieee.org)" c. "John Wiley (www.wiley.com)" d. "Science Direct (www.sciencedirect.com)" e. "Springer Link (link.springer.com)" f. "Google Scholar (scholar.google.com)"

- *Inclusion and Exclusion Criteria*: In order to include and exclude the manuscripts, the following inclusion and exclusion criteria, as given in Table 9.2, were considered.

Table 9.2: Inclusion and exclusion criteria

Inclusion Criteria	Exclusion Criteria
"Articles must be written in English language and it should be available as a full text article."	"Articles which have not discussed about any DevOps challenge"
"Manuscripts must be reported to journal, conference, magazine and book chapters."	"Articles written other than English language."
"Studies must be focused on the challenges of in DevOps implementation."	"Unpublished graduation project, master thesis and Ph.D. thesis."
	"Studies not related to the software development i.e. civil engineering."
	"Duplicity of the manuscripts."

- *Quality Check of Selected Papers*: The quality assessment of selected articles was evaluated using the quality criteria defined by Kitchenham *et al.* [13]. Five questions were used to assess how well the selected papers define the quality of the SLR, as shown in Table 9.3. The following points system was considered to determine the individual criteria scores: Yes (Y) = 1 point, Partial (P) = 0.5 point, No (N) = 0 point. After summing up the four individual criteria scores, a total quality score for each selected paper was calculated. Thus, the total quality score for each selected paper ranged between 0 (very poor) and 4 (very good). A paper with a quality score of more than 3 was considered a good quality paper and considered in our SLR study [1].

Table 9.3: Quality evaluation criteria.

Questions for QA	Score
"Are there readers able to understand the motive of research?"	"No = 0, Partial = 0.5, Yes = 1"
"Do the findings of the study clearly discuss about the improvement in DevOps practices?"	"No = 0, Partial = 0.5, Yes = 1"
"Does the study discuss any challenge for DevOps implementation in software development?"	"No = 0, Partial = 0.5, Yes = 1"
"Are the logical arguments well-presented and justified in the articles?"	"No = 0, Partial = 0.5, Yes = 1"
"Are the results related to the research questions discussed in the study?"	"No = 0, Partial = 0.5, Yes = 1"

9.2.2 Stage-2: Conducting the Review

- *Selecting the Primary Studies*: The whole process of selecting relevant articles was performed in four sequential stages [14]. Initially, 1520 articles were extracted from the selected digital databases after using the developed search string (2.1.2) and the inclusion and exclusion criteria as described in Table 9.2. After reading the title and abstract of the papers, 304 papers were selected in Stage-2. In Stage-3, 96 related papers were extracted after reading the introduction and conclusion sections of the papers, which was followed by the final Stage-4 from the selected list of articles in Stage-3, based on reading the whole text of the papers. After the four scanning phases, the total 24 relevant papers were retrieved as primary studies to address the research questions, as discussed in Section 9.1. Finally, a quality assessment criterion (Table 9.3) was performed on the selected papers. A list of the papers finally selected along with their quality score is presented in Appendix A.

Table 9.4: Search process.

Digital libraries	1st phase	2nd Phase	3rd Phase	4rd (final phase)	Percentage of final selected papers
ACM	75	21	1	1	04
IEEE	290	43	20	5	21
John Wiley	50	32	16	4	17
Science direct	218	93	11	4	17
Springer	317	51	18	4	17
Google scholar	570	64	30	6	25
Total	1520	304	96	24	**100**

- *Data Synthesis*: Data synthesis was performed by the project teams and a list of challenges was created from 24 articles extracted from the final phase of the selection process. The research questions were evaluated using the data extracted from the selected articles.

9.2.3 Stage-3: Reporting the Review Process

9.2.3.1 *Distribution of Final Selected Papers Based on Their Type*

The 24 final selected articles included 12 journal articles, 10 conference papers, 01 workshop articles, and 01 book chapters. Most of the selected studies (65 out of 78) are journal and conference articles.

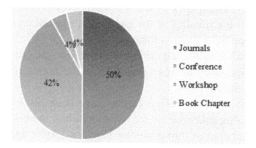

Figure 9.1: Reporting the review process.

9.3 Results

In this section, the factors are extracted from the finally selected articles based on the research questions discussed in Section 9.1.

9.3.1 RQ1 (Challenges Identified in the Literature)

To answer RQ1, Table 9.3 provides a list of challenges investigated using the SLR approach. These factors were identified from the 24 extracted primary studies. The most frequent challenges are identified in Table 9.5.

Table 9.5: Identified challenges.

S. No	Challenges	Frequency	Percentage (%) of Occurrences
Ch1	**Cultural change**	**16**	**67**
Ch2	Lack of a Standard Definition for DevOps	13	54
Ch3	**Lack of training**	**20**	**83**
Ch4	Shortage of Tool Knowledge	13	54
Ch5	**Optimizing Deployment Pipeline**	**20**	**83**
Ch6	**Lack of Sharing Knowledge**	**19**	**79**
Ch7	**Managing Multiple Environments**	**17**	**71**
Ch8	**Securing Your Infrastructure**	**18**	**75**
Ch9	**Lack of Infrastructure**	**17**	**71**
Ch10	**Lack of Adopt a DevSecOps Model**	**15**	**63**
Ch11	Use of immature automated deployment tools	12	50
Ch12	**Using unsuitable performance metrics for security evaluation**	**17**	**71**
Ch13	Lack of Automated testing performance measures for security	14	58
Ch14	Lack of tools for continuous automated testing.	13	54
Ch15	**Lack of motivation**	**21**	**88**
Ch16	Lack of effective team performance	11	46
Ch17	**Lack of planning for DevOps transformation**	**15**	**63**
Ch18	Lack of transparency	13	54

9.3.2 RQ2 (Most Critical Challenges)

Rockart [14] introduced the concept of critical constructs in order to identify the information needed from the chief executives of the projects; this was conceptualized in perception factors from the management literature [15, 16]. Khan *et al.* [17] identified the most critical barrier as the need for software process improvement in the GSD environment. The lack of attention on these challenges by the software development firms can lead to poor project performance. The criticality of the challenges may change over time because it depends on the demographic structure of the organization [9, 11, 17].

In our study, we used the following criteria to determine the criticality of the factor. If a factor exists with a frequency of more than 60% in the literature study, then it will be considered as the most critical factor.

The above criteria to evaluate critical factors have been discussed by researchers in many fields [14,19]. Using this criteria, we have identified the critical challenges which play the most significant role in implementing DevOps. After analyzing the frequency, seven challenges were identified in SLR as critical challenges in the DevOps context. The identified critical challenges along with their percentages follow: Cultural change (67%), lack of training (83%), optimizing deployment pipeline (83%), lack of knowledge sharing (79%), managing multiple environments (71%), securing your infrastructure (75%), lack of infrastructure (71%), lack of adopt a DevSecOps model (63%), using unsuitable performance metrics for security evaluation (71%), Lack of motivation (88%), lack of planning for DevOps transformation (63%).

9.3.3 RQ3 (Development and Operation Analysis)

We have categorized the identified challenges between the developers and operations teams. The categorization was carried out by taking responses of the practitioners who were part of the developers and operations teams of DevOps. A total of 12 practitioners (06 Developers, and 05 Operations) of DevOps were requested to take part in our study. After getting their consents, the process of categorization was started in which the list of the identified challenges was shared with them and they were requested to categorize the factors into Developers and Operations categories. The details of the practitioners who participated in the categorizations of the factors are given in Appendix B.

A Fisher's exact test was performed to test the differences and similarities of challenges between the developers and operations teams of DevOps. The findings of the Fisher's test shown that both developer and operation teams of DevOps have more similarities than differences for the identified challenges.

Following are the results of the categorization of challenges presented in Table 9.6: Cultural change (Ch1: 83% and 80%), lack of training (Ch3: 83% and 80%), shortage of tool knowledge (Ch4: 83% and 80%), optimizing deployment tool (Ch5: 83% and 80%), managing multiple environments (Ch7: 83% and 80%), lack of adopt DevSecOps model (Ch10: 83% and 80%), use of immature automated deployment tools (Ch12: 83% and 80%), Lack of motivation (Ch15: 83% and 80%), lack of planning for DevOps transformation (Ch17: 83% and 80%), lack of transparency (Ch18: 83% and 80%).

Table 9.6: Categorization of the challenges based on development and operations teams.

S.No	Challenges	Development (Dev) (06)		Operation (Ops) (05)		Fisher's test
		Frequency	%	Frequency	%	
Ch1	Cultural change	5	83	4	80	0.843
Ch2	Lack of a Standard Definition for DevOps	4	67	4	80	0.623
Ch3	Lack of training	5	83	4	80	0.843
Ch4	Shortage of Tool Knowledge	5	83	4	80	0.843
Ch5	Optimizing Deployment Pipeline	5	83	4	80	0.843
Ch6	**Lack of Sharing Knowledge**	**3**	**50**	**4**	**80**	**0.036**
Ch7	Managing Multiple Environments	5	83	4	80	0.843
Ch8	**Securing Your Infrastructure**	**3**	**50**	**4**	**80**	**0.036**
Ch9	**Lack of Infrastructure**	**5**	**83**	**3**	**60**	**0.048**
Ch10	Lack of Adopt a DevSecOps Model	5	83	4	80	0.843
Ch11	Use of immature automated deployment tools	4	67	3	60	0.873
Ch12	**Using unsuitable performance metrics for security evaluation**	**3**	**50**	**4**	**80**	**0.036**
Ch13	**Lack of Automated testing performance measures for security**	**3**	**50**	**4**	**80**	**0.036**
Ch14	**Lack of tools for continuous automated testing.**	**5**	**83**	**3**	**60**	**0.048**
Ch15	Lack of motivation	5	83	4	80	0.843
Ch16	**Lack of effective team performance**	**5**	**83**	**2**	**40**	**0.026**
Ch17	Lack of planning for DevOps transformation	5	83	4	80	0.843
Ch18	Lack of transparency	3	50	2	40	0.88

9.4 Discussion and Summary

The objective of this research was to investigate the challenges that need to be addressed for successful implementation of DevOps.

To answer RQ1, a total of 18 challenges for effective implementation of DevOps have been identified from the 24 selected primary studies. The identified challenges represent the key areas where the software practitioners need to focus to improve the DevOps management practices in the software development.

To address RQ2, the criticality of each of the investigated challenges is determined using the criteria discussed in Section 9.2. A total of eleven challenges were found as most critical challenges: Ch1: cultural change, Ch3: lack of training, Ch5: optimizing deployment pipeline, Ch6: lack of knowledge sharing, Ch7: managing multiple environments, Ch8: securing your infrastructure, Ch9: lack of infrastructure, Ch10: lack of adopt a DevSecOps model, Ch12: using unsuitable performance metrics for security evaluation, Ch15: lack of motivation (88%), Ch17: lack of planning for DevOps transformation.

We have classified the identified factors between developer and vendor categories in order to address RQ3. The results of the Fisher's exact test analysis shows that both development and operations teams have more similarities than differences between the identified challenges. The most common challenges encountered between development and operations teams while implementing DevOps are identified as: cultural change (Ch1: 83% and 80%), lack of training (Ch3: 83% and 80%), shortage of tool knowledge (Ch4: 83% and 80%), optimizing deployment tool (Ch5: 83% and 80%), managing multiple environments (Ch7: 83% and 80%), lack of adopt DevSecOps model (Ch10: 83% and 80%), use of immature automated deployment tools (Ch12: 83% and 80%), Lack of motivation (Ch15: 83% and 80%), lack of planning for DevOps transformation (Ch17: 83% and 80%), lack of transparency (Ch18: 83% and 80%).

9.5 Threats to Validity

There are several possible threats to validity in this study [17, 18]. The first possible threat is related to the SLR process. All the steps involved in the selection of primary studies were collected by the first author. However, all the authors discussed how to improve this threat by observing any issues that are unclear. However, a higher risk of biases exists because a single researcher could be biased and extract wrong data continuously. One possible threat is related to the internal validity of the study, which is referred to as the overall discussion and evaluation of the results. The outcomes of the discussion with the DevOps experts and practitioners provides an acceptable level of internal validity of categorizations of the factors between the developers and operations categorizations. One possible limitation is related to the review process used to extract the challenges. We might miss some of the relevant challenges because the scope of SLR is limited to five digital libraries (IEEE, Science Direct, ACM, Springer, John Wiley and Google Scholar) and a limited number of search keywords could be missed in the number of articles related to the implementation of DevOps. However, this is not a systematic omission as the SLR process has supported search strategy based on the previous SLR studies [17, 18]. The authors believe that the selected digital libraries and search strings are sufficient enough to investigate the recent DevOps literature for investigating the challenges to implement DevOps.

9.6   Conclusions and Future Study

Presently, the software organizations are following the DevOps framework for efficiently and effectively developing software product in order to develop a commercially viable quality product to satisfy their clients. The increasing trend of implementing DevOps in software development motivated us to investigate the challenges that negatively impact the implementation of DevOps practices. The SLR approach has been used and a total of 24 primary studies have been selected. A total of 18 challenges were investigated from the selected primary studies. Moreover, the identified challenges were categorized between development-operations teams. The results indicated that most of the challenges are the same for both development and operations teams of DevOps. This categorization could help both DevOps researchers and practitioners effectively in software organizations by addressing both development and operation teams.

In a future study, a multivocal literature review study will be conducted for investigating additional factors that impact negatively on the DevOps practices. Moreover, we also plan to conduct an empirical study to investigate and validate the factors identified in the literature. In this study, we only investigated the challenges, but this study can be extended by conducting pairwise comparisons between the factors and developing a priority-based framework which could help the DevOps practitioners address these challenges based on their priorities.

References

1. Leite, L., Rocha, C., Kon, F., Milojicic, D., & Meirelles, P. (2019). A survey of DevOps concepts and challenges. *ACM Computing Surveys (CSUR)*, 52(6), 1-35.

2. Díaz, J., López-Fernández, D., Pérez, J., & González-Prieto, Á. (2021). Why are many businesses instilling a DevOps culture into their organization?. *Empirical Software Engineering*, 26(2), 1-50.

3. Lwakatare, L. E., Kilamo, T., Karvonen, T., Sauvola, T., Heikkilä, V., Itkonen, J., ... & Lassenius, C. (2019). DevOps in practice: A multiple case study of five companies. *Information and Software Technology*, 114, 217-230.

4. Agarwal, A., Gupta, S., & Choudhury, T. (2018, June). Continuous and integrated software development using DevOps. In *2018 International Conference on Advances in Computing and Communication Engineering (ICACCE)* (pp. 290-293). IEEE.

5. Khan, A. A., & Shameem, M. (2020). Multicriteria decision-making taxonomy for DevOps challenging factors using analytical hierarchy process. *Journal of Software: Evolution and Process*, 32(10), e2263.

6. Riungu-Kalliosaari, L., Mäkinen, S., Lwakatare, L. E., Tiihonen, J., & Männistö, T. (2016, November). DevOps adoption benefits and challenges in practice: a case study. In *International Conference on Product-Focused Software Process Improvement* (pp. 590-597). Springer, Cham.

7. Diel, E., Marczak, S., & Cruzes, D. S. (2016, August). Communication challenges and strategies in distributed DevOps. In *2016 IEEE 11th International Conference on Global Software Engineering (ICGSE)* (pp. 24-28). IEEE.

8. Jones, S., Noppen, J., & Lettice, F. (2016, July). Management challenges for DevOps adoption within UK SMEs. In *Proceedings of the 2nd International Workshop on Quality-Aware Devops* (pp. 7-11).

9. Shameem, M., Kumar, C., Chandra, B., & Khan, A. A. (2017, December). Systematic review of success factors for scaling agile methods in global software development environment: A client-vendor perspective. In *2017 24th Asia-Pacific Software Engineering Conference Workshops (APSECW)* (pp. 17-24). IEEE.

10. Gupta, Viral, Parmod Kumar Kapur, and Deepak Kumar. "Modeling and measuring attributes influencing DevOps implementation in an enterprise using structural equation modeling." Information and software technology 92 (2017): 75-91.

11. Shameem, M., Kumar, C., & Chandra, B. (2017, January). Challenges of management in the operation of virtual software development teams: A systematic literature review. In *2017 4th International Conference on Advanced Computing and Communication Systems (ICACCS)* (pp. 1-8). IEEE.

12. Shameem, M., Chandra, B., Kumar, R. R., & Kumar, C. (2018, December). A systematic literature review to identify human related challenges in globally distributed agile software development: towards a hypothetical model for scaling agile methodologies. In *2018 4th International Conference on Computing Communication and Automation (ICCCA)* (pp. 1-7). IEEE.

13. Kitchenham, B. (2004). *Procedures for performing systematic reviews.* Keele, UK, Keele University, 33(2004), 1-26.

14. Rockart, J. F. (1979). Chief executives define their own data needs. *Harvard Business Review,* 57(2), 81-93.

15. Sánchez-Gordón, M., & Colomo-Palacios, R. (2018, October). Characterizing DevOps culture: a systematic literature review. In *International Conference on Software Process Improvement and Capability Determination* (pp. 3-15). Springer, Cham.

16. Erich, F., Amrit, C., & Daneva, M. (2014, September). Cooperation between information system development and operations: a literature review. In *Proceedings of the 8th ACM/IEEE International Symposium on Empirical Software Engineering and Measurement* (pp. 1-1).

17. Khan, A. A., Keung, J., Niazi, M., Hussain, S., & Shameem, M. (2019). GSEPIM: A roadmap for software process assessment and improvement in the domain of global software development. *Journal of Software: Evolution and Process,* 31(1), e1988.

18. Shameem, M., Chandra, B., Kumar, C., & Khan, A. A. (2018). Understanding the relationships between requirements uncertainty and nature of conflicts: a study of software development team effectiveness. *Arabian Journal for Science and Engineering,* 43(12), 8223-8238.

19. Khan, A. A., Keung, J., Hussain, S., Niazi, M., & Kieffer, S. (2018). Systematic literature study for dimensional classification of success factors affecting process improvement in global software development: client–vendor perspective. *IET Software,* 12(4), 333-344.

20. Shameem, M., Kumar, R. R., Nadeem, M., & Khan, A. A. (2020). Taxonomical classification of barriers for scaling agile methods in global software development environment using fuzzy analytic hierarchy process. *Applied Soft Computing,* 90, 106122.

21. Badshah, S., Khan, A. A, & Khan, B. (2020). Towards Process Improvement in DevOps: A Systematic Literature Review. In *Proceedings of the Evaluation and Assessment in Software Engineering (EASE '20).* Association for Computing Machinery, New York, NY, USA, 427–433. DOI:https://doi.org/10.1145/3383219.3383280

22. Zhou, P., Khan, A. A., Liang, P., & Badshah, S. (2021). System and Software Processes in Practice: Insights from Chinese Industry. In *Evaluation and Assessment in Software Engineering* (pp. 394-401).

23. Bao, T. N., Huynh, Q. T., Nguyen, X. T., Nguyen, G. N., & Le, D. N. (2020). A Novel Particle Swarm Optimization Approach to Support Decision-Making in the Multi-Round of an Auction by Game Theory. *International Journal of Computational Intelligence Systems,* 13(1), 1447-1463.

24. Le, D. N. (2017). A new ant algorithm for optimal service selection with end-to-end QoS constraints. *Journal of Internet Technology*, 18(5), 1017-1030.

25. Le, D. N., Nguyen, G. N., Garg, H., Huynh, Q. T., Bao, T. N., & Tuan, N. N. (2021). Optimizing Bidders Selection of Multi-Round Procurement Problem in Software Project Management Using Parallel Max-Min Ant System Algorithm. *CMC-COMPUTERS MATERIALS & CONTINUA*, 66(1), 993-1010.

Appendix A. Selected Primary Studies

Table 9.7: Selected primary studies.

S.No	Reference of the selected primary studies	Q1	Q2	Q3	Q4	Q5	Total quality score
PS1	Rafi, Saima, et al. "Prioritization Based Taxonomy of DevOps Security Challenges Using PROMETHEE." *IEEE Access* 8 (2020): 105426-105446.	1	1	1	1	1	5
PS2	Leite, Leonardo, et al. "A survey of DevOps concepts and challenges." *ACM Computing Surveys (CSUR)* 52.6 (2019): 1-35.	1	0.5	1	1	0.5	4
PS3	Riungu-Kalliosaari, Leah, et al. "DevOps adoption benefits and challenges in practice: a case study." *International conference on product-focused software process improvement*. Springer, Cham, 2016.	1	1	1	0.5	0.5	4
PS4	Senapathi, Mali, Jim Buchan, and Hady Osman. "DevOps capabilities, practices, and challenges: insights from a case study." *Proceedings of the 22nd International Conference on Evaluation and Assessment in Software Engineering 2018*. 2018.	1	0.5	1	1	0.5	4
PS5	Diel, Elisa, Sabrina Marczak, and Daniela S. Cruzes. "Communication challenges and strategies in distributed DevOps." *2016 IEEE 11th International Conference on Global Software Engineering (ICGSE)*. IEEE, 2016.	1	1	1	0.5	1	4.5
PS6	Jones, Stephen, Joost Noppen, and Fiona Lettice. "Management challenges for DevOps adoption within UK SMEs." *Proceedings of the 2nd International Workshop on quality-aware devops*. 2016.	1	0.5	1	1	0.5	4
PS7	Nogueira, Ana Filipa, et al. "Improving la redoute's ci/cd pipeline and devops processes by applying machine learning techniques." *2018 11th international conference on the quality of information and communications technology (QUATIC)*. IEEE, 2018.	1	1	1	0.5	0.5	4
PS8	Diaz, Jessica, et al. "Why are many business instilling a DevOps culture into their organization?." *arXiv preprint arXiv:2005.10388* (2020).	1	0.5	1	1	0.5	4
PS9	López-Peña, Miguel A., et al. "DevOps for IoT Systems: Fast and Continuous Monitoring Feedback of System Availability." *IEEE Internet of Things Journal* 7.10 (2020): 10695-10707.	1	1	1	0.5	0.5	4
PS10	Lwakatare, Lucy Ellen, et al. "DevOps in practice: A multiple case study of five companies." *Information and Software Technology* 114 (2019): 217-230.	1	0.5	1	1	0.5	4
PS11	Gupta, Viral, Parmod Kumar Kapur, and Deepak Kumar. "Modeling and measuring attributes influencing DevOps implementation in an enterprise using structural equation modeling." *Information and software technology* 92 (2017): 75-91.	1	1	1	0.5	0.5	4
PS12	Luz, Welder Pinheiro, Gustavo Pinto, and Rodrigo Bonifácio. "Adopting DevOps in the real world: A theory, a model, and a case study." *Journal of Systems and Software* 157 (2019): 110384.	1	1	1	1	1	5
PS13	Jabbari, Ramtin, et al. "Towards a benefits dependency network for DevOps based on a systematic literature review." *Journal of Software: Evolution and Process* 30.11 (2018): e1957.	1	1	1	1	0.5	4.5
PS14	Bheri, Sujeet, and SaiKeerthana Vummenthala. "An Introduction to the DevOps Tool Related Challenges." (2019).	1	1	1	0.5	1	4.5
PS15	Zaydi, Mounia, and Bouchaib Nassereddine. "DevSecOps PRACTICES FOR AN AGILE AND SECURE IT SERVICE MANAGEMENT." *Journal of Management Information and Decision Sciences* 22.4 (2019): 527.	1	1	1	1	0.5	4.5
PS16	Khan, Arif Ali, and Mohammad Shameem. "Multicriteria decision-making taxonomy for DevOps challenging factors using analytical hierarchy process." *Journal of Software: Evolution and Process* 32.10 (2020): e2263.	1	1	0.5	0.5	1	4
PS17	Daoudagh, Said, Francesca Lonetti, and Eda Marchetti. "An automated framework for continuous development and testing of access control systems." *Journal of Software: Evolution and Process* (2020): e2306.	1	1	1	0.5	0.5	4
PS18	Kamuto, Morgan B., and Josef J. Langerman. "Factors inhibiting the adoption of DevOps in large organisations: South African context." *2017 2nd IEEE International Conference on Recent Trends in Electronics, Information & Communication Technology (RTEICT)*. IEEE, 2017.	1	1	1	1	0.5	4.5
PS19	Mandepudi, Snehitha. "Communication Challenges in DevOps & Mitigation Strategies." (2019).	1	1	1	1	0.5	4.5
PS20	Faustino, João, et al. "Agile information technology service management with DevOps: an incident management case study." *International Journal of Agile Systems and Management* 13.4 (2020): 339-389.	1	1	1	1	1	5
PS21	Babar, Zia, Alexei Lapouchnian, and Eric Yu. "Modeling DevOps deployment choices using process architecture design dimensions." *IFIP Working Conference on The Practice of Enterprise Modeling*. Springer, Cham, 2015.	1	1	1	1	0.5	4.5
PS22	Hemon, Aymeric, et al. "From agile to DevOps: Smart skills and collaborations." *Information Systems Frontiers* 22.4 (2020): 927-945.	1	1	1	0.5	1	4.5
PS23	Riungu-Kalliosaari, Leah, et al. "DevOps adoption benefits and challenges in practice: a case study." *International conference on product-focused software process improvement*. Springer, Cham, 2016.	1	1	1	0.5	0.5	4
PS24	Muñoz, Mirna, Mario Negrete, and Jezreel Mejía. "Proposal to avoid issues in the devops implementation: A systematic literature review." *World Conference on Information Systems and Technologies*. Springer, Cham, 2019.	1	1	1	1	0.5	4.5

Appendix B. DevOps Practitioners

Table 9.8: DevOps practitioners.

S. No	Designation	Experience (Years)	Country	Primary roles in DevOps
1	DevOps Engineer	3	India	Development
2	Release manager	4	India	Operation
3	Release manager	3	UAE	Operation
4	Tester	3	China	Development
5	Data Analyst	6	Pakistan	Development
6	Production manager	7	India	Operation
7	DevOps architect	3	UAE	Development
8	Security engineer	4	Australia	Development
9	Data Analyst	8	Brazil	Development
10	QA engineer	4	USA	Operation
11	Associate Professor	3	China	Operation

10

DevOps' Culture Challenges Model (DC2M): A Systematic Literature Review Protocol

Muhammad Shoaib Khan[1], Abdul Wahid Khan[1], Javed Khan[1]

[1] University of Science and Technology Bannu, Pakistan
Email: mshoaibkhan102@gmail.com, wahidkn@gmail.com

Abstract

Development and operations (DevOps) is a cultural movement or framework that aims to build a bridge between IT development and operation with the purpose of efficiently shortening the development cycle at low cost. Many organizations are adopting DevOps practices due to the substantial benefits that have been shown such as a significantly faster time to market and reliability. However, there is a lack of meaning and literature on the key concepts, methods, tools and challenges of adopting DevOps strategies. The purpose of this systematic literature review protocol (SLR) is to investigate and discuss challenges related to DevOps culture and its practices. This includes how DevOps works in an organization and provides a detailed definition of the concept of DevOps and identifies the cultural challenges faced by organizations during the adoption of DevOps. SLR has been conducted to identify ways to successfully adopt the DevOps approach. The identified data will be validated by empirical study and finally analytic hierarchy process (AHP) techniques will be applied to give an alternate solution. Finally, the ultimate goal of this protocol is to develop DevOps' Culture Challenges Model (DC2M) to improve collaboration, understanding and trust and reduce the barriers between development team and operation team.

Keywords: DevOps, culture, culture challenges, systematic literature review, practices, software development

10.1   Introduction

Development and operations (DevOps) is one of the hottest and most favorable practices in the software delivery process in recent years. Software organizations are under pressure these days because they want an immediate supply of products to market [1]. DevOps aims to increase software production with speed and quality by means of new infrastructure, procedures and potency of automation [2]. DevOps is a set of practices and cultural values that aim to improve collaboration and resolve obstacles between development personnel and IT operation personnel [3-5]. DevOps is a shifting culture whose main objective is to integrate the development and operation to gain business benefits by means of appropriate technology [6]. The word "DevOps" describes the objective to break down the wall between the development team and operation team and bring together both teams by collaborative culture [7]. Time and quality are the two main constraints infecting software development [2]. At a DevOps organization, an independent team takes care of both development as well as IT operations department [8]. The key objectives of DevOps are to mitigate time, boost automation, resolve silos and user feedback between development and IT operation during the software delivery process without affecting the software quality [9, 10]. It aims to integrate teams with new practices and improve communication and automation techniques between the development team and operations teams [11].

Since DevOps is a new trendy and innovative approach in software engineering, its popularity is growing day by day. Most software organizations achieve their business goals by means of this new practice. Today's most popular software companies, like Google, Facebook, Amazon, Netflix and LinkedIn, adopt DevOps practices that enable fast software production, reduce time and reply quickly to user requests [12]. DevOps greatest emphasis is on productivity and its business-oriented ability to pave the way for organizational culture change and rapid learning [13]. Adoption of DevOps has many advantages, it allows greater collaboration and communication, and reduces the time it takes to market and release new updates of software [14]. However, adoption of this new approach is not an easy task. Several organizations have faced difficulties while changing from legacy infrastructure to new DevOps infrastructure. Transitioning from traditional organization to DevOps organization is a very costly, time-consuming, tedious process requiring great effort [4]. The DevOps practices need a solid and continuous link between the development department and IT operation in order to create a cross-functional team where every member is expected to do the task of the other member [15].

Various literature has been studied and published about DevOps practices with the main objective of finding an ultimate definition of DevOps [7]. Recent and previous scientific literature reveals that the critical challenge is that there is no standard and formal definition for it [2, 16]. A systematic literature review shows that DevOps rapidly spread from 2014 to 2015, and the related papers are low ranking in quality [10]. A systematic literature review (SLR) and empirical study (ES) is required to adopt DevOps practices to improve product quality, automation of operation services and fast delivery of software at low cost.

Since DevOps is a union of development and operation, and development members and operation members work together, there are always conflicts between them which affect the DevOps environment in an organization. Many critical challenges are faced by the development team and operation team. One of the most critical issues is "culture." DevOps culture focuses on the collaboration and integration of development and operation teams, which enhance the maturity of the software process, and quality and knowledge sharing among teams [17]. One main reason which can cause the entire process to fail is the temporary employee in an organization who is not part of the long-established DevOps culture

[18]. Another reason is the geographical distribution, which creates issues like communication, time zone, and social relationship, which are core elements for organizational culture [19].

10.2 Background

Software organizations are shifting from traditional approaches to new practices to deliver fast and smooth applications in the market. Conventional software processes are linear and performed sequentially. Each stage is completed after the completion of the previous stage. Traditional or waterfall model software is monolithic and executes in an isolated environment [20]. Traditional approaches become more challenging and create instability in the software development process [21]. One main disadvantage of traditional methodologies is that they delay the release of new software updates, causing users to become disheartened when errors are found in the updated version of software or it doesn't work as expected [16].

Conversely, the Agile model is an iterative and incremental software development process. The Agile software development model first appeared in 2001, and created a better relationship between software programers and business organizations [22]. The agile approach was developed by software companies due to the inefficiency of traditional methods to fulfill the desired goals of both software developers and business management. The agile concept has a set of guidelines for the software development process and focuses on the delivery of software in increments. Scrum is an agile application which has been broadly used in software development processes [23].

The term "DevOps" was invented by Petrick Debois in 2009, and he is also known as the father of DevOps [24]. From previous studies it is revealed that issues, such as lack of collaboration, and conflicts between development and operation, adversely impact on the quality, time and delivery of software production [25]. DevOps is a recent practice which breaks down the wall between the development team and operation team. It aims to integrate all team members into a collaborative organization.

DevOps is an evolution of agile approaches in the software development [2,7,26]. It does not have approaches like Scrum and extreme programming (XP), therefore organizations can apply DevOps practices by training their personnel [12]. DevOps is a continuous loop of integrated processes. Every process has its own specific tool which automates deployment and operations processes. The fast growth of DevOps ensures remarkable benefits of automation and acceleration of delivery and deployment of applications in the software industry [27]. Industrial DevOps is a vision to enable sustainable adaptation and improvement in industrial manufacturing by making industrial data available to multiple stakeholders [28]. The DevOps environment needs skillful technical staff as well as a wide variety of tools to maintain a continuous integration pipeline [9].

Despite the numerous advantages of DevOps, every organization cannot adopt this approach. It is not an easy job to adopt DevOps practices. DevOps is a culture shift and it requires various practices, tools, personnel and technology changes and upgradation. According to the literature, researchers have found many challenges while adopting DevOps. One of the most important and critical challenges faced by many organization is "Culture." The core elements of DevOps culture are face-to-face communication, motivation, trust, responsibility, and respect [29].

- Hüttermann *et al.* [19] describe DevOps as a multifaceted word with four major characteristics: culture, automation, measurement and sharing.

- Rembetsy *et al.* [9] stated that Etsy, an e-commerce company, converted his company culture into a DevOps culture.

- Luz *et al.* [5] stated that the key category for DevOps adoption is a collaborative culture which resolves the conflicts between the development team and IT operation team and carries out all tasks from the first day.

- Luz *et al.* [3] built a model based on grounded theory, which highlighted that for DevOps adoption a collaborative culture is a central element for practitioners.

From an organizational point of view, the top priorities are company culture and people and how they use DevOps practices in an organization [30]. Those in the DevOps culture need to have the correct mindset to learn new techniques, tools, and additional new tasks; and every member in the organization needs to closely work with colleagues to communicate and understand the new architecture design. Respect and trust are core elements in DevOps culture. Blaming each other can cause the failure of the entire project.

From the literature it is revealed that many researchers have tried to overcome the challenge of the DevOps culture. Researchers have created theories, theoretical models, maturity models, competency models and other techniques to resolve the culture issue in DevOps. In spite of that, it is a new approach in which some studies are carried out using the SLR protocol on the DevOps culture. However, many studies are limited and do not address the culture issues.

10.3   Systematic Literature Review Protocol

This study deals with designing the systematic literature review protocol for DevOps' culture challenges model (DC2M) by using the guideline of Kitchenham [31]. Systematic literature reviews are different from general literature surveys; the results are more accurate, authoritative and less biased than general literature surveys [32,33]. SLR is a procedure of collecting knowledge about a specific topic and its main objective is to be as unbiased, repeatable and auditable [34]. From the studies it has been demonstrated that SLR assists in organizing and focusing results related to a specific research question in software engineering [35,36]. The SLR is based on the three main phases of systematic review, i.e., planning the review, conducting the review and reporting the review [35]. We first performed the SLR procedure to identify key challenges for DC2M and develop a protocol. We have defined our search strings, related digital libraries, the inclusion and exclusion criteria, and data extraction process [37].

Research Questions:

- RQ1: What are the culture challenges that should be avoided by vendor organizations in DevOps development process?

- RQ2: What are the practices discussed in the literature to overcome culture challenges in DevOps process?

- RQ3: What are the real-world practices that should be adopted to overcome culture challenges?

10.4   Creating the Search String

After constructing the research questions, the following terminologies assist in the design for creating search terms. Table 10.1 show the search terms construction.

Table 10.1: Search string construction.

Intervention	Challenges, barriers, issues, problems
Population	DevOps Culture, Vendor Organization
Outcome	DevOps Culture Solution

Experimental Design: Empirical studies, systematic literature review, theoretical studies, experts' opinions, and AHP techniques are used in experimental design.

Table 10.2, 10.3, and Table 10.4 specify the search terms construction for RQ1, RQ2, and RQ3 respectively.

Table 10.2: RQ1 search terms construction.

Intervention	What culture challenges are avoided by …
Population	Vendor organization in....
Outcome	DevOps Culture Solution

Table 10.3: RQ2 search terms construction.

Intervention	What are the practices….as culture challenges
Population	Are discussed in literature ….. DevOps process
Outcome	DevOps Culture Solution

Table 10.4: RQ3 search terms construction.

Intervention	What are the real world practices.... as culture challenges
Population	Should be adopted ….. DevOps process
Outcome	DevOps Culture Solution

10.5   Search Strategies

10.5.1   Trial Search

In order to search the most relevant literature available about DevOps culture, the trial search is carry out in online electronic databases, which are IEEE Xplore, ACM Digital Library, Springer Link, Google Scholar, and Science Direct.

(DevOps AND Culture AND Challenges AND practices AND vendor)

Now we expand our trial search string for more details:

((DevOps OR "development operations" OR "cross-function collaboration" "software development" OR "product development" OR "IT operation" OR "collaborative culture" OR "continuous integration" OR monitoring OR management OR sharing) AND (culture OR values OR Society OR literature OR lifestyle OR growth) AND (challenges OR problems OR barriers OR obstacles OR issues) AND (practices OR training OR exercise OR implementation OR execution OR methods OR activities OR approach OR techniques OR procedure) AND (vendor OR supplier OR provider OR broker OR developer OR dealer OR agent OR merchant))

10.5.2 Recognizing Search Terms Attributes

For constructing the search string/term the following search approach is used:

a. Research questions are used for the extraction of major terms, by identifying population, intervention and outcome.

b. Alternative spellings and synonyms are found for the major terms.

c. Keywords are verified in any relevant paper.

d. Boolean operators such as 'OR' for the concatenation of alternative spellings and synonyms and 'AND' for the concatenation for the major terms.

10.5.3 Results for a

- RQ1: DevOps, culture, challenges, vendor

- RQ2: practices, culture, challenges, DevOps process

- RQ3: practices, culture, challenges, DevOps development

10.5.4 Results for b

- RQ1

  - DevOps: (DevOps OR "development operations" OR "cross-function collaboration" "software development" OR "product development"

  - OR "IT operation" OR "collaborative culture" OR "continuous integration" OR monitoring OR management OR sharing)

  - Culture: (culture OR values OR Society OR literature OR lifestyle OR growth)

  - Challenges: (challenges OR problems OR barriers OR obstacles OR issues)

  - Vendor: (vendor OR supplier OR provider OR broker OR developer OR dealer OR agent OR merchant)

- RQ2

  - Practices: (practices OR training OR exercise OR implementation OR execution OR methods OR activities OR approach OR techniques OR procedure)

– Culture: (culture OR values OR Society OR literature OR lifestyle OR growth)

– Challenges: (challenges OR problems OR barriers OR obstacles OR issues)

– DevOps process: (DevOps OR "development operations" OR "cross-function collaboration" "software development" OR "product development" OR "IT operation" OR "collaborative culture" OR "continuous integration" OR monitoring OR management OR sharing)

- RQ3

  – Practices: (practices OR training OR exercise OR implementation OR execution OR methods OR activities OR approach OR techniques OR procedure)

  – Culture: (culture OR values OR Society OR literature OR lifestyle OR growth)

  – Challenges: (challenges OR problems OR barriers OR obstacles OR issues)

  – DevOps development: (DevOps OR "development operations" OR "cross-function collaboration" "software development" OR "product development" OR "IT operation" OR "collaborative culture" OR "continuous integration" OR monitoring OR management OR sharing)

10.5.5 Results for c

DevOps, DevOps development, DevOps process, DevOps culture, culture, challenges, culture challenges, vendor, vendor organization, practices

10.5.6 Results for d

- RQ1:

  ((DevOps OR "development operations" OR "cross-function collaboration" "software development" OR "product development" OR "IT operation" OR "collaborative culture" OR "continuous integration" OR monitoring OR management OR sharing) AND (culture OR values OR Society OR literature OR lifestyle OR growth) AND (challenges OR problems OR barriers OR obstacles OR issues) AND (vendor OR supplier OR provider OR broker OR developer OR dealer OR agent OR merchant))

- RQ2:

  ((practices OR training OR exercise OR implementation OR execution OR methods OR activities OR approach OR techniques OR procedure) AND (culture OR values OR Society OR literature OR lifestyle OR growth) AND (challenges OR problems OR barriers OR obstacles OR issues) AND (DevOps OR "development operations" OR "cross-function collaboration" "software development" OR "product development" OR "IT operation" OR "collaborative culture" OR "continuous integration" OR monitoring OR management OR sharing))

- RQ3:

  ((practices OR training OR exercise OR implementation OR execution OR methods OR activities OR approach OR techniques OR procedure) AND (culture

OR values OR Society OR literature OR lifestyle OR growth) AND (challenges OR problems OR barriers OR obstacles OR issues) AND (DevOps OR "development operations" OR "cross-function collaboration" "software development" OR "product development" OR "IT operation" OR "collaborative culture" OR "continuous integration" OR monitoring OR management OR sharing))

10.6 Final Search String Construction

In order to find the most relevant literature, we chose the following five scientific databases:

- Google Scholar[1]

- ACM Digital Library[2]

- ScienceDirect[3]

- SpringerLink[4]

- IEEE Xplore[5]

We constructed a single search string from all three research questions. Within databases the search string was not filtered and also the date range was not selected for the purpose of getting a wide overview. We used the following final search string from the three research questions.

((DevOps OR "continuous integration" OR "software automation" OR "cross-function collaboration" OR "continuous deployment") AND (culture OR values OR literature) AND (challenges OR issues OR barriers) AND (vendor OR supplier OR trader) AND (practices OR methods OR implementation))

Table 10.5: Detail of search results of different databases.

Name of the Database	Search Result
Google Scholar	6580
ACM Digital Library	114
ScienceDirect	1233
SpringerLink	3543
IEEE Xplore	25
Total	**11495**

[1]https://scholar.google.com
[2]https://dl.acm.org/
[3]https://www.sciencedirect.com/
[4]https://link.springer.com/
[5]https://ieeexplore.ieee.org/

10.7 Selection Criteria and Search Process

In order to find the relevant data to the research questions, the primary selection first takes place on the basis of research paper title, research paper abstract and research paper keywords. The following Table 10.6 shows the primary selection of papers by search results.

Table 10.6: Detail of primary selected papers.

Name of Database	Search Result	Primary Selection
Google Scholar	6580	184
ACM Digital Library	114	31
ScienceDirect	1233	53
SpringerLink	3543	110
IEEE Xplore	25	2
Total	**11495**	**380**

The search results gave us the primary selection and then we used the following inclusion and exclusion criteria for selecting papers for the final publications.

10.7.1 Inclusion Criteria

Inclusion criteria are used to explain which part of the studies (articles, technical reports, or "grey literature") is built by the search term which will be used for data extraction phase. The focus has been on DevOps culture challenges and practices and papers written in English language and electronically available. The inclusion criteria are defined below:

- Research papers which are explicitly related to DevOps culture.

- Research papers which describe the culture challenges by vendor organizations in DevOps development processes.

- Research papers which describe the practices to overcome culture challenges.

- Research papers which describe the relationship between vendor organization and DevOps culture.

- Research papers which describe the real-world practices for the successful adoption of DevOps culture.

- Research papers are included which are written in English language.

- Research papers are included whose title is related to DevOps culture.

- Research papers are included whose keywords are matched with the keywords as defined in search strings.

10.7.2 Exclusion Criteria

Exclusion criteria are used when the literature is not related to our research project and excludes all irrelevant literature which is not used for data extraction process. The exclusion criteria are defined below:

- Research papers which are not related to our research questions.

- Research papers which are not related to DevOps culture.

- Research papers which are not related to the vendor organization.

- Research papers which do not describe the DevOps culture and its challenges.

- Research papers which do not describe practices in DevOps culture.

- Research papers which do not satisfied DevOps culture and practices in software organizations.

- Research papers repeated in more than one electronic library.

- Exclude papers which are not written in English language.

10.7.3 Selection of Primary Sources

The main goal of primary selection is based on reviewing the title, keywords and abstract of the papers. The objective of these findings helps us to remove all research papers which are not related to our topic. For the final selection of papers, check the results against inclusion/exclusion criteria by reviewing the articles completely. A secondary reviewer is needed to review the data if there is any uncertain situation regarding inclusion/exclusion criteria. The primary source record is effectively maintained regarding inclusion/exclusion criteria and is required when deciding whether to include or exclude it for the final review.

10.8 Assessment of Publication Quality

Quality criteria are used to ensure the quality of the final publication and the assessment of quality is performed in parallel at the time of data extraction. The quality of publication is carried out purely on the basis of the following questions:

- Has the author noticeably recognized the challenge which affects the DevOps culture in software organizations?

- What practices are adopted by the author to overcome culture challenges in DevOps?

The abovementioned questions will be marked as 'YES' or 'NO' or 'NA'.
The supervisor (secondary reviewer) will also contribute in scoring of small subset for the validation.

10.9 Data Extraction Stage

10.9.1 Initiation of Data Extraction Phase

After studying the primary selected publications the data extraction stage begins, which is focused on satisfying the research questions. The data below will be extracted from each of the research papers:

- Details of publication (title, authors, journal/conference title, volume, location year etc.).

- The following data will be extracted that is related to the research questions:

  - For RQ1, background information and challenges/risks/obstacles that point out the influence of the DevOps culture in vendor organization.

  - For RQ2, background information as well as practices and solutions related data will be extracted to overcome culture challenges in DevOps processes.

  - For RQ3, background information and practices or solution are identified in the literature for the DevOps culture.

10.9.2   Presentation of Data Extraction

The extracted data will be presented in the following format:

Table 10.7: Data extraction format.

- Date of Review
- Paper Title
- Authors
- Reference
- Conference / Journal Name
- Database / Resource
- Methodology (i.e. Interview, Survey, Case study, Report etc.)
- Sample Population
- Target Population
- Quality of Publication Description
- Organization Type (i.e. Software House, University, Research Institute etc.)
- Company Size (i.e. small, medium, large)
- Country (i.e. Location of Analysis)
- Year
- Challenges (i.e. identifies those barriers / issues which impact DevOps Culture)
- Practices (i.e. which are adopted to overcome culture challenges)

10.9.3   Data Extraction Process

In the data extraction process, the primary researcher who is responsible for data extraction from the publications commences the primary review. In the case where an issue needs to be dealt with in data extraction, the secondary reviewer provides guidance to the primary reviewer to tackle the issue. The primary reviewer is responsible for extracting data from the selected publications. The secondary reviewer also contributes to selecting the the data randomly from that already chosen by the primary reviewer. The secondary reviewer chooses the data independently and compares his/her results with the results of the primary reviewer.

10.9.4   Data Storage

After the data extraction process, the summarized data will be kept as an SPSS document and it will be stored on a local drive at the University of Science and Technology Bannu, Pakistan.

10.10   Data Synthesis

In the data synthesis stage, one summary table is constructed having columns as well as S No., DevOps Culture Challenges, Frequency, Percentage, etc., which spotlights the list of all challenges in DevOps culture with their frequencies and percentages.

10.11   Discussion

We have conducted this study to explore the various challenges in the DevOps development process faced by vendor organizations. We have used the SLR method to identify key challenges from the literature as given in Table 10.8.

Table 10.8: List of critical challenges.

S No	Challenges	Frequency (N=66)	Percentage
1	Lack of Collaboration and Communication	45	68
2	Lack of Skill and Knowledge	37	56
3	Criticism Practices	33	50
4	Lack of DevOps Approach	31	47
5	Lack of Management	30	45
6	Trust and Confidence Problems	30	45
7	Complicated Infrastructure	23	35
8	Poor Quality	22	33
9	Security Issues	19	29
10	Legacy Infrastructure	15	23

Table 10.8 lists a total of 10 critical challenges identified by the SLR. The challenge "lack of collaboration and communication" (68%) has the highest frequency. The distance of cooperation between communication, development and work will lead to problems such as team conflict and failure [38]. When the conversation is in English, which is not the mother tongue of the seller or the client, it creates natural challenges for communication [39]. Lwakatare *et al.* describe the problem of poor communication between teams in an organization, which can be identified by the limited common knowledge between people [40]. If there is a lack of communication and collaboration between IT managers and vendor organizations, then it creates misunderstandings and confusion, which results in a lot of work and time [41].

"Lack of skill and knowledge" (56%) is the second major challenge on this list. Implementing successful DevOps techniques in an organization requires knowledgeable and skilled staff in both development and operations departments [38]. Many organizations do not have enough skilled staff to create the right environment for IT projects and this is a key factor in project failure [42].

"Criticism practices," which has a reported 50% frequency in the literature, is a major challenge that has a negative impact on DevOps culture. If there is a culture of blaming and pointing fingers and people do not change their behavior, we will never learn anything. The literature shows that people resist changing their attitudes, which is the biggest obstacle to the success of organizational change [43].

In our study, the "lack of DevOps approach" (47%) has been identified as a key challenge in the implementation of DevOps culture. The biggest challenge in adopting the DevOps approach is learning new methods and tools as it requires changing mindsets and attitudes in specific contexts [44]. Due to its multifaceted nature, it is difficult to adopt the DevOps approach, because its vague definitions and goals confuse organizations and individuals, leading to a negative perception of resistance to the adoption of DevOps [45].

In every organization, management plays a vital role in achieving goals and objectives. "Lack of management" (45%) is also a critical challenge in our list. The management and DevOps teams do not have a common goal, which results in resource allocation as well as delays in delivery dates, which has a negative impact on stakeholders [46]. If there is friction between the management level as well as the members of other levels, then an undesirable atmosphere is created [47].

"Trust and confidence problems" (45%) also affects the DevOps culture and is a challenge for adoption of DevOps practices. Achieving goals is impossible if there is a lack of trust among team members. Lack of trust is easily established when the development team and the operations team cannot trust each other [48]. People generally resist and fear the loss of changing culture and jobs because they have insufficient expertise in both development and operation areas [45].

"Complicated infrastructure" (35%) is a serious problem that affects the overall performance of the organization. DevOps is a movement from a legacy structure to a highly integrated system, making it more difficult for IT services to become modern, reliable and efficient [44]. It is very difficult to be agile when a complex organization and culture is unintentionally slow [49].

Another challenge on the list is "poor quality" (33%). Poor quality is a major obstacle to project success due to the unavailability of a proper user company. When the development and operations team pays too much attention to non-functional requirements, they release substandard products into the market [39]. The high turnover of team members in an organization also affects the quality and volume of work [47].

Security is the backbone of any organization's success. In our literature, we have found that "security issues" are a major problem in the adoption of DevOps and our list of key challenges includes 29% frequency in security matters. When an organization does not have security experts, the development team focuses more on production than on "big fixes," which leads to products with poor quality as well as error-prone areas [50]. Another major mistake of the DevOps organization is that it does not pay attention to the security aspect and the employee has access to the database and can possibly install malware in the system and steal confidential information [46].

"Legacy infrastructure" is the last major challenge on our list and is identified by its 23% frequency in the literature. Because DevOps is a new practice that transforms the traditional structure into a new complex and integrated infrastructure, legacy infrastructure does not support new technologies, new software versions, and new ways of working with tools [51-55]. The traditional system creates resistance to the current way of working to adapt the organization's role, structure, decision-making and DevOps [40].

10.12 Validation of Review Protocol

This protocol will be submitted to the secondary reviewer (Supervisor, Dr. Abdul Wahid Khan) for the purpose of reviewing the protocol.

10.13   Limitation

A limitation to this study is that only real-world practices from RQ3 (questionnaire survey, interviews, etc.) will be generated. Another limitation to this study is that since DevOps is a new concept, the literature on DevOps culture is limited. Moreover, Google Scholar shows only 184 results out of 6580.

References

1. Wang, Y., Pyhäjärvi, M., & Mäntylä, M. V. (2020, October). Test Automation Process Improvement in a DevOps Team: Experience Report. In *2020 IEEE International Conference on Software Testing, Verification and Validation Workshops (ICSTW)* (pp. 314-321). IEEE.

2. Sánchez-Gordón, M., & Colomo-Palacios, R. (2018, October). Characterizing DevOps culture: a systematic literature review. In *International Conference on Software Process Improvement and Capability Determination* (pp. 3-15). Springer, Cham.

3. Luz, W. P., Pinto, G., & Bonifácio, R. (2018, October). Building a collaborative culture: a grounded theory of well succeeded devops adoption in practice. In *Proceedings of the 12th ACM/IEEE International Symposium on Empirical Software Engineering and Measurement* (pp. 1-10).

4. Senapathi, M., Buchan, J., & Osman, H. (2018, June). DevOps capabilities, practices, and challenges: insights from a case study. In *Proceedings of the 22nd International Conference on Evaluation and Assessment in Software Engineering 2018* (pp. 57-67).

5. Luz, W. P., Pinto, G., & Bonifácio, R. (2019). Adopting DevOps in the real world: A theory, a model, and a case study. *Journal of Systems and Software*, 157, 110384.

6. Ebert, C., Gallardo, G., Hernantes, J., & Serrano, N. (2016). DevOps. *IEEE Software*, 33(3), 94-100.

7. Leite, L., Rocha, C., Kon, F., Milojicic, D., & Meirelles, P. (2019). A survey of DevOps concepts and challenges. *ACM Computing Surveys (CSUR)*, 52(6), 1-35.

8. Govil, N., Saurakhia, M., Agnihotri, P., Shukla, S., & Agarwal, S. (2020, June). Analyzing the Behaviour of Applying Agile Methodologies & DevOps Culture in e-Commerce Web Application. In *2020 4th International Conference on Trends in Electronics and Informatics (ICOEI)(48184)* (pp. 899-902). IEEE.

9. Erich, F. M. A., Amrit, C., & Daneva, M. (2017). A qualitative study of DevOps usage in practice. Journal of Software: *Evolution and Process*, 29(6), e1885.

10. Bolscher, R., & Daneva, M. (2019, May). Designing Software Architecture to Support Continuous Delivery and DevOps: A Systematic Literature Review. In *ICSOFT* (pp. 27-39).

11. Rowse, M., & Cohen, J. (2021, January). A Survey of DevOps in the South African Software Context. In *Proceedings of the 54th Hawaii International Conference on System Sciences* (p. 6785).

12. Díaz, J., Almaraz, R., Pérez, J., & Garbajosa, J. (2018, May). DevOps in practice: an exploratory case study. In *Proceedings of the 19th International Conference on Agile Software Development: Companion* (pp. 1-3).

13. Mubarkoot, M. (2021, June). Assessment of factors influencing adoption of devops practices in public sector and their impact on organizational culture. In *Proceeding International Conference on Science (ICST)* (Vol. 2, pp. 475-483).

14. Lwakatare, L. E., Kuvaja, P., & Oivo, M. (2016, November). Relationship of DevOps to agile, lean and continuous deployment. In *International Conference on Product-focused Software Process Improvement* (pp. 399-415). Springer, Cham.

15. Hemon, A., Lyonnet, B., Rowe, F., & Fitzgerald, B. (2020). From agile to DevOps: Smart skills and collaborations. *Information Systems Frontiers*, 22(4), 927-945.

16. Wiedemann, A., Forsgren, N., Wiesche, M., Gewald, H., & Krcmar, H. (2019). Research for practice: the DevOps phenomenon. *Communications of the ACM*, 62(8), 44-49.

17. Khan, A. A., Shameem, M., Nadeem, M., & Akbar, M. A. (2021). Agile trends in Chinese global software development industry: Fuzzy AHP based conceptual mapping. *Applied Soft Computing*, 102, 107090.

18. Morales, J. A., Yasar, H., & Volkman, A. (2018, May). Implementing DevOps practices in highly regulated environments. In *Proceedings of the 19th International Conference on Agile Software Development: Companion* (pp. 1-9).

19. Smeds, J., Nybom, K., & Porres, I. (2015, May). DevOps: a definition and perceived adoption impediments. In *International Conference on Agile Software Development* (pp. 166-177). Springer, Cham.

20. Khan, A. A., & Shameem, M. (2020). Multicriteria decision-making taxonomy for DevOps challenging factors using analytical hierarchy process. *Journal of Software: Evolution and Process*, 32(10), e2263. DOI: 10.1002/smr.2263

21. Mishra, A., & Otaiwi, Z. (2020). DevOps and software quality: A systematic mapping. *Computer Science Review*, 38, 100308.

22. Zhou, P., Khan, A. A., Liang, P., & Badshah, S. (2021). System and Software Processes in Practice: Insights from Chinese Industry. In *Evaluation and Assessment in Software Engineering* (pp. 394-401).

23. Srinivasan, R., Eppinger, S. D., & Joglekar, N. (2019, July). The Structure of DevOps in Product-Service System Development. In Proceedings of the Design Society: International Conference on Engineering Design (Vol. 1, No. 1, pp. 3111-3120). Cambridge University Press.

24. Badshah, S., Khan, A. A, & Khan, B. (2020). Towards Process Improvement in DevOps: A Systematic Literature Review. In *Proceedings of the Evaluation and Assessment in Software Engineering (EASE '20)*. Association for Computing Machinery, New York, NY, USA, 427–433. DOI: https://doi.org/10.1145/3383219.3383280

25. Lwakatare, L. E., Kilamo, T., Karvonen, T., Sauvola, T., Heikkilä, V., Itkonen, J., ... & Lassenius, C. (2019). DevOps in practice: A multiple case study of five companies. *Information and Software Technology*, 114, 217-230.

26. Bobrov, E., Bucchiarone, A., Capozucca, A., Guelfi, N., Mazzara, M., Naumchev, A., & Safina, L. (2020). Devops and its philosophy: Education matters!. In *Microservices* (pp. 349-361). Springer, Cham.

27. Rong, G., Jin, Z., Zhang, H., Zhang, Y., Ye, W., & Shao, D. (2019, May). DevDocOps: Towards automated documentation for DevOps. In *2019 IEEE/ACM 41st International Conference on Software Engineering: Software Engineering in Practice (ICSE-SEIP)* (pp. 243-252). IEEE.

28. Henning, S., & Hasselbring, W. (2021). The Titan Control Center for Industrial DevOps analytics research. *Software Impacts*, 7, 100050.

29. Bisandu, D. B. (2018). Cloud DevOps future of E-Business. *International Journal of Latest Technology in Engineering, Management & Applied Science-IJLTEMAS*, 7(11), 19-23.

30. Yasar, H., & Kontostathis, K. (2016). Where to integrate security practices on DevOps platform. *International Journal of Secure Software Engineering (IJSSE)*, 7(4), 39-50.

31. Kitchenham, B. A. (2012, September). Systematic review in software engineering: where we are and where we should be going. In *Proceedings of the 2nd international workshop on Evidential Assessment of Software Technologies* (pp. 1-2).

32. Khan, A. A., Keung, J., Niazi, M., Hussain, S., & Ahmad, A. (2017). Systematic literature review and empirical investigation of barriers to process improvement in global software development: Client–vendor perspective. *Information and Software Technology*, 87, 180-205.

33. Khan, A. A., Keung, J., Hussain, S., Niazi, M., & Kieffer, S. (2018). Systematic literature study for dimensional classification of success factors affecting process improvement in global software development: client–vendor perspective. *IET Software*, 12(4), 333-344.

34. Kitchenham, B., Pretorius, R., Budgen, D., Brereton, O. P., Turner, M., Niazi, M., & Linkman, S. (2010). Systematic literature reviews in software engineering–a tertiary study. *Information and Software Technology*, 52(8), 792-805.

35. Kitchenham, B. (2004). *Procedures for performing systematic reviews*. Keele, UK, Keele University, 33(2004), 1-26.

36. Muñoz, M., Negrete, M., & Mejía, J. (2019, April). Proposal to avoid issues in the devops implementation: A systematic literature review. In *World Conference on Information Systems and Technologies* (pp. 666-677). Springer, Cham.

37. Khan, A. W., & Khan, S. U. (2015). Solutions for critical challenges in offshore software outsourcing contract. *Pakistan Academy of Sciences*, 52, 331-344.

38. Yiran, Z., & Yilei, L. (2017). *The Challenges and Mitigation Strategies of Using DevOps during Software Development*.

39. Seppä-Lassila, T., Järvi, A., & Hyrynsalmi, S. (2017). An assessment of DevOps maturity in a software project. *Computer Science*.

40. Jonker, M. (2017). DevOps Implementation Model for Large IT Service Organizations.

41. Baig, A. (2019). Implementation of Agile Software Development Methodology in a Company–Why? Challenges? Benefits?.

42. Wiedemann, A., & Wiesche, M. (2018). Are you ready for Devops? Required skill set for Devops teams.

43. Mayner, S. W. (2017). Transformational leadership and organizational change during agile and devops initiatives (Doctoral dissertation, Capella University).

44. Blomberg, V. (2019). Adopting DevOps Principles, Practices and Tools. Case: Identity & Access Management. in *Practice*, 29(6), 1-14.

45. 45. Pérez Hoyos, L., DevOps: IT Development in the Era of Digitalization. 2018.

46. Plant, O. H. (2019). DevOps under control: development of a framework for achieving internal control and effectively managing risks in a DevOps environment (Master's thesis, University of Twente).

47. Nader-Rezvani, N., Nader-Rezvani, & McDermott. (2019). *An Executive's Guide to Software Quality in an Agile Organization*. Apress.

48. Hamunen, J. (2016). Challenges in adopting a Devops approach to software development and operations.

49. Atwal, H. (2020). DataOps Technology. In *Practical DataOps* (pp. 215-247). Apress, Berkeley, CA.

50. Casagni, M., Lead, M. I. T. R. E., Hanf, D., Area, C., Malhotra, P., Heeren, M., ... & Kristan, M. FEDERAL DEVOPS SUMMIT.

51. Katal, A., Bajoria, V., & Dahiya, S. (2019, March). DevOps: Bridging the gap between Development and Operations. In *2019 3rd International Conference on Computing Methodologies and Communication (ICCMC)* (pp. 1-7). IEEE.

52. Ravichandran, A., Taylor, K., & Waterhouse, P. (2016). DevOps Finetuning. *In DevOps for Digital Leaders* (pp. 151-169). Apress, Berkeley, CA.

53. Feijter, R., Vliet, R., Jagroep, E., Overbeek, S., & Brinkkemper, S. (2017). Towards the adoption of DevOps in software product organizations: A Maturity Model Approach. *Technical Report Series*, (UU-CS-2017-009).

54. Le, D. N. (2017). A new ant algorithm for optimal service selection with end-to-end QoS constraints. *Journal of Internet Technology*, 18(5), 1017-1030.

55. Khan, A. A., Keung, J., Niazi, M., Hussain, S., & Shameem, M. (2019). GSEPIM: A roadmap for software process assessment and improvement in the domain of global software development. *Journal of Software: Evolution and Process*, 31(1), e1988.

11

Critical Challenges of Designing Software Architecture for Internet of Things (IoT) Software System

Noor Rehman[1,*], Abdul Wahid Khan[1]

[1] Department of Computer Science, University of Science and Technology, Bannu, Pakistan
Email: Noorkust301@gmail.com, Wahidkn@gmail.com

Abstract

Software architecture plays a pivotal role in the utilization of every software system according to user satisfaction. In the initial stage of development, the software architecture design for the internet of things (IoT) is considered essential. Software architecture is also considered the backbone of any software and is the cause of the entire system failing if it is not designed properly. The IoT is a new paradigm in the field of artificial intelligence and the digital world, which is considered the most significant approach for an automated system. In this chapter, we have identified various challenges faced by the software architecture team/vendor for IoT software design. These challenges were analyzed across different continents to determine their significance. The list of the identified different challenges include lack of common development, lack of poor architecting, lack of reliability, lack of management issues, environment issues, development limitation, cost issues, lack of knowledge for highly skilled resource pool, lack of proper technology, traditional co-located model, lack of privacy, lack of communication workflow, lack of trust, market expansion and growth issues, framework integration issues, lack of effectiveness, lack of assessment issues, and poor scheduling. The findings of this chapter demonstrate the similarities and dissimilarities across different continents.

Keywords: Software architecture, internet of things, software outsourcing, challenges/ risks, architectural models

11.1   Introduction

Today's world is a digital world where everything moves with rapid speed, including computations and submissions. Everything needs to be digitized in today's world, and the internet of things is the latest concept in this regard. Designing such a system from the perspective of a desired angle can fulfill the basic and desired needs of a user [1], which can lead to user satisfaction and ease of work. Software architecture is considered the base of every system. It provides the blueprint of a system regarding its use and its actual operation by the intended user [2]. Software architecture plays a significant role in the development and formulation of a software system for the IoT. In current research technology, the IoT is considered the most prominent technology, which is based on connecting physical objects or things to the digital world's objects in order to change future objects [3]. Software architecture is a basic part of the system that can express the good scalability and bad scalability of the system. As the technology of the IoT has commercial possibilities, a considerable amount of R&D goes into the technology embedded into devices, along with the endless progression of the number of smart things [4]. However, the issues arise when IoT applications have poor scalability and high coupling, which results in the breakdown of the IoT application [5].

Software architecture is the process of gaining suitable origins and recommendations for the specific software systems that are going to be developed before their actual commencement. Software systems that are affected are likely to be smaller and are associated with the design decisions and the anticipated quality attributes demonstrated in the intended software architecture [6]. This chapter aims to provide an outline of the principles related to software architecture reliability and delivers insights on how the structuring of a software system at the architectural level is important for the development of software systems. With this in mind, our intention is to show how reliability should be considered at the architectural level when developing software systems. Existing architectural approaches do not explicitly consider the dependability aspects, hence the need to know what are the general principles associated with software architectures, what is being developed in terms of dependable technologies, and what are the challenges that lie ahead [7]. The IoT has become an efficient paradigm to overcome all problems faced with manual systems [8]. Recently, there has been a growing trend of using machine learning to expand IoT applications and deliver IoT services such as traffic engineering, security, network management, quality service optimization, and internet traffic classification. As the reputation and widespread use of the IoT continues to grow, devices and sensors are generating considerable amounts of data and many IoT applications are being developed according to their efficient architecture for delivering more precise fine-tuned services to users. Most IoT systems are increasingly vibrant, complex and heterogeneous. Thus, the management of such IoT systems is difficult for the vendor, which may cause the failure of the actual system in the near future [8, 9].

We have achieved many IoT architecture framework issues through the literature with the help of a systematic literature review (SLR). One of the key issues that came up were structuring issues, such as software complexity, requirement, diagram formalization, and module design, for which we have proposed the term "lack of common development"; and the rest were elaborated based on the high frequency of occurrence [10, 11]. To redress the findings with the help of SLR, we formulated the following two research questions:

- RQ1: What are the challenges faced by the software outsourcing vendor organization when designing software architecture for IoT software systems?

▪ RQ2: How do the identified challenges vary from continent to continent?

We have planned the sections of this chapter as follows: in Section 11.2 we present some background on the topic; in Sections 11.3 and 11.4 we discuss the comprehensive research methodology; in Section 11.5 results of the SLR are analyzed and discussed; in Section 11.5 the challenges of this research are mentioned; in Sections 11.6 and 11.7 we give our conclusions and future direction of this research work.

11.2 Background

Architecture has already developed its own significance for every developer and user who interacts with it. The software architecture design challenges model for IoT software systems has its own significance, which will cover the limitations and issues in the existing architecture models [12]. Software architecture is a supportable part of every software and is an efficient component for the development process of object-oriented software applications [13].

The quality of any system is evaluated according to the architecture model to which it has been developed. Thus, it is of paramount importance to the initial development of any IoT or general software system. The IoT uses everyday devices/objects to gather and share data over networks, with or without human interaction, which is eventually used to create useful information for the specific goal of business [14].

Despite this, the initial stage of developing any kind of system is more important due to its proper architecting. With the help of efficient outsourcing, the developed system could be used freely because it will give results efficiently due to its proper development. Thus, the vendor should consider this stage as the most critical during the development of any software system for a specific job/task, etc. There are many factors that can negatively affect the development of any software with the help of outsourcing, which is nowadays used as a common approach for the development of any software system. Twelve Vietnamese participants in a study identified credibility, cultural understanding, capabilities, and personal visits as significant factors in gaining the trust of a client early on, while communication strategies, cultural understanding, contract conformance, and timely delivery were strong factors in maintaining that trust [15, 16].

Throughout the literature, it was found that the 89% failure of any software system is caused by its improper development, which means its architecting. The disturbance in architecture is mainly caused by the low and unusual communication between two parties, who are the vendor and client. Thus, outsourcing in this stage has been highly preferred due to its efficient role in the successful completion of any project [17]. It has also been observed that in the development of any software architecture, the main factor of the prosperous completion of the project is outsourcing contract management. However, due to the increasing scope and efficiency of outsourcing, it faces a poor understanding of the coordination between client and vendor, which may result in the failure of any system after its utilization [18]. We conducted a systematic literature review and received many challenges faced by software organizations during the development phase of any software. To carry out a systematic literature review means to evaluate or interpret all available evidences for a specific goal or issue. Some of the latest software architecture modeling approaches from the existing literature are illustrated below.

11.2.1   Layered Architecture Pattern

This pattern of architecture is the most commonly used pattern for the development of architecture for a software system. The model view controller (MVC) is also the structure of the layered architecture pattern. Drupal, Java EE, and Express are some examples of models of layered architecture styles or patterns. In this pattern of software architecture style, there are four layers that are led by this architectural pattern. The presentation layer contains the graphical representation and the general design of the system. Whereas, the business layer is concerned with the inclusion of models and logic for the explicit problem of a business. The application layer or database layer is processed between the presentation and business layer for the purpose of providing abstraction. Whereas, the persistence layer processes the code to access the database layer, while it also manipulates database queries and statements of the database, etc. [19]. Figure 11.1 represents the layered pattern of architecture design.

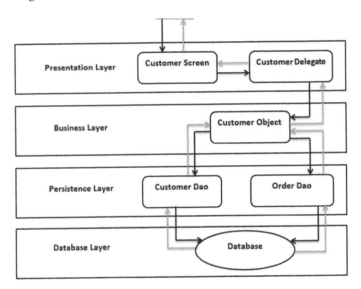

Figure 11.1: Layered architecture.

The majority of developers are more acquainted with the layered pattern of architecture than the others. This pattern also provides easy ways for writing organized and well-defined testable software applications [19]. There are also some drawbacks of this architecture pattern. This pattern of architecture leads to monolithic applications that are hard to split up.

11.2.2   Microservices Software Architecture

This architectural style or pattern is considered as an assemblage of services that are loosely coupled, independently deployable, highly maintainable, and testable, organized around business capabilities, and owned by a small team. Microservices is an architectural pattern that is used to develop services-based applications based on small, loosely coupled services. In this software architecture pattern, microservices have their own divergence responsibilities and a team can develop them autonomously like other microservices [20]. Figure 11.2 represents the graphical overview of microservices architectural style.

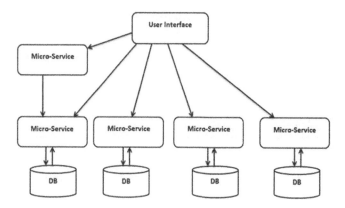

Figure 11.2: Graphical representation of microservices architecture pattern.

This layer gives accessibility to the developer for naming and arranging microservices unconnectedly. Microservices architecture is easy to scale because of the less dependent and loosely coupled services modules. There are some drawbacks of this architectural pattern. A user's action can pass through various microservices, which is why there are more chances of failure when something is done incorrectly in the process.

11.2.3 Event-Driven Software Architecture Pattern

Event-driven architecture pattern is one of the software paradigms used for promoting the detection, production reaction to events, and consumption of events. This architectural model acts like a robotic system and activates when some events occur. An IoT software system is mainly developed using this software architecture pattern due to its artificial intelligence [21]. This software architectural model is also used for developing of those systems which directly interact with humans for the accomplishment of some specific task, etc. Figure 11.3 shows the graphical representation of an event-driven software architecture pattern.

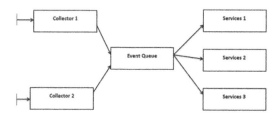

Figure 11.3: Event-driven architecture pattern.

An event-driven architecture pattern works by receiving events from the collector and gives a response accordingly. More than one event is also queued in the event queued box as shown in Figure 11.3.

11.2.4   Blackboard Software Architecture Pattern

A blackboard architecture pattern also deals with the concept of artificial intelligence. This architectural pattern is also considered as a useful pattern for the development of IoT software systems. It has components of a blackboard which act as a central repository of data [22]. This architectural pattern is often useful for those problems which have no deterministic solutions or strategies. Figure 11.4 shows a graphical representation of blackboard software architecture.

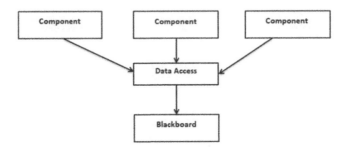

Figure 11.4: Graphical representation of blackboard software architecture.

The independent components are communicated exclusively through a common global data repository, or it may be a blackboard. A heuristic problem in artificial intelligence (AI) is the basic core example of the blackboard software architecture pattern.

11.2.5   Systematic Literature Review for SADM

For the process of protocol development, especially for the software architecture designing challenges model (SADCM) for the IoT software system, we studied and analyzed many survey-based approaches in the process of collecting data for analysis. We found that the literature review (SLR) was the most specific approach for data collection, identification, and solution of research questions. Stapić *et al.* [23] stated that the three phases of SLR are planning, conducting, and reporting. The main focus of this study will be the planning phase. This assessment will help settle quality-related issues and challenges in the field of software architecture outsourcing. The review is totally based on the research questions [24]. After the finalization of our research questions, we will initiate the trial search on different databases and will define a type of strings. After searching the relevant information, we will also specify the inclusion-exclusion measurement for the literature and for the data extracted.

11.3   Research Questions

The main objectives of using a systematic literature review are given in the following research questions:

- RQ1: What are the challenges faced by software outsourcing vendor organization for software architecture designing challenges model for IoT software systems?

- RQ2: What are the practices to handle the identified challenges by software outsourcing vendor organization for designing software architecture for IoT software systems?

- RQ3: What are the real-world practices to handle the challenges by software out-sourcing vendor organization for designing software architecture for IoT software systems?

11.4 Research Methodology

For the identification and processing of every object, this is just a unique way through which the said jobs or objects have been processed and completed. Thus, we have found the systematic literature review (SLR) to be the most proficient method for getting the latest results from already published articles whether our research questions fulfill the required amount of data or not for the subject matter [25]. The SLR analyzed the collected data using predefined inclusion and exclusion criteria. There are three phases of SLR: the planning phase, conducting phase, and reporting phase. The results of SLR are considered to be more accurate and reliable with less bias than a manual literature review. Our predefined research proposal [26] has already been validated and published in the International Conference at University of Swabi Journal (USJ), Pakistan, which is available online at the link: (http://www.uoswabi.edu.pk/cms/index/421). The said conference was held under the supervision of international professors and participants.

As mentioned in Subsection 11.4.6, we have found 20 challenges, as highlighted in Table 11.8, where the "lack of common development" and "lack of poor architecture" were marked as the most critical challenges/issues with frequency $>= 50\%$. The same approach has also been utilized in previous articles by many researchers [27, 29, 30].

11.4.1 Constructing Search Term Formulation

The following three basic formulation phases of a search show the details of each question separately. Population, Intervention, and Outcome (PIO) [31] is a particular context-based framework used mostly by researchers to integrate and formulate research questions and to assist the literature review.

Table 11.1: Search term construction composition.

Population	Client, Vendor, Outsourcing
Intervention	Challenges, Barriers, Issues, Limitations
Relevance outcomes	Software Architecture Designing Challenges Model for IoT software system
Exp Approach	Case, empirical studies, SLR, etc.

Tables 11.2, 11.3 and 11.4 express the search term construction for each question respectively.

11.4.1.1 Characteristics for Research Term Identification

a) For information gathering, we used research questions for data collection.

b) We used an alternative term for each string for valid data.

Table 11.2: RQ1 search terms construction.

Population	Vendor organization for software outsourcing
Intervention	What are challenges faced by... vendor
Outcomes	Architecture Design...

Table 11.3: RQ2 search terms construction.

Population	Software outsourcing... Vendor organization
Intervention	What are practices/ways...challenges
Outcomes	Solution and things to be avoided when designing software architecture for IoT software

Table 11.4: RQ3 search terms construction

Population	Defined in the literature... by vendor organization
Intervention	Real-world practices, to handle... challenges
Outcomes	To be avoided for software architecture design

c) We verified the search strings and their alternatives.

d) Boolean operators were used for concatenation purposes, where OR operators were used for the purposes of providing alternative synonyms and terms for getting meaningful data from the database. The other Boolean operator AND is also used for providing concatenation and plays the role of conjunction for the combination of two or more adjacent strings.

Results for a:

- RQ1: Software architecture, challenges, hindrance to vendor.

- RQ2: Software architecture designing challenges model practices, and justification of challenges.

- RQ3: IoT Architecture model, real-world practices, handles, challenges, issues, and proposed solutions.

Results for b:

- RQ1:

  - Software architecture: ("Software Architecture" OR "Software Construction")

  - Software outsourcing: ("Software outsourcing vendor" OR "Software subcontracting seller")

  - Challenges: ("Challenges" OR "Issues" OR "limitations").

  - Hindrance to vendor: ("hindrance to the vendor" OR "difficulties to developers" OR "Constraint to the service provider" OR "restriction to the seller")

  - IoT: ("Internet of things")

- RQ2:

  - Software architecture design: ("software manner planning" OR "software scheme development")

  - Practices: (Solution OR "Solving ways" OR "planned lesion")

  - Justification of challenges: (Exploration of challenges OR "identification of issues" OR "elaboration of limitations")

  - IoT: ("internet of things")

- RQ3:

  - Architecture model: (Scheme layout OR "Pattern layout" OR "design draft")

  - Real-world practices: ("actual universe solution" OR "Tangible domain rehearses")

  - Software architecture design: ("software manner planning" OR "software scheme development")

  - Software outsourcing: ("Software outsourcing vendor" OR "Software subcontracting seller")

  - IoT: ("internet of things")

Results for c:

- Software architecture design, constraints, limitations, vendor views, client views, real-world practices, handling critical issues, software architecture designing challenges model for IoT software system.

Results for d:

- RQ1:

  (("Software Architecture" OR "Software Construction" OR "Software structure") AND ("Software outsourcing" OR "Software deployment") AND ("Challenges" OR "Issues" OR "limitations") AND ("Internet of things") AND ("architecture design" OR "pattern layout")).

- RQ2:

  ((practice OR solution OR exercises OR ways) AND ("software architecture" OR "software construction" OR "software structure") AND ("software planning" OR "software designing") AND (Solutions OR exercises OR methods) AND ("Exploration of challenges" OR "identification of issues" OR "elaboration of limitations") AND ("internet of things")).

11.4.1.2 *Search Process and Practice*

The planning for the SLR was conducted as:

- Definition of search terms in the process of identifying population, intervention, and outcomes.

- Identification of substitute spellings and synonyms.

- Validated key words of search terms in pertinent deducted literature.

- Use Boolean operators (AND, OR) for the guidance of search engines (if applicable) for precise search.

A trial search was performed for the identification for getting the relevant literature from different digital libraries. The following trial search was performed in different digital libraries, i.e., IEEE Xplore, ACM, SpringerLink and Google Scholar.

(("Software architecture" OR "Software Structure" OR "Software Construction") AND ("Software outsourcing" OR "Software deployment" OR "Software utilization") AND ("Internet of things" OR IoT) AND (challenges OR limitation OR issues) AND (Solution OR methods OR practices OR ways)).

The search string used for the final search was:

Results from IEEE & Google Scholar: (("Software outsourcing" OR "Software deployment" OR "Software utilization") AND ("Software architecture" OR "Software construction" OR "Software structure") AND ("internet of things" OR IoT) AND (vendor OR developer) AND (challenges OR issues OR limitations OR barriers) AND (Solution OR Recommendation)).

By applying the final search string, we found the following list of research articles in the different digital libraries shown in Table 11.5.

Table 11.5: Final search results.

Digital Libraries	Total Found Publications	Primary Selection	Final Selection
IEEE	19	3	0
ACM	2,661	107	15
Google Scholar	118	85	22
SpringerLink	1,813	28	17
		Total	**54**

We got low data in the final selection, thus we decided to perform the snowballing technique for the final selection chapter in order to enhance the quality of our research. Adi Bhat [32] stated in his article that snowballing is a referral chain sampling which is defined as a nonprobability sampling technique in which the samples have qualities that are rare to find. This is a sampling procedure in which the existing subjects provide referrals to convert the samples required for a specific research study. After applying successful snowballing, we received the results shown in Table 11.6.

Table 11.6: Snowballing technique results.

Digital Library	Total Found Publications	Final Selection
ACM	25	21
Google Scholar	20	13
SpringerLink	55	22
	Total	**56**

The snowballing technique enhanced our results from 55 chapters to 110 chapters, so it has been considered valid for further review to be adopted.

11.4.1.3 Publication Selection and Quality Assessment

The quality of each publication will be determined by its analysis and assessment. The criteria for publication selection will purely be based on the following conditions:

- The authors of publications must recognize the limitations and challenges in software architecture outsourcing.

- Which practices will be conducted and which will be assumed for resolving the challenges faced by the vendor in designing a software architecture model.

11.4.2   Publication Selection Process

In this section of our research, the task to be carried out is of inclusion and exclusion of raw and useful data from the collected materials/data. We will include only those data of research publications which are relevant to our research questions aim of vendor outsourcing for the software architecture designing challenges model for IoT software development.

11.4.2.1 Inclusion Measures

In the data analysis part of the process, we will include only those data considered relevant to our research question. The string of that paper should be related to the research question being searched for. For this purpose, we will use a data extraction strategy.

The inclusion measures would be actionable in the following format:

- Those data would be the part of this study from the found material which is related to our research questions.

- The data that contain challenges and limitations as well as design concepts will be part of this study.

- To consider all those papers which are on software architecture and the internet of things.

- To include all those papers which have the challenges of software architecture and IoT.

11.4.2.2 Exclusion Measures

This part on the measure of data deals with the exclusion of material not related to our research, study or research string. The process of exclusion will likewise occur as follows:

- We will exclude those publications that are found to be duplicates or fakes.

- Those data that are not related to our research study software architecture designing challenges model for IoT software systems and current challenges in software architecture designing challenges model.

- Those data in which there is no citation of client, vendor and outsourcing.

- Papers that are short or not in English mode.

11.4.2.3 Selecting Previewer

At this stage, the preselecting viewer is done by checking the all the material received from the different databases: the title, author, paper type, date of publication, journal, authenticity, abstract and introduction of each research/article paper. Through secondary reviewers, the raw data has been excluded and in the primary study relevant data has been finalized for inclusion in the research study.

11.4.3 Quality Assessment of the Publication

The quality of each publication will be determined by quality analysis and assessment. The criteria for publication selection would purely be based on the following conditions:

- The authors of those publications must identify the challenges and limitations in software architecture outsourcing.

- Which practices will be handled and would be carried on for resolving the challenges faced by the vendor in the software architecture model design?

11.4.4 Data Extraction

11.4.4.1 Initialization of Data Extraction Phase

This phase of extraction of genuine data will be started after receiving data through the primary study on behalf of research question satisfaction. The format of data extraction during the extraction phase will be done under the following categorized conditions:

- We will check the full details of the extracted publication, e.g., its author's name, publication journal, year, title, keywords; and we will also check whether it is a journal, paper or conference paper, conference location, pages, etc.

- Data that are satisfying and cover RQ1, which is comprised of challenges in software architecture faced by vendors and client-side organizations.

- Data that satisfy RQ2 dealing with practices to be handled in software outsourcing contract for software architecture design.

- Data which express the real-world solution to handle challenges faced by vendor and client-side organizations.

11.4.5 Data Extraction Demonstration

The data which are preserved through primary and secondary studies on the allotted string are expressed in the format shown in Table 11.7.

Table 11.7: Data demo table.

- Date of assessment
- Title of the paper
- Authors of the paper
- Conference/journal Name
- Conference location
- Research methodology
- Publication description quality
- Type of organization
- Company volume
- Country
- Year
- Challenges/limitations
- Practices/solution or ways

11.4.5.1 *Data Extraction Process*

The job of data extraction is the responsibility of the primary reviewer. He/she will collect meaningful data from the existing literature. If the individual has problems or issues with the primary data, the secondary reviewer could help by providing related literature publications. The secondary reviewer should provide the literature independently to the primary reviewer. The data extraction will only be performed by the primary reviewer and the secondary reviewer should provide the related material. In case of any mismatch or issue, the secondary reviewer should guide the primary reviewer accordingly.

The review for the aforementioned search was performed both by primary and secondary reviewers. The already predefined protocol illustrated it in detail.

11.4.5.2 *Data Synthesis*

Data synthesis was performed by the primary reviewer with the help of the secondary reviewers. We found a list of 110 chapters as a final selection. The primary reviewer initially identified a list of 38 categories. These identified categories by the primary reviewer were again reviewed and some of them merged and finally we got a list of 20 risks, as shown in Table 11.8.

Table 11.8: Frequency-wise list of challenges.

S#	Challenges	Freq N=110	% (stage)
1	Lack of Common Development	67	60.9
2	Lack of Poor Architecture	62	56
3	Lack of Reliability	46	41.8
4	Lack of Development Issues	39	36
5	Lack of Management Issues	39	36
6	Lack of Environment	38	34.5
7	Cost Issues	37	33.6
8	Lack of Use of Technology	31	29
9	Lack of Knowledge for High Skilled Resources	31	28.2
10	Lack of Privacy	30	28
11	Tradition Co-located Models	31	27.3
12	Lack of Assessment Issues	29	27
13	Lack of Poor Scheduling	28	26
14	Lack of Trust	27	25
15	Communication Workflows	27	25
16	Market Expansion Growth	27	25
17	Framework Integration	27	25
18	Lack of Effectiveness	27	25
19	Fault Tolerance	19	17.3
20	Deliverance Issue	17	15.5

11.4.6   Findings

List of Challenges Found Through Systematic Literature Review (SLR): With the help of SLR, we found various issues/challenges faced by the development team, i.e., vendor-side organization, during the development of software. Two issues were noted as the most critical during our search, as they possess high frequency. The first was the "lack of common development" issue, with a frequency index of 61%. The "lack of common development" is further proposed by the group of following challenges: "structuring issues," "software complexity issues," "requirement issues," "diagram formalization issues," "module design," moved later in the development process. In 1972, Bengtsson [33] claimed that the way a software system disintegrates into modules affects its capabilities to meet levels of efficiency in certain aspects, e.g. performance, flexibility. Software architecture is concerned with which modules are to be used to develop a system and how these modules are related, i.e., the full structure of the system. The architecture of a software system sets the boundaries for its quality. Hence, to design the software architecture and to meet the quality requirements is to reduce the risk of not achieving the required quality levels. The design team vendor organization partaking in a deep level of situational consciousness in the beginning can also gather relevant information to be adopted and interpret it from different viewpoints of the involved stakeholders, exchange (well-grounded and reasonable) locations based on expectations, assumptions and predictions over the excellence of the resulting architecture with a client, and ultimately agree upon a single decision that will be interpreted later on [34].

The second most critical challenge found with the help of SLR is "lack of poor architecture," with a frequency index of 56%. Rick Kazman, a professor at the University of Hawaii, raised the well-known observation of John Zachman in his article about architecture that "architecture is architecture is architecture," which means that in all possibilities the system could be laid down by its scaled architecture [35]. Johan den Haan stated in his article [36] that the explanation of the term "designing" is required for making a distinction between the architecture and the design of a system. These terms refer to how systems will be constructed. According to [36], there are two different system notions present, the ontological and the teleological system notions. The teleological system notion refers to the function and the (external) performance of a system. This notion can be imagined with a black-box model. The teleological system notion is satisfactory for controlling or using a system. The ontological system notion, on the other hand, can also be used for changing or building a system. It is about the operation and the construction of a system and can be modeled with a white-box model. Our findings are presented in Table 11.8, which can facilitate the development team and the clients in overcoming the issue found with the help of SLR.

The third most important challenge found with the help of SLR is "lack of reliability," which is also considered a significant challenge. The said challenge is fixed with the frequency index of 41.8% as shown in Table 11.8. In his article, Eoin Woods [37] stated that every system is treated according to its reliability. This means that the software architecture should be concerned with enabling evaluation of the developed system.

The fourth and fifth challenges identified with the help of SLR for the development of the framework for software architecture designing challenges model for the IoT are recorded as "lack of development limitation," and "lack of management issues," with frequency indices of 36.0%. Both challenges were placed at the same number of frequency index due to their relevancy. Bernardo et al. [38] and Rubrich [39] specified the pivotal role that management plays at the beginning of every task or exercise. They further stated that the lack of management issues include ill-scheduled, unrevealed deliverance and period, unrecognized prices and checklists, and undefined goals, etc. They also emphasized that in software development outsourcing, the parties should adopt the proper checklist of arrangements. Without proper management, the workflow would be faced with failure ahead after the commencement of its utilization by the end user.

The sixth and seventh challenges of the software architecture designing challenges model are "lack of environment issues," with a frequency index of 34%, and "cost issues," with a frequency index of 33.6%. According to the statement of López *et al.* [40]. The IoT's products and life cycle are important and interoperable for the proposed architecture of software development for IoT software systems. Thus, due to the costly products for the development of an architecture for the IoT software system and the lack of consent from both the parties, i.e., vendor- and client-side organizations, difficulties may be created in outsourcing, which is also known as the failure of unsuccessful software outsourcing. Another important factor influencing the workflow of any software architecture are environmental issues, i.e., without having a proper environment for the development of an architecture for the IoT software system, the correspondence between client- and vendor-side organizations will also be affected. Yvnnx [41] also stated that lack of environmental awareness results in problems in the environment, such as loss of biodiversity, pollution and global warming, etc., which can also affect the flow of outsourcing during the development of software architecture for the IoT software system.

"Lack of technology" is the eighth challenge in Table 11.8 of the software architecture designing challenges model; it maintained the frequency index of 29.0%. Soto and his team [42] discuss the development of software architecture and state that the end-user being unfamiliar with the system they are interacting with and the nontechnical equipment used during the interaction, can also lead to system failure. The lack of technology refers to the improper equipment from the vendor-side organization used for the development of software architecture. As technology nowadays plays a significant role in making the daily lives of humans easier, "lack of knowledge for high skilled resources," with a frequency index of 28.2%, is known as the ninth uppermost challenge for the development of the software architecture designing challenges model for IoT software systems [43].

A system which doesn't have specific privacy would also be faced with failure due to the damage caused by lost data. Here, the "lack of privacy," with a frequency index of 28.0%, is considered as the tenth challenge for the designing software architecture model for the IoT software system. This refers to the highly automated, entirely automated, or even autonomous robot systems or vehicles with earlier unavailable intelligent capabilities requiring new techniques of architecture and development methods to grasp the highest mandatory stages of safety and security [44].

The eleventh and twelfth ranked challenges for the software architecture designing challenges model for the IoT software system are "traditional co-located models," with a frequency index of 27.3%, and "lack of assessment issues," with a frequency index of 27%. The traditional co-located model refers to the previous concept of model development and designing which are acting or performing the same task in different shapes and physical faces adapted by the developed system for a particular task [45]. Whereas, the lack of software assessment is the progression assessment, which is a self-controlled inspection of the software processes assumed or used by a company or organization, based on a development model. Our further investigation showed that the software assessment quality and structure is influenced by its development perspective, which is affected by the customer contribution, agility, which allows cooperation among the development teams; outsourcing; and human influences, i.e., innovation, developers' creativity, art and experience, which are not partial to development approaches but customer claim and feedback systems [46].

"Lack of poor scheduling" is also framed as a 13th challenge for the software architecture designing challenges model for the IoT software system. Earlier negotiations on the fixation of origins and other essential services of a system are also based on the successful system. The poor scheduling challenge also refers to the consequences of poor management scheduling, which is generally seen in the form of stress in the workplace, staff conflicts, time distribution, poor productivity, ultimately poor retention of trained workforce, and increased absenteeism. We mainly focus on the lack of poor scheduling and a random mixture of resource requests for interactive and batch applications in an architecture-independent state or procedure, etc.

The fourteenth, fifteenth, sixteenth, seventeenth, and eighteenth challenges have the same frequency, with only 25% from the extracted data of the literature review. These challenges are "lack of trust," "'communication workflow," "market expansion growth," "framework integration," and "lack of effectiveness." The lack of trust is a common challenge faced by software architecture vendor organizations. Some empirical insights of software practitioners on the role of trust in software outsourcing relationships are when the customer expectations are high, deliverance time is limited, and the other essential resources are found limited, then the vendor organization should ensure the arrangement of the essential services on time for the successful trustworthiness with the client-side organization [47]. Our literature study has also identified another challenge named "lack of communication workflow," as the source of failure of software development outsourcing. It means that the meager communication capabilities may be separated as the lack of proper language, accent, or slang while one speaks. It can be boosted by unfailing practice and wrought out by refining our soft communication skills [48]. The sixteenth challenge of our explorative study is "market expansion growth." It means suggesting the flow of a service or product to a broader section of a current market or into a new demographic, psychographic or geographic market. Instead, software architectures must be thoroughly designed and then executed using fragmentary growth, which suggests that software architects need to incrementally and iteratively refine, assess, and improve a software system [49].

The seventeenth challenge of the study is "framework integration issues." This issue of designing a software architecture involves integration frameworks that deliver a model for statement and interaction between mutually interconnecting software applications in service-oriented architecture (SOA). The management plan is comprised because the plan used by the organization is to achieve goals. As we have already stated, the IoT is trending in the market, so there will be more customer requests. The influence of the IoT on software development is yet to be known; as a part of this research we have composed software development models [50]. The eighteenth challenge of our research investigation is "lack of effectiveness." The maintenance and restoration of software design and architecture are often defenseless against rapid increases in size and complexity, changing requirements, and insufficient understanding of the required architectural design [51-55].

The nineteenth and twentieth challenges of our study are "fault tolerance," with a frequency index of 17.3%, and "deliverance issues," with a frequency index of 15.5%. Both challenges were considered as dropped from our research, investigation and analysis, as our critical percentage for each challenge was 25% and > 25%.

11.5   Continent-Wise Comparison of the Challenges Found

The challenges that were found have been compared continent to continent in order to know whether they are different or the same in each continent. We have selected five continents (Asia, Europe, North America, Africa, Australia). Table 11.9 illustrates the continent-wise presentation with its frequency index. For the analysis of the identified challenges, we used the Chi-square test to find out whether there were significant differences between the identified challenges in these five continents. According to Khan *et al.* [29], the Chi-square test is considered by researchers to be more powerful than Pearson's chi-square test.

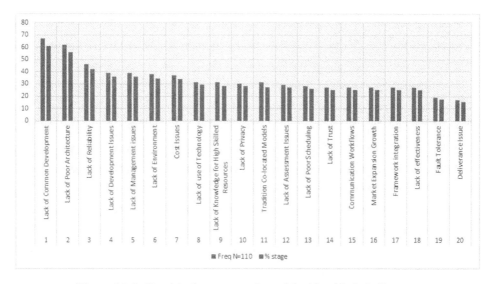

Figure 11.5: Graphical representation of the identified challenges.

In the early stages, we obtained 38 challenges, which have been merged. Finally, we achieved 20 challenges that were received from a different continent. These 20 challenges have been evaluated further and two challenge frequencies were considered less than 25. Therefore, only 20 challenges have been considered as critical, in which two challenges, "lack of common development" and "lack of poor architecture," have been highlighted as the most critical/considerable challenges among the rest. These two challenges have a frequency which is $>= 50$, as earlier discussed in detailed. The said frequency has been determined with the help of Statistical Package for Social Sciences (SPSS). The achieved frequency-wise outcomes were evaluated by SPSS while defining different relevant variables. Figure 11.5 gives a graphical representation of the identified challenges.

This research obtained the objective of determining the issues that affect the quality and chances of failure of the IoT software system.

11.6   Limitations

This research study indicates how efficient outsourcing is needed according to the identified challenges faced by vendor-side organizations in the development of a quality software system. We found limited data for extraction, but later applied the snowballing technique for increasing the number of chapters to be extracted for RQ1. A total of 38 groups of chal-

Table 11.9: Results of data from different continents.

Continent Name	Frequency	Percentage
Asia	32	29.1
Europe	51	46.4
North America	13	11.8
Africa	5	4.5
Australia	9	8.2

lenges were found and then some of them were merged and finally we obtained 20 groups to be considered as the main issues for the failure of any IoT software in the utilization stage. We plan to conduct an empirical study in the architecture and IoT software industry to validate our findings. Our systematic literature review (SLR) process will have missed some of the relevant data/chapters due to the considerable number of chapters.

11.7 Conclusion and Future Work

Our findings will provide safe shade to any IoT software in the initial development stage. Now, these identified challenges would be obvious to the vendor-side organization for pre-avoiding it in the development and in communication with the client, so the developed system will work properly as per user stratification. We identified a total of 20 challenges in which the 2 challenges indicated as the most critical issues were "lack of common development" and "lack of poor architecture," due to their high frequency received from multiple continents. The vendor should act according to our identified challenges in Table 11.8, which address the RQ1 for the successful completion of any software development. To address the RQ2, vendor organizations which are busy in the development process on various continents through outsourcing should concentrate on Table 11.10.

We will validate the identified challenges with the help of empirical studies in our future work by getting the consent of different software architecture stockholders for our developed architecture framework for the IoT software system.

In Table 11.10, we obtained three challenges whose P value is less than 0.05, which shows a significant difference between the continents. We considered the initial three continents, i.e., Asia, Europe and North America, as A and Africa and Australia as B. The market expansion growth challenge is considered essential in Continent A while less considered in continent B, where the same is also applicable to the "framework integration," which is considered highly essential in continent A and less considered in continent B. Another challenge whose P value is less than 0.05 is the "lack of assessment issue," which is essential in continent A and less essential in continent B.

Table 11.10: Continent-wise frequency.

Challenges	Sample Size find through Systematic Literature Review SLR (N=110)										Chi-square Test (Linear-by-Linear Association) α = .05		
	Asia N=32		Europe N=51		N. America N= 13		Africa N= 05		Australia N=09		X^2	df	p
	Frq	%	Frq	%	Frq	%	Frq	%	Frq	%			
Lack of common development	12	38	22	44	03	23	01	20	05	56	027	1	.869
Lack of poor architecting	19	60	29	57	05	39	03	60	07	78	.205	1	.851
Lack of reliability	10	32	23	46	07	54	00	00	06	67	1.590	1	.207
Lack of management issues	14	44	17	34	03	23	02	40	03	33	.581	1	.446
Environment issues	11	35	17	34	05	39	02	40	03	33	.019	1	.891
Development limitation	10	32	18	36	06	46	03	60	02	22	.079	1	.778
Cost issues	10	32	18	36	04	31	03	60	02	22	.000	1	.992
Lack of knowledge for high skilled resource pool	08	25	15	30	04	31	01	20	03	33	.127	1	.721
Lack of poor technology	13	41	14	28	01	08	02	40	01	11	3.472	1	.062
Traditional co-located models	06	19	18	36	02	15	03	60	01	11	.000	1	.986
Lack of privacy	07	22	17	33	03	23	01	20	02	22	.029	1	.865
Communication workflows	10	32	09	18	04	31	02	40	02	22	.007	1	.936
Lack of trust	07	22	11	22	03	23	04	80	02	22	1.165	1	.280
Market expansion and growth issues	02	07	15	29	04	31	04	80	02	22	5.017	1	.025
Framework integration issues	04	13	15	29	00	00	03	60	05	56	5.921	1	.015
Lack of effectiveness	09	29	15	29	00	00	01	20	02	22	1.098	1	.295
Lack of assessment issues	07	22	10	20	05	38	01	20	06	67	6.269	1	.012
Poor scheduling	09	28	12	24	05	38	01	20	01	11	.468	1	.494
Fault tolerance	06	19	09	18	02	15	00	00	02	22	0.060	1	.807
Deliverance issue	06	19	06	12	02	15	02	40	01	11	.003	1	.960

References

1. Stavropoulou, I., Grigoriou, M., & Kontogiannis, K. (2017). Case study on which relations to use for clustering-based software architecture recovery. *Empirical Software Engineering*, 22(4), 1717-1762.

2. Knodel, J., & Naab, M. (2017, April). How to Evaluate Software Architectures: Tutorial on Practical Insights on Architecture Evaluation Projects with Industrial Customers. In *2017 IEEE International Conference on Software Architecture Workshops (ICSAW)* (pp. 183-184). IEEE.

3. Patel, Z. D. (2018, May). A review on service oriented architectures for internet of things (IoT). *Proceedings of the 2nd International Conference on Trends in Electronics and Informatics (ICOEI 2018)*, (pp. 466-470). IEEE.

4. Ziegler, S., Nikoletsea, S., Krco, S., Rolim, J., & Fernandes, J. (2015, December). Internet of Things and crowd sourcing-a paradigm change for the research on the Internet of Things. In *2015 IEEE 2nd World Forum on Internet of Things (WF-IoT)* (pp. 395-399). IEEE.

5. Lin, N., & Shi, W. (2014, September). The research on Internet of things application architecture based on web. In *2014 IEEE Workshop on Advanced Research and Technology in Industry Applications (WARTIA)* (pp. 184-187). IEEE.

6. Herold, S., Blom, M., & Buckley, J. (2016, November). Evidence in architecture degradation and consistency checking research: preliminary results from a literature review. *In Proccedings of the 10th European Conference on Software Architecture Workshops* (pp. 1-7).

7. de Lemos, R. (2006, May). Software architectures for dependable systems: a software engineering perspective. In *Proceedings of the 28th International Conference on Software Engineering* (pp. 1065-1066).

8. Cui, L., Yang, S., Chen, F., Ming, Z., Lu, N., & Qin, J. (2018). A survey on application of machine learning for Internet of Things. *International Journal of Machine Learning and Cybernetics*, 9(8), 1399-1417.

9. Nechifor, S., Puiu, D., Târnaucă, B., & Moldoveanu, F. (2015). Autonomic aspects of IoT based systems: A logistics domain scheduling example. In *Interoperability and Open-Source Solutions for the Internet of Things* (pp. 153-168). Springer, Cham.

10. Cusick, J. J., Prasad, A., & Tepfenhart, W. M. (2008). Global software development: origins, practices, and directions. *Advances in Computers*, 74, 201-269.

11. Dias, J. P., & Ferreira, H. S. (2018). State of the software development life-cycle for the internet-of-things. *arXiv preprint arXiv:1811.04159.*

12. Woods, E. (2016). Software architecture in a changing world. *IEEE Software*, 33(6), 94-97.

13. Hasselbring, W. (2018). Software architecture: Past, present, future. In *The Essence of Software Engineering* (pp. 169-184). Springer, Cham.

14. Burd, B., Barker, L., Pérez, F. A. F., Russell, I., Siever, B., Tudor, L., ... & Pollock, I. (2018, July). The internet of things in undergraduate computer and information science education: exploring curricula and pedagogy. In *Proceedings Companion of the 23rd Annual ACM Conference on Innovation and Technology in Computer Science Education* (pp. 200-216).

15. Babar, M. A., Verner, J. M., & Nguyen, P. T. (2007). Establishing and maintaining trust in software outsourcing relationships: An empirical investigation. *Journal of Systems and Software*, 80(9), 1438-1449.

16. Mathrani, A., Parsons, D., & Mathrani, S. (2012). Knowledge Management Initiatives in Offshore Software Development: Vendors' Perspectives. *Journal of Universal Computer Science*, 18(19), 2706-2730.

17. Seth, F. P., Mustonen-Ollila, E., Taipale, O., & Smolander, K. (2015). Software quality construction in 11 companies: an empirical study using the grounded theory. *Software Quality Journal*, 23(4), 627-660.

18. Fraser, S., Anderson, L., Crocker, R., Gabriel, R., Fowler, M., Lopez, R., & Thomas, D. (2004, October). Challenges in outsourcing and global development: how will your job change?. In *Companion to the 19th annual ACM SIGPLAN Conference on Object-oriented Programming Systems, Languages, and Applications* (pp. 145-147).

19. Belle, A. B., El-Boussaidi, G., Desrosiers, C., & Mili, H. (2013). The layered architecture revisited: Is it an optimization problem?. In *SEKE* (pp. 344-349).

20. Márquez, G., & Astudillo, H. (2018, December). Actual use of architectural patterns in microservices-based open source projects. In *2018 25th Asia-Pacific Software Engineering Conference (APSEC)* (pp. 31-40). IEEE.

21. Filipponi, L., Vitaletti, A., Landi, G., Memeo, V., Laura, G., & Pucci, P. (2010, July). Smart city: An event driven architecture for monitoring public spaces with heterogeneous sensors. In *2010 Fourth International Conference on Sensor Technologies and Applications* (pp. 281-286). IEEE.

22. Stegemann, S. K., Funk, B., & Slotos, T. (2007). A blackboard architecture for workflows. In *CAiSE Forum* (Vol. 247).

23. Stapić, Z., López, E. G., Cabot, A. G., de Marcos Ortega, L., & Strahonja, V. (2012). Performing systematic literature review in software engineering. In *Central European Conference on Information and Intelligent Systems* (p. 441). Faculty of Organization and Informatics Varazdin.

24. Yulin, D., Shiying, L., & Yi, L. (2006, July). Information relevance management model-a new strategy in information security management in the outsourcing industry. In *5th IEEE/ACIS*

International Conference on Computer and Information Science and 1st IEEE/ACIS International Workshop on Component-Based Software Engineering, Software Architecture and Reuse (ICIS-COMSAR'06) (pp. 433-438). IEEE.

25. Sampaio, A. (2015). Improving systematic mapping reviews. *ACM SIGSOFT Software Engineering Notes*, 40(6), 1-8.

26. Rehman, M. N., & Khan (2020). Software architectecture designing challenges model for internet of things IoT software system. *USJ*, 1.1(1): p.9.

27. Khan, A. A., Keung, J., Hussain, S., Niazi, M., & Kieffer, S. (2018). Systematic literature study for dimensional classification of success factors affecting process improvement in global software development: client–vendor perspective. IET Software, 12(4), 333-344.

28. Magdaleno, A. M., Werner, C. M. L., & De Araujo, R. M. (2012). Reconciling software development models: A quasi-systematic review. *Journal of Systems and Software*, 85(2), 351-369.

29. Khan, S. U., Niazi, M., & Ahmad, R. (2009, December). Critical barriers for offshore software development outsourcing vendors: a systematic literature review. In *2009 16th Asia-Pacific Software Engineering Conference* (pp. 79-86). IEEE.

30. Khan, A. A., Keung, J., Niazi, M., Hussain, S., & Ahmad, A. (2017). Systematic literature review and empirical investigation of barriers to process improvement in global software development: Client–vendor perspective. *Information and Software Technology*, 87, 180-205.

31. Eldawlatly, A., Alshehri, H., Alqahtani, A., Ahmad, A., Al-Dammas, F., & Marzouk, A. (2018). Appearance of Population, Intervention, Comparison, and Outcome as research question in the title of articles of three different anesthesia journals: A pilot study. *Saudi Journal of Anaesthesia*, 12(2), 283.

32. Bhat, A. (2020). Snowball sampling: Definition, method, advantages and disadvantages.

33. Bengtsson, P. (1999). Design and evaluation of software architecture. University of Karlskrona/Ronneby: Sweden. p. 152.

34. Nowak, M., & Pautasso, C. (2013, July). Team situational awareness and architectural decision making with the software architecture warehouse. In *European Conference on Software Architecture* (pp. 146-161). Springer, Berlin, Heidelberg.

35. Clements, P., Kazman, R., & Klein, M. (2011). Evaluating software architectures. Beijing: Tsinghua University Press.

36. Den Haan, J. (2007). Architecture, A Definition http://www.theenterprisearchitect.eu/blog/2007/05/15/architecture-a-definition/, May, 2007: p. 3.

37. Woods, E. (2016). Software architecture in a changing world. *IEEE Software*, 33(6), 94-97.

38. Bernardo, M., Ciancarini, P., & Donatiello, L. (2002). Architecting families of software systems with process algebras. *ACM Transactions on Software Engineering and Methodology (TOSEM)*, 11(4), 386-426.

39. Rubrich, L. (2020). Lack of Management Leadership, Support Scuttles Lean Effort. https://www.reliableplant.com/Read/21642/lack-of-management-leadership,-support-scuttles-lean-effort

40. López, T. S., Brintrup, A., Isenberg, M. A., & Mansfeld, J. (2011). Resource management in the internet of things: Clustering, synchronisation and software agents. In *Architecting the Internet of Things* (pp. 159-193). Springer, Berlin, Heidelberg.

41. Lack of envromental awareness by yvnnx on prezi next. https://prezi.com/srmmti2jhm0m/lack-of-environmental-awareness/

42. Johnson, A. M., Jacovina, M. E., Russell, D. G., & Soto, C. M. (2016). *Challenges and solutions when using technologies in the classroom.* ERIC Clearinghouse.

43. Falessi, D., Babar, M. A., Cantone, G., & Kruchten, P. (2010). Applying empirical software engineering to software architecture: challenges and lessons learned. *Empirical Software Engineering*, 15(3), 250-276.

44. Kugele, S., Hettler, D., & Peter, J. (2018, April). Data-centric communication and containerization for future automotive software architectures. In *2018 IEEE International Conference on Software Architecture (ICSA)* (pp. 65-6509). IEEE.

45. Twomey, J. P., Johnston, J., Steinberg, J. L., & Morris, A. (2016). Whole-Person Care: Implementing Behavioral Health Integration in the Patient-Centered Medical Home.

46. Seth, F. P., Mustonen-Ollila, E., Taipale, O., & Smolander, K. (2015). Software quality construction in 11 companies: an empirical study using the grounded theory. *Software Quality Journal*, 23(4), 627-660.

47. de Andrade, H. S., Almeida, E., & Crnkovic, I. (2014). Architectural bad smells in software product lines: An exploratory study. In *Proceedings of the WICSA 2014 Companion Volume* (pp. 1-6).

48. Khan, A. A., & Shameem, M. (2020). Multicriteria decision-making taxonomy for DevOps challenging factors using analytical hierarchy process. *Journal of Software: Evolution and Process*, 32(10), e2263. DOI: 10.1002/smr.2263

49. Khan, A. A., Shameem, M., Kumar, R. R., Hussain, S., & Yan, X. (2019). Fuzzy AHP based prioritization and taxonomy of software process improvement success factors in global software development. *Applied Soft Computing*, 83, 105648.

50. Murari, B. T. (2016). Impact of Internet of Things on Software Business Model and Software Industry.

51. Schmidt, F. (2014). A multi-objective architecture reconstruction approach (Doctoral dissertation, Auckland University of Technology).

52. Zhou, P., Khan, A. A., Liang, P., & Badshah, S. (2021). System and Software Processes in Practice: Insights from Chinese Industry. In *the proceedings of 25th International Conference on Evaluation and Assessment in Software Engineering (EASE'2021)*.

53. Garg, S., Chatterjee, J. M., & Le, D. N. (2019). Implementation of Rest Architecure-Based Energy-Efficient Home Automation System. *Security Designs for the Cloud, Iot, and Social Networking*, 143-152.

54. Doss, S., Paranthaman, J., Gopalakrishnan, S., Duraisamy, A., Pal, S., Duraisamy, B., ... & Le, D. N. (2021). Memetic Optimization with Cryptographic Encryption for Secure Medical Data Transmission in IoT-Based Distributed Systems. *CMC-COMPUTERS MATERIALS & CONTINUA*, 66(2), 1577-1594.

55. Le, D. N., Bhatt, C. M., & Madhukar, M. (Eds.). (2019). *Security Designs for the Cloud, IoT, and Social Networking*. John Wiley & Sons, Incorporated.

12

Challenges to Project Management in Distributed Software Development: A Systematic Literature Review

SHER BADSHAH[1]

[1] Faculty of Computer Science, Dalhousie University, Halifax, Canada
Email: Sherbadshah46@gmail.com

Abstract

In recent decades, the development of organization software has been expanding across different continents due to a shortage of human resources and to save cost. The development of a software product among different geographically dispersed teams is a very challenging task. Software project management is one of the important challenges between distributed teams. This study aims to investigate project management (PM) challenges in global software development and provide solutions to overcome these challenges. We investigated these issues through a systematic literature review. The most common barriers that we have found are cultural differences, lack of communication and coordination, different time zones, language issues, different organization style and processes, and knowledge management between virtual teams. Our goal is to develop a PM framework for global software development.

Keywords: Global software development, distributed software development, global software engineering, project management, challenges

12.1 Introduction

The term/phenomena of distributed software development or global software development (GSD) is a common practice in software development organizations. GSD is the process in which an organization onshore or nearshore outsources their software development activities entirely or partially with another software development organization. The most important reason for an organization to decide to go for GSD is the lower development cost [1-3]. There are some other benefits that influence an organization towards GSD such as reduced cycle time [1,4-7], access to more extensive and multi-skilled labor forces [3,8], the effectiveness of time zones [1,3,9], closeness to market and customers [10], innovation and shares best practices [11]. However, the geographical, temporal, cultural, and organizational distances create challenges in GSD, including communication, coordination, control, and collaboration [2,12,13].

The geographical distance results in a lack of informal or limited communication [5], lack of awareness [14], and difficulties in knowledge management [15]. The temporal distance creates challenges, including restricted synchronous communication and delayed feedback [16]. The trust and confidence between sites are negatively affected due to socio-cultural distances [9,17-18]. The socio-cultural differences also introduce inconsistent process standards and minimized grapevine communication due to linguistic differences and diverse terminologies [11]. The level of experience, different process maturity levels, standards, tools, and different levels of experience are the challenges that occur due to the organizational differences [11,19]. As a result, it makes managing GSD projects more complex [11,19-22].

A large number of GSD projects have failed due to the absence of effective management [20]. It is imperative to perform improved and well-established PM approaches or practices to be successful in projects managed in the GSD environment. However, previously, it has been observed that GSD projects mostly failed due to poor PM activities. The most significant challenges dealt with PM issues and included, but were not limited to, "communication management, cultural differences awareness, specifying internal work processes and developing internal management skills" [19,21]. These challenges can affect the quality of GSD projects and can reduce profit [2]. Despite the importance of these problems, little research has been carried out to improve PM practices for GSD.

In this chapter, PM challenges encountered in GSD projects are investigated. In this regard, we conducted a systematic literature review (SLR) to report PM issues in GSD projects. The following research question (RQ) was designed to achieve the research objective of this study:

- RQ: What are the project management challenges in global software development?

The remaining contents of this chapter are organized as follows: Section 12.2 describes the background. The methodology used for this research is presented in Section 12.3. We present and discuss the results in Section 12.4. Finally, Section 12.5 presents our conclusions.

12.2 Related Work

Global software development (GSD) has become a key profit strategy for many organizations in the software industry. The following section describes the state-of-the-art literature review on the PM in the GSD environment. Da Silva *et al.* [21] performed the SLR and discovered the challenges, tools, and models used in the GSD projects. They included 54 studies published between 1998 and 2009. Based on the data extracted from these studies, they proposed an evidenced-based distributed software development PM improvement model.

Another study by Khan *et al.* [19] identified the challenges in global software development and stated that "geographical, temporal, cultural, and linguistic distances" all negatively impact coordination and cooperation. To overcome these challenges, the author also identified the areas in which the project manager can progress by considering the "organizational virtual team strategy, risk management, infrastructure, implementation of a virtual team process, team structure and organization, and conflict management."

Mishra and Alok [23] highlighted the research trends and management issues in GSD. The authors included the papers published between 2000 and 2011 in their review. After analysis, the authors pointed out that a lot of research had been done in requirement management, PM, knowledge management, and process management. However, little interest had been paid to configuration, risk, and quality management. The authors also highlighted the importance of research in these areas.

Niazi *et al.* [24] have identified the challenges of PM in GSD from the perspective of the client and vendor. They performed a two-fold study. First, they performed an SLR to identify the challenges of PM in GSD. Second, the challenges identified through SLR were validated through a questionnaire survey. They have identified nineteen challenges critical for the success of PM in the GSD setting. Lack of cultural understanding, lack of communication, and time management due to a difference in time region were the critical challenges with high frequency. In another study by Niazi *et al.* [25], the authors found the success factors related to successful PM in GSD environment. They performed a two-fold study: first, they identified the success factors in the literature related to successful project management in GSD and validated these factors in real-world practice. Second, they mapped the identified success factors to the ten areas of the project management body of knowledge (PMBOK). Their results show a positive correlation between the factors retrieved in the literature and the survey. They identified 18 success factors in the literature; organizational structure, skills, project management, communication, and collaboration are critical and the most common success factors with high frequency.

Jain and Suman [26] proposed a project management framework for global software development. They observed that the failure rate in GSD is high due to the lack of frameworks and standard procedures. In this study, the authors highlighted the standard procedures and frameworks introduced by the PMBOK for managing projects. However, these standards and frameworks are not commonly used by the organizations in GSD. The authors took the areas of PMBOK with the knowledge areas essential for the effective management of GSD. This framework will guide the project manager about the aspects to be considered while performing remote projects. The authors also highlighted that the framework would act as a baseline for the research in the global software project management domain.

12.3 Methodology

In this section, a systematic literature review (SLR) method is used to report PM challenges in the GSD environment. SLR is a method used to identify existing research studies relevant to specific research questions [27]. We followed the Kitchenham guidelines for conducting SLR. According to Kitchenham [27], an SLR consists of three phases: planning, conducting, and reporting [35]. Each phase is further divided into substeps (see Table 12.1).

Table 12.1: SLR process.

Number	Phase	Steps
1	Planning	1.1 Research questions
		1.2 Data sources
		1.3 Inclusion and Exclusion criteria
		1.4 Search strings
		1.5 Quality assessment
2	Conducting	2.1 Primary study selection
		2.2 Data extraction
		2.3 Data synthesis
3	Reporting	3.1 Reporting the results

12.3.1 Planning the Review

12.3.1.1 Research Questions

To report PM issues in GSD, we developed the following research question (RQ):

- RQ: What are the project management challenges in global software development?

12.3.1.2 Data Sources

In this part, electronic databases were identified to find solutions for our RQ. The data sources included:

- ACM Digital Library

- IEEE Xplore

- Google Scholar

- ScienceDirect

- SpringerLink

The search mechanisms in these repositories are different, so we incorporated our search terms accordingly.

12.3.1.3 Search Strings

The data sources were searched using search strings. We designed the search string according to the research question to extract relevant research articles. The following search string was applied to digital repositories:

("project management" AND "software project management" OR "managing software") AND (challenges OR problems OR issues OR barriers OR complications) AND ("global software engineering" OR "virtual teams" OR "distributed software development" OR GSD)

12.3.1.4 Inclusion and Exclusion Criteria

The inclusion criteria for research articles are the following:

- Papers written in English were included.

- Research papers published in conferences, journals, and magazines are included.

- Studies published between 2010 and 2018.

The exclusion criteria for studies are the following:

- Short papers, tutorials, notes or slides were excluded.

- Studies written in a language other than English were excluded.

- Studies published before 2010 were excluded.

12.3.1.5 Quality Criteria for Study Selection

In this step, quality criteria is defined for the assessment of articles. For the evaluation of the selected primary studies, we defined the quality assessment (QA) (see Table 12.2) criteria in the form of quality assessment questions as presented in [28]. Each study was valued against each QA question. We give a value of 1 to studies that comply with the QA criteria and 0 to studies that did not qualify for the QA checklist. Studies that partly answer the QA questions were assigned a score of 0.5. Finally, all scores of each study were summed up as a final score.

Table 12.2: Quality assessment.

S.no	Quality assessment questions
QA1	Are the results clearly presented in the paper?
QA2	Are the extracted articles reported in the research question?
QA3	Is the study methodology right to answer research questions?
QA4	Do the studies provide any empirical evidence?
QA5	Was the study conducted in the Global Software Engineering domain?

12.3.2 Conducting the Review

12.3.2.1 Primary Study Selection

The search string extracted research articles from identified data sources. We refined the extracted studies by the tollgate method proposed by Afzal *et al.* [29], which consists of five phases. In the first phase (1-Ph), relevant articles were extracted by searching using search terms. In, the second phase (2-Ph), the criteria for studies inclusion and exclusion were applied to the title and abstract. The introduction and conclusions were filtered in the third phase (3-Ph) based on inclusion and exclusion criteria. In phase four (4-Ph), inclusion-exclusion was based on the complete article. Final selection of studies was included in SLR in phase five (5-Ph).

The search strings retrieved 1722 initial studies from five different data sources based on the inclusion and exclusion criteria. The resultant articles were refined further using the tollgate approach and inclusion-exclusion criteria. Finally, a total of 33 sources were included in this review. The selected studies were evaluated based on the quality assessment criteria (see Section 12.1).

Table 12.3: Selection of studies using tollgate approach.

Electronic Databases	1-Ph	2-Ph	3-Ph	4-Ph	5-Ph
ACM Digital Library	67	43	24	9	4
IEEE Xplore	422	307	203	117	10
Google Scholar	809	543	324	155	9
ScienceDirect	281	177	151	88	8
SpringerLink	143	85	47	24	2
Total Studies	**1722**	**1155**	**749**	**393**	**33**

12.3.2.2 *Data Extraction and Data Synthesis*

We extracted the study's title, study type, research methodology, and year of publication to solve our research question. The selected primary studies were tagged as (*S*), which represent the study. The first and second authors reported the project management challenges occurring in GSD. The third author mapped the identified challenges with project management knowledge areas.

12.3.3 Reporting the Review

12.3.3.1 *Quality Attributes*

The selected primary studies were reviewed based on the QA checklist presented in Section 12.1. We calculated the final QA score of each study by adding the score of each QA checklist. The QA of selected primary studies shows that 75% of studies scored 3.0 and above, which illustrates that the articles meet our QA criteria.

12.3.3.2 *Research Methods*

The nominated articles consist of eighteen systematic literature reviews, three case studies, four questionnaire surveys, four interviews, and the remaining informal literature reviews and exploratory studies.

12.4 Results and Discussion

The SLR resulted in 25 PM challenges in GSD, as shown in Table 12.4. In this study, we found communication management as the most frequently occurring challenge in GSD projects. In a total of 33 studies, communication management was extracted from 31 (93%). From the selected sources, we observed that many GSD projects fail due to a lack of an effective mechanism for communication. One study claimed that 40% of GSD projects are not successful due to the lack of face-to-face communication [30]. The issue of face-to-face meetings decreases informal contact, leading to a lack of awareness and reduced trust [31]. The capabilities of communication management have an important impact on GSD projects. Therefore, a fundamental GSD challenge is that many of the techniques that function to coordinate work in a collocated environment are missing or disrupted [32].

Table 12.4: Project management challenges identified from selected primary studies.

S.no	Challenges	Frequency (n=33)	Percent %
1	Lack of communication management	31	93
2	Lack of culture understanding in teams	26	78
3	Lack of coordination	19	57
4	Geographical distances	18	54
5	Lack of trust and fear	18	54
6	Lack of management of time zone differences	17	51
7	Language barriers	17	51
8	Lack of knowledge management and knowledge transfer	16	48
9	Different processes	16	48
10	Risk management	13	39
11	No universal language	12	36
12	Tasks allocation	11	33
13	Lack of control	11	33
14	Lack of collaboration	9	27
15	Cost and effort estimation	7	21
16	Inadequate IT infrastructure	7	21
17	Requirement management	6	18
18	Lack of team awareness	6	18
19	Conflict management	5	15
20	Change management activities	4	12
21	Intellectual property issues	4	12
22	Lack of cooperation	3	9
23	Lack of configuration management mechanism	3	9
24	Integration activities	2	6
25	Quality management	2	6

The second most frequently occurring challenge in managing GSD projects is the lack of cultural understanding in teams. This challenge recorded 78% in selected primary studies. Software is developed in a multi-site, multi-cultural, distributed environment. The project manager faces formidable change on many levels, from technical to social and cultural [33]. Misunderstandings between virtual teams can occur due to cultural differences [34].

Mapping identified challenges with project management knowledge areas: The extracted PM challenges in GSD were mapped with PMBOK knowledge areas, as illustrated in Table 12.5.

Table 12.5: Project management knowledge areas, GSD challenges and PM implications in GSD.

Knowledge Area	GSD Challenges	PM Implications in GSD
Integration Management	• How changes in one side of a project leads to affect other sides?	• Lack of coordination
Scope Management	• What benefits can be achieved by engaging in the GSD projects?	• Change management activities • Requirement management activities
Time Management	• How time zone differences managed in a way that reduces project schedule and overcome coordination costs?	• Task's allocation
Cost Management	• What technique used to assure that cost savings are achieved, and coordination costs are decreased?	• Cost and effort estimation
• Quality Management	• How are quality management and control addressed in an offshore project, given the geographic distance?	• Different processes • Quality management
• Human Resource Management	• How can client assure that the best employees are assigned to their project, and that vendor employee turnover is managed?	• Lack of knowledge management and transfer among teams • Lack of trust • Lack of control • Conflict management • Lack of team awareness
• Communication Management	• How are the obstacles/challenges (cultural, language, and technology) addressed to safeguard effective and constructive communications in a largely remote environment?	• Lack of cultural understanding in teams • Lack of communication • Lack of management of time differences • Geographical distances • Language barriers
• Risk Management	• How are risks addressed in an IT offshoring project?	• Risk management • Protection of intellectual property • Lack of proper IT infrastructure • Integration activities
• Procurement Management	• Considering the complications (political, social, and cultural) associated with software projects outsourcing/offshoring, how does the firm find, choose and contract with the best/appropriate vendor for a specific project?	
Stakeholder Management		

12.5 Conclusion and Future Work

The advancements in information and communication technologies and lower development cost have led software organizations to distribute their work across different geographical locations. However, many GSD projects failed in achieving the expected advantages. One of the reasons behind the failure ratio of GSD projects was ineffective management.

In this chapter, an SLR was conducted to report PM challenges in GSD projects. The study resulted in 25 PM challenges in GSD projects. The most occurring challenge is the lack of communication management with the frequency of 31 (93%) out of 33 studies. Other challenges that recorded higher than 50% were lack of culture recorded, lack of cultural understanding in team, lack of coordination, geographical distances, lack of trust and fear, lack of time zone differences, and time zone differences coordination language barriers. Furthermore, all the extracted challenges were mapped with PMBOK knowledge areas.

In the future, we would like to continue this work by removing biases in mapping by applying fuzzy AHP. We also would like to propose a PM framework for GSD projects by considering the results of this study.

References

1. Ó Conchúir, E., Holmström Olsson, H., Ågerfalk, P. J., & Fitzgerald, B. (2009). Benefits of global software development: exploring the unexplored. International Conference on Global Software Engineering Exploring the Assumed Benefits of Global Software Development Development Global, *Software Process: Improvement and Practice*, 14(4), 201-212.

2. Nguyen-Duc, A., Cruzes, D. S., & Conradi, R. (2015). The impact of global dispersion on co-ordination, team performance and software quality–A systematic literature review. *Information and Software Technology*, 57, 277-294.

3. Ågerfalk, P. J., Fitzgerald, B., Olsson, H. H., & Conchúir, E. Ó. (2008, May). Benefits of global software development: the known and unknown. In *International Conference on Software Process* (pp. 1-9). Springer, Berlin, Heidelberg.

4. Pyysiäinen, J. (2003, May). Building trust in global inter-organizational software development projects: problems and practices. In ICSE Workshop on Global Software Development (pp. 69-74).

5. Khan, A. A., & Shameem, M. (2020). Multicriteria decision-making taxonomy for DevOps challenging factors using analytical hierarchy process. *Journal of Software: Evolution and Process*, 32(10), e2263. DOI: 10.1002/smr.2263

6. Bird, C., Nagappan, N., Devanbu, P., Gall, H., & Murphy, B. (2009, May). Does distributed development affect software quality? An empirical case study of Windows Vista. In *2009 IEEE 31st International Conference on Software Engineering* (pp. 518-528). IEEE.

7. Schwaig, K. S., Gillam, S. H., & Leeds, E. (2006). Project management issues in IT offshore outsourcing. *International Journal of e-Collaboration (IJeC)*, 2(4), 53-73.

8. Ó Conchúir, E., Holmström Olsson, H., Ågerfalk, P. J., & Fitzgerald, B. (2009). Benefits of global software development: exploring the unexplored. *Software Process: Improvement and Practice*, 14(4), 201-212.

9. Herbsleb, J. D., & Moitra, D. (2001). Global software development. *IEEE Software*, 18(2), 16-20.

10. Grinter, R. E., Herbsleb, J. D., & Perry, D. E. (1999, November). The geography of coordination: Dealing with distance in R&D work. In *Proceedings of the International ACM SIG-GROUP Conference on Supporting Group Work* (pp. 306-315).

11. Badshah, S., Khan, A. A, & Khan, B. (2020). Towards Process Improvement in DevOps: A Systematic Literature Review. In Proceedings of the Evaluation and Assessment in Software Engineering (EASE '20). Association for Computing Machinery, New York, NY, USA, 427–433. DOI:https://doi.org/10.1145/3383219.3383280

12. Khan, A. A., Shameem, M., Kumar, R. R., Hussain, S., & Yan, X. (2019). Fuzzy AHP based prioritization and taxonomy of software process improvement success factors in global software development. *Applied Soft Computing*, 83, 105648.

13. Al-Zaidi, A., & Qureshi, R. (2017). Global software development geographical distance communication challenges. *The International Arab Journal of Information Technology*, 14(2), 215-222.

14. Herbsleb, J. D. (2007, May). Global software engineering: The future of socio-technical coordination. In *Future of Software Engineering (FOSE'07)* (pp. 188-198). IEEE.

15. Desouza, K. C., Awazu, Y., & Baloh, P. (2006). Managing knowledge in global software development efforts: Issues and practices. *IEEE Software*, 23(5), 30-37.

16. Herbsleb, J. D., Paulish, D. J., & Bass, M. (2005, May). Global software development at siemens: experience from nine projects. In *Proceedings of the 27th International Conference on Software Engineering* (pp. 524-533).

17. Agerfalk, P. J., Fitzgerald, B., Holmstrom Olsson, H., Lings, B., Lundell, B., & Ó Conchúir, E. (2005). A framework for considering opportunities and threats in distributed software development (pp. 47-61), Austrian Comput. Soc.

18. Moe, N. B., & Šmite, D. (2008). Understanding a lack of trust in Global Software Teams: a multiple-case study. *Software Process: Improvement and Practice*, 13(3), 217-231.

19. Khan, A. A., Keung, J., Niazi, M., Hussain, S., & Shameem, M. (2019). GSEPIM: A roadmap for software process assessment and improvement in the domain of global software development. *Journal of Software: Evolution and Process*, 31(1), e1988.

20. Jain, R., & Suman, U. (2018). A project management framework for global software development. *ACM SIGSOFT Software Engineering Notes*, 43(1), 1-10.

21. da Silva, F. Q., Costa, C., França, A. C. C., & Prikladinicki, R. (2010, August). Challenges and solutions in distributed software development project management: A systematic literature review. In *2010 5th IEEE International Conference on Global Software Engineering* (pp. 87-96). IEEE.

22. Lanubile, F., Damian, D., & Oppenheimer, H. L. (2003). Global software development: technical, organizational, and social challenges. *ACM SIGSOFT Software Engineering Notes*, 28(6), 2-2.

23. Mishra, D., & Alok, M. (2011). Research trends in management issues of global software development: evaluating the past to envision the future. *Journal of Global Information Technology Management*, 14(4), 48-69.

24. Niazi, M., Mahmood, S., Alshayeb, M., Riaz, M. R., Faisal, K., Cerpa, N., ... & Richardson, I. (2016). Challenges of project management in global software development: A client-vendor analysis. *Information and Software Technology*, 80, 1-19.

25. Niazi, M., Mahmood, S., Alshayeb, M., Qureshi, A. M., Faisal, K., & Cerpa, N. (2016). Toward successful project management in global software development. *International Journal of Project Management*, 34(8), 1553-1567.

26. Jain, R., & Suman, U. (2018). A project management framework for global software development. *ACM SIGSOFT Software Engineering Notes*, 43(1), 1-10.

27. Kitchenham, B., Brereton, O. P., Budgen, D., Turner, M., Bailey, J., & Linkman, S. (2009). Systematic literature reviews in software engineering–a systematic literature review. *Information and Software Technology*, 51(1), 7-15.

28. Khan, A. A., Keung, J., Hussain, S., Niazi, M., & Kieffer, S. (2018). Systematic literature study for dimensional classification of success factors affecting process improvement in global software development: client–vendor perspective. *IET Software*, 12(4), 333-344.

29. Afzal, W., Torkar, R., & Feldt, R. (2009). A systematic review of search-based testing for non-functional system properties. *Information and Software Technology*, 51(6), 957-976.

30. Jain, R., & Suman, U. (2015). A systematic literature review on global software development life cycle. *ACM SIGSOFT Software Engineering Notes*, 40(2), 1-14.

31. Hossain, E., Bannerman, P. L., & Jeffery, D. R. (2011, June). Scrum practices in global software development: a research framework. In *International Conference on Product Focused Software Process Improvement* (pp. 88-102). Springer, Berlin, Heidelberg.

32. Kussmaul, C., Jack, R., & Sponsler, B. (2004, August). Outsourcing and offshoring with agility: A case study. In *Conference on Extreme Programming and Agile Methods* (pp. 147-154). Springer, Berlin, Heidelberg.

33. Khan, A. A., Shameem, M., Nadeem, M., & Akbar, M. A. (2021). Agile trends in Chinese global software development industry: Fuzzy AHP based conceptual mapping. *Applied Soft Computing*, 102, 107090.

34. Zhou, P., Khan, A. A., Liang, P., & Badshah, S. (2021). System and Software Processes in Practice: Insights from Chinese Industry. In *Evaluation and Assessment in Software Engineering* (pp. 394-401).

35. Khan, A. A., Keung, J., Niazi, M., Hussain, S., & Ahmad, A. (2017). Systematic literature review and empirical investigation of barriers to process improvement in global software development: Client–vendor perspective. *Information and Software Technology*, 87, 180-205.

13

Cyber Security Challenges Model: SLR-Based Protocol and Initial Findings

SHAH ZAIB[1], ABDUL WAHID KHAN[1], IQBAL QASIM[1]

[1] Department of Computer Science, University of Science and Technology, Bannu, Pakistan
Email: shahzebbiseb@gmail.com, shahzebbiseb@gmail.com, Iq_ktk@hotmail.com

Abstract

As cybercrime is increasing day by day and taking a wild shape in society, even highly reputable and government organizations' software are not safe from those attacks. So, the findings of this study will contribute to finding the reasons for how cyber attacks take place and how harmful they can be. A systematic literature review (SLR) is used to discover the negative effects of cyber attacks on vendor organizations in context of software development and also to tell us how to deal with the negative consequences of these attacks. We have identified 13 critical challenges through the SLR. Because of these findings we will get to know about the real-world practices which can be used to solve and overcome the negative consequences of cyber attacks. This chapter will provide a roadmap to conduct the research. The development of a cyber security challenges model (CSCM) is the conclusive aim of this protocol.

Keywords: Vendor, software development, cyber security, challenges, practices, systematic literature review

13.1   Introduction

The secure development of software is essential and basic in regard to the "confidentiality," "integrity," and "availability" of all product applications [1]. In the current thoroughly linked economy, persistent adaptive cyber (digital) threats have become the new standard. Current studies show that businesses, specifically small businesses, can be highly susceptible to cyber-attack risks [2]. In addition to precisely related financial impacts and data violations, analytical infrastructure, such as communications, economic structures, utilities and transportation systems, may even be undermined by cyber attacks [3, 4].

For many years the term cyber security was significantly considered in academia. Cyber security is defined by Shaw *et al.* [5] as the "practice of protecting critical systems and sensitive information from digital attacks." Despite the potential benefits, it's not easy to successfully deploy cyber security practices [6, 7]. The limitations in the existing cyber security practices significantly increase the risks of cyber attacks [8,9]. A threat intelligence management platform (TIMP) focuses on cyber threats and collects data from various origins to develop cyber security tools and approaches for a vast array of stakeholders [10, 11].

The existing cyber security frameworks and standards have different impacts in different scenarios. It is strongly demanded to propose specific techniques that explicitly focus on securing cyber data. One-third of the total world population uses online platforms to share data [12]. These times demand that government information technology bodies focus on providing secure and reliable data management platforms. Additionally, it is necessary to make internet users aware of cybercrimes and how to prevent them. It will increase their understanding of data security and privacy using internet sources [13]. Cyber attacks are incredibly costly for businesses, economies, and different organizations. Such attacks could undermine their data infrastructure [13, 14]. Various guidelines policies [16] and research studies [16] are documented to minimize cybercrimes. Based on these documents, we realized that the following are the five common threats of cyber crimes, and these threats could significantly hit businesses: "illegal access to IT systems," "cyberespionage," "data or system interference," "cyber extortion," and "internet fraud."

13.2   Related Work

Cyber security is getting a lot of attention because we are constantly astonished by the prevalent nature, determination, assortment and significance of cyberattacks. In recent years, some magnificent cybercrimes have been detailed, signifying, as in the case of Wannacry ([18], the cruel fact that thousands of individuals, public and private organizations can be harmed by even a single cyberattack. Across the world, governments and businesses think cyber security is a top concern and to secure themselves and the public from cybercrime they are paying out billions of dollars or euros [19, 20]. Only a few academic studies have tried to evaluate the harm and suffering of cybercrime, in spite of the growing concern about it and the educational awareness of cybercrime events [17, 21]. As for the effect, almost all studies in terms of price or losses (financial) consider the negative consequences of cybercrime (e.g., [21-23]).

Identifying the interrelationships amongst information systems, people and business processes, numerous public and private firms, such as Symantec and the World Economic Forum, can include resilience as a guiding principle for cyber security [24]. Conventional risk management approaches and obstacles like those outlined herein specifying the need to change plans continue to be applied by cyber security guidance and programs [25, 26]. Individually, different states approve the cyber security policies and guidelines [27]. Cyber security research shows that different researchers investigate the cyber security concepts and approaches [28, 29].

Cyber threats and advancement in technology are growing with the passage of time, so it's an important and formidable task to update a country's cyber security policy [27]. Due to challenging cyber security issues, small businesses are a specific class of organization that are habitually disregarded. The data collected from small-sized organizations reveal that cyber security is still a challenging and hard target issue for them. They don't have specific frameworks or standards that could assist them to effectively tackle the cyber security threats [30]. To secure the infrastructure of federal and private organizations against advanced cyber risks, there can be a significant requirement for cyber security talent [31]. Holt [32] recognizes that a cybercrime threat or vulnerability is crucial to locate in a multidisciplinary circumstance.

The majority of cyber security literature has bound its attention to information technology (IT) roles and the IT system [24]. The knowledge of the elements that influence the functioning of cyber attackers is restricted because of the deficiency of empirical research on them [13]. Cyber-attack results can go suddenly and unexpectedly from being compact to being vast [33].

The ISO 27032 standard provides a review of cyber security, probabilities for approximating risks and a description of the correlation between cyber security and other types of security. It also gives a framework to authorize stakeholders to cooperate on resolving cyber security issues. To prevent cyber security threats, several stakeholders have begun to cooperate in a coordinated manner [6]. The reasons why organizations strive to share information relevant to security dangers and threats, such as "standardization," "competition" and "trust," are nearly always highlighted by cyber security information sharing [34, 35].

The medium in which communication over the computer network takes place is referred to as the cyber world. Cyber security will widely become a research domain because of the fast-growing technologies, e.g., the internet of things (IoT), robotics, smart interactive networks, data sciences, artificial intelligence, and self-healing systems, where security is a significant factor. In most cases the organizational composition of the main owners and contributors of critical infrastructure services (public or private) consider the cyber world as a discrete and particular section [24].

Almost every country tries to secure their cyberspace by first preparing their cyberspace strategies. In general, a strategy arrangement consists of three successive procedures: Strategy formulation, strategy implementation and strategy evaluation [36].

The deployment of cyber security strategies developed by different organizations might be difficult to generalize in all the domains because they are developed in different contexts [37, 38].

To secure cyberspace an important step taken by many governments in their corresponding countries is to develop CSSs to their current information security status based on assessments [39-42].

The Cyber Security Agency (CSA) is the responsible organization to observe and implement the cyber security strategies [43]. All the proposed guidelines are included in the toolkit presented by the CSA [39-41, 44]. Moreover, Trim and Lee [45] proposed a generic cyber security framework to protect businesses, government organizations and society from cyber attacks.

13.3   Systematic Literature Review (SLR) Protocol

We have studied different systematic literature reviews for the development of protocol [46, 47]. In light of Kitchenham's guidelines [48], the foremost purpose of this research is the development of the SLR protocol for a cyber security challenges model (CSCM). As per Kitchenham [48], there are three phases of the SLR: Planning, conducting, and reporting. The planning phase will be the focus of this research. This review will help us negotiate issues faced by vendors due to cyber security in the software development field. This study is completely based on research questions. Once research questions are finalized, we will define some strings to start a test search on different databases. After completion of the search for literature, the criteria for exclusion and inclusion will be specified and can acquire the data. When the process of data extraction has been completed then data will be synthesized in tabular form.

13.4   Research Questions

Asking the following three research questions is the principal objective of our protocol:

- RQ1: "What are the cyber security issues faced by vendor organizations in software development that have a negative impact on the software industry?"

- RQ2: "What are the practices as discussed in the literature that should be adopted to overcome cyber security issues that have a negative impact on the software industry?"

- RQ3: "What are the real-world practices that should be adopted to overcome cyber security issues that have a negative impact on the software industry?"

13.5   Search Term Construction

The search terms are constructed based on the intervention, population and outcome concepts. The details are provided in Table 13.1.

Table 13.1: General format of the construction of a search term.

Intervention	Problems, challenges, issues
Population	Software development, vendors
Outcome	Cyber security, secure software development

Table 13.2 and Table 13.3 show details of search term construction for RQ1 and RQ2 respectively.

Table 13.2: RQ1 search term construction.

Intervention	What are the issues faced by...
Population	Vendor organization in... negative impact on software industry.
Outcome	Negative impact, cyber security

Table 13.3: RQ2 search term construction.

Intervention	What are the practices that...
Population	Should be adopted to ...that have negative impact on software industry.
Outcome	Outcome on cyber security issues.

13.6 Strategies for Searching

13.6.1 Trial Searching

To carry out a trial search on different resources or online digital libraries, i.e., IEEE, Google Scholar, ACM and SpringerLink, the following search string has been built by us.

> ((("Software development") AND ("Cybersecurity") AND (vendor) AND (Challenges) AND (practices))

13.6.2 Characteristics of Search Terms

The following perspective will be followed for construction of search terms or strings.

a) Identify main phrases for "population, intervention and outcome" from the research questions.

b) For main terms use alternative spelling and synonyms.

c) In relevant papers find the key words.

d) Use Boolean operators for conjunction purposes in such a way that main terms will connect through 'AND' operator while alternative terms will connect through 'OR' operator.

Output of a:

- RQ1: Software development, vendor, issues, cyber seurity.

- RQ2: Software industry, practices, issues, cyber security.

Output of b:

- RQ1:
  - Software Development: "Software development" OR "Software evolution" OR "Software maturing" OR "Software growth".
  - Vendor: Vendor OR supplier OR seller OR contractor OR trader.
  - Issues: Issues OR challenges OR problems OR barriers.
  - Cyber Security: "Cyber security" OR "cyber forensics" OR "cyber risks" OR "computing security" OR "IT security" OR "electronic information security".

- RQ2:
  - Software Industry: "Software industry" OR "software trade" OR "software business" OR "software field".

   – Practices: Practices OR procedures OR methods OR solutions.

   – Issues: Issues OR challenges OR problems OR barriers.

   – Cyber Security: "Cyber security" OR "cyber forensics" OR "cyber risks" OR "computing security" OR "IT security" OR "electronic information security".

Output of c:

- Software development, software growth, software evolution, software maturing, cyber security, cyber security issues, software industry.

Output of d:

- RQ1:

   (("Software development" OR "Software evolution" OR "Software maturing" OR "Software growth" OR "Secure software development") AND (Vendor OR supplier OR seller OR contractor OR trader) AND (Issues OR challenges OR problems OR barriers) AND ("Cyber security" OR "cyber forensics" OR "cyber risks" OR "computing security" OR "IT security" OR "electronic information security"))

- RQ2:

   (("Software industry" OR "software trade" OR "software business" OR "software field") AND (Practices OR procedures OR methods OR solutions) AND (Issues OR challenges OR problems OR barriers) AND ("Cyber security" OR "cyber forensics" OR "cyber risks" OR "computing security" OR "IT security" OR "electronic information security"))

13.7   Process of Search String

13.7.1   Development of Search String

On the basis of analysis for RQ1 and RQ2 in the previous Section 13.4 of this chapter, a search string has evolved to execute search activity on various libraries or resources, i.e., Google Scholar, IEEE, SpringerLink and ACM. For both research questions RQ1 and RQ2 we developed a single string because some libraries, i.e., IEEE, do not allow long string. Searching is a very monotonous and time-consuming process, which is why we developed a single string to save time. The search string for RQ1 and RQ2 is given below:

   (("Software development" OR "secure software development" OR "software evolution" OR "software maturing" OR "software growth") AND ("Cybersecurity" OR "cyber risks" OR "IT security" OR "cyber forensics" OR "computing security" OR "electronic information security") AND (vendor OR supplier OR trader OR seller OR contractor) AND (Challenges OR issues OR problems OR barriers) AND (practices OR solutions OR procedures OR methods))

As mentioned above, we made our final search string short in length for ScienceDirect to search relevant papers because ScienceDirect does not support lengthy strings. The said string is given below:

(("Software development" OR "software evolution" OR "software maturing") AND ("Cybersecurity" OR "cyber risks" OR "IT security") AND (vendor OR supplier OR trader) AND (Challenges OR issues OR problems) AND (practices OR solutions OR methods))

13.7.2 Resources to be Searched

When the search string is finalized, a search is performed on various resources/databases: Google Scholar, IEEE, SpringerLink, ACM, and ScienceDirect.

The search results of abovementioned databases are shown in Table 13.4.

Table 13.4: Search results of different resources.

Name of Resources	Search Result
Google Scholar	13900
IEEE	55
SpringerLink	2074
ACM	398
ScienceDirect	4795
Total	**21222**

13.8 Selection of Publication

At first, absolutely on the basis of paper title, abstract and keywords, primary selection of publication has materialized. The search results of selected papers on primary and final basis are shown in Table 13.5.

Table 13.5: Primary and final selected papers results.

Name of Resources	Search Result	Primary Selection	Final Selection
Google Scholar	13900	81	37
IEEE	55	2	0
SpringerLink	2074	33	3
ACM	398	22	0
ScienceDirect	4795	31	4
Total	**21222**	**169**	**44**

After primary selection; on the basis of reading full text and verification of inclusion and exclusion criteria discussed in Sections 13.8.1 and 13.8.2, respectively, of this protocol, the final selection of publications will occur.

13.8.1 Inclusion Criteria

The part of literature defined by the inclusion criteria will be used for the process of data extraction. Our inclusion criteria are based on the study of:

- Software development papers.

- Cyber security challenges in software development papers.

- Cyber security challenges faced by vendor organization papers.

- Cyber security negative impact on software industry papers.

- Solutions to control the negative impact of cyber security issues on software industry papers.

Furthermore, we have involved only English language research papers and match their titles, abstracts and keywords with our search string.

13.8.2   Exclusion Criteria

The criteria of exclusion aim is to define that section of literature which cannot be included in the data extraction process or is ignored. Our criteria for exclusion are simply based on the study of:

- "Not pertinent to software development."

- "Not matched with research questions."

- "Not about challenges and their solutions."

- "Not fulfilling the criteria of software development cyber security related issues."

- "Research papers which are in other languages instead of English language."

13.8.3   Support of Secondary Reviewer

The involvement of primary sources selection is completely based on just reviewing the title of paper, abstract of paper and keywords. In the case of specified criteria, the inclusion and exclusion is used just to check the results for final selection of papers. The secondary reviewer is requested to review the data, if there are any doubtful circumstances regarding inclusion/exclusion criteria.

13.9   Assessment of Publication Quality

After the final selection of publications, the quality of publication will be evaluated and this will be executed in parallel with the data extraction phase. The quality of publication will be completely based on the following questions:

- Has the author clearly identified those cyber security issues which affect software development?

- Which practices are adopted by the author to overcome these issues?

The abovementioned questions will be marked as Y or N after reading the research paper. Furthermore, for validation purposes the secondary reviewer will also take part in scoring of small subset.

13.10   Data Extraction Phase

13.10.1   Commencement of Data Extraction Phase

Afterscrutinizing the primary selected publications, the data extraction phase and all its importance will rest on satisfying the research questions. During data extraction phase the following data will be extracted:

- Detail of publication, i.e., title of paper, name of author(s), reference type, i.e., whether conference paper or journal paper, name of journal, name of conference, volume of journal, issue of journal, conference location, year of publication, pages, etc.

- Data interconnected with research questions, i.e.,

For RQ1 background information and those cyber security issues/challenges will be identified which are faced by vendor organization during software development.

For RQ2 background information and such practices/solutions-related data will be extracted which keep up with those challenges/issues which have a negative impact on the software industry during software development.

13.10.2   Presentation of Extracted Data

The extracted data will be presented in the following prescribed format as shown in Table 13.6.

Table 13.6: Data extraction presentation.

- Date of Review
- Title of Paper
- Author(s) of Paper
- Conference / Journal Name
- Name of Database / Resource
- Methodology (i.e. Interview, Survey, Case study, Report etc.)
- Quality of Publication Description
- Organization Type (i.e. Software House, University, Research Institute etc.)
- Company Size (i.e. small, medium, large)
- Country (i.e. Location of Analysis)
- Year
- Challenges (i.e. identifies those cyber security issues / problems which have impact software on development)
- Practices (as adopted by different vendor organizations in order to survive against challenges)

13.10.3   Data Extraction Process

The primary reviewer will only be responsible for the commencement of data extraction phase. During the data extraction process if any trouble is faced by the primary reviewer then the secondary reviewer will give guidance. From primary selected publications, the primary reviewer will extract data one after another. The secondary reviewer will also contribute in the process of data extraction and randomly select those papers from which data is already extracted by primary reviewer. The secondary reviewer selection will be completely unconventional; its main aim is just to compare his/her extracted results with the primary reviewer results. If there is any discrepancy in the results of primary reviewer with secondary reviewer results then the secondary reviewer will guide the primary reviewer properly.

13.10.4 Data Storage

Once the data extraction process is completed, then it will be summarized and will be stored in the form of a SPSS document. Furthermore, it will also be stored in the local drive of the Department of Computer Science, University of Science and Technology, Bannu.

13.11 Literature Search and Selection

For the identification of literature at numerous resources, such as ACM, Google Scholar, ScienceDirect, SpringerLink and IEEE Explore, an automatic search was conducted and we have found the literature from 2001 to Mid-2020 and selected papers on a primary basis as mentioned above in Table 13.4. As per predefined criteria of exclusion and inclusion, we have selected the research publications and initially, found 21222 papers from the five digital libraries as shown in Figure 13.1.

During selection on the primary basis, a total of 169 papers were selected by reviewing papers through title, abstract and keywords. After reading the complete text of the primary selected papers, thoroughly and applying the predefined criteria for quality assessment and inclusion/exclusion, a total of 44 papers are finally selected as shown in Table 13.5.

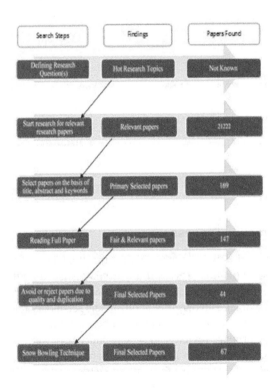

Figure 13.1: Searching and selection process of research articles.

13.12 Results

A list of total 13 challenges/issues have been identified in CSCM through SLR as given in Table 13.7. In this chapter, we have further analyzed the identified challenges based on database/digital libraries and methodology as given in the following subsections.

Table 13.7: List of challenges in CSCM identified through SLR.

S.No	Challenges in CSCM	Frequency (N=67)	Percentage of factors occurrence
1	Security Issues/Access of Cyber Attacks	39	58
2	Lack of Right Knowledge	32	48
3	Framework	32	48
4	Lack of Technical Support	29	43
5	Disaster Issues	27	40
6	Cost Security Issues	26	39
7	Lack of Confidentiality and Trust	25	37
8	Lack of Seriousness	22	33
9	Unauthorized Access Issues	21	31
10	Lack of Resources	19	28
11	Impact Issues	19	28
12	Administrative Mistakes during Development	18	27
13	Lack of Quality, Liability and Reliability	17	25

Table 13.7 shows a list of a total of 13 challenges identified through SLR. The challenge with the highest frequency is "Security Issues/Access of Cyber Attacks" (58%). Auret *et al.* [50] have discussed that "Government agencies, private-sector companies, and academic institutions all suffer from cyber vandalism, and denial-of-service attacks, by a spectrum of hackers, criminals, terrorists, and state actors." Our results show "lack of right knowledge" (48%) and "framework" (48%) as the first and second most common challenges, respectively. David Klaper and Eduard Hovy [49] stated that "It is impossible to react in a timely manner if the responsible people do not have the vocabulary to communicate what kind of attack it is."

Taylor Lusher [51] argued that "As demonstrated in past data breaches and attacks, network infiltration can occur by targeting the weakest users of a network." Our results, as mentioned in Table 13.7, represent other frequently cited challenges such as "lack of technical support, disaster issues, cost security issues, lack of confidentiality and trust, lack of seriousness, unauthorized access issues, lack of resources, impact issues, administrative mistakes during development, and lack of quality, liability and reliability."

13.12.1 Challenges in CSCM Based on Database/Digital Libraries

The challenges identified to answer RQ1 based on the database/digital libraries are represented in Table 13.8. We have searched a few databases/digital libraries, i.e., IEEE Explore, Google Scholar, ACM, Research Gate, SpringerLink and ScienceDirect and analyzed the identified challenges based on the searched databases/digital libraries used in searching in order to know the availability of these challenges in various databases/digital libraries. We have used the linear-by-linear association chi-square test to identify the significant difference between the identified challenges across the searched databases/digital libraries. As Chi-square linear-by-linear association is considered more powerful than Pearson's chi-squared test, we have used the chi-squared linear-by-linear association test to find the significant difference of the ordinal level data variable.

We have identified a total of 13 challenges for the searched databases/digital libraries. There is an inequality in the total number of challenges identified through the searched databases/digital libraries as shown in Table 13.8. i.e., the frequency of the total 13 challenges varies in the searched databases, some have the highest frequency while some have null value as shown in Table 13.8. We have used 25% criteria to identify the critical challenges and based on these criteria all the challenges we have identified are included in critical challenges, as shown in Table 13.8. The challenge "security issues/access of cyber attacks" (56%, 63%, 0, 75%, 50%, 33%) is considered a critical challenge in the searched databases. In this challenge, as we see there is variation in the frequencies of the searched databases/digital libraries. The "lack of right knowledge" (44%, 54%, 100%, 50%, 0, 50%) is also considered as a critical challenge of the cyber security challenges model in all searched databases except SpringerLink because it shows null frequency. There is variation in this challenge too, as we can see that its frequency is 100% in ACM but gives null value in SpringerLink. The rest of the identified challenges, i.e., "framework" (56%, 46%, 0, 25%, 50%, 67%), "lack of technical support"" (56%, 41%, 0, 50%, 50%, 33%), "disaster issues" (44%, 41%, 100%, 25%, 33%, 33%), "cost security issues" (44%, 37%, 0, 75%, 33%, 33%), etc., as shown in Table 13.8, have different frequencies in all searched databases/digital libraries as if one challenge has the highest frequency in one database then the other challenges has the lowest or null frequency in that database, so the frequencies of total identified 13 challenges has variations in their frequencies. It can be seen that if one challenge is largely covered in one database/digital library then it is completely ignored in other databases too, as seen in Table 13.8.

Table 13.8: Database/digital library-wise list of challenges.

Challenges	IEEE Xplore (N=9)		Google Scholar (N=41)		ACM (N=1)		Research Gate (N=4)		Springer Link (N=6)		Science Direct (N=6)		X2	df	P
	Freq	%	Freq	%	Freq	%	Freq	%	Freq	%	Freq	%			
Security Issues/Access of Cyber Attacks	5	56	26	63	0	0	3	75	3	50	2	33	1.125	1	.289
Lack of Right Knowledge	4	44	22	54	1	100	2	50	0	0	3	50	1.315	1	.252
Framework	5	56	19	46	0	0	1	25	3	50	4	67	.099	1	.753
Lack of Technical Support	5	56	17	41	0	0	2	50	3	50	2	33	.127	1	.721
Disaster Issues	4	44	17	41	1	100	1	25	2	33	2	33	.422	1	.516
Cost Security Issues	4	44	15	37	0	0	3	75	2	33	2	33	.002	1	.960
Lack of Confidentiality and Trust	4	44	14	34	1	100	2	50	3	50	1	17	.079	1	.779
Lack of Seriousness	3	33	13	32	1	100	1	25	3	50	1	17	.019	1	.891
Unauthorized Access Issues	3	33	15	37	0	0	0	0	1	17	2	33	.816	1	.366
Lack of Resources	2	22	13	32	0	0	0	0	2	33	2	33	.000	1	.987
Impact Issues	2	22	11	27	1	100	0	0	3	50	2	33	.542	1	.462
Administrative Mistakes during Development	3	33	12	29	0	0	0	0	2	33	1	17	.615	1	.433
Lack of Quality, Liability and Reliability	2	22	13	32	1	100	1	25	0	0	0	0	3.241	1	.072

Auret *et al.* [50] stated that the study of ICS-CERT showed that there are some ways in which attacks occur, where the percentage of those which are non-discoverable to their basic cause are 38% while 4% involved abuse of access authority. Barabanov *et al.* [52]

stated that due to the careless or incompetent actions of the software developer's personnel, unintentional information security threats may occur during software development processes. The condition of cyber security will remain poor as long as these individuals will remain negligent, uninterested and ignorant about their role in improving cyber security [53]. Möller and Haas [54] have discussed various data breaches as "At the most basic level, a cyberattack requires some form of access to the targeted system, and this is normally followed by some kind of exploit. The effects of the exploit phase can include data breaches such as: Defective system operation, Denial of service (DoS), Destruction of data systems, Exfiltration of data, Information removal or corruption, Unauthorized data access and others."

13.12.2 Challenges in CSCM Based on Methodology

To answer RQ1, the list of identified challenges based on methodology bases is shown in Table 13.9. The identified challenges have been analyzed across the various methodologies such as Literature Review, Case Study, Empirical Research, Survey, Interview, Questionnaire and Interview and Report by using linear-by-linear chi-squared test. In the final selection, a total of 67 research papers have been selected but only 60 papers have mentioned the methodologies shown in Table 13.9. We have found a total of 13 challenges for Literature Review, Case Study, Empirical Research and Survey whereas the remaining methodologies do not cover all the identified challenges. In Table 13.9, the first three challenges, i.e., "security issues/access of cyber attacks," "lack of right knowledge," and "framework," are considered critical for all the methodologies used. All these critical challenges are equally important for all methodologies used to consider seriously, so that they can properly use methodologies.

Table 13.9: Methodology-wise list of challenges.

Challenges	Literature Review (N=25) Freq	%	Case Study (N=14) Freq	%	Empirical Research (N=4) Freq	%	Survey (N=11) Freq	%	Interview (N=2) Freq	%	Questionnaire & Interview (N=2) Freq	%	Report (N=2) Freq	%	Other (N=7) Freq	%	X2	df	P
Security Issues/Access of Cyber Attacks	14	56	8	57	3	75	8	73	1	50	1	50	1	50	3	43	.181	1	.671
Lack of Right Knowledge	12	48	4	29	3	75	7	64	2	100	1	50	1	50	2	29	.000	1	1.000
Framework	14	56	3	22	2	50	6	55	1	50	1	50	2	100	3	43	.099	1	.753
Lack of Technical Support	9	36	6	43	1	25	9	82	2	100	1	50	1	50	0	0	.179	1	.672
Disaster Issues	12	48	3	22	3	75	5	45	1	50	0	0	1	50	2	29	.412	1	.521
Cost Security Issues	11	44	4	29	2	50	3	27	2	100	0	0	2	100	2	29	.012	1	.914
Lack of Confidentiality and Trust	8	32	4	29	2	50	4	36	1	50	1	50	0	0	5	71	2.306	1	.129
Lack of Seriousness	7	28	3	22	2	50	5	45	1	50	0	0	1	50	3	43	1.011	1	.315
Unauthorized Access Issues	6	24	2	14	2	50	6	55	0	0	1	50	2	100	2	29	2.161	1	.142
Lack of Resources	7	28	4	29	3	75	2	18	1	50	1	50	0	0	1	14	.488	1	.485
Impact Issues	6	24	3	22	2	50	4	36	1	50	0	0	1	50	2	29	.339	1	.561
Administrative Mistakes during Development	6	24	2	14	3	75	5	45	0	0	0	0	1	50	1	14	.000	1	1.000
Lack of Quality, Liability and Reliability	5	20	3	22	3	75	4	36	1	50	1	50	0	0	0	0	.233	1	.630

Our findings show that there are a total of 13 critical challenges identified for Literature Review, Case Study, Empirical Research and Survey, while it was discussed earlier that other methodologies do not cover all the critical challenges because in some challenges the frequencies of used methodologies comes to 0, such as "security issues/access of cyber attacks" (56%, 57%, 75%, 73%, 50%, 50%, 50%), "lack of right knowledge" (48%, 29%, 75%, 64%, 100%, 50%, 50%), "framework" (56%, 22%, 50%, 55%, 50%, 50%, 100%), "lack of technical support," etc.

13.13   Discussion

Through the SLR, we have found 13 challenges, as given in Table 13.7, faced by vendor organizations in software development in the shape of cyber security. We have considered all those challenges as critical in a study where the frequency is $>= 25\%$. These critical challenges are "security issues/access of cyber attacks, lack of right knowledge, framework, lack of technical support, disaster issues, cost of security issues, lack of confidentiality and trust, lack of seriousness, unauthorized access issues, lack of resources, impact issues, administrative mistakes during development, and lack of quality, liability and reliability."

13.14   Limitations

As far as limitations are concerned, for real-world practices RQ3 (i.e., questionnaire survey, interviews, etc.) will be developed. Furthermore, Google Scholar shows 13900 search results but only a very few are accessible.

As there has only been a small amount of work done in the field, we are doing the research, which is why we have found only 44 papers as our final sample for the data extraction in this study, which is a very low number, and we were not able to get our required results. So, we have conducted a snowballing technique and got 67 papers as our final sample for data extraction which is nearly an appropriate number to get our required results.

We have used a test of inter-rater reliability during primary selection and data extraction phase on a limited number of papers in order to mitigate the bias of the researcher. Our findings are based on the opinions of the authors of the papers in our final selection of papers. Most of these authors are academicians and some of these papers were published more than 10 years ago. Due to these reasons our findings need validation from the industry practitioners, and we plan to conduct an empirical study in the industry for validation of the SLR findings.

13.15   Conclusion and Future Work

Through SLR, we have identified a list of 13 challenges which are all marked as critical challenges for vendor organizations during software development in CSCM. The vendor organizations need to give proper attention to these critical challenges in order to avoid any risk of failure by not addressing them. In this chapter, we have answered what the challenges are. In order to answer how to address the identified challenges, we are working on the identification of practices through SLR, empirical study and analytic hierarchy process for industrial validation which will be published in the future.

We have further analyzed the identified challenges across the different databases/digital libraries, i.e., IEEE Explore, Google Scholar, ACM, Research Gate, SpringerLink and ScienceDirect. It has been found that the frequency of the challenges varies in all databases; for example, one challenge has the highest frequency in one database but gives null value in another database. On the other hand, we have analyzed the identified challenges across the different methodologies, where it has been noticed that only the literature review, case study, empirical study and survey covered all the critical challenges, whereas the remaining methodologies do not cover all the identified challenges but only some of them.

Our future research work in this research project is as follows:

- To find out the practices for the identified issues through SLR.

- To conduct a questionnaire survey for the validation of SLR findings.

- To conduct AHP and Fuzzy AHP techniques to analyze the identified data [55-60].

- To conduct a case study in real world to get feedback about the reliability of our proposed model.

The ultimate goal of this research project is to develop a cyber security challenges model (CSCM) and this study contributes to one component of our proposed model. The findings of this study will contribute to find the reasons for how cyber attacks take place and how harmful these attacks can be. It will tell us about the negative consequences of cyber attacks on vendor organizations in context of software development and also tell us about the solution to these negative consequences. Because of these findings we will get to know about the real-world practices which can be used to solve and overcome these cyber attacks. Through this research we will be able to educate the outsourcing software development organizations about the kinds of cyber security issues they should keep in mind while developing software.

References

1. Shahriar, H., Shalan, A., & Tarmissi, K. (2019, June). Towards Secure Password Protection in Portable Applications. In *National Cyber Summit* (pp. 3-13). Springer, Cham.

2. Lepofsky, R. (2014). Payment Card Industry (PCI) Data Security Standard Template for Report on Compliance for use with PCI DSS v3. 0. In *The Manager's Guide to Web Application Security*: (pp. 179-196). Apress, Berkeley, CA.

3. Kelic, A., Collier, Z. A., Brown, C., Beyeler, W. E., Outkin, A. V., Vargas, V. N., ... & Linkov, I. (2013). Decision framework for evaluating the macroeconomic risks and policy impacts of cyber attacks. *Environment Systems and Decisions*, 33(4), 544-560.

4. Rinaldi, S. M., Peerenboom, J. P., & Kelly, T. K. (2001). Identifying, understanding, and analyzing critical infrastructure interdependencies. *IEEE Cntrol Systems Magazine*, 21(6), 11-25.

5. Caulkins, B. D., Badillo-Urquiola, K., Bockelman, P., & Leis, R. (2016, October). Cyber workforce development using a behavioral cybersecurity paradigm. In *2016 International Conference on Cyber Conflict (CyCon US)* (pp. 1-6). IEEE.

6. Zibak, A., & Simpson, A. (2019, August). Cyber threat information sharing: Perceived benefits and barriers. In *Proceedings of the 14th International Conference on Availability, Reliability and Security* (pp. 1-9).

7. Young, W., & Leveson, N. G. (2014). An integrated approach to safety and security based on systems theory. *Communications of the ACM*, 57(2), 31-35.

8. Symantec, C. (2019). Internet security threat report.

9. Tounsi, W., & Rais, H. (2018). A survey on technical threat intelligence in the age of sophisticated cyber attacks. *Computers & Security*, 72, 212-233.

10. Brown, S., Gommers, J., & Serrano, O. (2015, October). From cyber security information sharing to threat management. In *Proceedings of the 2nd ACM Workshop on Information Sharing and Collaborative Security* (pp. 43-49).

11. Roberts, S. J., & Brown, R. (2017). *Intelligence-Driven Incident Response: Outwitting the Adversary.* " O'Reilly Media, Inc.".

12. Union, I.T. (2011). The world in 2011: ICT facts and figures. ITU.

13. Jacob, J., Peters, M., & Yang, T. A. (2019, June). Interdisciplinary Cybersecurity: Rethinking the Approach and the Process. In *National Cyber Summit* (pp. 61-74). Springer, Cham.

14. Tirumala, S. S., Sarrafzadeh, A., & Pang, P. (2016, December). A survey on Internet usage and cybersecurity awareness in students. In *2016 14th Annual Conference on Privacy, Security and Trust (PST)* (pp. 223-228). IEEE.

15. Fielden, K. (2011). An holistic view of information security: a proposed framework. International Journal, 4(1), 427-434.

16. Malby, S., Mace, R., Holterhof, A., Brown, C., Kascherus, S., & Ignatuschtschenko, E. (2013). Comprehensive study on cybercrime. *United Nations Office on Drugs and Crime, Tech. Rep.*

17. Anderson, R., Barton, C., Böhme, R., Clayton, R., Van Eeten, M. J., Levi, M., ... & Savage, S. (2013). Measuring the cost of cybercrime. In *The Economics of Information Security and Privacy* (pp. 265-300). Springer, Berlin, Heidelberg.

18. Goldman, R. (2017). What we know and don't know about the international cyberattack. New York Times, 13.

19. Veiligheid, K. I. Veiligheid 2016-2019.(2016). Brussel: Federale Overheidsdienst Binnenlandse Zaken.

20. Volz, D., & Hosenball, M. (2016). Concerned by cyber threat, Obama seeks big increase in funding. Reuter.

21. Klahr, R. (2017). Cyber security breaches survey. A Survey Detailing Business Action or Cyber Security and the Costs and Impacts of Cyber Breaches and Attacks. *United Kingdom: Department for Culture, Media; Sport*, 2017.

22. McAfee, N.L. (2014). Estimating the global cost of cybercrime, economic impact of cybercrime ii. *Center for Strategic and International Studies.*

23. PWC, H., Government (2015). Information security breaches survey. *Technical Report.*

24. Roege, P. E., Collier, Z. A., Chevardin, V., Chouinard, P., Florin, M. V., Lambert, J. H., ... & Todorovic, B. (2017). Bridging the gap from cyber security to resilience. In *Resilience and Risk* (pp. 383-414). Springer, Dordrecht.

25. Lambert, J. H., Parlak, A. I., Zhou, Q., Miller, J. S., Fontaine, M. D., Guterbock, T. M., ... & Thekdi, S. A. (2013). Understanding and managing disaster evacuation on a transportation network. *Accident Analysis & Prevention*, 50, 645-658.

26. Parlak, A. I., Lambert, J. H., Guterbock, T. M., & Clements, J. L. (2012). Population behavioral scenarios influencing radiological disaster preparedness and planning. *Accident Analysis & Prevention*, 48, 353-362.

27. Alexander, A., Graham, P., Jackson, E., Johnson, B., Williams, T., & Park, J. (2019, June). An analysis of cybersecurity legislation and policy creation on the state level. In *National Cyber Summit* (pp. 30-43). Springer, Cham.

28. Horowitz, B., & Crawford, J. (2007). Application of Collaborative Risk Analysis to Cyber Security Investment Decisions. *Financial Services Technology Consortium Innovation J*, 2(1), 2-5.

29. Pfleeger, S., & Cunningham, R. (2010). Why measuring security is hard. *IEEE Security & Privacy*, 8(4), 46-54.

30. Imsand, E., Tucker, B., Paxton, J., & Graves, S. (2019, June). A survey of cyber security practices in small businesses. In *National Cyber Summit* (pp. 44-50). Springer, Cham.

31. Insight, N. E. (2017). *The cybersecurity threat–fighting back.* Retrieved November, 2.

32. Holt, T. J. (Ed.). (2016). *Cybercrime through an interdisciplinary lens*. Taylor & Francis.

33. Borg, S. (2005). Economically complex cyberattacks. *IEEE Security & Privacy*, 3(6), 64-67.

34. Robinson, N. & E. Disley (2012), Incentives and challenges for information sharing in the context of network and information security.

35. Mavroeidis, V., & Bromander, S. (2017, September). Cyber threat intelligence model: an evaluation of taxonomies, sharing standards, and ontologies within cyber threat intelligence. In *2017 European Intelligence and Security Informatics Conference (EISIC)* (pp. 91-98). IEEE.

36. David, F. R., David, F. R., & David, M. E. (2013). *Strategic management: Concepts and cases: A competitive advantage approach*. Upper Saddle River: Pearson.

37. Haley, C. B., Moffett, J. D., Laney, R., & Nuseibeh, B. (2006, May). A framework for security requirements engineering. In *Proceedings of the 2006 international Workshop on Software Engineering for Secure Systems* (pp. 35-42).

38. Whitman, M. E., & Mattord, H. J. (2011). *Principles of information security*. Cengage Learning.

39. House, W. (2009). Cyberspace policy review: Assuring a trusted and resilient information and communications infrastructure. Washington, DC Available at http://www.whitehouse.gov/assets/documents/Cyberspace_Policy_Review_final. pdf.

40. Suid-afrika, R. (2010). South African National Cybersecurity Policy. Available at: South African National Cybersecurity Policy.

41. Cabinet Office. (2010). A strong Britain in an age of uncertainty: the national security strategy (Vol. 7953). The Stationery Office.

42. Estonia (2008). Cyber Security Strategy. Estonia Ministry of Defence Tallinn.

43. Atoum, I., Otoom, A., & Ali, A. A. (2014). A holistic cyber security implementation framework. *Information Management & Computer Security*, 22(3), 251-264.

44. Phahlamohlaka, L. J., Jansen van Vuuren, J. C., & Coetzee, A. J. (2011). Cyber security awareness toolkit for national security: an approach to South Africa's cyber security policy implementation.

45. Trim, P. R., & Lee, Y. I. (2010, June). A security framework for protecting business, government and society from cyber attacks. In *2010 5th International Conference on System of Systems Engineering* (pp. 1-6). IEEE.

46. Khan, A. A., Keung, J., Niazi, M., Hussain, S., & Ahmad, A. (2017). Systematic literature review and empirical investigation of barriers to process improvement in global software development: Client–vendor perspective. *Information and Software Technology*, 87, 180-205.

47. Khan, A. A., Keung, J., Hussain, S., Niazi, M., & Kieffer, S. (2018). Systematic literature study for dimensional classification of success factors affecting process improvement in global software development: client–vendor perspective. *IET Software*, 12(4), 333-344.

48. Kitchenham, B., & Charters, S. (2007). *Guidelines for performing systematic literature reviews in software engineering*.

49. Klaper, D., & Hovy, E. (2014, June). A taxonomy and a knowledge portal for cybersecurity. In *Proceedings of the 15th Annual International Conference on Digital Government Research* (pp. 79-85).

50. Auffret, J. P., Snowdon, J. L., Stavrou, A., Katz, J. S., Kelley, D., Rahman, R. S., ... & Warweg, P. (2017). Cybersecurity leadership: Competencies, governance, and technologies for industrial control systems. *Journal of Interconnection Networks*, 17(01), 1740001.

51. Lusher, T. (2018). *Present and Future Solutions for the Lack of Cybersecurity Professionals* (Doctoral dissertation, Utica College).

52. Barabanov, A. V., Markov, A. S., Grishin, M. I., & Tsirlov, V. L. (2018, October). Current taxonomy of information security threats in software development life cycle. In *2018 IEEE 12th International Conference on Application of Information and Communication Technologies (AICT)* (pp. 1-6). IEEE.

53. Sen, R. (2018). Challenges to cybersecurity: Current state of affairs. *Communications of the Association for Information Systems*, 43(1), 2.

54. Möller, D. P., & Haas, R. E. (2019). *Guide to Automotive Connectivity and Cybersecurity*. Springer International Publishing.

55. Khan, A. A., Shameem, M., Nadeem, M., & Akbar, M. A. (2021). Agile trends in Chinese global software development industry: Fuzzy AHP based conceptual mapping. *Applied Soft Computing*, 102, 107090.

56. Khan, A. A., & Shameem, M. (2020). Multicriteria decision-making taxonomy for DevOps challenging factors using analytical hierarchy process. *Journal of Software: Evolution and Process*, 32(10), e2263. DOI: 10.1002/smr.2263

57. Khan, A. A., Shameem, M., Kumar, R. R., Hussain, S., & Yan, X. (2019). Fuzzy AHP based prioritization and taxonomy of software process improvement success factors in global software development. *Applied Soft Computing*, 83, 105648.

58. Le, D. N., Nguyen, G. N., Garg, H., Huynh, Q. T., Bao, T. N., & Tuan, N. N. (2021). Optimizing Bidders Selection of Multi-Round Procurement Problem in Software Project Management Using Parallel Max-Min Ant System Algorithm. *CMC-COMPUTERS MATERIALS & CONTINUA*, 66(1), 993-1010

59. Le, D. N. (2017). A new ant algorithm for optimal service selection with end-to-end QoS constraints. *Journal of Internet Technology*, 18(5).

60. Bao, T. N., Huynh, Q. T., Nguyen, X. T., Nguyen, G. N., & Le, D. N. (2020). A Novel Particle Swarm Optimization Approach to Support Decision-Making in the Multi-Round of an Auction by Game Theory. *International Journal of Computational Intelligence Systems*, 13(1), 1447-1463.

14

A Process Assessment Model for Human Resource Skill Development Enabling Digital Transformation

EBRU GÖKALP[1,2]

[1] Department of Computer Engineering, Hacettepe University, Ankara, Turkey
[2] Institute for Manufacturing, Cambridge University, Cambridge, England
 Email: ebrugokalp@hacettepe.edu.tr, eg590@cam.ac.uk

Abstract

Human resource skill development plays a critical role in the success of digital transformation (DX) in organizations. As a result of the literature review, it is seen that there is a lack of systematic guidance on how to improve the quality of the process of DX human resource skill development for the organizations. ISO 330xx, the set of standards, provides a process assessment framework that can also be used as a baseline to generate process capability models for different specific domains. We utilized this approach by developing process definitions of DX human resource skill development based on the standard to assess the current process capability level and generate a road-map for process improvement. To observe the benefits and usability of the approach, we have performed a case study, including assessing an organizations' DX human resource skill development process capability level and developing an action plan for process improvement. The findings show that the proposed approach is applicable for identifying the current capability level and can provide a roadmap for moving to the next level.

Keywords: Process assessment, digital transformation, maturity model, human resource skill development

14.1 Introduction

The utilization of emergent technologies in the business environment is ushering in a new era known as digital transformation (DX). Although organizations are aware of the potential advantages of this transformation, they have faced problems creating a clear path to reshape their existing human resource skills in line with these emergent technologies. Empirical evidence shows that investment in new technologies provides the expected benefits if, and only if, the investment is integrated with adequate upskilling of the workforce [1-3]. The literature review [4], survey results [5,6], and interviews with practitioners show that organizations that face the most significant challenges in their DX journey are insufficient internal skills and resistance to change. DX is not just about technology: successful DX initiatives should include gearing up and aligning the strategy, culture, workforce, and processes to embrace this rapidly changing environment. Cultural change should be implemented before the process transformation begins. Thus, it is necessary to improve the process of DX human resource skill development as part of a successful DX initiative. Correspondingly, DX initiatives should cover assessing and improving DX human resource skill development process enabling DX in the organizations.

There are various well-accepted process capability and maturity models, such as software process improvement and capability determination (SPICE) [7-10], and capability maturity model integration (CMMI) [11] for the software industry. These models are an evaluative and comparative basis for process improvement and assessment, assuming that higher process capability is associated with better performance. They are developed to perform assessments of software and systems processes. As a result of the practical benefits of these models, including cost savings, increased involvement of employees, improved and predictable quality as well as productivity, generating consistency regarding process capture and use [12], customizing them to different domains other than software development is the subject of increasing interest in the literature. Accordingly, many initiatives have been proposed for various domains such as the automotive sector [13], knowledge management [14], internal financial control [15], industrial processes [16], medical devices [17], government [18-24], and industry 4.0 [25].

We have utilized a similar approach to assess and improve DX human resource skill development process. It pursues a structured and standardized approach by assessing this process to perform quality improvement initiatives consistently and repeatably. The approach enables organizations to determine the capability level of their DX human resource skill development practices against a benchmark that other organizations also use. Furthermore, it helps them establish a continuous human resource development program, set priorities for DX human resource skill development improvement actions, integrate DX human resource skill development with process improvement and obtain a culture of excellence.

This study aims to develop a process assessment model for DX human resource skill development enabling digital transformation of a maturity model to assist organizations by providing current DX human resource skill development capability/maturity determination, derivation of a gap analysis, and creating a comprehensive roadmap for improvement in a comprehensive, structured, objective, complete, and standardized way. In order to satisfy this necessity, the approach aims to fulfill four high-level requirements: enabling the organization to evaluate its process of DX human resource skill development in detail; identifying the current state of the process capability; comparing itself against other organizations evaluated with the same model; generating a roadmap for improving the process capability level of the organization. This paper is organized into six sections. A literature review is provided in the second section, followed by a high-level description of the developed process assessment model for DX human resource skill development. After this, the case study results are analyzed, and the roadmap derived for improvement in the organization is presented. Finally, the conclusion is given.

14.2 Literature Review

14.2.1 Human Resource Skill Development

Several well-known studies in the literature [26-29] emphasize the importance of an effective DX human resource skill development process. It is also suggested that process improvement within the human resource department is fundamental to an organization-wide structured quality improvement approach [30-32]. Evidence from an increased amount of literature on failure indicates that quality programs' human resource development aspect is generally ignored. Many experts assert that entirely successful and self-sustainable quality management requires a comprehensive refashioning of DX human resource skill development practices because cultural change should be implemented before the process transformation begins. Human resources skills development, organizational structure management, sustainable learning management, and organizational change management are essential for organizations' DX journey.

As a result of the literature review, it is observed that studies related to improving quality in the DX ignore the importance of the process aspect of human resource skill development and do not focus on improving human resource quality through the use of a standardized approach for assessment and improvement purposes. Accordingly, this study aims to satisfy this need by developing a process assessment model for DX human resource skill development to help organizations improve the capabilities related to their DX human resource skill development practices for a successful digital transformation initiative.

14.2.2 Theoretical Background

Process capability assessment is the systematic process of identifying gaps in organizational performance between what is and what could/should be. High process capability can be achieved by applying an iterative procedure of process capability assessments and improvement. The output of the assessment is a list of improvement opportunities for increasing effectiveness and efficiency.

SPICE, also known as ISO/IEC 330xx [33-35], a revised version of ISO/IEC 15504 [7-10], provides a structured process assessment framework, facilitating a basis for process capability and maturity level improvement. It assumes that a higher level of process capability or organizational maturity is associated with better performance. It consists of technical standards documents for process improvement and capability determination; it is a reference model for the maturity models. SPICE comprises two dimensions, process, and capability. The process dimension in SPICE includes software-development process definitions; and the capability dimension consists of process capability levels, which are, in turn, composed of process attributes (PA), including base practices (BPs) for Level 1 and generic practices (GPs) covering Level 2 to Level 5. Process Attributes (PA) represent measurable characteristics which are required to manage the corresponding process and improve its capability. BPs refer to the unique functional activities of the process.

The process assessment model for human resource skill development enabling DX was developed based on the family of standards ISO/IEC 3300xx [33-35]. The primary reasons for selecting it as a benchmark are its well-established and widely recognized structure. It presents a process viewpoint of process assessment, providing a clear set of requirements for the process assessment process and the resources required to implement it effectively. It consists of technical standards, including the requirements for MM design [34], process definition [35], planning and execution of process capability/maturity assessments [36], and the application of process improvement based on the process assessment [37-40]. The developed process assessment model for DX human resource skill development is given in the next section.

14.3   Process Assessment Model for Human Resource Skill Development

The developed process assessment model for DX-HRSD provides a basis for the process improvement in a structured manner. It provides to perform the DX-HRSD process quality improvements in a consistent and repeatable manner. It is established based on ISO/IEC 330xx [33-35], also has two dimensions, process, and capability, as explained below.

14.3.1   Process Dimension

The process dimension includes the process definition for the DX-HRSD process defined by following the requirements defined in ISO/IEC 33004 [35]. The process definition of the DX-HRSD process is given in Table 14.1.

14.3.2   Capability Dimension

The capability dimension, which is applicable to any process, was adapted from SPICE [7]. It includes the same capability levels, PAs, BPs, and GPs defined in ISO/IEC 3300xx [33-35]. It includes six levels, from Level 0: Incomplete to Level 5: Innovating, as seen in Figure 14.1.

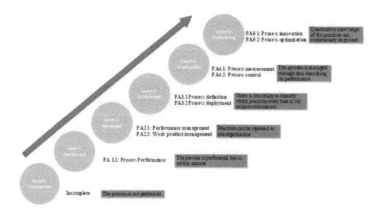

Figure 14.1: The measurement framework (adapted from ISO/IEC 330xx).

Table 14.1: The process definition of DX-HRSD.

Process	DX Human Resource Skill Development
Purpose	The purpose of the process is to provide the organization and project with individuals who possess the needed skills and knowledge in digital transformation to perform their roles effectively.
Outcomes	As a result of Successful DX Human Resource Skill Development Process;
	1. Organization's current and strategic workforce needs related to DX technologies are defined.
	2. Necessities for DX-related skills are determined.
	3. Skill development activities are prioritized.
	4. The DX-related skill development plan is published.
	5. Training, mentoring, or other services for skill development are provided.
	6. Employee performance are managed.
	7. The DX-related skill development plan is dynamically managed.
Base Practices	1. Define the organization's current and strategic workforce needs related to DX Technologies.
	2. Determine necessities for DX-related skills.
	3. Prioritize skill development activities to align with cost, schedule, and other business considerations.
	4. Establish a DX-related skill development plan.
	5. Review and revise the DX-related skill development plan on a periodic and event-driven basis.
	6. Provide training, mentoring, or other services for skill development
	7. Assess and recognize/reward employee performance.
	8. Track progress in meeting the objectives of the skill development plan.
	9. Skill-based experience and information are captured and made available.

Work Products	
Input	**Output**
Current Employee Skill Set [Outcome:1,2]	DX related skill development plan [Outcome 4]
	Employee Performance Report [Outcome:6]
	Training records [Outcome:5]

Level-1 assessment is performed to check if the BPs, defined in the process definition in Table 14.1, are conducted according to the corresponding PA 1.1. The rating of PAs is performed based on the gathered evidence, as shown in Table 14.2.

Table 14.2: Scale definitions.

Scale	Achievement	Definition
Not Achieved	0 – 15%	There is no or little evidence of application for the PA.
Partially Achieved	16 – 50%	There is some evidence of application for the PA.
Largely Achieved	51 – 85%	There is some evidence of application for the PAs and some weaknesses can exist.
Fully Achieved	86-100%	There is complete evidence of application for the PAs.

The process capability level ratings, adapted from ISO/IEC 33002, are given in Table 14.3.

Table 14.3: Process capability level ratings (adapted from ISO/IEC 33002).

Process Attributes	Level 1	Level 2	Level 3	Level 4	Level 5
P.A.1.1 Process Performance	L.A. or F.A.	F.A.	F.A.	F.A.	F.A.
P.A.2.1 Performance Management	-	L.A. or F.A.	F.A.	F.A.	F.A.
P.A.2.2 Work Product Management	-	L.A. or F.A.	F.A.	F.A.	F.A.
PA3.1 Process Definition	-	-	L.A. or F.A.	F.A.	F.A.
PA3.2 Process Resource	-	-	L.A. or F.A.	F.A.	F.A.
PA4.1 Process Measurement	-	-	-	L.A. or F.A.	F.A.
PA4.2 Process Control	-	-	-	L.A. or F.A.	F.A.
PA5.1 Process Change	-	-	-	-	L.A. or F.A.
PA5.2 Continuous Improvement	-	-	-	-	L.A. or F.A.

14.4   Application of the Process Assessment Model for DX-HRSD

An exploratory case study was conducted to observe if the proposed approach is applicable and usable for the process capability level assessment of DX-HRSD and the achievement of roadmaps for improvement. The process capability level of the DX-HRSD process performed in an organization was determined, and a guideline for process capability improvement was generated due to the assessment. A qualitative case study was performed by following the protocol template proposed by Yin [38], as described below:

- *The research question of the case study is*: How can an organization improve its DX-HRSD process by assessing its process capability?

- *The measure used* is the process capability level of the DX-HRSD process.

- *Field procedure, data collection, and limitations of the case study*: The assessment is conducted by following the requirement defined in ISO/IEC 33020, which is provided to ensure planning, performing, data collecting, and report the assessment in a structured manner.

- *The objectivity of the judgment*: The measurement framework, adapted from ISO/IEC 33020, yields to the theory of measure related requirement. Additionally, the requirement of data collection includes evidence reducing subjectivity.

The assessment was conducted in the organization to gather evidence. The semi-structured interviews with the DX and human resource department heads were conducted through on-line meetings because of the pandemic circumstances.

14.5 Findings and Discussions

During the assessment, it was observed that the DX had been initiated in the company. There is a DX roadmap for the short-term. Moreover, the DX department has been established in the organization, although the number of employees working in there is small. On the other side, there is a long DX journey waiting for the company department to achieve the highest DX human resource skill development process capability level. As a starting point, the organization should focus on the acquisition of DX-related training; enterprise culture and current challenges can be considered as beginning steps.

Capability Level 1 assessment of DX human resource skill development process is given in Table 14.1. During the Capability Level 1 assessment, the BPs defined in the process definition were assessed and the rate of PA 1.1, Process Performance was determined as largely achieved, as given in Table 14.5. Then, the Level 2 assessment was carried out. The GPs defined in ISO 15504-Part-5 were used for the assessment and PA 2.1, Performance Management and PA 2.2, Work Product Management were rated as largely achieved, as given in Table 14.4. As defined in ISO 33002, the capability level of the process will be determined as Level X if all PAs below Level X are rated as fully achieved, and the PAs at Level X are rated as fully achieved or largely achieved. Since PA 1.1. was not rated as fully achieved, the requirements of being Capability Level 2 were not satisfied, and it was concluded that the process capability level of DX human resource skill development process is Level 1 based on the collected and validated evidence, according to ISO 33020.

Table 14.4: Capability Level 1 assessment of DX-HRSD process.

Base Practices (BPs)	Rate of BP	Rate of PA 1.1
BP1. Define the organization's current and strategic workforce needs related to DX Technologies.	Fully Achieved	
BP2. Determine necessities for DX-related skills.	Largely Achieved	
BP3. Prioritize skill development activities to align with cost, schedule, and other business considerations.	Largely Achieved	
BP4. Establish a DX-related skill development plan.	Largely Achieved	
BP5. Review and revise the DX-related skill development plan on a periodic and event-driven basis.	Partially Achieved	**Largely Achieved**
BP6. Provide training, mentoring, or other services for skill development	Partially Achieved	
BP7. Assess and recognize/reward employee performance.	Partially Achieved	
BP8. Track progress in meeting the objectives of the skill development plan.	Not Achieved	
BP9. Skill-based experience and information is captured and made available.	Not Achieved	

Table 14.5: Capability level assessment of DX-HRSD process.

Level 1	Level 2		Level 3		Level 4		Level 5		Process Capability Level
PA 1.1	PA 2.1	PA 2.2	PA 3.1	PA 3.2	PA 4.1	PA 4.2	PA 5.1	PA 5.2	
Largely Achieved	Largely Achieved	Largely Achieved	-	-	-	-	-	-	Level 1

Based on the assessment results, a guideline for increasing the process capability level of the process to the next level, Level 2, was generated. The roadmap aims to move the capability level to Level 2 by achieving all BPs as fully achieved and all GPs in PA 2.1 and PA 2.2, as largely or fully achieved, as described in Table 14.5.

The main drivers of the roadmap include: generating, publishing and dynamically managing the DX-HRSD plan, acquiring training, mentoring, or other services for skill development, developing an Employee Performance Management System by identifying knowledge, skills and experience to perform the DX-related processes; managing key performance indicators for employee performance; evaluating employee performance; providing feedback for the existing performance; identifying and giving rewards to employees having highest performance; providing a lessons learned database by publishing skill-based experience and information; document job definitions; manage performance management.

A meeting with the assessment team and the process owners in the company occurred to present these assessment results, explaining the rating mechanism and sharing the generated roadmap for process improvement. They gave feedback as they realized the need for process assessment and improvement due to this assessment.

14.6   Conclusion

Although the process improvement models are customized for the different domains rather than software development, their application to the DX domain, and specifically the DX-HRSD process, has not been extensively studied in the literature. Correspondingly, A process assessment model for DX-HRSD was developed and validated with an exploratory case study to check the applicability and usability of the model in this study to fulfill this gap in the literature. As a result of the assessment, the process capability level of the DX-HRSD process performed in the organization was acquired, and a roadmap for improving the process capability level to the next level was generated. The case study findings show that the proposed model can identify the capability level and provide a roadmap for improving the DX-HRSD process.

There is a limitation of the study, which is the number of case studies. That restricts the generalizability of the proposed model. As a future study, additional case studies in different organizations with different sizes, sectors, and DX adoption levels are planned to generalize the results.

References

1. Autor, D. H., Levy, F., & Murnane, R. J. (2003). The skill content of recent technological change: An empirical exploration. *The Quarterly Journal of Economics*, 118(4), 1279-1333.

2. Morrison, A., Pietrobelli, C., & Rabellotti, R. (2008). Global value chains and technological capabilities: a framework to study learning and innovation in developing countries. *Oxford Development Studies*, 36(1), 39-58.

3. Fu, X., Pietrobelli, C., & Soete, L. (2011). The role of foreign technology and indigenous innovation in the emerging economies: technological change and catching-up. *World Development*, 39(7), 1204-1212.

4. Kagermann, H., Helbig, J., Hellinger, A., & Wahlster, W. (2013). Recommendations for implementing the strategic initiative INDUSTRIE 4.0: Securing the future of German manufacturing industry; *Final Report of the Industrie 4.0 Working Group*. Forschungsunion.

5. Koch, V., Kuge, S., Geissbauer, R., & Schrauf, S. (2014). Industry 4.0: Opportunities and challenges of the industrial internet. *Strategy & PwC*, 5-50.

6. Leaders, C. (2018) Digital Transformation Readiness Survey Summary.

7. ISO (2012) ISO/IEC 15504-5: Information technology - Process assessment - Part 5: An exemplar Process Assessment Model.

8. ISO (2003) ISO/IEC 15504-2: Information technology - Process assessment - Part 2: Performing an assessment.

9. ISO (2004) ISO/IEC 15504-4: Information technology – Process assessment - Part 4: Guidance on use for process improvement and process capability determination.

10. ISO (2004) ISO/IEC 15504-3: Information technology – Process assessment - Part 3: Guidance on performing an assessment.

11. Team, C. P. (2010). CMMI for Development, Version 1.3, Improving processes for developing better products and services. *Software Engineering Institute*, 433-454.

12. Goldenson, D., & Gibson, D. L. (2003). Demonstrating the impact and benefits of CMMI: an update and preliminary results.

13. Automotive, S.I.G. (2010) Automotive SPICE Process Assessment Model. Final Release, v4, 4, 46.

14. Barafort, B., Renault, A., Picard, M., and Cortina, S. (2008) A transformation process for building PRMs and PAMs based on a collection of requirements-Example with ISO/IEC 20000. SPICE, Nuremberg, Ger.

15. Ivanyos, J. (2007). Implementing process assessment model of internal financial control. The *International SPICE Days, Frankfurt/Main*, Germany.

16. Coletta, A. (2007). An industrial experience in assessing the capability of non-software processes using ISO/IEC 15504. *Software Process: Improvement and Practice*, 12(4), 315-319.

17. Mc Caffery, F., & Dorling, A. (2010). Medi SPICE development. *Journal of Software Maintenance and Evolution: Research and Practice*, 22(4), 255-268.

18. Gökalp, E., & Demirörs, O. (2014, November). Government process capability model: an exploratory case study. In *International Conference on Software Process Improvement and Capability Determination* (pp. 94-105). Springer, Cham.

19. Gökalp, E., & Demirörs, O. (2015, June). Proposing an ISO/IEC 15504 based process improvement method for the government domain. In *International Conference on Software Process Improvement and Capability Determination* (pp. 100-113). Springer, Cham.

20. Gökalp, E., & Demirörs, O. (2016, June). Developing process definition for financial and physical resource management process in government domain. In *International Conference on Software Process Improvement and Capability Determination* (pp. 169-180). Springer, Cham.

21. Gökalp, E., & Demirörs, O. (2014). Kamu Kurumları için Süreç Yetenek Modeli Geliştirilmesi. *UYMS*.

22. Gökalp, E., & Demirörs, O. (2016) Towards a Process Capability Assessment Model for Government Domain, in Software Process Improvement and Capability Determination: 16th International Conference, SPICE 2016, Dublin, Ireland, June 9-10, 2016, Proceedings (eds.Clarke, M.P., O'Connor, V.R., Rout, T., and Dorling, A.), Springer International Publishing, Cham, pp. 210-224.

23. Gökalp, E., and Demirörs, O. (2015) ISO/IEC 15504 Standardının Devlet Kurumları için Uyarlanması.

24. Gökalp, E., & Demirörs, O. (2017). Model based process assessment for public financial and physical resource management processes. *Computer Standards & Interfaces*, 54, 186-193.

25. Gökalp, E., Şener, U., & Eren, P. E. (2017, October). Development of an assessment model for industry 4.0: industry 4.0-MM. In *International Conference on Software Process Improvement and Capability Determination* (pp. 128-142). Springer, Cham.

26. Crosby, P.B. (1980). *Quality is free: The art of making quality certain*, Signet Book.

27. Deming, W.E. (1986) Out of the crisis: Quality. Product. Compet. Position, Massachusetts, USA.

28. Ishikawa, K. (1985) *What is total quality control? The Japanese way*, Prentice Hall.

29. Juran, J.M. (1989) Leadership for quality: An executive handbook. Free.

30. Blackburn, R., & Rosen, B. (1993). Total quality and human resources management: lessons learned from Baldrige Award-winning companies. *Academy of Management Perspectives*, 7(3), 49-66.

31. Bowen, D. E., & Lawler III, E. E. (1992). Total quality-oriented human resources management. *Organizational Dynamics*, 20(4), 29-41.

32. Vouzas, F. (2004). HR utilization and quality improvement: the reality and the rhetoric–the case of Greek industry. *The TQM Magazine*, 16(2), 125-135.

33. ISO (2015) ISO/IEC 33000: Information Technology - Process Assessment, International Organization for Standardization.

34. ISO (2015) ISO/IEC 33004: Information technology - Process assessment - Requirements for process reference, process assessment and maturity models.

35. ISO (2015) ISO/IEC 33020: Information technology - Process assessment - Process measurement framework for assessment of process capability.

36. ISO (2015) ISO/IEC 33002:2015, Information technology - Process assessment - Requirements for performing process assessments. 2015.

37. ISO (2013) ISO/IEC TR 33014 Information technology - Process assessment - Guide for process improvement.

38. Yin, R.K. (2013) Case study research: Design and methods, Sage publications.

39. Creswell, J. W., & Creswell, J. D. (2017). *Research design: Qualitative, quantitative, and mixed methods approaches*. Sage publications.

40. Le, D. N., Nguyen, G. N., Garg, H., Huynh, Q. T., Bao, T. N., & Tuan, N. N. (2021). Optimizing Bidders Selection of Multi-Round Procurement Problem in Software Project Management Using Parallel Max-Min Ant System Algorithm. *CMC-COMPUTERS MATERIALS & CONTINUA*, 66(1), 993-1010.

Printed and bound by CPI Group (UK) Ltd, Croydon, CR0 4YY

27/10/2024

14580137-0001